Personal and Family Economics

· · · · · · · · · · · · ·

Grady Kimbrell
Educational Consultant
Santa Barbara, CA

Patti Wooten Swanson
Ph.D Consumer Science and Family Economics
Bethel College, San Diego, CA

WEST PUBLISHING COMPANY

Minneapolis/St.Paul   New York   Los Angeles   San Francisco

Copy Editing:	Angie Vogl
Composition:	American Composition & Graphics, Inc.
Interior photos:	Dana C. White, Elisa Haber—Dana White Productions, Inc.; David Hanover, Hanover Photography; Superstock. Complete photo credits and acknowledgments appear following the index.
Cover and opener photos:	Dana C. White, Dana White Productions
Indexing:	Terry Casey

WEST'S COMMITMENT TO THE ENVIRONMENT

In 1906, West Publishing Company began recycling materials left over from the production of books. This began a tradition of efficient and responsible use of resources. Today up to 95 percent of our legal books and 70 percent of our college and school texts are printed on recycled, acid-free stock. West also recycles nearly 22 million pounds of scrap paper annually—the equivalent of 181,717 trees. Since the 1960s, West has devised ways to capture and recycle waste inks, solvents, oils, and vapors created in the printing process. We also recycle plastics of all kinds, wood, glass, corrugated cardboard, and batteries, and have eliminated the use of Styrofoam book packaging. We at West are proud of the longevity and the scope of our commitment to the environment.

Production, Prepress, Printing and Binding by West Publishing Company.

British Library Cataloguing-in-Publication Data. A catalogue record for this book is available from the British Library.

Library of Congress Cataloging-in-Publication Data

Kimbrell, Grady.
    Personal and family economics / Grady Kimbrell.
        p.   cm.
    Includes index.
    ISBN 0-314-04518-X
      1. Home economics.   2. Consumer education.   I. Title.
TX148.K56 1995
640--dc20   94-28844
                                                            CIP

Contents in Brief

Table of Contents

Unit 4 CONSUMER CREDIT 98

Unit 5 FINANCIAL SECURITY — 130

Unit 7 CLOTHING 194

Unit 11 HEALTH CARE 332

INTERACTING WITH TECHNOLOGY

To The Student

Our ancestors, a hundred years or so ago, didn't have much of a problem with becoming informed consumers. Most of them lived on farms and raised crops that would become their food. They made many of their clothes, and they raised horses or mules for their transportation. They were largely self-reliant. They bartered with neighbors, trading excess produce for things they needed. They had little money, and they made few purchases.

Today, more than 90 percent of Americans live in towns or cities. Unlike our self-reliant ancestors, we depend upon others for almost everything. Food, clothing, transportation, housing, furniture, appliances, healthcare, and entertainment are produced by others for us to purchase.

The way we spend money determines, in large part, the way we live—our lifestyle. If we don't plan our spending according to what will bring the greatest satisfaction, we waste our purchasing power. Due to poor planning, many people waste somewhere between 10 percent and 30 percent of their income. As we begin the twenty-first century, the average person in high school today is expected to earn about $3 million throughout his or her lifetime. Those who don't plan their spending for the greatest satisfaction will waste somewhere between $300,000 and $900,000! That is, they will have spent a very large sum on things that, in the long run, didn't really matter much. Later in life, of course, they will think of many ways to spend that much on things that would truly be satisfying.

How can you avoid wasting so much of your purchasing power? The answer, of course, is by becoming an informed consumer and by following a spending plan. You can achieve this through an understanding of personal and family economics.

In this text, *Personal and Family Economics*, you will learn to be a responsible consumer. Units 1 and 2 deal with consumer decision making and consumer rights and responsibilities. You will learn why we buy what we buy and how to make consumer decisions. You will learn what to do when a retailer or manufacturer of a product acts irresponsibly.

In Units 3 and 4, you will learn how to manage your money and how to use credit wisely. You will learn how to set up a spending plan so that your earnings will provide the greatest satisfaction.

Unit 5 deals with financial security. This includes how to set up a savings plan, how to insure your future income, and how to invest for the future.

In Units 6 through 11, you will learn how to become a more effective consumer of food, clothing, transportation, housing, furniture and appliances, and health care.

Unit 12 addresses the need for greater responsibility in caring for our environment. This includes protecting our land, air, water, and energy sources.

In Unit 13, you will learn the significance of your career to your future lifestyle. You will also learn how to evaluate alternatives in education and how to find and apply for a job. Finally, you will learn how to apply consumer principles to recreation.

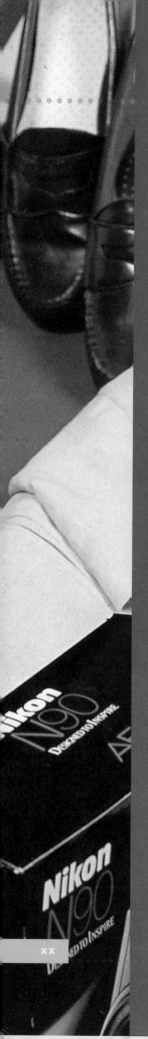

CONSUMER DECISION MAKING

CHAPTERS

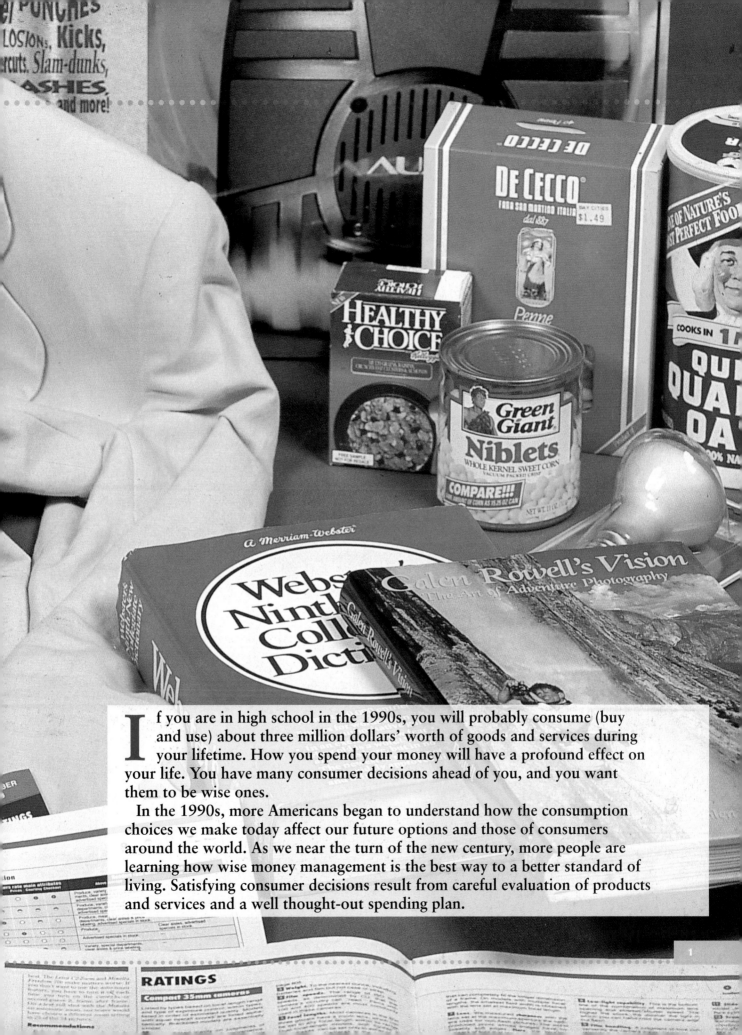

If you are in high school in the 1990s, you will probably consume (buy and use) about three million dollars' worth of goods and services during your lifetime. How you spend your money will have a profound effect on your life. You have many consumer decisions ahead of you, and you want them to be wise ones.

In the 1990s, more Americans began to understand how the consumption choices we make today affect our future options and those of consumers around the world. As we near the turn of the new century, more people are learning how wise money management is the best way to a better standard of living. Satisfying consumer decisions result from careful evaluation of products and services and a well thought-out spending plan.

CHAPTER 1

The Role of the Consumer

OBJECTIVES

After completing this chapter, you will be able to do the following:
1. Explain the purpose of an economy.
2. Name three major types of economic systems and explain how they differ from one another.
3. Explain how, in the United States, consumer spending habits affect producers.

TERMS

capital
consumer demand
consumers
economy

free enterprise
goods
Industrial Revolution

marketplace
producers
services

Everyone needs and wants goods and services. However, making wise consumer decisions is not always easy. How can we know we're getting the best value for the money we spend?

As **consumers**, we use goods and services that are produced by those known as **producers**. **Goods** are the products that we buy and use, such as food, clothing, CD players, and automobiles. **Services** are the activities and accommodations that we purchase. The **marketplace** (the world of trade and business) provides a way for consumers and producers to meet to buy and sell goods and services.

In early America, several generations often lived together as an extended family. Parents and older children worked together with grandparents, uncles, aunts, cousins, and in-laws—and they produced nearly everything the family needed. In the late 1600s, a few ambitious individuals in Europe began a new system of production.

These individuals made products in large quantities and sold them at a profit. This approach to production led to the **Industrial Revolution**. It, in turn, brought great changes in where and how people lived.

From the end of the 1600s through the middle 1900s, most people moved from farms to cities to take jobs in industry. The large extended family had been an asset on the farm, but it was difficult to support in the city. Industrial jobs were often taken by only one or two members of a family, which resulted in breaking up the extended family into smaller units known as *nuclear* families composed of father, mother, and dependent children.

Families supported by specialized jobs were no longer self-sufficient. They

---

consumers
. . . .
users of goods and services

producers
. . . .
suppliers of services and makers of goods

goods
. . . .
products for sale, merchandise

services
. . . .
activities or accommodations required by buyers

marketplace
. . . .
the world of trade and business

Industrial Revolution
. . . .
a period during the late 1600s during which economic changes were brought about by the production of large quantities of goods for sale for profit

INTERACTING WITH TECHNOLOGY

SHOPPING TO PLEASE THE CUSTOMER

A re you one of those people who love to shop? Maybe you are a person who hates busy stores and wants to make your shopping as painless as possible. Regardless of your style, electronic shopping may be just the ticket for you.

Home-shopping on popular channels such as QVC is just the beginning of what may be available in the future. Interactive shopping using TVs that contain powerful computers offers a wide range of new possibilities for home-shopping. This powerful equipment may allow the consumer to personalize shopping without ever having to leave home. For example, it is possible that some day you may be able to order your clothing through interactive equipment and have it custom-tailored; 3-D scanners may allow you to scan your measurements and transmit this information electronically. Menus like those found in personal computers may allow you to specify color, fabric, and style. Does this seem unlikely? Most experts agree that this kind of shopping is several years off, but there are some new services that will be available much sooner.

Plans are underway to provide a home video service that will allow you to rent a movie from the comfort of your home. You will select a title from an extensive menu of movies, instruct the computer to bill it to your account number, which is already programmed into the system, and sit back to enjoy your viewing.

Additional savings will be available to consumers as shopping services develop systems that make it possible to comparison shop from home. In the future it will be possible to read detailed descriptions of products on the screen as well as

view many of these products. Once you have decided what you want, you will be able to generate a computer search to find the best bargain. With a brief transaction, you will be able to place an order and have the product delivered directly to you.

Other proposals take advantage of the merchandise available in modern shopping malls. Interactive programs are being designed that would allow you to "enter" these stores, "walk" down the aisles, and look at merchandise from various angles on your TV screen. Will new services such as these change the way we shop? Retailers are betting they will and are scrambling to find ways to make them attractive to consumers. The success of these ventures will depend on how well these new services are able to provide what the customer wants.

had to depend on others to grow their food and to produce whatever other goods and services they needed. Even families that remained on farms saw that profits could be made in the new marketplace. They, too, began to spe-

Businesses exist because consumers demand the goods and services businesses provide. However, businesses are consumers, too. Do you see how businesses are also consumers?

cialize. For example, the dairy farmer produced milk and butter but had to depend on other producers for other consumer needs, such as clothing.

Today, we continue to depend on others to produce most of the goods and services we consume. Of course, producers are also consumers. Without consumers, there would be no reason for any business to produce goods and services—so consumers are an important part of the economy.

ECONOMIC SYSTEMS

An **economy** is a system for producing and distributing goods and services to satisfy the needs of consumers. Needs are satisfied in different ways (and to different degrees), according to the type of government under which the economy exists.

There are three major types of economic systems:

- communism
- socialism
- capitalism

Under communism, there is little or no individual freedom. The government decides what will be produced, what prices will be charged and where the goods will be sold. This economic system was rejected by most formerly communistic countries in Europe (such as East Germany and the U. S. S. R.) in the 1980s and 1990s.

Under socialism, the government makes decisions for most major industries, limiting which companies can produce certain goods and services and also limiting competition. This, in turn, limits consumer choices and may increase prices. However, socialism does allow for some privately owned and privately directed businesses.

Capitalism is a system based on freedom of choice. Anyone who wishes to start up a business may do so; thus, capitalism is also known as a **free enterprise** economy. This freedom leads to increased competition and more consumer choices, usually at lower prices.

The economy of the United States is based on capitalism. A business may produce almost anything that its directors think will sell and earn enough profit for the business to survive. Even under capitalism, though, there are cer-

economy
....
a system of producing and distributing goods and services

free enterprise
....
the practice of allowing a capitalistic economy to function with minimum government regulation

Under the free enterprise system we have the freedom to open almost any business that will make a profit. What are some reasons a business might have to close?

tain governmental constraints on production. For example, the government makes laws prohibiting the sale of certain goods and services, such as those considered harmful to individuals or that are against the public interest.

THE AMERICAN CONSUMER

As consumers, we exercise a great deal of control over the American economic system. We are free to buy whatever we want (and can afford). The choices we make determine which products and services can be produced successfully. When we, as a group of consumers, stop buying a product, the producer is forced to stop making it, reduce the price, or modify the product. The business may even have to close. Sometimes we see a new product that we think we can't live without. In that case, we may demand products faster than they can be made, and the business hires more workers to produce more of that product to meet the **consumer demand**.

Besides hiring more workers, an expanding business will need to buy more equipment and may need to buy or build larger buildings. All this, of course, requires **capital** (invested money). In order to expand production, a business may have to borrow money—and this borrowing provides work and profits for the banking industry. As you can see, the choices we make as consumers have far-reaching effects.

Consumer choices are not usually as simple as just deciding what we want. Most of us want far more than we can ever afford. You will want to spend your money wisely—because when you do, you will get the greatest satisfaction for dollars spent. If you have a

Offering a good product at a fair price can help increase consumer demand for that product. What things might decrease consumer demand?

family, you will want to see that your consumer decisions improve their lives as well as your own.

You can become a more effective consumer by recognizing needs, analyzing values, and setting goals in relation to needs. Then you can identify and evaluate alternatives, make choices, and evaluate those choices. Our modern economic system presents many obstacles to wise consumer decisions. Exaggerated or misleading advertising, defective products, and consumer fraud are just a few of these obstacles. If you learn the consumer decision-making concepts presented in this book, you will be well prepared to make satisfying consumer decisions.

Summary

- Wise money management is the best way to a better standard of living.
- Spending your money wisely gives the greatest satisfaction.
- We (consumers) depend on others (producers) to provide most of the goods and services we consume.
- Communism, socialism, and capitalism are the three major types of economic systems.
- Capitalism is an economic system based on freedom of choice.

consumer demand
. . . .
the quantity of goods or services that buyers will purchase at a given price

capital
. . . .
money invested in business

CHAPTER REVIEW
1

E NRICHING YOUR VOCABULARY

Number your paper from 1–10. Beside each number write the word or phrase that matches that definition. Choose your answers from the following list.

capital
consumer demand
consumers
economy

free enterprise
goods
Industrial Revolution

marketplace
producers
services

1. The world of trade and business
2. The practice of allowing a capitalistic economy to function with minimum government regulation
3. Money invested in business
4. The quantity of goods or services that buyers will purchase at a given price
5. Activities or accommodations required by buyers

6. A period during the late 1600s during which economic changes were brought about by the production of large quantities of goods for sale for profit
7. A user of goods and services
8. Products for sale, merchandise
9. A system for producing and distributing goods and services
10. Suppliers of services and makers of goods

R EVIEWING WHAT YOU HAVE LEARNED

1. What is the purpose of an economy?

2. Name the three major types of economic systems in the world today. Explain briefly how they are different from one another.

U SING YOUR CRITICAL THINKING SKILLS

1. In the United States, how do consumer spending habits affect producers?

2. How do consumer spending habits affect other consumers?

A PPLYING WHAT YOU'VE LEARNED

1. Collect newspaper and magazine articles dealing with topics of interest to consumers.

Share these with the class, then file them according to the chapters of this book.

CHAPTER 2

Why We Buy What We Buy

OBJECTIVES

After completing this chapter, you will be able to do the following:
1. List six steps in the decision-making process.
2. List five categories of human need.
3. Name seven influences that help shape our personal preferences.
4. Name and define three advertising techniques.

TERMS

decision-making process
fraud
goals
infomercial

lifestyle
personal preferences
pluralistic society
propaganda

status symbols
values

How effective are you as a consumer? Many Americans don't know how to spend money so that it gives the greatest satisfaction. Clever advertising convinces many of us that we must buy certain brands of clothes, cars, and cosmetics because those brands are what beautiful, successful, popular people buy. We may think certain brands will increase our own appeal and popularity, but a week or a month after we make a purchase, we may wish we had bought a different brand. We may realize that we overestimated our financial resources. Maybe we should have saved the money in order to make a more satisfying purchase later. Advertising has become so effective and so intrusive in our lives, especially on TV, that we must make consumer decisions very carefully.

THE DECISION-MAKING PROCESS

decision-making process
....
a series of steps that will lead the decision maker to a final choice

All of us can improve our effectiveness in making satisfying purchases. Those who get the best results often follow a **decision-making process**, a series of steps leading to a final choice. Try using these steps to guide your decision making (see Figure 2.1):

1. Understand how every purchase is a reaction to a need.

2. Identify alternatives (find other choices or ways of meeting the need).

3. Gather information on alternatives.

4. Evaluate the alternatives (weigh one against the other).

5. Analyze your financial resources.

6. Make your choice.

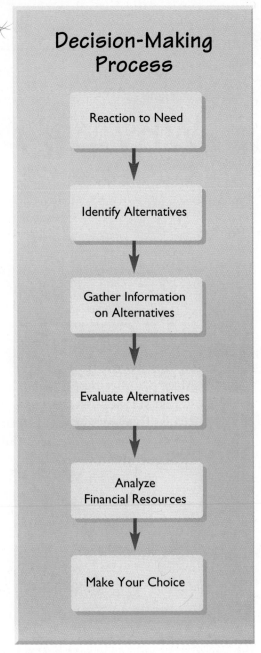

Decision-Making Process

- Reaction to Need
- Identify Alternatives
- Gather Information on Alternatives
- Evaluate Alternatives
- Analyze Financial Resources
- Make Your Choice

Figure 2.1
....

Using a step-by-step decision-making process can help you avoid making decisions you will regret later. Think of a purchase you would like to make. Now use the decision-making process to determine whether that will be a good purchase. Don't forget to evaluate your decision.

Always evaluate your decisions after you have made them. This will help you make wiser, more satisfying consumer decisions.

DECISIONS ARE BASED ON NEEDS

Every action that you take is taken for a reason. Every consumer decision is based on need. Even our "wants"—including those impulse purchases that we later regret—are based on some need. Sometimes it is a need, however temporary, to feel good about ourselves (self-esteem). Our needs can all be traced to one or more of five basic needs.

Basic Human Needs

The psychologist Abraham Maslow studied human needs and determined that everyone has the same basic needs.

These basic needs can be divided into five categories (see Figure 2.2):

1. survival—the need for food, clothing, and shelter
2. safety and security—the need to be free from physical harm and to feel economically secure
3. social—the need for a sense of belonging, to love and be loved
4. self-esteem—the need for a feeling of self-respect, to feel worthy
5. self-actualization (fulfillment)—the need to be creative, to find and use one's own special talents, to reach personal and social goals through one's own efforts

Dr. Maslow's studies suggest that these needs are hierarchical (sequential). That is, needs at each level must be satisfied before we start to be greatly concerned about the next level. For example, the first level is the need for survival. This need must be satisfied before we give much thought to social and security needs. We make consumer decisions to satisfy our own individual needs, and these decisions can be re-

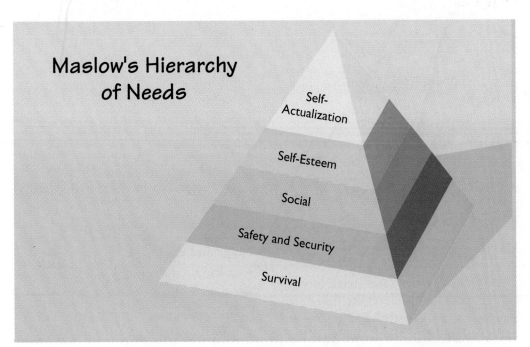

Maslow's Hierarchy of Needs

Self-Actualization

Self-Esteem

Social

Safety and Security

Survival

Figure 2.2
. . . .
Maslow's Hierarchy of Needs indicates that basic needs such as those for food, clothing, and shelter, must be met before a person can move on to "higher" needs. Try to determine at which level you are right now. How can you reach a higher level?

Making Consumer Decisions

Shari had worked hard and saved enough money to buy a pair of rollerblades. She had tried out a pair that belonged to her friend, Chris, and really liked them. She decided to get the same brand. When she went shopping, however, she discovered that this was one of the most expensive models around. To make matters worse, she had procrastinated and not shopped for the rollerblades during the winter, when prices were down and sales were going on. Now it was spring, when companies were promoting sporting goods and prices were up, but she wanted these blades now, to use this summer.

Shari went to a few sporting goods shops and even went to a larger city nearby in hopes of finding better prices. The news was the same everywhere, though—this model was still relatively new and was not going to be offered at a sale price for some time to come. Each store she went to pointed out that many other models were on sale and that she could get a better "deal" if she would consider other models and brands.

Shari wished she could try out some of the other brands, but of course, the stores couldn't let her do that. Although Shari had enough money saved to buy the more expensive brand, she had worked hard for her money and didn't want to spend more than she had to. On the other hand, she had *really* liked the ones she had borrowed from Chris. Tough decision! Finally, she decided to be "economical" and get a less expensive model.

Unfortunately, when she started using the new rollerblades, she discovered that they weren't quite as quick as Chris's and weren't as much fun. Now, she's sorry she didn't spend the extra money to get the better pair. To make matters worse, a few months later, at the end of the summer season, the rollerblades she had really wanted did go on sale!

What did Shari do wrong in her decision-making process? What did she do right? What other strategies could she have used to help her make an informed and wise decision? What decision would you have made?

lated to Maslow's system of basic human needs.

DECISIONS ARE BASED ON PERSONAL PREFERENCES

Everyone has the same basic needs, but our **personal preferences** (likes and dislikes) vary greatly. For example, some people buy used luxury cars, while others buy new economy models. Some prefer to own and live in suburban homes, and others prefer apartment living and freedom from the responsibilities of home ownership. Personal preferences are influenced by many factors, including the following:

- values
- goals
- age and sex
- cultural background
- family influences
- peer pressure
- advertising influences

personal preferences
....
the things that an individual likes and/or dislikes

Values

How we spend our money depends a great deal on our values. **Values** are our ideas of what is important, and they are influenced by our cultural heritage—especially our family and friends. We develop our values as we grow up. The first persons to influence our values are our parents. Other family members, friends, our schools, and our religions also affect our developing values. We learn values from people we respect and care about and because of this, we have an emotional attachment to our values. During our growing years our values are constantly changing as we search for the value system that will become a basic part of our personality and then remain fairly constant. For many of us, our values are fairly well fixed by the time we graduate from high school. Others among us are still struggling to clarify our value systems. Our values guide us in developing a **lifestyle**, our way of living, which determines how we spend our time and money.

Having a clear understanding of your personal values, knowing what is truly important to you, will help you make consumer decisions that are satisfying.

Analyzing Values. There are a number of value-appraisal scales that can help you recognize the relative importance you give certain values. These scales may help you rate the importance of a number of values in your own life. These values may include family, fame, religion, money, power, humanitarianism, health, aesthetic appreciation, and involvement in intellectual, creative, and social activities. It is your own balance of values that helps you decide what is important in terms of people, places, situations—even consumer products and services. Your values, then, are your guideposts in decision making. They influence how you spend

Our values are greatly influenced by family and friends. Whose influence affects you the most when you're considering a purchase?

your time and money, so they influence your overall lifestyle. (See Figure 2.3 on the next page.)

Sometimes a desired purchase makes us give up something else we value. It may mean that we won't be able to afford something else that we want very much. Suppose your old TV set shows only part of the picture on the screen. You have a new friend whom you like very much who enjoys coming to your house—and who also likes to watch TV. You have saved money for a new coat. Should you make your old coat last another season and spend the money to get your TV repaired? Maybe you should buy the new coat and hope to entertain your friend some other way? You will have to analyze the consequences of these choices. Then you will make a decision based on what is most important to you.

Sometimes there is a conflict between a desired purchase and giving up the *time* needed to make that purchase. Buying food provides a good example. In most areas, grocery stores advertise

values
....
the things a person feels are important or believes are right or wrong

lifestyle
....
the typical way a person or group of people lives

This is a sample of the type of items you would find on a values inventory. The higher your score for an item, the more important that item is to you. If you're interested in learning more about your values, check with your school counselor about taking a values inventory.

Discovering Your Values

	True	Mainly True	Not Sure	Mainly False	False
1. If I were in a play, I would rather be an actor than part of the stage crew.	5	4	3	2	1
2. I would enjoy having an expensive car.	5	4	3	2	1
3. When I'm with friends, I like to be the one who decides what we're going to do.	5	4	3	2	1
4. I attend religious services regularly.	5	4	3	2	1
5. I like to give things to people who don't have as much as I have.	5	4	3	2	1
6. I enjoy spending time with my family.	5	4	3	2	1
7. I exercise regularly.	5	4	3	2	1
8. I like to browse in art galleries.	5	4	3	2	1
9. Developing new ideas is something I enjoy doing.	5	4	3	2	1
10. I prefer being with other people rather than alone.	5	4	3	2	1

goals
......
aims or purposes that a person intends to accomplish or achieve

"specials" (low prices on certain items) in the local newspaper on the same day each week. Suppose one store has the lowest price on bread and eggs this week, but another store has a special on chicken, fish, and meats. Then you notice that still another store has a special on soft drinks, fruits, and canned goods. There are other stores with specials on certain items, too. You could drive to every market with the lowest price on each item—but you know that if you do, you will use up what you save in food to pay for gasoline. If you ride your bike and don't buy too much, you can really save money. Unfortunately, you will spend a lot of time shopping. Again, you have to decide which is worth more—your time or the money saved by going to several stores for lower-priced goods.

Goals

Our values help to guide us as we set our **goals**. A goal is an aim or a purpose, what we intend to accomplish or achieve. Goals are important because they give us things to work toward. They make daily efforts seem worthwhile and cut down on wasted time and money. Long-range goals are what you hope to achieve in the next three, four, five, or more years. Set long-range goals first. Do this by daydreaming about where and how you would like to be living when you are twenty or thirty or even forty! Long-range goals might include living in a large home in an affluent neighborhood. Perhaps you would like to travel several months each year or just have time to pursue some favorite hobbies. Your long-range goals can help you plan your intermediate goals, which you hope to reach in the next one to three years.

Intermediate goals may include getting married and having children and/or advancing in your career. They may also include moving to a larger home. Your intermediate goals should help in setting your short-range goals, which you hope to reach next week, next month, or within a year.

Some of your short-range goals will likely lead to achieving your intermediate and long-range goals. An example would be establishing a savings program that will provide the money you will need when you begin your own family. For high school students, short-range goals often include saving money for college or other post-high school education. They may include saving money for a CD player or TV, the purchase of a car, moving into an apartment or house, and buying furniture.

Our goals are like mountains—the closer they are, the more clearly we can see them. Our long-range goals may seem a little fuzzy, but our short-range goals are clear. Unless we set and consider long-range goals, though, we are likely to spend all of our resources (time and money) on short-range goals unrelated to the longer term. Thus, we may reach middle age (or older) unsatisfied with our accomplishments and lifestyle. Goals, like interests, may change—but goals guide us in our financial planning. The effects of goal-setting on financial planning will be discussed in Chapter 8.

Age and Sex

Have you noticed that your spending habits have changed in the last several years? As we get older, our needs and

Spending time dreaming about your future can help you determine your long-range goals. Once you've determined some long-range goals, you can begin setting intermediate and short-range goals to help you reach the long-range goals. What goals—from short-range to long-range—have you set for yourself?

wants change. An eight-year-old looks for transportation and independence and gets it in the form of a bicycle. An eighteen-year-old may seek the same thing in the form of a car. Generally, as we become adults, satisfying our needs and wants costs more.

Young men spend money differently from young women. Transportation and entertainment costs are often the biggest items in a young man's spending plan. Young women often spend more on clothes, cosmetics, and personal items.

Cultural Background

The United States has long been considered the "melting pot of the world." People who came from other countries to live in the United States often put aside their old cultural ways to assimilate, or "become Americans." Among recent newcomers, however, are groups that prefer to keep as much of their former culture as possible. As a result, many different cultures exist within American society, so we say we have a pluralistic society. For many first- and second-generation immigrants, cultural background is likely to have a strong influence on consumer spending. Preferences based on cultural background are often apparent in clothing, food, and music.

Family Influences. Among those who most influence the way we spend our money are members of our own family. We may discuss many of our prospective purchases with them. Older family members may have already researched which brand gives the best service for the money, or they may have determined which brand has the best warranty. They may have even bought the same type of product that you are

considering, so their experiences can be very helpful. Unlike people who write advertisements, members of your own family have your interests in mind when they make a recommendation.

Peer Pressure. You will recall that Maslow's social needs include the need for a sense of belonging. Most of us want to be liked by those in our own social group or age group. Because of this need to be accepted, we may adopt many of the ideas of our peers. Among teenagers, this is most apparent in dress, hairstyles, and music.

Older adults are not immune to peer influence, however. Have you heard the expression "Keeping up with the Joneses"? It refers to those who buy expensive items because their peers or neighbors (the Joneses) buy them. Such purchases are considered status symbols because they show off financial status. Of course, many people who buy expensive homes or cars do so mainly because they enjoy the comfort of such luxuries. Even so, our peers influence our purchases by the things they buy and by what they say is good or desirable.

Advertising Influences

Advertising is among the strongest influences on how we spend our money. This is not surprising. In the early 1990s, about a hundred billion dollars was spent every year on advertising to influence our purchases. The most expensive advertising appears on TV. A 30-second commercial during the 1994 Super Bowl cost $900,000! The price is worth it to the advertiser because more than thirty million people were watching. If only one person in a thousand buys the product, the result is thirty thousand sales.

status symbols
....
expensive items that show off a person's financial position

pluralistic society
....
a community or nation that has people of different ethnic, social, and religious groups

CONSUMERS AND MAIL SERVICES

Advertisers often send ads to people whose names are on mailing lists. You can have your name added to certain lists in order to get advertising mail that you want, or you can have your name removed and receive less advertising mail. The Direct Marketing Association allows you to do either of these things through its Mail Preference Service. The service is free. See the Appendix for the address of the Association.

The U.S. Postal Service can help you in many ways. If you have a question, a suggestion, or a complaint, you may fill out a Consumer Service Card. These cards are available from your letter carrier or from your local post office.

You may refuse to accept mail that is delivered to your mailbox. The U.S. Postal Service will return first-class mail to the sender. If you receive merchandise you did not order, you need not return it—it is legal to keep unordered merchandise—and you do not need to pay for it, even if you receive a bill.

WHY DOES ADVERTISING WORK?

The goal of those in the advertising business is to influence us to buy the products and services they advertise. They try for the most urgent-sounding messages possible. The most effective advertising approach for a particular product often depends on the product itself. For example, a strong advertisement for an office computer might stress its efficiency. The advertisement might say the computer will let workers get more tasks done in half the time. An effective advertisement for breakfast cereal might appeal to our needs for good nutrition. Sometimes advertising a product as more interesting than others will cause us to buy it (for example, a cereal that pops, crackles, and "talks" to you).

Advertising Techniques

Some advertising is straightforward and honest. The ad points out the good features of a product or service. Often this kind of advertising does not convince us to spend as much money as the producers would like. So advertising companies study human psychology to learn how to take advantage of human weaknesses. Much of the advertising today makes an emotional appeal. Most of us listen to, see, or read more than 1,500 advertisements every day—and we remember about 30. We usually can recall five for information only, but the other 25 appeal to our emotions, which may cause us to buy things we don't need or can't afford.

Many advertisements, especially TV commercials, use special techniques that are designed to control our thoughts and actions. These techniques are called propaganda. One or more of these techniques appear in many advertisements today.

propaganda
....
techniques that are designed to control thoughts and actions by deceiving the audience or by distorting the truth

Advertisers use many different techniques to make us want to buy their products. What types of advertisements do you like the most? Which do you like the least? Why?

price of plain jeans. The advertising sold millions of jeans at high prices because young consumers began to consider it "in" to own and wear them.

Plain-Folk Ploy. The plain-folk ploy is a reverse kind of snobbery. Some people like to think of themselves as "just plain folk." They look down on sophisticated, fast-living lifestyles—and effective advertising takes advantage of this. A handsome but modest-looking actor talks to viewers about some common feelings among "us plain folk." Of course, one of those things held in high regard among us is the fine product being advertised. The actor says he hopes we'll buy it. If we buy the plain-folk approach, there's a good chance that we'll buy the product as well.

infomercial
....

an advertising presentation that lasts from 30 minutes to an hour and is designed to look like an informative television program

Image-Building. The technique that appeals to our need for self-esteem is image-building. Advertisers try to convince us that using a certain product will improve our social status. It's difficult to pass up a product that promises to make us more attractive, popular, or successful. Advertisers may use testimonials by respected or beautiful people for image-building. When these people say how much they enjoy this or that product, we may want to buy it to be more like them. Movie, TV, and sports stars are often seen in such commercials.

Snob Appeal. Some advertisements suggest that a product is "not for everyone." This technique is known as "snob appeal." The implication is that only those of us who are a cut above ordinary people buy the product. This approach is often used to advertise a product that is more expensive than its competition. Dozens of companies have used this technique to sell jeans for high profits. "Designer" jeans, with distinctive stitching on the pockets, have sold for two or three times the

Television Infomercials

A newer type of advertising presentation, called an **infomercial**, may be seen on many channels during late night or Saturday morning television. An infomercial is a presentation, usually lasting a half-hour or an hour, designed to *look* like an information program. You may have watched an infomercial for a few minutes before you realized that it was more commercial than informational.

Infomercials are used to sell products that have mass appeal, products with a "can't live without it" quality. For example, millions of people would like to lose a few pounds, so infomercials are used to sell diet programs and exercise equipment. (Many other types of products are sold through infomercials, too.) Usually one person makes the presentation (gives information about a product) and another stands by and looks amazed at the product's effectiveness. A studio audience (which is usually paid) applauds loudly whenever the product is shown to be effective.

Misleading and Fraudulent Advertising

Advertisements should not make promises that cannot be proved. For example, advertisements for facial creams that promise teenagers beautiful skin are often misleading, and advertisements such as these may come close to being fraudulent (dishonest). Most teenage skin problems are due to hormone imbalances, and serious problems can be corrected only through a doctor's care. (See Figure 2.4.)

Some advertisements are indeed fraudulent. It is important for consumers to be able to recognize fraud. Fraud is the cheating or tricking of consumers. Recognizing fraud and knowing what to do if you are "ripped off" will be discussed in Chapter 5.

The Value of Advertising

You may be thinking that advertising is beneficial only to the producers, sellers, advertising agencies, and advertising media. Advertising has value for us as consumers, too. Through advertising, we learn what products are available and when new products are introduced. However, we need to rec-

ognize that the purpose of advertising is to persuade us to buy a product, so we must evaluate the advertising message carefully. This will be discussed further in Chapter 3 under "Gathering Consumer Information" on alternative products and services.

DECISIONS ARE BASED ON FINANCIAL RESOURCES

We know that there are many influences on how we spend our money. The biggest influence of all is the amount of money we have to spend. That determines what we can and cannot buy. Some Americans can hardly afford the necessities of life: food, housing, and medical care. Others have enough financial resources to pay for these necessities and some luxuries as well. However, even the wealthy among us do not have an unlimited supply of money. We are constantly being offered products and services that we think would make life more interesting, fun, and satisfying. Therefore, we must constantly analyze our

fraud
....

the cheating or tricking of consumers

Figure 2.4
....

This cartoon demonstrates what often happens when a consumer reads an advertisement that is "too good to be true." What do you think has happened in this cartoon?

Our financial resources determine how much money we have to spend at any given time. If this shopper can't really afford to buy this product at this time, but does anyway, what purchases might she have to give up tomorrow or next week?

financial resources. How will each purchase affect our ability to make other purchases tomorrow, next week, next month, and next year?

Summary

- Following a decision-making process can help you spend your money more wisely.
- Consumer decisions are based on needs, personal preferences, and financial resources.
- Personal preferences are influenced by: values, goals, age and sex, cultural background, family influences, peer pressure, and advertising.
- Advertising is a powerful influence on how we spend our money.
- Some advertising techniques try to control our thoughts and emotions, and some are misleading. Being aware of this can help in making wise spending decisions.

CHAPTER REVIEW
2

ENRICH YOUR VOCABULARY

Number your paper from 1–10. Beside each number write the word from the following list, along with a brief definition.

decision-making process   lifestyle   status symbols
fraud   personal preferences   values
goals   pluralistic society
infomercial   propaganda

REVIEWING WHAT YOU HAVE LEARNED

1. List six steps in the consumer decision-making process.

2. Name at least five influences that help to shape our personal preferences.

3. Name and define three advertising techniques.

4. Give one example for each of the following:
   A. short-range goal
   B. intermediate goal
   C. long-range goal

USING YOUR CRITICAL THINKING SKILLS

1. Discuss and evaluate a recent consumer decision you have made.

2. Use the decision-making process to select a service or product for your school or class.

3. What is the role of advertising in a free enterprise system?

4. How is advertising helpful to consumers?

APPLYING WHAT YOU HAVE LEARNED

1. Our goals add meaning to our daily lives. For your own use, write down three of your long-range goals, three intermediate goals, and three short-range goals. Will your short-range and intermediate goals help you achieve your long-range goals? Review your goals from time to time to see if you are making progress toward achieving them or to see if your goals have changed.

2. Collect samples of different advertising techniques and prepare a display to show the various types.

3. Prepare a script and act out a "commercial" for TV that makes use of one of the three advertising techniques discussed in the chapter.

CHAPTER 3

Making Consumer Decisions

OBJECTIVES

After completing this chapter, you will be able to do the following:

1. List four types of consumer information you should gather when researching alternatives for a major purchase.
2. Determine whether a manufacturer of a product will pay for repairs.
3. List eight sources of information about products and services.

TERMS

alternatives	decision matrix	suggested retail prices
consumable	implied warranty	warranty

Wise consumers research product alternatives. Because they do, they tend to be more satisfied with their purchases. Think of a purchase you have not been happy with. Do you think you might have made a wiser choice if you had researched the alternatives?

Do you usually know all you need to know about a product to make a wise decision? Some people make decisions to buy without considering alternative choices. They see something that is attractive and make a purchase immediately, but the most satisfying purchase is one that is made after considering *pertinent information about a variety of alternative products.* Then you feel good because you know you've made the best choice. Spending a large amount of money without going through this process often results in disappointment when better buys or more desirable products are seen after the purchase is made.

IDENTIFYING ALTERNATIVES

Suppose your old CD player is broken, and you are considering buying a new CD player so that you can have great sound when you have friends over (thus satisfying a social need). You determine that you can afford the cost. Then, since you want to follow a logical decision-making process, you refrain from buying the first one that looks good to you. You consider many alternatives that have the features you want and that are in the price range that you can afford. There are many alternatives to a given make and model of CD player. See what various stores have available in the general size and type of CD player that you want to buy.

alternatives
....
different choices

GATHERING CONSUMER INFORMATION

After identifying a number of possible alternatives, gather information about the products or services you are considering. The amount of information you want to gather before making a purchase will depend, of course, on the type of product or service. Many items are consumable. That is, they will be used up or thrown away after use. You would probably not spend a lot of time researching alternatives to inexpensive, consumable items such as bread, soap, and razor blades. (Even for these small items, though, you can still compare prices to get good buys.)

For reasonably expensive items, researching alternatives makes a satisfying purchase more likely. Gather as much information as possible on each product or service, especially regarding:

- **Quality.** Is the product well constructed? Will it be durable? (If you are selecting a service, talk to others who have used this service so that you will know what to expect.)

consumable
....
items that will be used up or thrown away after use

- **Cost.** What is the lowest price for this product or service in relation to quality and expected use?
- **Availability.** Where is it available? Is it in stock? Will it have to be ordered? How much time will be required for delivery?
- **Warranty.** A warranty is a written guarantee, and it is legally binding. Things to look for in a warranty include:

    a) If it needs service, will it be repaired for free during the first ninety days, year, or two years?

    b) Does the warranty cover the labor required to repair the product, or just the parts?

    c) For how long is the warranty in effect?

    d) If the product must be sent away for repair, who pays the cost of shipping and handling?

    e) What is required to keep the warranty in effect?

    f) Who is responsible for the terms in the warranty: the seller, manufacturer, importer? What do you do if you have a problem with the product?

CONSUMER PROFILE

Fred was ready to invest in his own camping stove. He asked his family and friends what they liked or didn't like about their stoves. They discussed the advantages and disadvantages of different types and models of stoves. Fred also studied the various stoves available through catalogs.

By asking questions in a couple of sporting goods shops, he found that a lesser-known brand was available that offered the same quality and warranty as the "name" brand. In fact, it actually had some advantages over the "name" brand and was much less expensive!

"Thank goodness I asked questions! I really ended up with a product I'm happy with!" Fred exclaimed.

Sources of Information

Information about products and services is available from a variety of sources:

- family and friends
- advertising
- sales and informational brochures
- catalogs
- magazine and newspaper articles
- consumer product-testing organizations
- in-store information
- manufacturers

Family and Friends. Whether you're making a small or large purchase, your family and friends are good sources of information. Ask around. People you know are likely to have fairly accurate information on who sells what and for how much. They may have bought one or more of the alternative products or services that you are considering. If so, their experience should be helpful to you in making a decision. Did their purchase need servicing? Ask if the repairs were completed promptly, either under the warranty or at a fair cost.

Advertising. Advertising helps us identify alternatives to a particular product or service. It often provides information on availability, and remember, the way we learn what's new on the market is frequently through advertising.

Some advertisements state exact prices, but others mention suggested retail prices. This means that the actual price may be different in the store (usually lower). Advertising is often helpful in identifying special features of a product, and some ads give information on warranties. Because the purpose of advertising is to persuade you to buy the product and not consider others, it's best to look elsewhere for details on product quality and warranties. Also, don't depend on advertisements to determine the reputation of the company or companies involved in producing and selling a product or service.

Sales and Informational Brochures. Product manufacturers and distributors often prepare sales or informational brochures (booklets). The ultimate purpose of the brochures is to sell products, but brochures are usually more factual than other forms of advertising.

Company brochures are often the best source of product specifications, and the details given often indicate the quality of the product. Sometimes the brochures contain information on warranties and on what to do if the product needs repair. Brochures are usually available where the product is sold. If not, call or write the distributor or manufacturer. Their telephone numbers and addresses are often given in magazine or newspaper advertisements.

Catalogs. You may be shopping for clothing, furniture, recreational equipment, or any of a thousand other products. No matter what you want to buy, mail-order catalogs provide a quick reference. In the comfort of your own home, you can compare features and prices of similar items from the different catalogs. Then you can compare the features and prices of items in the catalogs with those of items available in your local retail stores. (Remember to add the cost of shipping and handling to the cost of items ordered through the mail.)

Magazine and Newspaper Articles. Every magazine rack or newsstand has publications that include articles on new products. You can read different articles about the type of product you want and learn a lot about product quality and serviceability (usefulness). Some magazines, such as *Modern Photography*,

Magazines, catalogs, and sales brochures provide important information on product alternatives. Libraries usually have many magazines from which you can gather information.

publish issues devoted to information on new products. Some, such as *Mechanix Illustrated*, regularly test products of special interest to their readers. Popular home magazines, sold mainly in food markets, generally have a variety of articles giving information that helps in making consumer decisions.

Consumer Product-Testing Organizations. There are two major independent, nonprofit consumer product-testing organizations. These are Consumers Union, which publishes *Consumer Reports*, and Consumers' Research, which publishes *Consumers' Research Magazine*. These organizations buy products for testing from retailers. They do this to be sure that their test samples are representative of what consumers buy. The test results are published monthly, and they list brand names according to quality.

Consumers Union, the larger and more influential of these organizations, also publishes an annual *Consumer Reports Buying Guide*. The products most often tested by Consumers Union are automobiles. Other frequently test-

CONSUMER PROFILE

Erica plays on the girls' basketball team. On TV, she saw some of her favorite professional athletes wearing and advertising a particular brand of sport shoe. She thought that if she had a pair of these shoes, they might improve her game. Besides, the more popular girls on the team had these shoes.

Somehow she convinced her mother to buy her a pair. Although Erica liked her new shoes, unfortunately they did not improve her basketball skills. They didn't make her any more popular either!

Advice from Erica, "Buy things because *you* like them, not because you think they will make you more successful or popular!"

ed products include stereo and TV sets, cameras, recreational equipment, refrigerators, and washing machines. Hundreds of other products are tested too, and the reports are prepared and published in *Consumer Reports*. Characteristics of tested products are discussed, then each brand that was tested is ranked (first, second, and so forth) or rated as "acceptable" or "unacceptable." *Consumer Reports* and *Consumers' Research Magazine* are usually available in your local library.

In-Store Information. American consumers are accustomed to asking questions about products and examining them in the store before making a purchase. Information that salespeople give can be very helpful, but they may tell you only the good things about the product. Also, some salespeople may say whatever they think will influence you to buy from them, including unsupportable claims and promises. For important or expensive purchases, ask all the questions you want of the salespeople—but take time to gather information from other sources, too. Reliable in-store information is often available in the form of:

- labels
- seals
- warranties

The name and address of the manufacturer are given on the label, along with some specifications and how to use and take care of the product safely. (See Chapters 18 and 20 for more about labels.)

Seals are used to identify products that are "approved," "commended," "certified," or "tested." Seals are given to products that meet the requirements of the organization that issues the seal

Many consumer magazines offer excellent product-comparison information. They will often have comparison charts, and rate the products that have been researched.

Among the most widely used seals is the Good Housekeeping Seal, carried by products advertised in the magazine *Good Housekeeping*. If one of these products proves defective, the publisher of the magazine agrees to replace the product or refund the purchase price. Information on other seals is presented in Chapter 4.

Information on the warranty of a specific product is available in the store. By law, you should be able to read the warranty of any product costing fifteen dollars or more before you make the purchase.

In addition to written warranties, every product has an implied warranty. This means that the product can be used for its intended purpose and will give reasonable service. For example, a cassette tape player must function properly in playing tapes. If not, it may be returned to the seller for a refund.

Salespeople might make *verbal* promises (spoken, rather than written) that go beyond a product's reasonable service. These promises may or may not be supported by the store or manufacturer. Verbal promises are not binding. (There is no legal obligation to keep verbal promises.)

Manufacturers. Suppose you have a specific question about a product, but you can't find an answer from the sources we have discussed. If this happens, you can write or call the manufacturer. The address can usually be found on a product warranty or in an information brochure—or you can ask the retail salesperson.

If you want a quick answer, use the telephone—and be prepared to state your question clearly. Many companies have 800 numbers, so the call will cost you nothing. To find a toll-free number, dial 1-800-555-1212 for directory assistance. If the company does not have a toll-free number but you know the city and state, dial 1, the area code for the city, and then 555-1212.

Gathering information on alternatives takes time and may cost some money for gasoline and phone calls.

implied warranty

the unwritten guarantee that a product can be used for its intended purpose and will give reasonable service

A warranty is a legally-binding contract. However, consumers who don't read the warranty, don't know what their rights are if a product proves to be defective. Locate a warranty for a product you have at home. Determine your rights as the purchaser of the product.

However, it is worth the time and effort when the cost of the product is high and the cost of information-gathering is low. Information-gathering is most helpful when product costs or quality vary greatly. Gathering information will help you get more for your money, and you will usually avoid the unhappy experience of finding a better buy after you have made your purchase.

EVALUATING ALTERNATIVES

After gathering information on a variety of choices that you think would satisfy your need, evaluate your alternatives. This can be done in several ways. Some people do it entirely in their minds. Others make a few notes, listing the advantages and disadvantages. Then the best decision becomes clear to them. Although it takes a bit more time, probably the best way to evaluate alternatives for really important purchases is to use a **decision matrix**. This is a form that you can use to compare products. The procedure can be done in five steps:

1. Write the name, price, and source of each product as a column head.

2. List the desirable features for this kind of product on the left side of the page.

3. Rate the importance of each feature. (A scale from one to ten is useful.) This rating is a "weight factor." Include an "X" since each weight factor will later be multiplied by your ranking for each feature. When this is done, your decision matrix will look something like Figure 3.1 below.

Figure 3.1
· · · · · · · · · · · ·

This decision matrix shows the information that a consumer might want to gather before purchasing a personal computer. Are there any features that you would weight differently?

Decision Matrix

Features	Weight Factor	GB-13 Computer Shop $2,500		PI-720 Computer Masters $1,800		CD2000 Computers and More $2,200		X311 Turbo SoftWare House $3,200		System 24-1 The PC Place $3,000		LX-T3 Premier Computers $2,700	
		Rank	Score	Rank	Score	Rank	Score	Rank	Score	Rank	Score	Rank	Score
Price	10x												
RAM	8x												
HD size	8x												
CPU size	8x												
Expansions	6x												
Bundles	4x												
CD drive	7x												
Modem	5x												
Connections	6x												
Size	3x												
Total													

Decision Matrix

Features	Weight Factor	GB-13 Computer Shop $2,500 Rank	Score	PI-720 Computer Masters $1,800 Rank	Score	CD2000 Computers and More $2,200 Rank	Score	X311 Turbo SoftWare House $3,200 Rank	Score	System 24-1 The PC Place $3,000 Rank	Score	LX-T3 Premier Computers $2,700 Rank	Score
Price	10x	4	40	6	60	5	50	1	10	2	20	3	30
RAM	8x	5	40	1	8	4	32	6	48	3	24	2	16
HD size	8x	6	48	1	8	4	32	5	40	3	24	2	16
CPU size	8x	5	40	1	8	4	32	6	48	3	24	2	16
Expansions	6x	5	30	1	6	6	36	4	24	3	18	2	12
Bundles	4x	2	8	3	12	4	16	1	4	6	24	5	20
CD drive	7x	yes	7	no	0	yes	7	yes	7	no	0	no	0
Modem	5x	yes	5	yes	5	no	0	no	0	yes	5	no	0
Connections	6x	3	18	6	36	5	30	4	24	2	12	1	6
Size	3x	1	3	6	18	3	9	2	6	4	12	5	15
Total			239		161		244		211		163		131

Figure 3.2
....
This completed decision matrix includes information for all of the features for the different models listed. According to this matrix, which computer would be the best purchase?

4. Rank the quality of the products for each feature. Start with the first feature listed. If there are six products, use the numbers one through six. Give the biggest number, six, to the product that is best on the first feature. Give a five to the product that is next best. Rank all the other products down to the worst, which gets the lowest number, one. (Give the same rank number to products that are tied.) Rank the products for each of the other features, then multiply each rank times the weight factor for each feature and write in your answers.

5. Total the column of numbers that you calculated for each product. The product with the highest total should be the best buy. If for any reason you feel seriously that the results are not right, you may want to revise your weight factors for some features. When complete, your matrix will look something like Figure 3.2 above.

MAKING A DECISION

A decision matrix makes it easy to choose the best alternative. If you do not use the matrix, you will still make your decision on the basis of whatever information you have gathered—along with your personal preferences. Once you have evaluated the alternatives and feel comfortable with your choice, you may want to make your purchase without too much delay. If you wait several

REDUCING YOUR PHONE BILL

The phone is so easy to use that we may not think about the charges, but they can add up quickly. To keep them to a minimum you can do some basic planning.

When you move to a new place, you will probably have to pay a telephone connection charge. If new equipment is installed by the phone company, there will be additional charges. If you own your own telephone, you won't have to rent one.

In many places, you have a choice of several types of phone service. One type lets you make any number of calls for a fixed monthly charge. Another type of service is charged by the call; and if you don't make a lot of calls, this service may save you money.

The easiest way for phone bills to get out of hand is through long-distance calls. When visiting with friends or family members in another state, the minutes go by—and the charges mount up!

You can help yourself cut back on long-distance calling time by planning what you want to say before you make your call. During the call, use a timer—or avoid the call by writing instead.

Call long-distance when the rates are low (at night or on weekends), and dial directly rather than asking for operator assistance. Unless you need to call several times to locate someone, avoid person-to-person calls. Use toll-free ("800") numbers whenever possible, as they involve no charge to the caller. Many consumer affairs offices and service agencies have toll-free numbers.

You can get useful information about charges and services from your phone company business office. Call there, too, if you have questions about your bill, such as calls mistakenly charged to you—which you are not required to pay.

The front pages of your phone book are a valuable consumer guide about phone service. If you consult these sources and do some planning, you can meet your phone needs economically.

weeks or months, the costs and features may change.

EVALUATING YOUR DECISION

After you make a purchase, evaluate your decision. Most of us do this without thinking about it. If we are happy about a purchase some weeks later, we may tell a friend or family member that we are very happy about it. If we later decide that we are not very happy about a purchase, we should try to analyze the reason why we aren't happy. The explanation may help us in future decisions.

Summary

- When considering an expensive purchase, research your choices before you buy. Get information regarding quality, cost, availability and warranty.

- There are numerous sources of information about products and services. These include: family and friends, advertising, sales brochures, catalogs, magazine and newspaper articles, consumer product-testing organizations, stores, and manufacturers themselves.

CHECKLIST FOR DECISION MAKING

The remaining chapters of this book deal with how to get the most for your money in your consumer buying. Each chapter covers a major area of consumer spending, but decision making is much the same no matter what the purchase. The following checklist can help you make wise consumer decisions—so when you are considering a purchase, ask yourself each of these questions. We shall refer to this general checklist and to more specific checklists as we continue to discuss consumer decision making.

___ Which basic human and personal needs will be satisfied?

___ How does the purchase fit in with my short-, intermediate-, and long-range goals?

___ Will it save time?

___ Will it provide satisfaction for a long or short period of time?

___ Will it delay a more satisfying or more important purchase?

___ What other product or service might be just as satisfying?

___ How does the quality of this product or service compare to the alternatives?

___ Will this product or service last as long as the alternatives?

___ How does the cost of this product or service compare to the cost(s) of the alternatives?

___ How does the warranty of this product or service compare to those of the alternatives?

___ How does the reputation of the producer or distributor of this product or service compare to those of the alternatives?

___ Do I have enough information to make a good choice?

___ Overall, which product will be most satisfying?

___ Is there money available to pay for this product or service?

___ How much time, effort, and money will be required for the use, care, and upkeep of the product?

___ How will my family and friends feel about it?

___ After time has passed: Was the choice a wise decision? (If I had it to do over again, would I make the same decision?)

CHAPTER REVIEW 3

ENRICH YOUR VOCABULARY

Read the following pairs of sentences. Write the sentence that correctly uses the underlined word or phrase on your paper.

1A. An <u>implied warranty</u> lists the terms of the guarantee in writing.

1B. An <u>implied warranty</u> is an unwritten guarantee that a product will give reasonable service.

2A. A <u>warranty</u> is legally binding.

2B. A <u>warranty</u> is not as legally binding as a guarantee.

3A. An actual price may vary from the <u>suggested retail price</u>.

3B. An actual price is usually much higher than a <u>suggested retail price</u>.

4A. <u>Consumable</u> items are any items that are purchased by consumers.

4B. <u>Consumable</u> items are either used up or thrown away after use.

5A. Comparing cost and quality is part of the process of considering <u>alternatives</u>.

5B. American consumers usually have no <u>alternatives</u> to choose from when shopping.

6A. Using a <u>decision matrix</u> makes it unnecessary to evaluate alternatives.

6B. Using a <u>decision matrix</u> is a good way to evaluate alternatives.

REVIEWING WHAT YOU HAVE LEARNED

1. Name four pieces of consumer information you should gather when researching alternatives.

2. Where would you look to find out whether the manufacturer of a product will pay for repairs?

3. List eight sources of information about products or services.

4. List six things to look for in a warranty.

5. What kind of product information can consumers expect to find in stores?

6. What is the purpose for preparing a decision matrix?

USING YOUR CRITICAL THINKING SKILLS

1. Which source(s) of product information could tell you both advantages and disadvantages of a product? Which one(s) would you consider most reliable?

2. Name two types of products that you might evaluate using a decision matrix, and explain why you would use this method of comparison.

3. Why is it important to evaluate your decision after making a purchase?

4. Select an item such as breakfast cereal. List the things you would consider before purchasing the item. Tell why you would look for these things.

CHAPTER REVIEW
3

APPLYING WHAT YOU HAVE LEARNED

1. Select a product that you are interested in purchasing, gather information on alternative products, and prepare a decision matrix.

2. Write a brief evaluation of your decision to purchase a product that you bought within the past year.

3. Select an item, such as a TV or CD player, that many people you know own. Interview several of the people to find the features they looked for when shopping for the item. Make a list of the features and compare with your classmates.

UNIT

2

CONSUMER RIGHTS AND RESPONSIBILITIES

CHAPTERS

W e consumers "wear many hats." We produce goods and services, and we buy them—and as such we are part of the economy (Chapters 1 and 2). But consumers are also citizens, members of society with rights and responsibilities. We are entitled to have our needs met as consumers, but we are also responsible for maintaining and improving the way all of us are treated as consumers.

35

CHAPTER 4

Increasing Consumer Awareness

OBJECTIVES

After completing this chapter, you will be able to do the following:
1. Describe methods businesses use to give consumers information that will help them make good decisions.
2. Explain the difference between a full and a limited warranty.
3. Describe what your actions would be if you had a consumer complaint.

TERMS

American Gas
   Association (AGA)
Better Business Bureaus
boycott
caveat emptor
certification seals
Consumer Action Panels
   (CAPs)

consumer complaint
Consumer Product Safety
   Commission
Consumers Union
guarantee
Magnuson-Moss
   Warranty Act
product standards

regulate
Underwriters
   Laboratories (UL)

Consumer interests have taken on a new importance, and as consumers we are speaking up more and more. We express our wishes and opinions about goods and services to those who produce them, and producers are becoming more sensitive to consumer needs. The government as well as the producer is listening to the consumer, and the government has passed laws to regulate the production and sale of goods and services. The consumer movement is now a major force in our society.

THE CONSUMER MOVEMENT

The consumer movement began about 100 years ago, in the late 1800s. During those years, many people left their farms and self-sufficient lifestyles. They moved to the cities, where they had to rely on others for the things they needed for their families. As our industrialized society grew, poor housing and working conditions were reported, abuse of consumers and workers increased, and the first consumer groups were formed to investigate poor sanitation and production of impure food at meat-packing houses.

In 1929, F. J. Schlink started Consumers Research, Inc. to conduct independent testing of consumer goods. Consumers Union was founded in 1936, and today it publishes *Consumer Reports*—a monthly magazine that gives us independent test results on consumer products. (See p. 322.)

During the 1940s and 1950s, little action was taken in the consumer movement. But at the start of the 1960s, critics of American industry spoke out, denouncing industry's lack of concern for the environment and the effect of industry's economic policies on the poor. They also questioned the safety of many consumer products.

In 1962, President John F. Kennedy gave his speech on "The Consumers' Bill of Rights" (see p. 48). In 1964, President Lyndon B. Johnson appointed the first consumer affairs officer of the United States. This was Esther Peterson, appointed as Special Presidential Assistant for Consumer Affairs. Ralph Nader came on the scene in the late sixties and quickly became a national champion of the consumer movement with his attempts to improve automobile safety.

Consumer laws were passed, and many industries set up Consumer Action Panels and consumer affairs divisions to handle consumer concerns. Today, consumers, producers, and government cooperate more than in the past. Consumers use their spending power and join together to support legislation. By doing these things, consumers have shown they can influence business practices and industry's products.

Consumers Union
....
independent nonprofit organization that tests consumer products for quality and price

Consumer laws have been passed to help protect consumers from producers. However, some producers still try to take advantage of consumers. Think of a time when you felt you were taken advantage of by a producer. What did you do about it?

Business has become aware of the need to be accountable to society, and business now must openly take responsibility for its decisions. Government has played a needed role by regulating businesses that have had bad effects on the environment and consumers.

THE CONSUMER STORY

There are three characters in the consumer story—the producer, the consumer, and the citizen—and we all play all three roles. As citizens, we need to consider how our activities as producers and consumers affect others. Do we produce products harmful to others? Do we buy more than we need? Do we consume in a wasteful manner?

The Producer

The producer in our society is responsible for providing a variety of goods and services. Then, we as consumers may choose those that best meet our needs or wants. Communication is needed between producers and consumers. Producers may respond to our wishes by making the products and offering the services that we will buy, or producers may create the desire for a product. How do producers and consumers communicate?

Advertising. One way that producers inform people about their products is by advertising. Today's consumer wants more information than in the past, for several reasons. There are more products to choose from and more brands of the same product, and there is easier access to different stores. In many self-service stores, there are no salespeople to provide information. Through truthful advertising and your own consumer research, you can learn about products before you buy.

Advertising tells us about new products, prices, product features, brands, stores, and sales. But sellers may present only their own views in their ads. They may exaggerate the good side of their products, or they may leave out important information.

Suppose a new soft drink is introduced. A TV commercial shows a group of young people at a party, everyone having a great time and drinking CalCola. Then an announcer says that in a recent survey, nine out of ten soft-drink lovers preferred Cal-Cola. Would you be impressed enough to try it? What if that survey consisted of only ten people's comments—and those people were all employees of the CalCola Company? The commercial would not be false, but it would surely be misleading.

The slogan caveat emptor is what people say as a warning about doubtful claims. It means, "Let the buyer beware." The Federal Trade Commission (FTC) has the responsibility for checking advertising, making sure that false or misleading claims by manufacturers are corrected.

Consumer Action Panels and Warranties. Many industries have established Consumer Action Panels (CAPs) during the past few years. These panels are composed of people who are not employees in that industry, but who listen to consumer complaints and help resolve them. For example, automobile dealer associations have set up AutoCAPs (Automobile Consumer Action Panels).

Toll-free telephone numbers are provided by many companies, and this "direct response" improves communi-

caveat emptor
....
let the buyer beware

Consumer Action Panel (CAP)
....
a group of persons not employed in a particular industry that is responsible for handling consumer complaints in that industry

CONSUMER FOCUS

SERVICE GUARANTEED?

When you buy a product such as a CD player, you expect it to work properly. If it doesn't work properly, you would expect it to have a warranty stating that it will be fixed or replaced. But what about services such as pizza delivery? Would you expect that to be guaranteed?

Many companies, in order to give themselves a more competitive edge, do just that; they guarantee their service. Pizza restaurants that deliver often guarantee delivery within 30 minutes or the pizza is free. A bottled gas delivery company in New Jersey also guarantees on-time delivery or there is no charge to the customer. A pest control firm guarantees customers a full refund if any live bug is found in an area treated regularly by that company.

Are customers willing to pay for these services? They seem to be. Companies that guarantee their service often charge more than companies that don't, but the higher prices don't seem to hurt sales. In fact, in many cases, sales are increasing rapidly.

LIMITED ONE YEAR WARRANTY

---

cation between companies and consumers. The 800 numbers provide consumers with immediate responses to their questions and complaints, and the companies use the opportunity to do brief consumer surveys. Consumer complaints and comments are logged into computers and analyzed to improve customer satisfaction.

Another method producers use to tell about their products is the warranty or guarantee. (These terms may be used interchangeably.) The warranty is a contract spelling out your rights as a consumer.

The Magnuson-Moss Warranty Act (1975) was passed by Congress to help clarify the warranty issue. It requires that warranties be written in ordinary language, not "legalese," so that you may have an accurate and understandable warranty before you buy. It may be either a full or limited warranty. According to a full warranty, a defective product will be fixed or replaced without charge. A limited warranty covers less than the full warranty, such as repair charges for parts but not labor. You will recall from Chapter 3 that products automatically have implied, unwritten warranties that the product will serve the purpose for which it was made. A toaster will toast, and a stove will heat.

It is important to read and understand the warranties of products and services you purchase—and to *keep the warranties* with your records. Some states provide warranty rights in addition to those stated in the warranty. A local or state office of consumer affairs can provide you with information about your rights in your state.

Seals of Approval. Today, many manufacturers use seals of approval on their products, and these seals provide added information to the consumer.

guarantee

a written contract (warranty) spelling out consumer rights

Magnuson-Moss Warranty Act

federal law passed in 1975 requiring that warranties be written in ordinary language

CONSUMER PROFILE

Skyler bought a fancy telephone with an answering machine for $180 at a large electronic equipment store. The machine came with a one-year warranty. Skyler had heard from friends that answering machines didn't seem to have a long life and broke down frequently. So, when the salesperson offered him an "extended service policy" which added a year to the warranty, he bought it for $39. The "service policy" would guarantee Skyler that if the machine broke at any time during the next two years, he could return it with the receipt and the store would repair or replace it free-of-charge, OR give him full credit toward anything else in the store.

Skyler saved his receipt and filed it with other receipts for household items. Many months later, the machine did break down. When he found his receipt, he discovered that he had purchased it just over a year ago. If he hadn't bought that extended warranty, it would have been a total loss. But since he had the extended warranty, he just took the machine and his receipt back to the store. With no questions asked, the store gave him a brand-new machine equal in value to the original price. Skyler is really glad he got that extended warranty—and kept his receipt!

certification seals

stamps of approval indicating that products have met certain established standards

American Gas Association (AGA)

private nonprofit organization that sets standards for gas appliances governing use, durability, and safety

Underwriters Laboratories (UL)

private nonprofit organization that tests products for safety

Some are very useful, others are not. What do these seals mean?

Certification seals are placed on items that meet certain standards set by industries or other private organizations. The Association of Home Appliance Manufacturers is an example of a certification agency. The certification process helps consumers compare products.

Professional standards for products are set by several private, national associations. Two of these are the **American Gas Association (AGA)** and **Underwriters Laboratories (UL)**. Gas companies and businesses that manufacture gas appliances finance AGA, and the AGA seal on an appliance means that it has met certain minimum standards of use, durability, and safety.

Underwriters Laboratories Inc. (UL) is an independent, not-for-profit organization that tests materials and products for safety. It also tests methods and systems for hazards that may affect life and property. UL provides a follow-up service, too. It checks products marketed with the UL Certification Mark. When you see the UL mark, you can be sure that the product has met UL safety standards.

Magazine Seals and Ratings. Seals that often appear on labels and in product ads are magazine seals, and some magazines have their own testing laboratories. Their seals are promises that products are "as advertised" in their magazines. *Good Housekeeping* is an example of such a magazine. (See Chapter 3.)

Magazine seals do not provide consumers with any facts about a product. They probably should not be used as the basis for buying a product, but there are magazines that provide independent test results to help consumers make decisions. *Consumer Reports* is such a magazine. It is published by Consumers Union, one of the largest nonprofit consumer product-testing organizations.

Consumer Reports accepts no advertising. All of the test data in the magazine are based on regular product samples. The products are bought in the same way any consumer would buy them, then the products are tested.

What does a rating in *Consumer Reports* mean? Testers rank the products for overall quality—and if a product is also low in price, it may receive a "best buy" rating. These ratings have proved to be very useful and factual for consumers, but remember one thing about the articles tested for *Consumer Reports*. Though there may be many brands and models of an item, the testers do not buy them all. The ratings are good only for those that were tested. The ratings also reflect the values expressed in the article, and these may not be the same values that are important to the consumer. For example, a car that receives a high rating because of its repair record may not satisfy the consumer's desire for a certain design or style.

The Consumer

In our society, the consumer is responsible for gathering information and examining alternatives before making a purchase decision. Individually or in groups, consumers are free to buy whatever products they choose.

Communicating Consumer Opinions. Each consumer is responsible for communicating his or her opinions to retailers and producers. Occasionally you may feel that you did not get a good buy. Maybe the hair dryer broke after one week, or the eyeliner smeared after swimming, even though the ad said it would not. Sometimes a product simply does not perform as advertised or as expected. Informing the retailer and the producer when this happens can make them aware of a problem, and it may also keep other consumers from making the same mistake you made.

Consumers Working Together. Consumer movements have been effective in correcting some consumer problems, and this was especially true in the sixties and seventies. If consumers demand change and make their wishes known, changes are made. Improved product labels and pollution controls are two examples. Consumers may contact the Office of Consumer Affairs in Washington, which receives more than 7,000 complaints each month from consumers trying to influence the marketplace.

As a group, consumers may **boycott** a product by withholding their dollars and refusing to buy the product because of their feelings about it. Con-

Well-organized boycotts send powerful messages to producers about their products or practices. Have you ever been involved in a boycott? If so, what was the reason? What was the outcome of the boycott?

sumers may feel the product is unsafe, or they may disagree with the methods used to produce it. Communicating with producers by means of a boycott can be dramatic when many consumers join together. Sometimes, when all other methods fail, consumers resort to this organized withholding of funds.

Consumer Interest Groups. Government responds to requests from large groups of people who are interested in the same thing. Producers have known this for a long time and have hired people to lobby for them in Washington and in state legislatures. But consumer groups have been slow at organizing and speaking with one voice. Consumers are all different, so they make different buying decisions. It is hard to organize such a diverse group of people, but several national organizations are now representing consumers.

Better Business Bureaus, funded by contributions from local business people, are located in many larger cities. A Better Business Bureau will take a

boycott
....
organized refusal to buy certain products as a means of sending a message to the producer

Better Business Bureaus
....
organizations supported by local businesses for the purpose of assisting consumers with information and complaints

consumer complaint to the business in question, but if the business refuses to act, the Bureau cannot force it to do so. Better Business Bureaus can tell you if a certain company has a good record in handling previous complaints or if the company is safe to deal with. If you are unfamiliar with the community and need a reference for a business, the local Better Business Bureau can help you.

The Citizen

Besides being a producer and a consumer, each of us is a citizen. As a citizen, each of us has responsibilities, including the responsibility to pay taxes. We need to make our wishes known to all levels of government, and this can be as simple as voting in all elections or attending city council meetings.

You can become personally involved by talking to your council representatives. Tell them what you want and don't want them to do. You can also join with others to form groups that represent consumer interests. When you are qualified, you can run for election to a government office, or you can earn an appointment to a government committee concerned with protecting consumer interests.

Government Agencies. How does the government respond to consumer wishes? There are several steps that federal and state governments can take to help consumers. Governments strive to make products safer, they provide

MAKING CONSUMER DECISIONS

Katie shopped around for a new dresser for her bedroom. She finally found a lovely one at a small, out-of-the-way furniture store she'd never heard of. She was happy with her "find" since she had seen the same dresser at a department store for $100 more! For $25 extra, Katie arranged for it to be delivered to her home.

A few days later, when the dresser arrived, she discovered a large scratch on it. The delivery man said, "Sorry, I'm just the delivery person. You'll have to call the store where you bought it." When she called the store and spoke with her salesperson, he said, "Sorry. It must have happened during delivery. That's the delivery company's responsibility. You'll have to call them." When she called the delivery company, they said it was the store's responsibility. And so on. Katie was in a panic.

Eventually, she called the Better Business Bureau to see if they could be of any help. They couldn't help her, but did say that they had received complaints about that furniture company before. A little late for this news!

With some research, Katie found that, in this case, the furniture company was responsible for the goods arriving in satisfactory condition. Katie was rather shy and somewhat intimidated by this whole situation and wanted to just forget the whole thing. However, with advice of friends and family, she decided to take the furniture company to small-claims court to get her money back. In court, the judge ruled in her favor, and Katie did get her money.

Would you have gone to this much trouble to get your money back? What else could Katie have done to let others know about this dishonest company? Was it Katie's responsibility to not let this store "get away with" what they were doing?

consumer information, and they try to ensure that producers tell the truth. Generally, the handling of consumer problems is divided among many different agencies, and some are described here. Addresses for these and others are listed in the Appendix.

Federal agencies do not resolve individual consumer complaints, but they do investigate companies that have a record of many complaints from consumers. It is important to contact these federal agencies to make them aware of problems.

The United States Postal Service is responsible for controlling and stopping mail fraud. Advertisements for "get-rich-quick" schemes and "work-at-home" money-makers are popular types of mail fraud. (See the next chapter for more about mail fraud.)

The Interstate Commerce Commission (ICC) is responsible for regulating shipments across state lines in trucks and other vehicles. The Federal Communications Commission (FCC) grants licenses to radio and TV stations. The Food and Drug Administration (FDA) is responsible for the safety and labeling of food products.

The Consumer Product Safety Commission (CPSC) is one of the newest agencies. It has the responsibility and authority to set safety standards on products, and it can ban from the market any products that are found to be unsafe.

Some states, counties, and cities have their own consumer protection agencies that help consumers. Many of these agencies have toll-free numbers and are listed in your telephone directory. If you have a consumer problem, you may also appeal to a state regulatory agency. These agencies watch the activities of banking, insurance, utilities, and other areas of interest to consumers.

Many states also have agencies that license people within the state in some

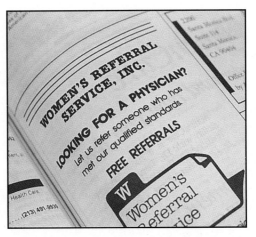

Many areas have referral services that list names of professionals in particular fields, such as physicians. The service will be able to answer many questions about the professionals listed. Check the telephone book to find any referral services in your area.

occupations. Doctors, lawyers, and real estate brokers may be licensed. Often, licensing agencies will give helpful information to consumers who are looking for reputable professionals— and these agencies also keep track of complaints against people they license.

Government Regulation. Congress has given some government agencies the power to regulate certain products and processes. The rules the agencies make must be followed in production, distribution, advertising, and selling. There is much disagreement about whether regulation is good or bad.

Many people in industry consider much of the government regulation costly and time-consuming. They feel it decreases competition and discourages new practices, but they would rather have federal regulation than state regulation in most cases. That way, a company may have to worry about only one regulation instead of fifty (one for each state). For instance, a detergent company could have to make fifty different types of Brand X in order to meet different regulations in all fifty states, but when the federal government makes one regulation, the company can sell the same product in every state.

Most consumers believe some regulation is needed. Regulations protect our

regulate
. . . .
to control the production, distribution, sales, and advertisement of products

Consumer Product Safety Commission
. . . .
federal agency responsible for establishing product safety standards

INTERACTING WITH TECHNOLOGY

RESPONSIBLE SOFTWARE USE

What's your favorite computer game? Which word processing or draw program do you like best? How would you feel if those computer programs were no longer available? Could it happen? Maybe.

With today's technology, it's very easy for people to copy computer programs to give to friends or to take home and put on their own computer. "Everyone does it," you might be thinking. So what's the problem? The problem is that copying computer programs is illegal; it's stealing. But copying one little program to give to a friend doesn't hurt anything. Right? Wrong. Stop and think about how many people are copying just "one" program to give to a friend or to take home. Those programs add up to thousands of dollars in sales that are lost. You might think that the software companies have lots of money and it won't really matter if they lose sales. That's not true. If the companies don't make money from software sales, they won't be able to pay people to develop new games and programs. They might not have the money needed to make additional copies of the software that's already been developed. Eventually the companies might have to close and lots of people would lose their jobs.

Have you ever come up with a great idea, told it to a friend, and had that friend start sharing the idea as if it were his own? How did that make you feel? You probably wanted credit for what you created. Well, the people who develop computer programs (programmers, designers, artists, writers, etc.) put their imagination and creativity into those programs. If someone copies a program and uses it without paying for it, it's like stealing those ideas.

Computer software is protected by copyright laws. Those laws say that it is illegal to make copies of software to avoid paying for it. Making copies to save money is called *piracy*. The Software Publishing Association (SPA) says that over $2 billion in sales are lost in the United States because of illegal copying of software. Because of this, many software companies are using investigators to track down software pirates. Some pirates have been caught and prosecuted in court. The fines and monetary judgments that the convicted pirates must pay are far more than the cost of legally purchased software.

Besides being illegal, there are other disadvantages to software piracy. If you obtain copied software, you will not have documentation, manuals, warranties, or access to technical support from the software company.

Since many software pirates are students, organizations such as the SPA are developing education programs to help students realize that they are hurting people by copying software programs. It is hoped that students such as yourselves will develop a sense of ethics and a sense of respect for the property of others.

health and safety, as unsafe products may be removed from stores. Products that might pollute the environment are taken out of production.

Some industries may argue that regulation costs consumers more than it is worth—but most consumers disagree. For both the producer and the consumer, there is a trade-off between initial and lifetime costs. A product may have a higher purchase price because of regulation. For example, pollution-control devices may make cars more expensive, but regulation may mean that there will still be trees and fresh water for the next generation.

Product Standards. One method used to regulate consumer products is setting **product standards**. Product standards are generally set by government agencies, and these standards state requirements for a type of product. For example, the Food and Drug Administration has set a standard for mayonnaise which requires that any product labeled "mayonnaise" must have specific ingredients. There are also standards for car tires and energy standards for appliances. Light bulbs must conform to standards of safety and size.

Today, there are more than 40,000 government standards in effect, and some standards are international. Without product standards, every producer could do his or her "own thing." Our products would not be as interchangeable as they are now, and we would be less sure of what we were buying.

Regulation is one of the main responsibilities of the government, but we have a responsibility, too. We should let government know if we agree or disagree with regulations that are being passed.

Summary

- Through the consumer movement, businesses have become more accountable to society, and government has passed laws which regulate businesses.

- There are three characters in the consumer story—the producer, the consumer, and the citizen—and we each play all three roles.

- One way that producers inform people about their products is by advertising.

- Many industries have established Consumer Action Panels (CAPs) that listen to consumer complaints and help resolve them.

- *Consumer Reports* is a magazine that provides independent test results on products in order to help consumers make decisions.

- Many different government agencies handle consumer problems: the United States Postal Service, the Interstate Commerce Commission (ICC), the Federal Communications Commission (FCC), the Food and Drug Administration (FDA), and the Consumer Product Safety Commission (CPSC).

- Product standards state requirements for a type of product and are generally set by government agencies.

- It is our responsibility to let government know if we agree or disagree with regulations that are being passed.

product standards
....
stated requirements for types of products

CHAPTER REVIEW
4

E NRICHING YOUR VOCABULARY

Number your paper from 1–14. Beside each number write the word from the following list, along with a brief definition.

American Gas Association
   (AGA)
Better Business Bureaus
boycott
caveat emptor
certification seals

Consumer Action Panels
   (CAPs)
consumer complaint
Consumer Product Safety
   Commission
Consumers Union

guarantee
Magnuson-Moss Warranty Act
product standards
regulate
Underwriters Laboratories
   (UL)

R EVIEWING WHAT YOU HAVE LEARNED

1. What methods do businesses use to give consumers information that will help them make good decisions?

2. What is the difference between a full and a limited warranty?

3. What are some things you can do if you have a consumer complaint?

U SING YOUR CRITICAL THINKING SKILLS

1. Work in groups of three. Let one person take the role of the consumer, and let another person take the role of the producer, and another, the citizen. From the point of view of the role you are playing, discuss your views about the following: soft-drink containers, aerosol cans, and government regulations.

A PPLYING WHAT YOU HAVE LEARNED

1. Examine two advertisements in your local paper. Analyze the information they provide.

2. Find at least three products at home or school that have seals of approval. Cut out, draw, or list the seals, and tell what each one indicates.

3. Write a letter of complaint to the manufacturer of a product you have been dissatisfied with. If you have not had a problem, for the sake of an example, pretend the antenna on your portable radio does not work properly.

CHAPTER 5

Basic Consumer Rights

OBJECTIVES

After completing this chapter, you will be able to do the following:
1. Name the four consumer rights in the "Consumers' Bill of Rights."
2. List three examples of consumer fraud.
3. List the requirements for a legal contract.

TERMS

Consumers' Bill of Rights
contract
Equal Credit
   Opportunity Act

Fair Debt Collection
   Practices Act
monopoly

oligopoly
tariff

Rights and responsibilities cannot be completely separated. They are like two sides of the same coin. Many consumers are not aware of their rights under the law, so they fail to be responsible consumers. Well-informed consumers protect their rights by living up to their responsibilities.

BASIC AND EXPECTED RIGHTS

Consumers' Bill of Rights

a list that states that consumers have the right to safety, to be informed, to choose, and to be heard

On March 15, 1962, President John F. Kennedy presented the first **"Consumers' Bill of Rights."** This list included the right to safety, to be informed, to choose, and to be heard. In addition to these four basic rights, consumers may expect several other rights in our free enterprise system, and they include:

- the right of all consumers to have equal access to the available goods and services;
- the right to find out about all the alternatives available to consumers without having anyone try to stop the comparison of alternatives;
- the right to be treated in a courteous manner while in a store, even though a purchase is not made;
- the right to expect producers to consider the effect of each product on the environment;
- the right to expect good-quality design and workmanship in a product;
- the right to consumer education.

THE RIGHT TO SAFETY

As consumers, we ask questions about products. We ask about prices, materials, or colors—but we seldom ask, "How safe is this product?"

Consumer Responsibilities

Not long ago, the Consumer Product Safety Commission conducted a survey to find out the factors that consumers actually considered when buying a product. Of the thousands of consumers surveyed, not one listed safety as something they looked for. When asked why, they said they just assumed that if a product was for sale, it was safe. What a mistake! Always make safety a consideration.

As consumers, it is our responsibility to read the directions before using a

Safety cannot be taken for granted. We must all do our part to keep ourselves and others safe. Safety devices such as seat belts are of no use unless they are used properly.

product. We must use a product only for its intended purpose, and we must store it and dispose of it properly.

Producer Responsibilities

Safety is a joint effort between the consumer and the producer. Just how much protection should a producer have to provide? Producers cannot always give complete protection. Some products (such as razor blades) can never be 100 percent safe, but sometimes the producer can make a product safer at little additional cost. Sometimes the damage from misuse could be life-threatening. In either case, the manufacturer should take safety measures. If the manufacturer produces an unsafe product, the Consumer Product Safety Commission may remove the product from the market.

THE RIGHT TO BE INFORMED

Generally, today's consumers have access to adequate information about products, and most of this information is free of charge. It is in newspapers and magazines, on TV, and on the radio. Special brochures are published by the government and by local consumer agencies and cooperative extension services. Our libraries have a lot of product information, but many consumers do not bother to get this information, or they don't make good use of the information they have. Evaluating information is important, but how do you decide which information source to believe? How can you tell if advertisements contain accurate or exaggerated claims? You need to know about and read reliable sources, then you can make good decisions.

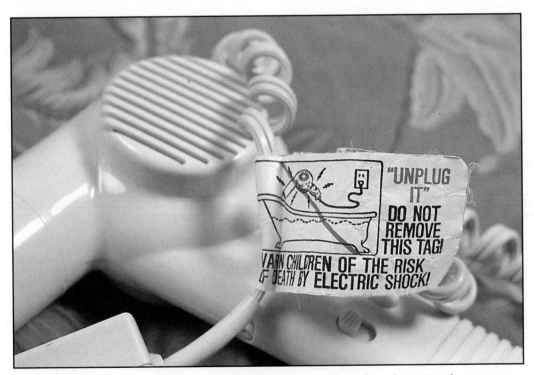

Producers and consumers are both responsible for the safety of products. Producers must provide warnings and consumers must follow the warnings. Can you think of an instance when an injury occurred because of improper use of a product?

Consumer Fraud

Some information is misleading, exaggerated, or simply untrue. People who prepare this information trick consumers out of millions of dollars through schemes called frauds.

Mail-fraud schemes are a good example of distorted or false information, and such schemes are among the major consumer problems today. They sound good and are difficult to investigate, so dishonest promoters design schemes that appeal to basic human nature and weakness. They know that a certain percentage of the people who receive an ad will respond no matter what is offered for sale. Generally, victims who lose less than ten dollars never complain.

Some of the most common schemes involve land sales in which people try to sell inaccessible land or land that does not exist. Other schemes involve education, such as correspondence courses that provide useless training at very high prices. Charity rackets and work-at-home schemes are also common. For example, a scheme may suggest you send in a fee to find out if you qualify for a specific type of employment. Then you are notified that you do not qualify, but your money is not returned.

Fraudulent items offered for sale include "magic potions" that increase your IQ or memory. Then there are the ones that give you instant beauty or melt away extra pounds. Watch out for the gadgets that are supposed to save fantastic amounts of energy. Investigate all purchases before you invest!

Taking Time for Research

We can expect better results from our consumer decisions if we research a product or service before buying or investing. Of course, research is often costly and may include money spent on telephone calls or gasoline for the car. Other expenses might include time spent away from your job. And the cost may not be money—you may have a recreational activity in which you would rather participate. Of course, some people enjoy shopping and don't feel they are giving up anything while searching for additional information. As you know, you generally spend more time shopping if you are interested in buying an expensive product, such as a car.

Buying from a Door-to-Door Salesperson. Be cautious about buying items from people selling door-to-door. You have little or no time for research. As a result, you may make a purchase that you will later regret.

Some companies that use door-to-door selling methods are honest and give you good service. Other companies are not trustworthy. Sometimes, when a salesperson comes to your door, you may know the company, or you may want or need the product or service. If so, you may want to do business with them. If you do not know the company, proceed carefully. First of all, if you don't want or need the product or service, don't be persuaded to buy it. Say no! If you *might be* interested in buying, check to see whether the salesperson has a selling permit that may be required in your area. If none is required, ask to see some other form of identification.

If you decide to buy, the salesperson may ask you to sign an agreement. Read this carefully before you sign, make certain that what you are buying is clearly stated, and be sure that you fully understand all the terms of the agreement.

If you sign an agreement or make a purchase for twenty-five dollars or more, you may still change your mind,

Shopping at home can be very convenient, but it's still important to research the services and products offered. What services or products are offered for in-home sale in your area?

but you must write to the company within three days. This is according to a regulation made by the Federal Trade Commission. Ask yourself if you have any doubts about the company, the product or service, or the agreement. If you do, your best protection is to avoid making a commitment.

Home Shopping

Many consumers welcome the convenience of shopping from their homes. Catalogs offering everything from baby clothes to electrical appliances arrive daily in the mail in many homes. Television offers additional home shopping opportunities. Entire stations are dedicated to displaying goods for sale. Also, television "infomercials," usually twenty- to thirty-minute presentations and demonstrations, have become a popular way to get information about products and services to the public.

By shopping from home, you can save on car expenses and avoid the fuss of crowded parking lots and stores. Ordering is easy. Usually, the catalog or TV advertisement has a toll-free 800 phone number to call to place your order and pay with a credit card. If you don't want to use a credit card, you can mail in your order with a personal check—or a money order, which is required by some companies.

As with all your shopping, it is important to remember that some companies are reputable and some are not. Just because a product is advertised on TV and a celebrity says it's fantastic, doesn't necessarily mean that product is reliable or something you need. Research a product or service before you buy it whenever possible—and if the item is available locally, call a local store to compare the price. If you are dealing with an unfamiliar company, look for this motto: "Satisfaction fully guaranteed, or your money back." This means that the company is willing to stand behind its product.

Contracts

Consumers today buy many of their purchases with credit or long-term con-

contract
··········
an agreement between two or more people that is enforceable by law

Equal Credit Opportunity Act
··········
a law that states that a lender cannot deny credit because of race, sex, color, religion, national origin, age, or martial status

Fair Debt Collection Practices Act
··········
a law that controls debt-collecting practices

tracts. (Credit is discussed in Chapters 10–12 and buying houses on contract in Chapter 27.) A **contract** is an agreement between two or more people that is enforceable by law. The requirements include:

• The people must agree on all terms.

• There must be money or something of value exchanged.

• People must understand what they are doing.

Federal Laws Regarding Credit Contracts. There are federal laws to make sure consumers are well informed about credit and credit contracts. These laws allow consumers to make better credit decisions. One such law is the **Equal Credit Opportunity Act** (1974). This states that a lender cannot deny credit because of race, sex, color, religion, national origin, age, or marital status. It also allows women to apply for credit using their own names, either maiden or married names.

Lenders cannot ask questions about your spouse, child support, or welfare payments. If you are denied credit, you must be notified of the reason you were denied.

It is usually difficult for teenagers to obtain credit in their own names. Most teens have no regular source of income, and they have not had a chance to establish a credit rating. (See Chapter 12.)

The **Fair Debt Collection Practices Act** (1977) controls debt-collecting practices. There are more than 5,000 debt-collection agencies in the United States. They are trying to collect over five billion dollars in debts that consumers have failed to pay. Before this act was passed, some collectors used harassment and even threats to collect their money. These practices are now illegal. (Other credit laws, the Fair Credit Reporting Act, and the Truth in Lending Act are discussed in Chapter 12.)

THE RIGHT TO CHOOSE

You learned earlier that the American market system is a free enterprise system. (See Chapter 1.) Under this system, consumers have the opportunity to choose what they buy. They can choose from a wide variety of goods from all over the world and at all price levels. Different companies offer different products and services, and the companies compete for the consumer's dollar.

Competition

In the United States, we encourage competition in selling products and services. For example, there are more than forty different brands of tennis shoes on the market. And in most communities, there is more than one doctor or

Competition can make shopping confusing. The next time you're in the supermarket, count the number of different brands of the same kind of cereal, such as corn flakes. How can you know which is the best product for you?

Competition allows us to have more products available at the best prices possible. Can you think of a situation in which competition might be a bad thing?

lawyer, so you may choose the person who you think will provide the best service.

When there is competition among producers of goods and services, they are encouraged to operate as efficiently as possible. That way, they can keep their prices low and quality high. One company may produce good stereo tapes, but other companies will try to make their tapes as good or even better—and at the same price. Sometimes, though, competition is not the method used to provide services and products for the consumer.

Monopoly. Sometimes a business gains control of a product or service and there is no competition. This condition is called a **monopoly**. The electric and gas companies are examples of monopolies in the United States, but the government regulates these monop-

olies. They are allowed because costs would probably be greater and service less efficient without them. For example, having several electric companies run separate wires in one area would be a waste.

In 1890, the Sherman Anti-Trust Act was passed. It was intended to stop the formation of large monopolies and to help ensure competition. Some groups today feel that too many large corporations are joining together to form monopolies. Representatives of industry disagree, and there will surely be much discussion about this. Is the consumer's best interest served by allowing more monopolies to form?

Oligopoly. When just a few producers control the market for a product, we call the industry an **oligopoly**. For example, there are many different types of cereal and detergent on the store

monopoly
. . . .
a condition in which a business gains control of a product or service and there is no competition

oligopoly
. . . .
a situation in which a few producers control the market for a product

tariff

......

a price charged to keep prices of imported goods competitive with U.S. products, so foreign companies must raise the prices of their products to cover the cost of the tariff

shelves, but most are made by a few companies. Can you name these companies? Do you really have as much choice as you thought?

Government Import Policies. Government policies concerning import quotas and tariffs affect the number of products you have to choose from. Restrictions on imported clothing are discussed in Chapter 20. The need to ensure jobs in the United States is one reason the government sets quotas. Tariffs are charged to keep prices of imported goods competitive with U.S. products, so foreign companies must raise the prices of their products to cover tariff costs.

Financial Limitations

Generally, the less money you have, the fewer choices you will have. One reason for this is simply that you cannot afford to buy some of the higher-priced products. You may want to do comparison shopping or take advantage of specials and sales, but perhaps you cannot get to different stores to do these things.

When you have limited money and access, you often have to buy products at hand. They may or may not be your first choices. Lower-income consumers may be forced to buy milk at the corner grocery rather than at the supermarket across town, so they may have to pay a higher price. If you cannot afford to pay cash for a product, you also have to add the cost of credit to your purchases.

CHECKLIST FOR CONSULTING SOURCES OF CONSUMER INFORMATION

When you research a product or service, consider the following:

____ Ask others about their experiences with various companies.

____ Go to the library and read about the items you are thinking of buying.

____ Talk to experts who will give you objective information about the subject. Make sure your expert is unbiased.

____ Check on professional services with professional associations, or check lists of people who are licensed in certain professions.

____ Check with the Better Business Bureau to see if complaints have been filed about the company you may buy from.

____ Make use of government resources that are available from local and state agencies. (See the Appendix.)

____ Ask questions of salespeople before buying. Some consumers feel shy or fear they will appear "dumb" if they ask questions.

____ Don't allow yourself to be pressured into buying something if you have doubts about it. If the seller uses the old line, "It may not be here when you get back," be sure to shop around!

____ If you cannot understand the language in a document, take it to a lawyer or a legal-aid group that can help you. Never sign anything until you read and understand the entire document.

Summary

- The "Consumers' Bill of Rights" includes the right to safety, to be informed, to choose, and to be heard.

- Safety is a joint effort between the consumer and the producer.

- Investigate before you purchase.

- Consumers today buy many of their purchases with credit or long-term contracts.

- Competition among producers of goods and services is healthy; it encourages the producers to keep their prices low and quality high.

ENRICHING YOUR VOCABULARY

Use the following words or phrases to complete the sentences below. Write the completed sentences on your paper.

Consumers' Bill of Rights   Fair Debt Collection   oligopoly
contract   Practices Act   tariff
Equal Credit Opportunity Act   monopoly

1. Countries wanting to sell goods to the American consumer may be charged a

2. The federal law that protects against discrimination in lending practices is called the

3. The right of a consumer to expect good workmanship in a product is guaranteed by the

4. When one business gains control of a product or a service, it is said to have a

5. A legal agreement between two or more people is a

6. The federal law that makes it illegal to use threats in attempts to collect debt is the

7. The control of a business or product by a few companies is called an

REVIEWING WHAT YOU HAVE LEARNED

1. What are the four consumer rights in the "Consumers' Bill of Rights"?

2. List three examples of consumer fraud.

3. List the requirements for a legal contract.

USING YOUR CRITICAL THINKING SKILLS

1. Do you think we need stricter product safety laws in the United States? Explain why or why not.

2. Suppose you know that a certain product is dangerous. You have contacted the manufacturer, but no action was taken. Which government agency could you contact?

3. What are the advantages and disadvantages to having only one electric company provide service in your community?

APPLYING WHAT YOU HAVE LEARNED

1. A young man comes to your door selling CDs. You can pay later, he says, if you will just sign the contract now. What would you do? How would you find out if he has a good product and if he is a reliable salesperson?

CHAPTER 6

Solving Consumer Problems

OBJECTIVES

After completing this chapter, you will be able to do the following:
1. Name the five major reasons consumers complain.
2. Describe the steps a consumer should follow in filing a complaint.
3. List five consumer responsibilities.

TERMS

arbitration   legal action   small-claims court
class-action suit

THE RIGHT TO BE HEARD

Have you ever returned a product you purchased? Were you ever so dissatisfied with a product or service that you contacted the company that produced it? Even the most careful consumer will buy products now and then that are defective or of inferior quality. Sometimes a consumer may receive poor service. In these cases, consumers have an obligation to themselves and others to complain.

By complaining effectively, the consumer makes it harder for the questionable manufacturer or retailer to continue doing business. At the same time, complaints to responsible manufacturers and businesses help all consumers. Reliable companies want to know why their products have failed or in what way their service was poor. Most businesses are concerned with serving their customers well.

Most consumer complaints fall into one of five categories:

- Delivery failures—a product was delivered late or not at all, or it was damaged when delivered.

- Performance failures—a product did not work, and the company failed to correct the defect.

- Misrepresentation and deception—a product did not perform as advertised.

- Failure to communicate—there was disagreement about a price or service.

- Environmental effects—for example, fumes came from a product and made people sick or had a bad effect on the environment.

Today, the people who sell us products are generally not the same people who produced them. You usually cannot go directly to producers with your complaint, but instead you must talk with a salesperson or retailer who may be a thousand miles away. You must rely on that person to understand your problem and decide who was at fault. This can be very frustrating—but if you feel something is wrong, it is important that you complain.

Complaining Effectively

Settle complaints with the retailer from whom you purchased the product if you can. If this is not possible, call or write a letter to the company, making

CHECKLIST FOR AVOIDING BUYING PROBLEMS

There is an old saying that "an ounce of prevention is worth a pound of cure"—meaning that preventing problems is wiser than trying to resolve them after they have occurred. The following points will help minimize consumer buying problems:

____ Select a seller with a good reputation.

____ Read all material you can about the product. Read ads, consumer publications, leaflets from the government, and information from local consumer agencies.

____ Obtain a warranty, or as much assurance in writing as possible.

____ If possible, buy on a trial basis with the option to exchange or return.

____ When a product is delivered, check it thoroughly before accepting it.

____ Maintain a good financial reputation, and you will be in a good bargaining position if a problem does occur.

____ Finance through a credit agency, then withhold some payment until you are sure the product will work and is what you thought you were buying. Purchasing an item on a credit card will give an opportunity to be sure you are satisfied. You may dispute the payment of any item within 60 days after it first appears on your bill.

Arbitration is becoming popular as a means of settling consumer complaints without legal action. Is there a time when you feel you might have benefited from arbitration?

small-claims court
....

a special court in which consumers and sellers with small claims (usually less than $1,500) present their case to a judge who makes the final decision

arbitration
....

a process in which a complaint is referred to an impartial person whose decision the consumer and seller must agree to accept and comply with

your complaint clear, concise, and polite. You will get a reply much quicker than the consumer who is angry and not sure of all the facts.

Some communities have *Consumer Action Lines* through local radio or TV stations. A call from a station often causes a manufacturer to respond to your concern quickly, and public discussion can help other consumers with their own problems. Consumer Action Panels can also help solve problems between consumer and manufacturer.

Resolving Difficult Problems

Most complaints can be settled easily, but you may not be satisfied with the action of a company. Or you may be upset by the lack of action. If so, you can take other steps.

Arbitration. More and more consumer complaints are being handled through arbitration. In this process, a complaint is referred to an arbitrator, a person who is impartial. Both the consumer and the seller must agree to accept the decision of the arbitrator and then comply with the recommendations.

Small-Claims Court. In the United States, small-claims courts are becoming more common. Usually, consumers with claims of less than $1,500 are the ones who use these courts, but maximum amounts vary greatly from state to state. There are court costs. You may have to pay between $10 and $15 or even more to go to court. Here again, amounts vary.

Generally, no lawyers are involved in small-claims court. The seller and the consumer present their reports to the judge, who makes the final decision. The judge may direct the seller to pay the consumer—but if the seller does not pay, the consumer must file a formal lawsuit to collect. Perhaps the biggest problem with the small-claims-court procedure is that decisions cannot be enforced.

Many small-claims courts have established mediation programs to help citizens settle their own disputes and work out their own agreements. The courts have found that these methods are often satisfactory with both parties.

Class-Action Suits. A **class-action suit** is a case in which many consumers have similar complaints against the same company or person. If the consumers win the case, the company generally must produce a remedy for all consumers who bought the product.

Legal Action. Consumers can take **legal action** beyond small-claims court. This requires hiring a lawyer and usually takes much time and money, so it is used only as a last resort.

Consumers' Voices in the Government

Government decisions affect us and the items we want to buy. We need to be aware of these decisions and make our voices heard when the decisions are being made. Today, we rely on consumer action groups to speak for us at the state and federal levels, but each of us needs to be involved locally. Learn what is happening in your city and county. Take an interest in water rates, housing codes, street-widening projects, school crossing guards, and other issues.

Government decisions need consumer input. Each of us has the responsibility to let the decision makers know what we think.

BEING A RESPONSIBLE CONSUMER

As consumers, we have been given certain rights under the law. We have the freedom of choice and the right to safe products and services. We have the

class-action suit
....
a case in which many consumers have similar complaints against the same company or person

legal action
....
hiring a lawyer to settle one's claim

CONSUMER FOCUS

SHOPLIFTING

Shoplifting is stealing. Who is affected by shoplifting? Retailers suffer the loss of their merchandise. Shoplifters themselves are guilty of a crime, and all consumers suffer because retailers must raise prices to cover their losses. An estimate of the value of the losses is about 7 percent of sales, amounting to billions of dollars.

What are the penalties for shoplifting? Laws provide for fines and/or jail sentences. At best, being caught for shoplifting is humiliating—but worse, it can brand the shoplifter with a police record that affects the person in many ways. For example, employers may not want to hire a shoplifter.

What do retailers do about shoplifting? They watch carefully and may hire others to watch—and, in many stores, they may use devices that trigger alarms when merchandise is stolen from their stores. Many retailers prosecute shoplifters, mainly to deter other people from shoplifting.

What can you do about shoplifting? Of course, don't do it yourself, and discourage others from doing it. If you see someone shoplifting, tell the storekeeper. Remember, shoplifting is costly to everyone.

CONSUMER PROFILE

T.J. bought a new shirt with a colorful print which looked great with his blue trousers. When it came time to clean the shirt, he threw it in with the rest of his laundry and his mother washed it. Unfortunately, it came back all limp and misshapen, with the print on it blurred together. The laundry had ruined his new shirt! T.J. was totally furious with his mother. When they looked at the label on the shirt, it said, "Dry Clean Only." T.J. was still furious with his mother. She should have read the label and not washed it! She felt it was his responsibility to have read the label before he bought it. What do you think?

CHECKLIST FOR MEETING CONSUMER RESPONSIBILITIES

As a consumer, you are responsible for determining the values and goals that direct your spending. You also have the responsibility to plan your budget to meet the needs of your family. These are personal responsibilities. As a consumer, your general responsibilities include the following:

____ Stay aware of legislation affecting consumers.
____ Be an ethical shopper—treat sellers honestly and fairly.
____ Use information provided for you by manufacturers and the government.
____ Report any unsafe products and help to keep others from being injured.

In the Store:

____ Be courteous to salespeople and to other shoppers.
____ Handle all merchandise carefully, whether you are planning to buy it or not. (For example, do not squeeze the tomatoes or get makeup on clothing you are trying on.)
____ If you change your mind about buying an item, return it to the place in the store where you found it.
____ Never shoplift!
____ If you receive too much change from a purchase, return it to the salesperson.
____ Always pay your bills!

right to obtain truthful and useful information, and we have the right to be heard through the complaints we make and through our votes on important issues. Along with these rights come responsibilities.

Failing to meet these responsibilities can raise costs for producers or retailers. These higher costs in turn mean higher prices for consumers, so when one consumer cheats or abuses her or his responsibilities, everyone suffers the consequences.

Considering the Rights of Others

Consumer decisions are not made in a vacuum; every decision you make affects others. You have the responsibility as a consumer to choose products and services with others in mind. Your choices should be safe for the environment and should not infringe upon the rights of others.

Summary

- Consumers have an obligation to themselves and to others to complain when the goods or services they receive are not satisfactory.
- Settle complaints with the retailer from whom you purchased the product if you can.
- Difficult consumer problems can be resolved through arbitration, small-claims court, class-action suits, or legal action.
- We have been given certain rights as consumers; along with these also come responsibilities.

CHAPTER REVIEW
6

E NRICHING YOUR VOCABULARY

Read the following pairs of sentences. Write the sentence that correctly uses the underlined word or phrase on your paper.

1A. The lawyer's arbitration convinced the jury.

1B. The ownership dispute was settled through arbitration.

2A. Several parties that had been injured in the same model car with faulty steering filed a class-action suit against the manufacturer.

2B. The judge ruled that all the driving citations would be treated as a class-action suit.

3A. The injured woman took legal action by hiring a lawyer to represent her.

3B. The injured woman took legal action by agreeing to arbitration.

4A. The lawyer represented his clients' million-dollar class-action suit in small-claims court.

4B. The buyer and seller settled their dispute in small-claims court.

R EVIEWING WHAT YOU HAVE LEARNED

1. What are the five major reasons consumers complain?

2. What steps should consumers follow in filing a complaint?

3. List four general consumer responsibilities.

4. List four "in the store" consumer responsibilities.

U SING YOUR CRITICAL THINKING SKILLS

1. Why is it best to settle complaints by first going to the salesperson involved? Why not take your complaint straight to the company president or to court?

2. Why is it important to let government officials know how we feel about consumer decisions?

A PPLYING WHAT YOU HAVE LEARNED

1. Find out the exact terms of the warranties for three brands of the same product. How are the warranties different from each other? How are they the same?

UNIT

3

MONEY MANAGEMENT

CHAPTERS

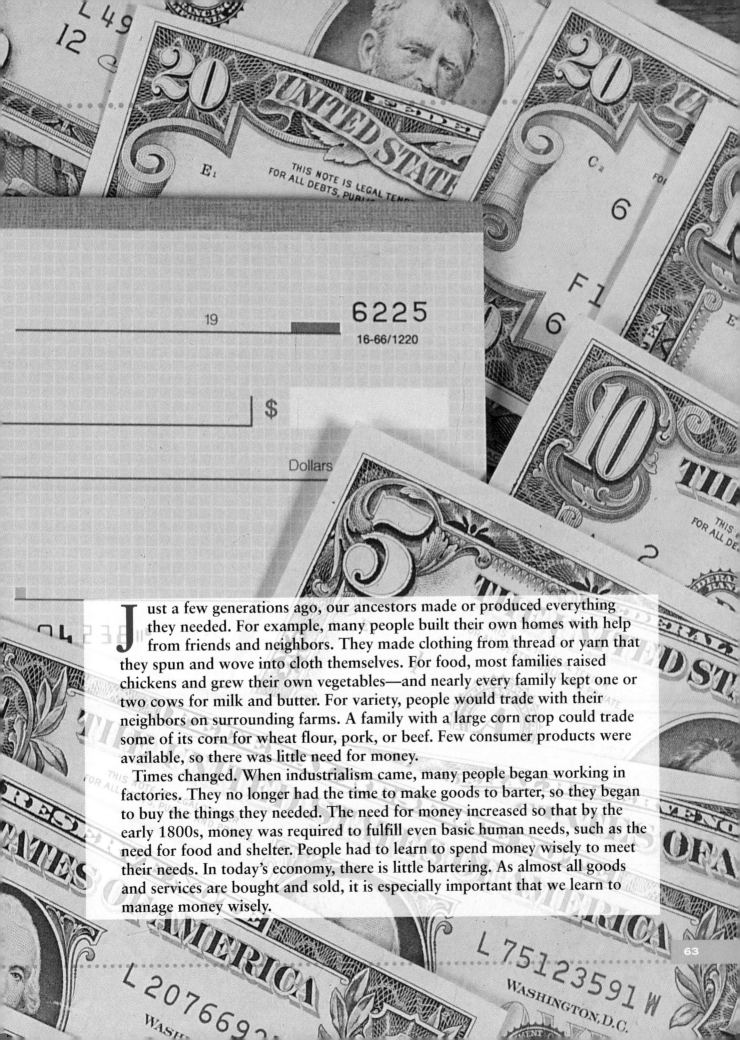

Just a few generations ago, our ancestors made or produced everything they needed. For example, many people built their own homes with help from friends and neighbors. They made clothing from thread or yarn that they spun and wove into cloth themselves. For food, most families raised chickens and grew their own vegetables—and nearly every family kept one or two cows for milk and butter. For variety, people would trade with their neighbors on surrounding farms. A family with a large corn crop could trade some of its corn for wheat flour, pork, or beef. Few consumer products were available, so there was little need for money.

Times changed. When industrialism came, many people began working in factories. They no longer had the time to make goods to barter, so they began to buy the things they needed. The need for money increased so that by the early 1800s, money was required to fulfill even basic human needs, such as the need for food and shelter. People had to learn to spend money wisely to meet their needs. In today's economy, there is little bartering. As almost all goods and services are bought and sold, it is especially important that we learn to manage money wisely.

CHAPTER 7

The Economy and the Consumer

OBJECTIVES

After completing this chapter, you will be able to do the following:
1. Name five freedoms or rights that businesses have in the United States.
2. Name four responsibilities of businesses in the United States.
3. Name and describe the three phases of the business cycle.
4. Explain the law of supply and demand.

TERMS

business cycle
competition
constraints
Consumer Price Index
   (CPI)
debts
deficit spending
demand
depression
federal budget

federal debt
Federal Reserve Bank
   System (FRBS)
inflation
interest rate
invest
law of supply and
   demand
productivity
profit

progressive tax
prosperity
recession
recovery
reinvested
standard of living
stock
unemployment

As consumers, our thoughts about the economy are often limited to how much money we have and whether we can afford to buy what we want. But we need to learn about the whole system of producing and distributing goods and services. (See Chapter 1.) There was a time when what happened in another part of the nation may not have affected our own local economy, but this is no longer true. As we finish the 1990s and move into a new century, we have an integrated *global economy*. That is, what happens across the nation and around the world affects each one of us. The way cars and computers and all other consumer products are made in Japan and around the world affects the type, availability, and price of the products we buy. If we understand the national economy and the effects of other nations' economies in an integrated global economy, we can make better decisions about our spending.

THE FREE ENTERPRISE SYSTEM

You know that the economic system in the United States is a capitalistic system. Under capitalism, the means of production and distribution of goods and services are controlled by individuals. People are free to start almost any business they choose, so capitalism is known as the free enterprise system. This system gives many freedoms, but accepting or using the freedoms means also accepting responsibilities and obeying laws and regulations. If this freedom is not used wisely, one person or business could infringe upon the rights of others. By being responsible and using freedom wisely, the rights of all are protected.

There are laws that prohibit or regulate the sale of unsafe or damaged goods. Consumers who buy goods that are not usable for the purpose for which they are sold can have the purchase price refunded or have the goods replaced.

The Freedoms

The freedom of choice in business is an important strength of the U.S. economy. Many different individuals may start the same kind of business or company, then each business or company can try to produce a better product or perform a service better than the others. Each also may try to keep production or service costs low so that it can charge the lowest price. This is **competition**.

Freedoms include rights, and people in business have many rights. They have a right to own their own businesses. If they wish, they may sell **stock** (shares) in a business and form a corporation.

People in business may distribute products almost whenever and wherever they wish (within the United States). They may increase or decrease production as they wish.

People in business have a right to make a fair **profit**, which is the money left after all expenses are paid. And they are also free to spend or **invest** profits (use them to make more money) as they wish. ”

The Responsibilities

To maintain freedom within the free enterprise system, people in business meet certain responsibilities. They plan the use of labor, capital (money and possessions used to earn a profit), and materials carefully. They try to keep workers on the job throughout the year and avoid layoffs—although this is not always possible. (There were many layoffs in the early 1990s.) Usually some profits are **reinvested** in the business to make the business even more profitable. For example, money may be spent to improve production methods.

Businesses accept the consequences of their own actions. For example, sometimes the **demand** for products is overestimated and more goods are made than will sell at the planned price. When that happens, the products may have to be sold at a discount or even at a loss.

The Safeguards

The economy of the United States is a "controlled" free enterprise system, because the government places some **constraints** on total freedom. For example, unsafe products ordinarily cannot be sold. Businesses are responsible for the goods they produce, and there is an implied warranty that any product can be used for the purpose for which it is sold. Thus, defective products must be replaced or repaired.

Today, workers are protected, but this wasn't always true. For example, in the early years of the Industrial Revolution, there was no governmental control, so businesses paid very low wages and working conditions were poor. Workers often used machinery that was dangerous, and even children worked long hours in factories. Now federal and state labor laws ensure a better work environment and limit the number of hours of work for young workers.

Both rights and responsibilities are important in a working economy. Businesses that are not responsible will infringe on the rights of consumers, and consumers who are not responsible may infringe on the rights of business or other consumers. Businesses and consumers need established rights and recognized responsibilities for themselves in order to maintain a fair system for everyone. Chapters 4 and 5 provided details about business regulations and consumer rights. As you continue to think about the ways in which rights and responsibilities must stay in balance, develop your own picture of

---

demand
....
quantity of goods buyers will purchase

competition
....
producing the best product or service at the best price

constraints
....
restrictions

stock
......
shares in a business

profit
......
money remaining after expenses are paid

invest
......
use money to make more money

reinvested
....
put back into the business

Employment greatly affects the economy. Think about the area in which you live. Is employment high or low? How has this affected the economy in your area?

how business and the consumer are parts of the same economic system.

THE BUSINESS CYCLE

Consumers are a vital part of the economy. When we, as consumers, spend money on products and services, businesses succeed, companies expand, and more workers are hired. When most people are employed and spending money, there is **prosperity**. Sometimes consumers spend too much money and borrow heavily, and they must cut their spending for a while in order to pay their **debts**. When this happens among the population in general for more than six months, a **recession** is likely. A recession is a time when sales of goods and services are reduced, resulting in lower profits for businesses. Some workers may be laid off until consumers start buying again. When workers are laid off, they can't afford to buy as many goods and services.

If sales are off drastically during a recession and many workers are laid off, a **depression** can result. This is a period of very low business activity when many people are out of work, so very few goods and services can be sold. You no doubt have read about or heard stories about the *Great Depression* of the 1930s.

A recession or depression continues until needs increase or new markets open up. Then businesses begin to produce and sell more goods and services, and the economy enters a **recovery** stage. If more people are hired and sales of goods and services continue to increase, a new period of prosperity occurs. These periods of prosperity and recession (or depression) and back to prosperity make up the **business cycle**.

prosperity
....
economic condition in which people have money to spend

debts
....
money owed

recession
....
period of reduced business activity

depression
....
period of low business activity and high unemployment

recovery
....
increase in sales and production following a recession or depression

business cycle
....
periods of prosperity and recession

HOW THE ECONOMY AFFECTS THE CONSUMER

Consumer Price Index (CPI)

....

monthly government list of how much average prices have gone up or down

As consumers, we have an impact on the economy—but the economy also has an impact on us. We must deal with the economic problems of inflation, unemployment, and changing interest rates.

INFLATION

inflation

....

the rising cost of goods and services

Inflation is a sustained rise in the level of prices. Prices go up, but the goods and services you buy stay the same. You may have heard your grandparents talk about going to movies when they were teenagers and paying a quarter. In most cities, admission to movies today is at least seven dollars.

That's a 2,700 percent increase in two generations! How much do you suppose your grandchildren will have to pay to see a movie? In some years, inflation has frequently been the top story in the news. Every month, the federal government releases its **Consumer Price Index** (see Figure 7.1), listing how much average prices have gone up or down. Since about 1939, with few exceptions, prices of consumer goods have continued to rise. Notice that there have been only brief periods in which prices remained constant, and these have usually occurred during a recession or the recovery following a recession.

Inflation Factors

What causes inflation? There is no simple answer, but we know there are several factors that contribute to inflation. They include the supply of and demand for goods and services, wage increases, strikes, declines in produc-

Figure 7.1

....

The Consumer Price Index measures changes in average prices for specific goods and services used by average households. Have you noticed an increase in prices for goods or services you use? If so, what goods and services have increased in price?

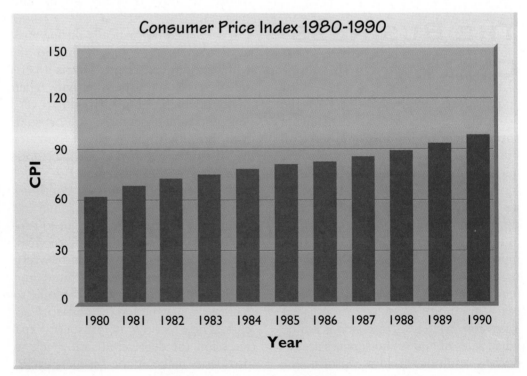

UNIT 3 MONEY MANAGEMENT

tivity, and deficit spending by the government.

Supply and Demand. "When supply exceeds demand, prices fall; and when demand exceeds supply, prices rise." This is known as **the law of supply and demand**. A limited supply of goods needed for manufacturing products that are in demand can be especially inflationary. For example, there are many cars in the United States, and most of them run on gasoline—which is made from oil—so the demand for oil is great. During the early 1970s, the United States started running out of oil. People waited, sometimes for an hour, in long lines at service stations for their turn to buy gasoline. Large amounts had to be imported from other countries. The continued increase in demand, combined with a limited supply of oil, caused the price of gasoline to triple between 1973 and 1980! For example, a person who paid 40¢ per gallon in 1973 was probably paying more than $1.20 in 1980. Gasoline prices remained fairly steady until the early 1990s, when prices again began to increase.

Standard of Living. Another inflation factor is the effort made by workers to maintain or even raise their **standard of living**. This is the level of necessities and comforts that people expect to be able to buy. Workers request and sometimes receive increases in wages, which are usually followed almost immediately by employers raising prices of goods and services to cover the wage increases. Then workers must pay higher prices for what they buy, so they again ask for wage increases. This upward spiral of prices and wages is an inflationary cycle.

Strikes. Strikes are particularly inflationary. They may result from poor management decisions, but most often are the result of a lack of understanding between management and workers. Whatever the causes, strikes are very costly to companies that make the products we consume. Workers receive

law of supply and demand
· · · · · · · · ·
relationship between quantity and price

standard of living
· · · · · · · · · · · · ·
level of necessities and comforts that a group of people expect to be able to buy

The demand for gasoline continues to rise as more Americans drive cars. Talk to someone who remembers the gas lines of the 1970s. How did they feel about the price and availability of gasoline at the time?

A strike is a work stoppage by employees to force the employer to meet the demands employees have made, or to protest some act or condition that relates to their jobs. Strikes are not good for the economy.

interest rate
....
price paid to borrow money

productivity
....
amount of output per unit of input

deficit spending
....
spending more money than is taken in

no wages during a strike, and no goods are produced—yet companies must continue to pay many other expenses. Goods made after the strike is over must be sold for a higher price to make up for losses during the strike.

Decline in Productivity. Productivity is related to wages, as **productivity** is the amount of output achieved by a certain amount of input. You can easily see the results of productivity in a factory. For example, one worker may produce five units of a certain product for five dollars, while another worker may produce ten of that product, also for five dollars. The second worker is more productive because that worker produces more output with the same amount of input. The cost of making each product would be one dollar for the first worker and only fifty cents for the second worker. The selling price must cover the cost of producing the product—so if productivity is lower and demand remains steady, prices will be higher.

Deficit Spending by the Government. **Deficit spending** by the government is a major cause of inflation.

When a city, state, or the federal government spends more money than it takes in, it must borrow. Thus, government competes for loan funds (money available to loan) with businesses that need capital to expand and to hire more workers to produce more goods.

The rate of interest charged for using borrowed money is a percent of the amount borrowed, and an increased demand for loan funds causes the **interest rate** (price of money) to go up. In recent years, the U.S. government has spent hundreds of billions more than it has taken in and in 1993 had accumulated a total debt of more than four trillion dollars! Because this reduces the supply of money available for loans, the price of money goes up. Economic recessions such as the one in 1991–1993 (and downward pressure on rates by the Federal Reserve Board) may result in lower interest rates due to less demand for loans. Future deficit spending by the government may help push interest rates still higher.

Coping with Inflation

The rate of inflation is measured as a percentage of increase or decrease in the cost of selected products. The highest rate of inflation in the United States was 14.6 percent, which occurred in 1974. In 1979, it was still 13.8 percent; but the rate of inflation decreased gradually throughout the 1980s. In the early 1990s, the inflation rate stayed below 5 percent. Many people thought that an inflation rate of 5 percent on a permanent basis would be all right. Some still think so, but the effect of inflation is compounded with every increase. This means that every year's increase is figured on the inflated price from the year before. You may be surprised at future prices based on a 6 or 10 percent inflation rate. Can you imagine paying more than $2,500 for

Effects of Inflation

	Amount of Inflation	New Price
1st year	10% of $1.00 = $.10	$1.00 + $.10 = $1.10
2nd year	10% of $1.10 = $.11	$1.10 + $.11 = $1.21
3rd year	10% of $1.21 = $.12	$1.21 + $.12 = $1.33
4th year	10% of $1.33 = $.13	$1.33 + $.13 = $1.46
10th year	$.23	$2.59

	Rent Currently $250		Lunch Currently $2.28	
	6% Inflation	10% Inflation	6% Inflation	10% Inflation
After 10 years	$445	$648	$4.08	$5.91
After 40 years	$2571	$11,315	$23.45	$103.19

Figure 7.2

The top part of this figure shows how to calculate the new prices caused by inflation. After 10 years of inflation at 10%, an item that 10 years ago cost $1.00, now costs $2.59. Calculate what the price of a car that now sells for $10,000 will be after ten years of inflation at 10%.

one month's apartment rent? Or $103 for lunch? (See Figure 7.2)

As long as there is inflation, it will continue to cut away at what our dollars will buy. There is no way to avoid the effects of inflation completely, but it is helpful to be aware of projected costs of goods and services you expect to buy in the future. This information can serve as a guide when you develop a financial plan. For example, you may need to save more than you thought in order to make large purchases in the future.

UNEMPLOY-MENT

During an economic recession, sales of goods and services are down, so businesses lay off workers. In a depression, a great many more workers lose their jobs. Thus, unemployment is another way the economy affects us. Usually those who are first to lose their jobs during a recession are either the last workers hired or the least-productive workers. When workers are laid off, they have little money to buy goods being produced, and when producers cannot sell their products it is usually necessary to lay off more workers. This makes it difficult for the economy to recover from a recession. In the 1990s, many companies reorganized by *downsizing*—laying off workers and reassigning work responsibilities for greater efficiency.

Interest Rates

American businesses and consumers must compete with government agencies for whatever money is available for loans, and this produces a large demand for loan money. The more that governments, businesses, and consumers borrow, the less money there is for loans. This reduces the supply of loan money for withdrawals. With high demand and low supply, the cost of borrowing money—the interest rate—goes up. When demand falls, as it did in the recession of 1991–1993, interest rates decline.

unemployment

the state of being without a job involuntarily

TRILLIONS OF DOLLARS

To spend one trillion dollars, you'd have to spend thirty million dollars a day for more than ninety years. You'd probably find such massive spending hard to keep up. In the United States, trillions of dollars are spent in just one year, and in 1993, the federal debt was around four trillion dollars. Just how much is a trillion dollars?

One thousand (1,000) is an easier number. If you had 1,000 thousand-dollar bills, you would be a millionaire—a million (1,000,000) is a thousand thousand. You would need a million times that to have a trillion dollars. A trillion (1,000,000,000,000) is a million million!

Imagine such wealth in terms of one-dollar bills. Placed end to end, one trillion dollars would stretch more than the distance from the earth to the sun. Sewn together, they could form a money quilt covering the Grand Canyon or almost two million football fields. They could pave a mile-wide road across the United States.

Trillion-dollar sums are staggering, but understanding them is important because we live in a trillion-dollar economy.

federal debt

....

amount of money owed by the federal government

Federal Reserve Bank System (FRBS)

....

federal organization that controls the amount of money available for loans

Interest rates also depend on the current policy of the Federal Reserve Board. The Board, through its Federal Reserve Bank System, has considerable control over the amount of money available for loans. Banks are required by law to maintain reserve supplies of money, and the Board sets the amounts that must be held in reserve, which affects the money supply. More in reserve means less can be added to the money supply in loans, and the supply of money affects the rate of interest that must be paid for loan funds. A smaller supply means a higher rate of interest. Banks also decide what rate of interest they will charge different types of borrowers. For example, a person seeking a loan to buy a car usually pays a higher rate of interest than a person getting a loan to buy a house.

Aside from setting reserve requirements, the Federal Reserve Board influences interest rates in other ways. It sets the rates that banks pay to borrow money from other banks and from the Federal Reserve System. The more that the banks pay, the more they charge their customers for loans. In this way, businesses and consumers must pay higher rates of interest when the Federal Reserve Board raises the rates for banks. The rates increased from the middle 1970s to the early 1980s, and decreased in the early 1990s.

Most businesses like low interest rates because it is less costly to borrow money needed for building and operating a business. Most consumers like lower interest rates, too, because it is less costly to borrow money to buy a house or a car. But some consumers, such as older, retired workers who live off savings in the bank, lose money when interest rates decline. As a group, consumers can reduce interest rates by borrowing less and saving more of their income. If we do this, the amount of money available for loans will increase and interest rates will decline.

THE FEDERAL BUDGET

We talked about how the economy affects us through inflation, unemployment, and interest rates. The economy also affects the **federal budget**—the plan for spending federal tax money. The federal income tax is a **progressive tax**—which means the more we earn, the higher the rate we must pay.

Sometimes the economy does not seem to do what is needed for the good of the people, and the government tries to help people through the federal budget. When money is needed, taxes are raised; which in turn affects most Americans directly in the pocketbook. When most people have less money to spend, the economy is affected—sometimes leading to a recession.

We Americans are understanding our economic problems better, and we are taking steps to correct them. Labor is realizing that lower wage increases will help the economy. Management is realizing that they must seek long-range goals and not just short-range profits. The federal government is recognizing the need to control spending, but this is proving to be a very big and very complex problem. Together, Americans are working for a sound economy.

Summary

- If we understand the national economy, we can make better decisions about our own money management.

- The free enterprise system includes certain freedoms, responsibilities, and safeguards.

- The behavior of consumers affects the overall economy and vice versa. The economy can heavily affect the consumer in the form of inflation, unemployment, and changing interest rates.

- Several factors can contribute to inflation: supply and demand for goods and services, wage increases, strikes, declines in productivity, and deficit spending by the government.

federal budget

the plan for spending federal tax money

progressive tax

tax that increases in relation to increased earnings

ENRICHING YOUR VOCABULARY

Number your paper from 1–25. Beside each number, write the word or phrase that matches that definition. Choose your answers from the following list.

business cycle	federal debt	progressive tax
competition	Federal Reserve Bank System	prosperity
constraints	(FRBS)	recession
Consumer Price Index (CPI)	inflation	recovery
debts	interest rate	reinvested
deficit spending	invest	standard of living
demand	law of supply and demand	stock
depression	productivity	unemployment
federal budget	profit	

1. Shares in a business
2. Quantity of goods that buyers will purchase
3. Use money to make more money
4. Economic condition in which people have money to spend
5. Periods of prosperity and recession
6. Plan for spending federal tax money
7. Increase in sales and production following a recession or depression
8. Monthly government list of how much average prices have gone up or down
9. Amount of output per unit of input
10. Money owed
11. Money remaining after expenses
12. Put back into the business
13. Spending more money than is taken in
14. Tax that increases in relation to increased earnings
15. Level of necessities and comforts that a group of people expect to be able to buy
16. The state of being without a job involuntarily
17. Federal organization that controls the amount of money available for loans
18. Period of low business activity and high unemployment
19. Period of reduced business activity
20. Restrictions
21. Relationship between quantity and price
22. Producing best product or service at best price
23. Price paid to borrow money
24. Amount of money owed by the federal government
25. The rising cost of goods and services

CHAPTER REVIEW 7

REVIEWING WHAT YOU HAVE LEARNED

1. Explain the five freedoms or rights that businesses have in the United States.

2. Name at least four responsibilities of businesses in the United States.

3. Name and describe the three phases of the business cycle.

4. Explain the law of supply and demand. How does this law apply to interest rates?

5. Inflation, unemployment, and high interest rates are three important economic problems. Choose one of these problems and explain how it affects consumers.

USING YOUR CRITICAL THINKING SKILLS

1. How does competition work for the consumer?

2. Some of the constraints placed on businesses in our "controlled" free enterprise system increase consumer costs. For example, controlled logging increases the price of lumber. Do you agree with the concept of some constraints? Why or why not? Try to find examples to support your ideas.

APPLYING WHAT YOU HAVE LEARNED

1. Collect newspaper and magazine articles dealing with one of the three major economic problems—inflation, unemployment, or high interest rates. Keep the articles in order according to when they were written—you may want to keep them in a scrapbook. At the end of the course, review what has been done about each problem. Prepare a report, and answer these questions: Has progress been made toward solving the problem? Has the problem worsened? Do you think world events had an influence on the problem, and if so, how?

CHAPTER 8

Financial Planning

OBJECTIVES

After completing this chapter, you will be able to do the following:
1. List four steps leading up to making a spending plan.
2. Name two examples of fixed expenses.
3. Explain how you can use your spending plan to provide money for future goals.
4. Name two obstacles to good money management.

TERMS

credit rating
discretionary spending
fixed expenses

impulse buying
flexible essential expenses
paying yourself first

payroll deduction plan

Achieving your life's goals, your *lifestyle* goals, depends directly upon good financial planning. Good financial planning can help you get more value and satisfaction for your money, and it begins with developing a spending plan.

You will need a financial record book, an inexpensive loose-leaf notebook fills this need quite well. Stationery stores sell a variety of spending plan forms that you can use, or you may want to make up your own forms. Financial planning involves the following four major steps:

- setting financial goals
- estimating income
- estimating expenses
- planning your spending

SETTING FINANCIAL GOALS

You read in Chapter 2 about the importance of goals if you are to take charge of your own life. The first step in making your spending plan is to review your goals. If you are a single person, start by writing down your long-range goals, your intermediate goals, and your short-range goals. This will help you plan your savings.

Making a spending plan as a single person is fairly simple since it does not involve compromises to satisfy the goals of others. Making a spending plan for a family is more complex because the values and goals of each family member are likely to differ. For this reason, if you do not live alone, include all family members in a discussion. Decide together what is most important to each member and to the family as a whole, so that individual and family needs and interests can be considered. Then review individual and family goals at least once a year. As the size, age, income, and interests of the family change, so will its goals.

When you write down your goals, be as specific as you can. Then refer to your written goals as you begin to outline your spending plan. You will refer to them again and again later as you revise your spending plan for future years. A spending plan can cover any period of time, but most plans cover one year.

ESTIMATING INCOME

Before you can plan your spending, you must know how much money you will have, so the next step is to estimate your income. Write down all the income you expect to receive during your planning period. If your planning period covers one year and you are paid once a month, estimate your income separately for each of the twelve months. If you are paid once a week, estimate your income separately for each of the fifty-two weeks. To keep our examples simple, they will be based on monthly income for one year. Start by writing down wages and other income that you can count on regularly—then, add other income that you expect, such as gifts, interest from savings accounts and bonds, tips, or money from other sources.

Income from seasonal jobs, sales commissions, and self-employment often varies greatly from month to month. If your income is irregular, make two estimates of your total yearly income. Consider your past experience and figure both the smallest and the largest amounts you can reasonably expect. Plan first on the basis of the

The entire family can participate in setting financial goals. Has your family set any financial goals? If not, encourage your family to develop a financial plan that will fit with your lifestyle.

lower amount, then plan how you will use extra money if you receive it.

ESTIMATING EXPENSES

After estimating your income, estimate your expenses using the same planning period as before. You will find that some expenses (such as rent) are paid every week or every month. Others (such as insurance premiums) are paid periodically, maybe every three months or even once a year. Some expenses are **fixed expenses** that must be paid, such as for rent, insurance, or payments on loans or credit card balances. Fixed expenses do not vary. They are the same amount (or nearly the same) each time that you pay them. Other expenses, including such essentials (necessities) as food and clothing and such non-essentials as recreation,

are *flexible* expenses. The amount you spend on flexible expenses will vary from month to month. You will have to estimate the monthly cost of **flexible essential expenses** based on averages for these items over the past months.

The exact cost of utilities varies from month to month. For example, in cool climates, the bill for heating the house is higher in winter. Still, utilities are usually considered fixed expenses. You may get a more accurate picture if you average utility bills over several months or even for a whole year.

If you have kept records of your spending in recent months, use these to guide you in setting up your spending plan. Checkbook records, bills, and sales receipts will help you estimate your expenses. If you have no records, write down your spending for the next several months in order to identify actual spending patterns. A simple listing of goods or services purchased and amounts paid is sufficient for planning purposes.

flexible essential expenses

payments for necessary items, such as food and clothing, that vary from month to month

fixed expenses

payments such as rent and insurance that are the same amount each time you pay them

Reviewing Spending Practices

Review your spending records carefully. Do you want to continue your present spending practices? Would you rather make some changes?

If all your spending has been for things you feel are important, include about the same expenses in your spending plan. You may find that you have been spending too much for things that don't give you much satisfaction. Careful planning will help you get more for your money.

Plan major purchases well in advance, keeping them separated by several months or years. A car and furniture, for example, are major purchases—and most people cannot afford to buy both during the same month, or even the same year. If you use credit for major purchases, plan how you will repay the loan.

Your income is, and probably always will be, limited. When you first begin working full-time, you may not have much left after paying for necessities. However, some savings should always be part of your plan from the beginning so that you will develop the habit of "**paying yourself first**." Develop the habit of saving by paying yourself first, and you will have a higher standard of living and a better personal economic outlook throughout your whole life. When your income is greater, you can increase your savings to meet your long-range goals.

paying yourself first
....
putting money in savings for later use before paying for essential and non-essential items

PLANNING YOUR SPENDING

After you have reviewed your goals and estimated your income and expenses, you are ready to prepare your

Computer programs can make it easy to keep track of your spending. However, they won't keep you from spending your money unwisely. Develop a personal spending plan to keep track of your own finances, and stick to it!

spending plan. Base your plan on two things:

- your goals or your family's goals
- your estimates of income and expenses

If you work part-time and live with your family, you may need only a simple plan—but when you begin working full-time, you will need a more complete plan. The following five-part plan is similar to plans used successfully by many individuals and families.

1. *The first part is to write down your estimate of income for the next twelve months.*

2. *The second part is to write down your obligations (what you must pay).* Make a separate section for fixed essentials (such as rent or house payments, insurance premiums) and another section for flexible essentials (such as food and clothing). Then add a section listing installment payments for things already purchased.

3. *The third part is to write down the difference between your estimated income and your estimated expenses for essential (necessary) items.* This is the amount you may save for the future or spend as you wish.

4. *The fourth part is to write down how much you plan to save to reach your goals or your family's goals.* Have you wanted to save for future goals but run out of money at the end of the month? The best approach is to set aside a certain amount regularly each month! When planning, treat savings as a fixed expense, and keep your savings separate. For example, you could use a savings account or buy government savings bonds. Then it won't be easy to dip into your savings to buy things you don't need—and your savings will grow

by earning interest. Probably the easiest way to save regularly is to have a certain amount deducted from each paycheck that goes directly into a savings account. Your employer may offer a **payroll deduction plan** that makes this easier.

5. *The fifth part is to write down how you plan to spend money left after paying essential expenses and saving for your goals.* This is the amount you may spend according to your own discretion (good judgment)—you may spend it as you want. This is **discretionary spending**, and you will use this money to pay for all items not listed as fixed or flexible essentials.

Following Your Spending Plan

To see how well you are following your spending plan, keep track of how you actually spend your money. It isn't necessary to write down every penny you spend, but you will need to know where your money goes.

Making Your Spending Plan Work for You

Try your spending plan for a month or two, then make whatever revision is necessary. Once you have a workable plan, there are several things you must do to make it run smoothly.

- Decide on a special place for your financial records, then keep them all together. Some people store records in a desk or cabinet, some keep them in a cardboard box. Most stationery stores sell metal boxes for storing records, and some of these boxes are insulated against heat (to protect important papers in case of

payroll deduction plan
. . . . .
an employer plan that allows employees to have money deducted from their earnings and put into a savings account before they receive their paycheck

discretionary spending
. . . .
using your money according to your own good judgment

fire). If you have a lot of records, you may decide to use a small filing cabinet.

- Pay monthly bills on a definite date or dates, always on time to avoid extra interest payments and late charges. By choosing a definite date or dates to pay your bills, you won't overlook payments. If all of your bills arrive early in the month, you might decide to write checks on the tenth of each month. If you receive bills throughout the month, you might decide to write checks on the tenth and the twenty-fifth of each month. This can save you money and protect your **credit rating**. (Your credit rating is based on records of how well you pay your bills, and this information is kept on file by three large credit report companies.)

- Stick with it. The most difficult thing about using a spending plan is following it. The best plan in the world is worthless if it isn't used! To stick with a spending plan, you will need to develop good buying habits.

- Review your spending plan regularly. Your spending plan should be helping you reach your financial goals—and if it isn't doing this, take time to study it. Remember, your plan must work for you, so adjust it to suit your needs. Even if your plan seems to be working, review it at least once a year.

OBSTACLES TO GOOD MONEY MANAGEMENT

One of the main obstacles to good money management is impulse buying. While shopping, we all see items that we would like but had not planned to buy. Many of these things don't cost very much, and we may buy them without considering our overall spending plan. This is impulse buying, and most of us do some of it—usually right after payday.

credit rating
· · · · · · · · · · · · ·
records that are kept by credit report companies, of how well you pay your bills

impulse buying
· · · · · · · · · · · · ·
purchasing items that we would like but had not planned to buy

MAKING CONSUMER DECISIONS

Adrian is learning to take responsibility for her own finances. She has gone through the four steps in financial planning—goal setting, estimating income and expenses, and arriving at a spending plan. Since she lives at home, her parents cover many of her expenses. Her part-time job provides enough money for her to pay some of the car insurance, put away some for savings, and have a some left over to spend as she likes.

Adrian's plan has been in effect for several months, and she has followed it successfully and stayed within her budget. This month, however, she has an opportunity to go on a special trip with another family. She has already spent most of her discretionary spending money for the month. She really wants to go on this trip, and thinks, "I could use my savings. That would cover my expenses for the trip, and I can always replace it later."

Do you think Adrian should use her savings to go on this trip? What other options could she consider?

Tracy is an avid reader and enjoys browsing in the many fine local bookstores. However, with inflation over the last several years, the price of paperback novels has risen from 25 cents to $5.95 and up. As much as Tracy loves books, such expenses are not within her budget.

Instead, Tracy has had to find alternative ways to get books. She uses the library, goes to bookstores that sell used books, and goes to swap meets and garage sales. In addition, she has contacted some of her mother's friends to see if they have books they don't want anymore. She also set up a "book exchange" day with her friends.

Being a good money manager sometimes means getting creative and looking for alternative solutions to needs!

Stores encourage impulse buying by setting up attractive displays of low-cost items in places where unsuspecting consumers are sure to see them. Some people spend hundreds of dollars impulsively, buying inexpensive items they had not planned to buy and don't really need—and these purchases add up to big bills at the end of the month.

Planning your spending carefully can help you avoid impulse buying. Have you ever bought an item impulsively, and regretted it later? Why did you regret it?

People who have a habit of impulse buying usually get the least satisfaction from their purchases, they seldom have enough money to achieve their long-range goals.

One thing more damaging to good money management than impulse buying is impulse buying on credit. Saying "Charge it" for things we don't need and haven't planned to buy is the quickest way to financial ruin. Yet it is easy to do. Many salespersons encourage us to buy on credit, saying, "It's only ten dollars a month—you'll never miss it!" Just a few of these "easy payments" can leave us without money to pay for basic necessities. Consumer credit is discussed in detail in Chapters 10, 11, and 12.

MANAGING TWO INCOMES

In many families, both the husband and wife work just to pay for the necessities of life. Some couples use the second income to provide a higher standard of living, and others save money to purchase a home.

When both husband and wife work outside of the home, there are added expenses. Transportation costs more, sometimes a second car is needed, and often it is necessary to buy extra clothing to be worn on the job. There may be less time for food preparation, so costly convenience foods are often purchased. Working couples tend to dine out more often, too. If there are small children, there is the added cost of child care.

Many working couples deposit both paychecks into one bank account, and keep one checkbook. Others prefer separate accounts. Checking accounts are discussed in detail in the next topic.

Many families need two incomes to be able to pay all of their bills. However, working outside the home increases some costs such as child care. Check with a child care facility in your area. How much does it cost for a child to stay there?

Summary

- Good financial planning can help you get more value out of your money and can help you reach long-term goals.
- Financial planning involves four major steps: setting financial goals, estimating income, estimating expenses, and planning your spending.
- Review your spending plan regularly and stick to it! It can help you reach your financial goals.
- Keep financial records and pay bills on time.

CHECKLIST FOR CONTROLLING SPENDING

Preparing and following spending plans takes some work, but it pays off by providing satisfaction in achieving goals. Make sure you understand the steps that have been described in this section:

____ Review your goals, and let them guide your spending.
____ Estimate your income.
____ Estimate your fixed and flexible essential expenses.
____ Use the difference between income and essential expenses to plan savings and discretionary spending.
____ Keep financial records.
____ Pay bills on time.
____ Review your spending plan regularly.
____ Stick with your plan.

CHAPTER REVIEW
8

ENRICHING **Y**OUR **V**OCABULARY

Use the following phrases to complete the sentences below. Write the completed sentences on your paper.

credit rating
discretionary spending
fixed expenses

flexible essential expense
impulse buying
paying yourself first

payroll deduction plan

1. When creating a spending plan, money spent for items such as food and clothing is considered a

2. Establishing an automatic savings plan is a good way of

3. Spending money on items that are not part of your spending plan falls under the category of

4. Expenses that do not vary and must be paid on a regular basis are called

5. Your employer may be able to help you establish a

6. Paying your bills on time will help you establish a good

7. Marketing techniques take advantage of

REVIEWING **W**HAT **Y**OU **H**AVE **L**EARNED

1. What are the four steps leading up to making a spending plan?

2. Give two examples of fixed expenses.

3. How can you use your spending plan to provide money for future goals?

4. Why is it a good policy to pay your bills on the same day each month?

5. What are two obstacles to good money management?

USING **Y**OUR **C**RITICAL **T**HINKING **S**KILLS

1. Does anyone you know buy on impulse? What products or types of products does this person buy?

2. What can be done to control impulse buying?

3. Some people believe financial planning is not necessary. Do you agree or disagree? Why?

4. What have you recently bought on impulse? Was it a good or bad decision? Why?

APPLYING **W**HAT **Y**OU **H**AVE **L**EARNED

1. Begin a financial plan for yourself that will include your spending plan for the coming year. Start by writing down your financial goals. Estimate your income for each week or month, then estimate your expenses for each week or month of the coming year by reviewing your recent spending practices. Then write out a spending plan appropriate to your lifestyle.

CHAPTER 9

Using Banking Services

OBJECTIVES

After completing this chapter, you will be able to do the following:
1. Explain the difference between a blank endorsement and a restrictive endorsement.
2. Name three advantages of paying bills by check.
3. List six services usually offered by banks.

TERMS

automatic teller
  machine (ATM)
bank statement
banks
blank endorsement
canceled checks
certificate of deposit
check
check register

commercial banks
credit unions
deposit
deposit slip
financial services
full endorsement
full-service banks
minimum balance
outstanding checks

passbook accounts
reconcile
restrictive endorsement
savings and loan
  associations
savings banks
service charge
signature card
withdraw

As consumers, we spend money and save money—but hardly anyone spends and saves with cash alone. Buying things with cash all the time can be inconvenient. For example, who would want (or could afford) to take twenty thousand dollars to a car dealer to buy a new car? Few people want to keep their savings stuffed in a mattress. (This was done by some people in the past, but it is *not* a safe place to keep money.) Today, people depend on banks and similar institutions.

Banks hold money for safety, to facilitate paying money to other persons or companies, to provide savings plans, and to make loans. The functions that banks perform are called **financial services**. Banks and similar institutions offer many kinds of financial services. As a consumer, you should know about these services—then you can decide which ones you want to use.

FINANCIAL INSTITUTIONS

As society moved from an agricultural economy to an industrial economy and the need for money increased, banks were established. At first, the main function of banks was the safekeeping of money. Today, banks have also become specialists in the transfer of money and credit.

Specific functions differ according to the type of bank. The two most common types of banks in the United States are **commercial banks** and **savings banks**. In addition, **savings and loan associations** and **credit unions** offer some similar services.

Commercial Banks

Many financial services are offered by commercial banks, sometimes ad-

Financial institutions offer a variety of services, but not all institutions offer all services. Do you already use the services of a financial institution? If not, do some research to find the right place that offers the right services for you.

vertised as **full-service banks**, including the following:

- checking accounts
- savings accounts
- savings certificates
- credit card services
- loans
- cashier's and traveler's checks
- safe-deposit boxes
- trust services

Commercial banks are organized as corporations and are chartered (licensed) by either the federal government or the state. They are in business to earn profits.

Savings Banks

Savings banks are chartered by the state. They, too, are in business to earn a profit. Their services are more limited than those of commercial banks, but savings banks do offer:

- savings accounts
- loans (including home mortgages)
- traveler's checks
- safe-deposit boxes

CONSUMER FOCUS

BANKING SERVICES

The banking services that you need will affect your choice of bank, but most banks offer the following services.

- Checking accounts: money in these accounts may be paid to individuals or companies by writing checks.
- Savings accounts: money left in these accounts earns interest.
- Savings certificates: these are also known as certificates of deposit. Money is left on deposit for a certain period of time at a fixed rate of interest. The interest earned is usually higher than in ordinary savings accounts, but a penalty is charged if money is withdrawn early.
- Money-market accounts: money in these accounts usually earns a high rate of interest, though the rate changes frequently. Consumers may write checks that draw on these accounts, but a considerable amount must be left on deposit in order to earn the high rate of interest.
- Credit card services: banks may issue credit cards and accept payment of credit card bills.
- Loans: consumers may apply to borrow money for the purchase of major appliances, automobiles, property improvement, or buying a home.
- Cashier's and traveler's checks: consumers may buy these checks, which are more widely accepted than personal checks. A cashier's check is typically used for large purchases. Traveler's checks are available in a variety of denominations.
- Safe-deposit boxes: consumers may rent these boxes, which are intended for safe storage of important papers and small but valuable possessions, such as jewelry.
- Trust services: a bank may manage the money or investments included in a "trust." This is for the benefit of people named in the trust agreement (such as young children who inherit money from their parents).
- Other services: most banks offer such conveniences as drive-up windows, automatic teller machines (ATMs), bill paying, and automatic deposit of payroll checks.

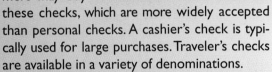

Savings and Loan Associations

Technically, savings and loan associations (S&Ls) are not banks, so they operate under a different set of regulations. Their services are generally limited to savings accounts, home mortgages, and checking accounts. Recent laws have expanded the services of savings and loan associations, and now they can compete more easily with commercial banks.

Savings and loan associations are in business to earn a profit. However, during the 1980s, many savings and loan associations made large real estate loans that could not be repaid. This caused a national crisis that required hundreds of billions of dollars in federal money to help pay off creditors. Still, many people who had savings in S&Ls lost money. By 1993, this crisis appeared to be over, and most savings and loan associations are now solvent (able to pay their debts) and safe places to save money.

full endorsement
....
a signature on the back
of a check with "pay to
order" instructions

Credit Unions

Credit unions are nonprofit institutions that accept money for savings and also loan money to their members. Membership usually consists of a group of people who work for the same employer or group of employers. For example, a teachers' credit union is made up of teachers (and their families) from a particular school district or county. Because they do not make a profit, credit unions often pay higher interest rates on savings and charge lower rates on loans than other financial institutions.

CHECKS

The first contact with banking services for most of us is when we are given a **check**. Checks are a way of transferring money. If you want money for your check, you may "cash" it by exchanging your check for the amount of money (cash) written on the front of the check. If you have a bank account, you may deposit the check in your account—or you may decide to pass the check on to someone else.

check
....
a document for
transferring money

Endorsing a Check

Whether you cash a check, deposit it, or pass it on, you must endorse your check. This means signing your name on the back of the check. Sign your name exactly as it appears on the front. If you write *only your name* on the back of the check, it is a **blank endorsement**—and if you lose such a check, anyone may cash it.

If you want to restrict what can be done with your check, use a **restrictive endorsement**. For example, if you plan to deposit the check in your own account, you may write "For deposit only" and then sign your name. If you

blank endorsement
....
a signature on the back
of a check with no
instructions

restrictive
endorsement
....
a signature on the back
of a check with
instructions limiting
what can be done with
the check

plan to pass a check on to someone else, you may write "Pay to the order of (the person's name)" and sign your name. This is a **full endorsement**. (See Figure 9.1 on the next page.)

Handling Checks

When you write a check, be certain that there is enough money in your checking account to cover (pay) each check. When you receive a check, cash it, deposit it, or pass it on promptly. When a check is held for weeks or months, the person who wrote it may forget that the check has not been paid—and there may not be enough money in the account to cover the check. Or the person who wrote the check may change banks or move away, in which case the account that was supposed to pay your check may be closed.

Cashing Checks

Some people write *overdrafts*—"bad" checks. That is, they write checks when there is no money in the bank to cover them. Of course, this is against the law, and the people or businesses accepting bad checks lose money. Sometimes honest people make mistakes, however. If you ever mistakenly write a "bad" check, pay the amount owed as soon as possible. Banks charge a fee for handling bad checks, and businesses charge a fee for the inconvenience caused by a bad check, too.

Whoever cashes your check will probably want to make certain it is good. If that person doesn't know you, you may be asked to show identification, such as your driver's license or a check guarantee card. The person cashing your check needs to be sure that you are really the person whose name is on the check.

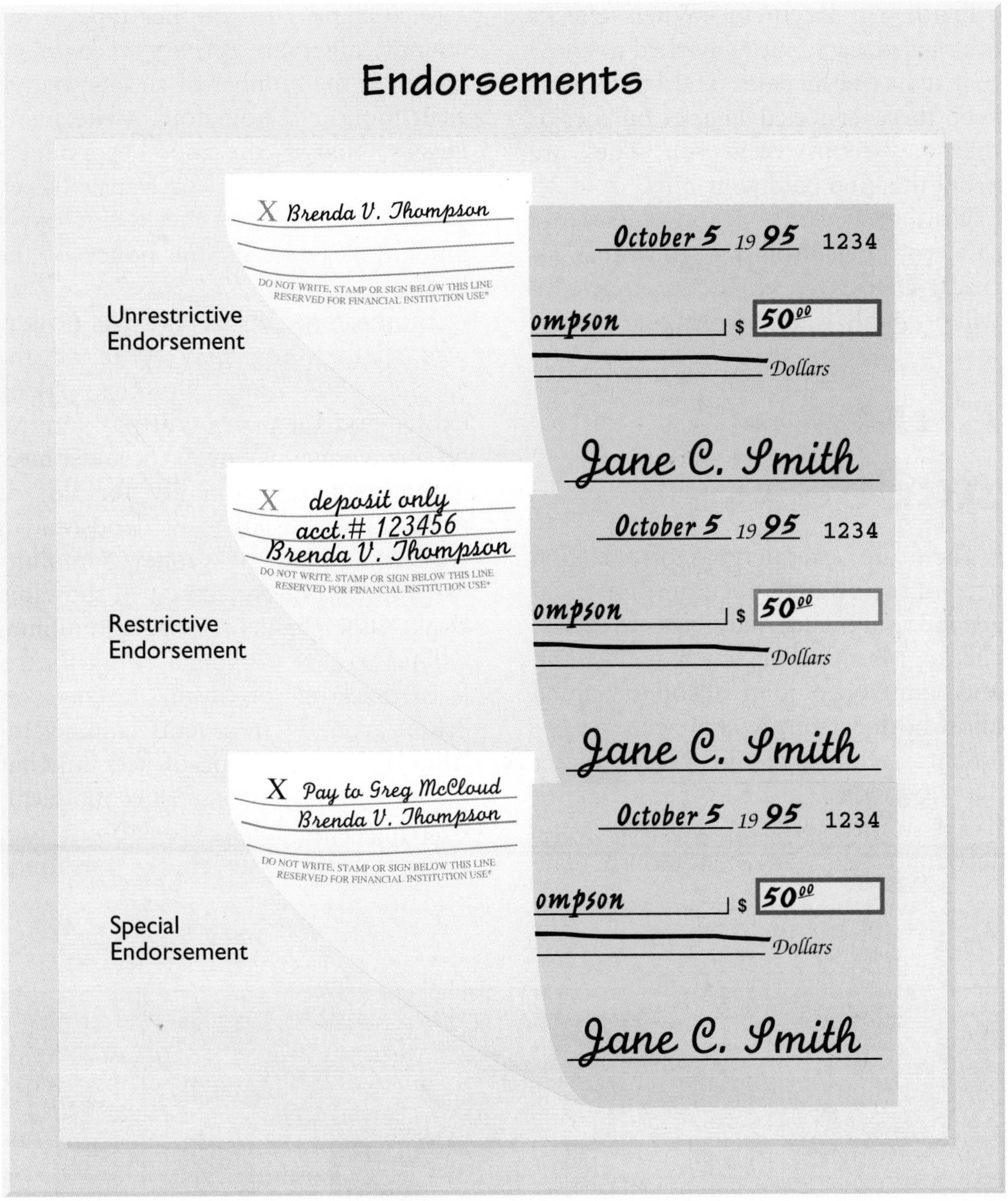

Endorsements

Unrestrictive Endorsement

X Brenda V. Thompson

DO NOT WRITE, STAMP OR SIGN BELOW THIS LINE
RESERVED FOR FINANCIAL INSTITUTION USE*

October 5 19 95   1234

ompson | $ 50⁰⁰

_____ Dollars

Jane C. Smith

Restrictive Endorsement

X   deposit only
    acct. # 123456
Brenda V. Thompson

DO NOT WRITE, STAMP OR SIGN BELOW THIS LINE
RESERVED FOR FINANCIAL INSTITUTION USE*

October 5 19 95   1234

ompson | $ 50⁰⁰

_____ Dollars

Jane C. Smith

Special Endorsement

X   Pay to Greg McCloud
    Brenda V. Thompson

DO NOT WRITE, STAMP OR SIGN BELOW THIS LINE
RESERVED FOR FINANCIAL INSTITUTION USE*

October 5 19 95   1234

ompson | $ 50⁰⁰

_____ Dollars

Jane C. Smith

Figure 9.1
....

Three types of endorsements are shown here; unrestrictive endorsement, restrictive endorsement, and special endorsement. Which of these endorsements would make it easy for anyone to cash a check?

Paying Bills by Check

Most people carry cash to pay for small purchases. For example, when we buy tickets to a local football game, we usually pay cash. If we want to buy a hot dog at the game, we spend cash for that, too. However, most people use a checking account for paying their bills.

Convenience, Economy, and Time. Some people pay their monthly bills with cash, but that requires driving around town to make payments. It is more economical to put a check in the mail for these expenses—and, of course, it saves time.

Safety. Mailing cash is not safe, so pay your out-of-town bills with a check. (If you haven't yet opened a checking account, you can buy a money order to pay an out-of-town bill, but this is rather expensive.) It's also safer to keep your money in the bank than in your house.

canceled checks
. . . .
checks that have been identified as paid

Proof of Payment. When checks are cashed, each one is marked to show that it has been paid. The banks may keep these canceled checks on file, or they may return them you. They are proof that you paid your bills.

Writing checks is a convenient and safe way to pay bills. If you don't already have a checking account, you will probably want to open one soon.

CHECKING ACCOUNTS

There are several types of checking accounts. You may open an individual account, allowing only you to write checks. Many people (such as husband and wife) open joint accounts which allow both persons to write checks.

Some accounts require you to pay a service charge. In one type, a flat fee based on the minimum balance in the account is charged each month. The

service charge
. . . .
fee paid to the bank for checking services

minimum balance
. . . .
the lowest balance in an account during a given accounting period

service charge for another type of account, called an *activity account*, is based on the number of checks written each month. If you don't write many checks, this is the most economical type of account. The cost is usually ten to fifteen cents per check—the exact amount depends on the policy of the bank.

Another type of account has no service charge. You may write all the checks you want without paying extra—and the bank will pay interest on the average balance! You must meet a requirement to qualify for this at most banks, usually by depositing a certain amount of money (amounts vary) in a savings account in the same bank. Other banks require a minimum balance in the checking account for the free checking privilege. It pays to "shop around" in several banking institutions for the type of account that fits your needs and is most economical.

Savings and loan associations, too, allow you to write checks for funds

Automatic teller machines (ATMs), discussed on page 92, have made it convenient to do banking at all hours. This convenience, however, has made ATM users easy victims of robbers. Care must be taken when using ATMs at any hour of the day or night.

INTERACTING WITH TECHNOLOGY

USING TECHNOLOGY TO MANAGE YOUR FINANCES

Record keeping is one of the most important parts of good financial planning and one of the most difficult for many people to organize. Software programs are available for personal computers that streamline record keeping and help produce an organized picture of personal finances.

These programs create budgets based on the actual record of your past spending pattern. Once the budget has been created, you can modify it to reflect the amount you would like to spend in each category, Then your budget print-out will show you how you're doing, compared to your plan. This information is updated with each transaction you enter.

Computer programs can be used to write checks and pay bills or to keep track of the checks you write from your checkbook. If you use the programs to write checks, the payments are made electronically through a central processing center. Even if the computer is not used to actually pay bills, these programs provide excellent check register systems. By entering all your banking transactions into a computer register, your bank account will automatically be balanced.

These computer registers also aid in organizing your finances. If each transaction is assigned to a category, the computer can use this information to create a variety of different reports about your finances. For example, any item that is tax-related can be identified and accessed in a report when you are ready to prepare your taxes. This information is available to you without your having to collect records and add up totals if your computer check register is up to date.

These programs can be used to track a variety of activities in addition to your checking transactions. They can keep track of savings accounts and investment accounts, and can be used to transfer funds from one account to another. They can also track loan balances and be programmed to remind you when regular loan payments are due. If you are using your computer to make electronic payments, you can program it to make loan payments automatically. Categories can be set up so that all your credit card purchases can be entered into your check register to help you keep track of these expenditures too. Having all this information stored in one place and readily available can be very helpful in looking at your finances. Successful financial planning depends on seeing the whole picture.

Glossary terms (margin)

automatic teller machine (ATM)

a computerized machine that allows deposits and withdrawals to be made when the bank is closed or from another city or state

deposit

to place money into an account

deposit slip

a form to accompany a deposit so that it is credited to the proper account

check register

a record of checks and deposits for a checking account

signature card

a card kept on file at the bank to verify the signature on checks

---

in certain types of accounts. For example, you can write checks on *negotiable order of withdrawal*—"NOW" accounts.

Money-market and Super NOW accounts offer checking services and may pay somewhat higher interest than other types of accounts. Find out the facts about the types of accounts being offered in your area, then choose the type that is best for you.

Almost all banks provide automatic teller machine (ATM) services. Using an electronically encoded card (along with your secret *personal identification number*—PIN) an ATM allows you to make deposits or withdraw money from your account when the bank is closed or when you're in another city or state.

OPENING A CHECKING ACCOUNT

Opening a checking account is easy. At the bank, ask for the person who can help you open a checking account. The person in charge of new accounts will need information about you, such as:

- name
- address
- telephone number
- place of work
- amount of deposit

You will also be asked to sign a signature card, and you will sign your name exactly as you will sign your checks. Later, bank employees will match the signatures on your checks with the signature on your card, making it less likely that someone else could write checks on your account.

Most banks have several styles of checks; and, for a fee, you can choose the style you like from samples. Your checks will have your name and address printed on them. Printing may take a couple of weeks so, for your immediate use, you may be given a book of pre-numbered checks (without an imprinted name).

Making Deposits

When you deposit money in a checking account, you must fill out a deposit slip. If you are depositing cash, write the amount beside the word "cash" on the deposit slips. When you deposit checks, use the next lines, labeled "checks," and list each check separately.

When you are depositing one or more checks in your account, you may want some cash. If so, write the amount of cash you want after the words "less cash received," subtract the cash from the "total" line, and write the difference on the "net deposit" line. You must sign your name to acknowledge that you received the cash. The bank teller will give you a receipt, or, if you are using an ATM, the machine will print out a receipt. Keep these receipts with your other financial records, as they are your records of the money you have deposited.

In the front of your checkbook is a check register. Use it to keep a record of deposits and checks written and to keep a running balance. Whenever you make a deposit, write the amount in the deposit column of your check register. Then add the deposit to the previous balance to see how much you now have in your account.

Writing Checks

The first step in writing a check is to record it in your check register. Write

Filling Out Your Own Checks

Figure 9.2
....

This figure shows a check that has been properly filled out. To whom was the check written? What was the reason for writing the check?

in the number of the check and the name of the person or company to whom you are writing the check. Write the amount of the check in the payment or debit column, then subtract the amount of the check from the previous balance. Also subtract any charge for writing the check. The result is how much you have left in your account after you write the check.

Now you are ready to write the check. Always use a pen. If you use a pencil, someone could easily change the amount of your check. After the words "Pay to the order of," write the name of the person or company to whom the check will be paid. Then write the amount of the check in figures, writing close to the dollar sign so that no one can write in an extra figure. On the next line, write the amount in words, using a fraction of a dollar to show the cents (for example, "50/100"). If the check is written for an even dollar amount, show the cents as "no/100." Draw a line from the fraction to the word "dollars." This makes it difficult for anyone to change

the amount of your check. After the word "memo," write the reason for writing the check. Finally, sign your name exactly as you did on your signature card. (See Figure 9.2.)

Reconciling the Bank Statement

Most banks return canceled checks or a list of checks you have written once a month, along with a **bank statement**, which shows your balance at the beginning of the accounting period. Then each check or other charge is listed and subtracted from the beginning balance. Deposits are listed, too, and added to the balance.

To make certain your own records match the bank statement, you must **reconcile** your bank statement. This procedure can be done in five steps.

1. Sort your canceled checks in numbered order.

2. Make a small check mark in your check register for each check that

bank statement
....
a monthly accounting of checking account activity and balance provided by the bank

reconcile
....
to match the balance in the check register to the bank statement

has been returned and for each deposit that has been recorded.

3. If you have made recent deposits that do not show on the bank statement, add the amount to the bank's closing balance. If you are paid interest on your account, add the interest shown on the bank statement to your check register.

4. List the numbers and amounts of checks you have written that have not yet been returned. These are known as **outstanding checks**. Add up the total of these outstanding checks and subtract the total from the bank's closing balance.

5. In your check register, list any service charge or fees shown on the bank statement—then subtract them from your register total.

The revised balances of your checkbook register and the bank statement should now be the same. If not, check your addition and subtraction, and make sure you have done everything right. If the balances still do not match, notify your bank and a bank employee will go over the statement with you.

Interest paid on savings accounts varies according to the type of account and the type of financial institution. Many institutions post the current interest being paid, or you can call financial institutions to find out the current interest being paid.

outstanding checks
....
checks that have been written but have not been paid

passbook accounts
....
savings accounts

withdraw
....
to remove money from an account

certificate of deposit
....
a savings account in which money is deposited for a given period of time

SAVINGS ACCOUNTS

Have you ever saved for weeks or months to buy something you wanted? If so, you know the happy feeling of setting a financial goal and reaching it. Banks can help you reach your goals by providing savings accounts. Remember money deposited in a savings account earns interest, so your money accumulates even faster. A formal savings program provides safety, it's easier to resist the temptation to spend impulsively, and it establishes a record of saving.

Passbook Accounts

When you open a savings account, you are issued a passbook to keep a record of your savings. Thus, savings accounts are called **passbook accounts**. A passbook shows how much you have saved and how much interest your savings have earned. Passbook accounts pay less interest than other types of savings, but you are free to **withdraw** (take out) your money at any time—including the interest earned.

Certificates of Deposit

If you deposit money for a fixed period of time, the bank will usually pay a somewhat higher rate of interest. You will be issued a **certificate of deposit**. These certificates are issued for various time periods, such as six months, one year, thirty months, or longer. In an emergency, you can withdraw your money—but if you withdraw your money early, you will lose much of the interest and may also pay a penalty.

A Guide for Saving

Some people never save any money—so when they make major purchases, they must buy on credit. When they do this, they obligate future income, making it difficult to start saving money at all. When an emergency comes along, these people either obligate even more future income, or they must sell something that they have finally paid off. Of course, there are times when it *is* wise to buy on credit, and this is discussed in Chapter 10.

How much should you save? This depends on both your income and your financial responsibilities, but the chart on this page can serve as a general guide.

Summary

- Many financial services are offered by commercial banks, savings banks, savings and loan associations, and credit unions.

- Having a checking account is a responsibility. Be sure there is enough money in your account to cover each check you write. When you receive a check, cash it or deposit it promptly.

- There are different types of checking accounts. Some require a minimum balance, some apply a service charge, some pay interest on the balance.

- Saving money regularly is part of good money management. The money in a savings account at a bank earns interest.

CONSUMER PROFILE

Edwin has had a checking account for almost a year now. He keeps track of his deposits and checks in his check register, and calculates his balance. What he doesn't do, however, is reconcile his monthly bank statement. He figures that he's "close enough."

Recently, Edwin received a note from his bank returning a check he had written. The note said he had "insufficient funds" to pay for the check. On top of that, the bank charged him a hefty $15!

When Edwin checked his register against all his old statements, he found that he had forgotten to write in a large ATM withdrawal. His balance was, indeed, a negative number! Edwin says, "What a hassle, and an extra expense! From now on, I'll reconcile my bank statement every single month!"

CHECKLIST FOR MONTHLY SAVINGS

If your monthly income after taxes is:	Each month, you should save:
$600 to $900	$21 to $90
$900 to $1200	$75 to $150
$1200 to $1500	$150 to $270
$1500 to $1800	$270 to $330
$1800 to $2100	$285 to $360
$2100 to $2400	$345 to $495
$2400 to $2700	$405 to $555
$2700 to $3000	$450 to $660

E NRICHING YOUR VOCABULARY

Number your paper from 1–25. Beside each number write the word or phrase that matches that definition. Choose your answers from the following list.

automatic teller
  machine (ATM)
bank statement
banks
blank endorsement
canceled checks
certificate of deposit
check
check register

commercial banks
credit unions
deposit
deposit slip
financial services
full endorsement
full-service banks
minimum balance
outstanding checks

passbook accounts
reconcile
restrictive endorsement
savings and loan associations
savings banks
service charge
signature card
withdraw

1. Match balance in check register to bank statement

2. Record of checks and deposits for a checking account

3. Monthly accounting provided by bank of checking account activity and balance

4. Signature on back of check with "pay to order" instructions

5. Fee paid to bank for checking services

6. Signature on back of check with instructions limiting what can be done with the check

7. Remove money from an account

8. Signature on back of check with no instructions

9. Full service bank offering a wide range of financial services

10. Institutions for the safekeeping of money and the transferring of money and credit

11. Functions performed by banks

12. Commercial banks

13. State chartered banks offering fewer financial services than commercial banks

14. Lowest balance in an account during a given accounting period

15. Checks that have been identified as paid

16. Place money into an account

17. Card kept on file at your bank to verify signature

18. Checks that have been written but have not been paid

19. Savings account in which money is deposited for a given period of time

20. Form to accompany deposit so that it is credited to the proper account

21. Savings accounts

22. Document for transferring money

23. Financial institution offering similar services to a bank but operating under different regulations

24. Nonprofit institution offering financial service for members only

25. A computerized machine that allows deposits and withdrawals to be made when the bank is closed or from another city or state

CHAPTER REVIEW
9

R EVIEWING WHAT YOU HAVE LEARNED

1. What is the difference between a blank endorsement and a restrictive endorsement?

2. Why should you cash or deposit a check without delay?

3. The person to whom you are writing a check asks to see two identifications.

A. What identification could you use to show that you are really the person whose name is on the check?

B. Why are people often asked to show identification when they want to write a check?

U SING YOUR CRITICAL THINKING SKILLS

1. How would you decide whether to use your money to open a passbook savings account or to buy a certificate of deposit?

2. Some people do not like to take the time to balance a check register, so they rely on the bank to inform them of their checking account balance. Is this a good way to handle a checking account? Why or why not?

A PPLYING WHAT YOU HAVE LEARNED

1. In five years, you plan to go to medical school; and today, your father gave you $1,000 to invest for medical school. Examine various savings plans available to you, and describe the plan or combination of plans that will give you the most money at the end of those five years. Compare your plan with your classmates' plans.

2. You are ready to open your first checking account. Go to several financial institutions in your area to obtain information about the kinds of checking accounts they offer. Select the account that you think best suits your needs. Explain your selection to your classmates.

UNIT
4

CONSUMER CREDIT

CHAPTERS

10. **Credit Can Help or Hurt**
11. **Types of Credit**
12. **Using Credit**

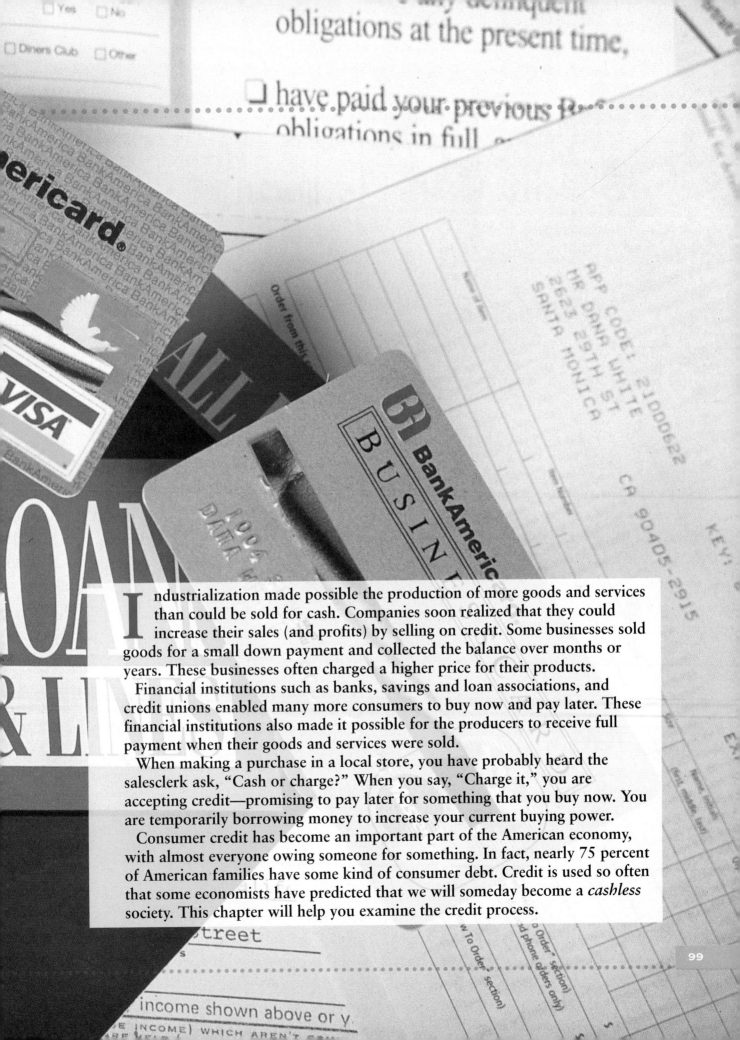

Industrialization made possible the production of more goods and services than could be sold for cash. Companies soon realized that they could increase their sales (and profits) by selling on credit. Some businesses sold goods for a small down payment and collected the balance over months or years. These businesses often charged a higher price for their products.

Financial institutions such as banks, savings and loan associations, and credit unions enabled many more consumers to buy now and pay later. These financial institutions also made it possible for the producers to receive full payment when their goods and services were sold.

When making a purchase in a local store, you have probably heard the salesclerk ask, "Cash or charge?" When you say, "Charge it," you are accepting credit—promising to pay later for something that you buy now. You are temporarily borrowing money to increase your current buying power.

Consumer credit has become an important part of the American economy, with almost everyone owing someone for something. In fact, nearly 75 percent of American families have some kind of consumer debt. Credit is used so often that some economists have predicted that we will someday become a *cashless* society. This chapter will help you examine the credit process.

CHAPTER 10

Credit Can Help or Hurt

OBJECTIVES

After completing this chapter, you will be able to do the following:
1. Explain the use of credit.
2. Describe the advantages and disadvantages of using credit.
3. Explain why consumers pay the bill for bankruptcies.

TERMS

bankrupt
bankruptcy

Bankruptcy Reform Act
    of 1978
credit

creditors
debtors

Credit is tempting to use because it lets you buy things without paying right away. If you use it properly, credit can help you get the things you want; but there are times when using credit can lead to serious problems. At those times, you may get what you want right away—but you may have financial troubles later on. Knowing the advantages and disadvantages of credit will help you decide when to use it and when not to.

ADVANTAGES OF CONSUMER CREDIT

Have you ever borrowed against next week's allowance? Or borrowed lunch money from a friend? Have you purchased anything on credit? Think about a specific purchase that you or someone you know made on credit. Why did you or the person you know use credit? There are many good reasons for buying on credit.

Convenience

Buying on credit is convenient. Sometimes you may be a little short on cash when a special sale comes up—but if you buy on credit, you can still make your purchase at the sale price.

You may charge any number of purchases that you make from a company (or one credit card) and only write one check when the bill arrives. And when a purchase is made with a credit card, you may withhold payment if the product is defective.

Suppose that you plan to purchase a CD player. You've decided that either of two models will satisfy your need, and you've checked prices from every source you know. Then, while buying some notebook paper, you see one of the models on sale for a very low price. Unfortunately, you haven't brought along your checkbook, and you don't have enough cash to pay for the CD

Credit makes it possible to purchase items when they are on sale, even if you don't have the money at the time. Do you know anyone who uses credit cards more often than they use cash? Why do you think they do this?

In his senior year of college, Chad was sent an offer in the mail for an all-purpose credit card. All his friends were getting them too. Evidently, the credit card company thought that young people who were about to graduate from college were good credit risks.

Chad filled out and returned the offer and, after about a month, his new credit card arrived. Chad had never had much experience with finances, so this card was like a new toy. The first purchase he made with the card was a thrill—he felt so adult.

Unfortunately, in Chad's mind, the new credit card had nothing to do with real money. "Charging" felt like getting something for nothing, like getting presents. He had no thought of the consequences that would come later.

By the time his first bill arrived, Chad had charged several hundred dollars' worth of new clothing and gadgets. He paid the minimum amount required on the bill and still felt as if he was getting a good deal. By the time Chad graduated, he had accumulated over $1,000 in charges. As it turned out, it was many months after graduation before Chad was hired in his chosen career. Meanwhile, he had no income and had to ask his parents to help make his credit card payments.

Chad had an "attitude problem" with his credit card. What would have been a healthier attitude toward his new credit card, given his situation? What is the ideal way to manage a credit card?

player. If you charge it, you can buy at the sale price and take your new CD player home that day.

The convenience and safety of credit cards also makes them useful for travel and entertainment expenses. (In fact, the first credit cards were issued for travel and entertainment.) When you plan to use a credit card for these expenses, you don't have to carry large sums of cash. You may even leave your checkbook at home.

Help in Emergencies

Although it is important to save for emergencies, many people don't have enough savings to take care of all unexpected expenses. If you or someone in your family were to become ill or injured, how would you pay the costs of medical care? There are many costs that are not paid by medical insurance. If you could not work for several months, how would you pay for food, housing, and other necessities? Credit can be helpful in managing unexpected expenses.

Forced Savings Program

Some people never seem to be able to save up enough money to pay for expensive items. For them, buying on credit is a forced savings program. If they didn't have to make payments on their major purchases, they might fritter away their money on lots of small, unimportant things. However, credit used in this way is costly to the consumer because of the interest or finance charges that must be paid in addition to the cost of the goods purchased. And the consumer also loses the advantage of interest that would be earned in a true savings program.

The price of a new car makes it difficult for most people to purchase one without using credit. Interest rates on car loans vary greatly at different finance companies. It pays to research a loan to get the best interest rate possible.

Earlier Use of Goods and Services

Months or even years may be required before you save enough money to pay for some of the expensive items you need or want, such as a car or a house. Suppose you have decided to buy a new car. How long would it take to save up, say, twenty thousand dollars? With credit, you can have these things immediately and use them while you are paying for them.

Help in Record Keeping

Companies from whom you make credit purchases will send you monthly bills. Each company will itemize your purchases for the month, and these lists make it fairly easy to keep track of where you spent your money.

CREDIT DISADVANTAGES

Credit can help us get what we want when we want it, sometimes at a special sale price, and it helps us with our record keeping. Because credit is useful, it may seem that we should use credit often, but there are some disadvantages to using credit, too.

Credit Costs Money

Some people take pride in using credit to purchase sale items, but credit usually costs money. The interest charged for the right to make monthly payments is often more than consumers realize. There are other charges for using credit, too. These are discussed in detail in Chapter 12.

People who misuse credit may end up in court because they cannot pay their creditors. Depending on the situation, those who owe may lose all of their assets and have a damaged credit record for many years to come.

Credit Increases Impulse Buying

Sometimes credit purchases are *too* easy. Suppose you see something that you would like to have, but you don't have the cash to pay for it. If you can charge it and pay just a few dollars a month, you may not think about the total cost. You may buy an item that you don't really need and later realize that it was just a passing impulse and regret making the purchase.

Misuse of Credit

A lot of people don't know how to set up a spending plan or aren't willing to follow a plan. When they run out of cash, they start charging everything they buy. In the past, this was not such a big problem. The amount a person could charge was quite limited. During the 1970s, credit became easier to obtain. The amount of consumer credit has risen steadily since then, and many more people are becoming overextended with credit debt.

We are constantly urged to buy now and pay later. Some people get so caught up in credit buying that they feel they have paid for purchases when they sign the charge slip. Many people, particularly younger adults, seem compelled to borrow in order to satisfy their wants. Some spend everything they earn and use all the credit they are allowed. This lack of discipline in the use of credit causes many financial problems, even forcing some people into bankruptcy.

Bankruptcy

When a person's or a family's debts are greater than their ability to repay over a reasonable period of time, they are said to be **bankrupt**. To wipe out debts, **debtors** (people who owe) can file for **bankruptcy**. Under the **Bankruptcy Reform Act of 1978**, individuals may file for one of two kinds of bankruptcy. The Wage Earner Plan allows the debtor to file a court plan to pay debts from future earnings. In severe cases where it is not possible for the debtor to repay the debt, a straight bankruptcy can be filed. With a straight bankruptcy, the debtor's assets are sold and the money is used to repay as much of the debt as possible. The remaining unpaid debts are cancelled.

bankrupt
....
having debts that are greater than the ability to repay over a period of time

debtors
....
people who owe debts

bankruptcy
....
a situation in which a person or company is unable to repay debts

Bankruptcy Reform Act of 1978
....
a law that allows for two types of bankruptcy: one in which the debtor may file a plan to repay debts from future earnings, and another in which the debtor's assets are sold and the money is used to repay as much of the debt as possible

INTERACTING WITH TECHNOLOGY

WHO MADE THAT CALL?

Consumer credit can be a wonderful thing. We can buy things now and pay for them later or, with service credit, we can use things like phone services now and pay for them later. The computer system at the phone company keeps an accurate account of the phone calls we make and charges us accordingly. Is the phone bill we receive really accurate? Most of the time it is. But, at one time or another, you may have heard your parents complain that they've been charged for a phone call they didn't make. How does this happen?

It's possible that someone has made an unauthorized phone call from your home; it could have been a friend, for example. It's also possible that someone has made a call from another phone and had it charged to your account.

One way this can happen is for someone outside of your family to know your calling card number. It is very important not to give this number out to people. It's also necessary to be sure no one is watching while you punch this number into the phone; people can memorize or write down the number and use it later. Another way a call can be charged to your phone is through computer access. Hackers are computer experts who gain illegal access to information in a computer system. They can get into a computer system at the phone company and charge calls to your account. Hackers can also gain direct access to long-distance lines, which enables them to make free phone calls.

Hackers have drawn a lot of attention from law enforcement personnel because their activities are illegal. Some intentionally steal information or charge things to others' accounts. Others have used the Internet network to get into military and other government computer systems. Security officials feel this could threaten the security of our country. Credit histories are also targets of hackers. They can permanently damage a person's credit or make it difficult for them to get credit in the future.

Security experts and phone company investigators have set up electronic stakeouts in an attempt to catch the hackers. The Secret Service and FBI also are investigating computer crime. When caught, hackers can be sent to prison.

What should you do if you get a phone bill with a charge that is not yours? Call the phone company and explain the situation to them. If the charge is for a call to a "900" number, there is probably a different number for you to call, the number of the "900" line carrier, which is listed on your phone bill. If you call this number they will check your account and, if the charge is small enough and you haven't claimed before that you were charged for a call that wasn't yours, they will send you a check for the amount you were charged. The check will be made out to your phone company. You can then send it in with your phone bill. It takes several weeks to get the check so you will need to contact your phone company to tell them why you won't be paying that part of your bill. They are very understanding and helpful when these situations arise. But don't try to take advantage of the phone company, you could lose the privilege of having a phone!

Under both plans, some debts, such as taxes, child support, and fines, cannot be wiped out by bankruptcy. Debtors who pay less than 70 percent of their remaining debts are not allowed to file for bankruptcy again for six years. Bankruptcy records remain in the debtor's credit record with the credit bureau for seven years. This makes it difficult for that person to obtain credit for several years.

Bankruptcy is a drastic move, and it should be used only when there is no other way out of financial ruin. Many debtors have used the 1978 bankruptcy law to wipe out their debts. Then, as soon as they could obtain credit again, they accumulated more large debts. Creditors who lose money through their debtors' bankruptcies pass the cost along to customers, so all of us pay for the cost of bankruptcies. We may pay higher prices for goods and services, or we may receive lower returns on our savings.

creditors
....
the people or companies to whom money is owed

Summary

- Consumer credit has become an important part of the American economy, with almost everyone owing someone something.

- Advantages of using credit include: convenience, help in emergencies, forced savings program, earlier use of goods and services, and help in record keeping.

- Some disadvantages of using credit are that credit costs money, credit increases impulse buying, and that credit can be misused.

CHAPTER REVIEW
10

ENRICHING YOUR VOCABULARY

Number your paper from 1–6. Read each sentence below. If the sentence is true, write "true" next to that number. If the sentence is false, rewrite it to make a true statement.

1. An individual is considered to be *bankrupt* if he or she has no money in the bank.

2. Persons making car payments are classified as *debtors*.

3. *Bankruptcy* must be established through the judgment of the court.

4. *Creditors* borrow money with the intent to repay later.

5. The *Bankruptcy Reform Act of 1978* established two kinds of bankruptcy.

6. *Credit* allows the consumer to purchase goods or services now and pay for them later.

REVIEWING WHAT YOU HAVE LEARNED

1. What is credit?

2. Describe the advantages and disadvantages of using credit.

3. Explain this statement: Consumers pay the bill for bankruptcies.

4. Explain the two types of bankruptcy established under the Bankruptcy Reform Act of 1978.

5. Define "impulse buying" and explain why it can be dangerous.

USING YOUR CRITICAL THINKING SKILLS

1. Should a consumer ever consider filing for bankruptcy? Why or why not?

2. Why do you think the government established the Bankruptcy Reform Act of 1978?

APPLYING WHAT YOU HAVE LEARNED

1. Talk with a number of people who have credit cards. Ask why they use the card(s): convenience, help in emergencies, forced savings program, earlier use of goods and services, help in record keeping, or a combination of several reasons. Also, ask what advice they would give a young person such as yourself, who will be getting his or her first credit card soon.

CHAPTER 11

Types of Credit

OBJECTIVES

After completing this chapter, you will be able to do the following:
1. Name two examples of service credit.
2. Explain the three kinds of short-term consumer credit.
3. Explain how credit cards are used.
4. Explain why department stores often prefer to issue their own credit cards instead of using all-purpose credit cards.
5. Identify the least expensive sources of cash loans.

TERMS

amortization schedule	grace period	revolving account
collateral	installment credit	sales credit
cosigner	line of credit	service credit
credit cards	long-term consumer	short-term consumer
debit cards	credit	credit
defaults	mortgage	signature loans
down payment	pawnshops	
foreclose	repossess	

Nearly everyone who lives in the United States will, at some time in his or her life, make use of consumer credit. Chances are that you will use it for many of your future purchases. When you decide that you can afford the payments and the extra cost of credit, you will have a choice of several types—including service credit, sales credit, and cash loans.

Service Credit

Many people begin using **service credit** without knowing it. The most widely used service credit is for utilities, such as electricity, gas, telephone, cable TV, water, and garbage collection. At the end of each month, the purchaser is mailed a bill.

If you have a telephone, you may call a friend in another state or even another country and talk for hours without paying until the next month. When you visit your dentist or doctor, you may be given credit until the first of the following month. In some areas, plumbers and appliance repairers perform their services and wait until the next month for payment. If bills for service are paid on time, there is usually no extra charge for service credit.

Sales Credit

Buying a product and paying for it later is **sales credit**, and the time allowed to pay for credit varies. If you charge a sweater at a local clothing store, you may be expected to pay the full amount within thirty days—usually without interest. If you obtain a loan to buy a house, you may have as long as thirty or forty years to pay for it—and you may pay more in interest than the original cost of the house.

service credit
. . . .
use of a service with agreement to pay later

sales credit
. . . .
purchase of a product with agreement to pay later

If you have a telephone, you have service credit. Telephone services can be used now, and paid for later. What other types of service credit does your family have?

SHORT-TERM CONSUMER CREDIT

There are several variations of short-term consumer credit. These include revolving accounts, installment credit, and credit card credit.

Revolving Accounts. In a revolving account, charges are allowed up to a specified amount, which is set by the store or company based on the income and credit record of the individual consumer. Part of the total amount owed must be paid each month, and interest is charged. You need not pay the entire amount before charging more.

Consider the following example of a revolving account. Suppose you are approved for a revolving account at a department store which allows you to charge purchases up to $1,000. You need some new clothes, so you decide to charge the $250 total to your new revolving account. Your payment is only $12 per month. Another day you

Installment credit can be used for the purchase of appliances, TVs, stereos, and many other things. Regular monthly payments must be made to repay the loan. Can additional purchases be added to an installment loan?

go out shopping on your lunch hour and make more purchases, bringing the total owed up to $350. Your payment is increased to $18 per month. You could continue charging purchases until you owed the company $1,000, and your monthly payments would go up as the total amount owed increased. However, if the amount owed is reduced, the amount of your payment may or may not be reduced accordingly. Read the credit information supplied by the company or store with which you have the account. Many consumers continue paying on and adding to their revolving accounts month after month, continually paying interest on their purchases. If the balance owed continues to increase, they even pay interest on interest.

Installment Credit. Many companies offer installment credit to customers who buy more expensive things, such as a TV or a car. Door-to-door salespeople may offer installment sales contracts to sell such things as vacuum cleaners, pots and pans, and encyclopedias. Usually a down payment is required, and a finance charge is added to the amount owed. Then the total is divided by the number of weeks or months that payments will be made, and the buyer signs a contract agreeing to make the payments on the due dates. Unlike a revolving account, new purchases may not be added to an installment contract.

An installment sale allows the buyer to use the goods purchased while paying for them, but ownership remains with the seller until the total amount has been paid. If the buyer defaults (doesn't pay in full), the seller may repossess the goods. Even if the goods are repossessed by the seller, the buyer may still be required to make payment. With interest and the added charges for credit checks and other costs, some consumers pay more than double the original price.

How much can you safely buy on installment credit? That, of course, depends on many factors, including your personal values. Many financial advisors recommend that no more than 20 percent of one's take-home pay should go for installment payments other than mortgage payments (home loans). This is a general guide. Some people spend as much as 30 percent, but such a large debt usually requires reductions in other expenses. You are the best judge of your own finances, but do remember that large debts may leave you with no way to meet future needs or emergencies.

Credit Cards

Credit cards are commonly used to buy items on credit. Credit cards are sometimes called "plastic money," and are used to charge such things as gasoline, clothing, food, airline tickets, and hotel lodging. In fact, almost anything can be purchased with credit cards. For the consumer, they are probably the most convenient way to make purchases.

Sellers of goods and services accept credit cards because they know that doing so increases their sales. Consumers with credit cards buy more on impulse than those who pay cash, so hundreds of companies issue credit cards. Before you apply for a credit card, be sure you understand repayment terms. Will you need to pay the entire bill each month—or just part of it? What is the rate of interest? Credit card interest rates vary widely, often ranging from 10 percent to 21 percent annually. Check with each company and store, and be sure that the right to use the card will be worth the cost.

There are basically three types of credit cards. These are single-purpose credit cards, cards for entertainment and travel expenses, and all-purpose (or bank) credit cards.

credit cards
....
cards used to charge purchases to an account

CONSUMER FOCUS

CREDIT DECISIONS

John Sanders graduated from high school two years ago, and he has a job. He shares an apartment with some friends. He has a checking account to pay bills, but he wanted the convenience of an all-purpose credit card.

He went to his bank and filled out an application. Because he'd always paid his bills on time, John thought he'd have no trouble getting the card. In a few weeks, he was surprised to be turned down.

Upset, John went to see a bank officer. "What's wrong?" he asked. She replied that John did not meet some of the bank's requirements. The length of time at his job and the time at his current residence were too short.

"Do you have a policy against young people who aren't married?" he asked. Her answer was no. It is illegal to deny credit to adults on the basis of age or marital status. Credit also can't be denied because of sex, race, color, religion, or nationality.

John was still unhappy about being denied credit, but he expected to have a better chance after some time has passed.

If you are denied credit, you can ask for the reason. If there are errors in your credit record, you can correct them. Sometimes the problem is just a clerical error.

There is no guarantee that you will be granted credit when you apply for it, but you can make sure that you have complete information and that your credit record is accurate.

Many airlines offer their own credit cards. Why do companies prefer customers to use company credit cards rather than all-purpose cards?

Single-Purpose Credit Cards. Single-purpose credit cards have been used for many years by customers of large department stores and major oil companies. These cards can be used to buy products only from the store or company that issues them. Department stores like to issue their own credit cards because this encourages customers to make more purchases at their stores. Oil companies, too, feel that credit cards increase their sales.

In recent years, oil companies have expanded direct mail offerings to their credit card holders to include such items as cameras, radios, and typewriters.

Both department stores and oil companies issue free cards. Most department store cards are issued for revolving accounts. If you always pay your bill on time, you will not be charged any more than if you had paid cash. (You may choose to pay only part of the total charges each month, but there is an interest charge on the unpaid balance.) Oil company credit card customers are usually expected to pay the total amount owed when they are sent the bill.

Airlines, hotels, and restaurants also issue their own credit cards, and some of these companies provide revolving credit. If you have one of their cards, you may choose to pay only part of the total charges each month. There is an interest charge on the unpaid balance.

Travel and Entertainment Cards. Entertainment and travel cards, such as Diner's Club and American Express, provide a convenient way to pay restaurant and hotel bills. Most airlines will also accept one or more of these cards, and many retail stores will now accept them as well. There is usually a fee for this type of card—thirty-five to fifty dollars a year. If you want an extra card for another family member, there is an additional fee. A good credit rating and higher than average income are required to obtain entertainment and travel cards.

All-Purpose Credit Cards. In the 1970s, all-purpose credit cards, usually issued by banks, became popular. More recently, these cards have been issued by a variety of financial institutions. Two widely accepted cards are Visa and MasterCard. As the names imply, you may charge almost any kind of purchase on these cards. When these cards are issued, you will be given a maximum amount that you may charge—depending on your credit rating and income. The credit available may range from one hundred to several thousand dollars. You may make your purchases from dozens of different stores, but you will receive only one bill per card. You will pay the institution that issued the credit card. If you pay the total amount due each month, you will not be charged interest if the card allows a **grace period** (a period of about 25 days following a purchase). However, you may choose to make only a partial payment, in which case you will be charged interest. The amount of interest charged varies from

grace period

time during which interest is not charged

state to state. In 1994, the interest rate on most all-purpose credit cards ranged between 10 percent and 18 percent annually.

In previous years, banks promoted the use of all-purpose credit cards by mailing cards to people with good credit records, even though the people had not applied for cards. This is no longer legal. In the 1980s, some banks began to charge a yearly fee for these cards, which usually varied from fifteen to fifty dollars. Presently, some institutions offer cards with no annual fees. If you are interested in obtaining an all-purpose credit card, shop around at various financial institutions to find one with terms that best suit your needs.

If Your Credit Card Is Lost or Stolen

Keep a list of the numbers on your credit cards in a safe, easy-to-find place. If a credit card is lost or stolen, immediately call the bank or company that issued it. Give the number of the card and when it was lost, then write a letter indicating the card number and the date on which it was lost. Make and keep a copy of the letter, send it by certified mail, and keep the receipt. If you do this immediately, you will not be charged more than fifty dollars for goods charged to your card by someone else. The bank or company that issued your card will then notify stores not to accept that card and will send you a new one.

Debit Cards

Debit cards are not the same as credit cards but are discussed here because of their appearance. They *look* like credit cards. (See Figure 11.1.) The only difference in the way they look

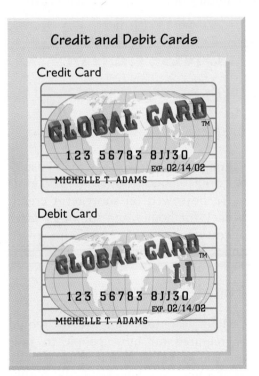

Credit and Debit Cards

Credit Card

GLOBAL CARD™
123 56783 8JJ30
EXP. 02/14/02
MICHELLE T. ADAMS

Debit Card

GLOBAL CARD II™
123 56783 8JJ30
EXP. 02/14/02
MICHELLE T. ADAMS

debit cards
....
cards used to deduct payment from checking accounts

Figure 11.1
....

Credit cards and debit cards may look very similar, but their uses are very different. Use of a credit card is borrowing money, use of a debit card is spending your own money. What advantages can you see for using a debit card? A credit card?

may be the number on the card, but debit cards offer no credit. They are, instead, a substitute for writing checks. When you use a debit card, the amount of the purchase is immediately deducted from your checking account.

Visa and MasterCard have established national debit-card networks called Interlink and Maestro, respectively. Many banks have added the Interlink or Maestro logo on the back of customers' ATM (automated teller machine) cards, allowing the ATM to be used as a debit card with merchants that display the logo.

Merchants like debit cards because they do not have the risk of a possible bad check, and customers typically buy more than when paying with cash. A 1993 survey by Wells Fargo Bank indicated that customers spend about 50 percent more when using a debit card than they do when paying with cash.

LONG-TERM CONSUMER CREDIT

Long-term consumer credit usually involves amounts of money too large to be borrowed on short-term credit. Money for homes and for other large or costly purchases is usually borrowed on long-term credit.

Home Loans

Many years or even a lifetime would be required for most people to save enough to buy a home. This is why people who buy homes usually obtain a **mortgage** (a loan secured by the home). They make a **down payment** of 10 percent to 25 percent of the selling price and arrange for a long-term loan to cover the balance.

Home loans are available from savings and loan associations, commercial banks, savings banks, mortgage bankers, credit unions, private lenders, and some insurance companies. These loans are usually paid off on an **amortization schedule** by which equal monthly payments, including principal (amount owed on a loan) and interest, are made for a specified number of years. The amount of the monthly payment depends on the amount borrowed, the interest rate, and the length of the loan. The time allowed to pay off home loans varies greatly, but it often ranges between twenty and forty years. If the borrower fails to make payments, the lender has the right to **foreclose** the mortgage, meaning that the lender starts legal action that may lead to the borrower's losing the home.

Buying a home may be the most expensive purchase in your life, so it should be done only after careful study of your long-term goals and your ability to pay. Generally, you are well advised to borrow no more than two to three times your total yearly income for the purchase of a home. In recent years, many have borrowed up to five times their yearly income, but then they have had to cut back on other costs of living. Another rule of thumb for purchasing a home is that the monthly mortgage payment should not exceed more than 25 percent of your monthly income. Details of obtaining a home loan are covered in Chapter 27.

CASH LOANS

Cash loans may be either short-term or long-term. Sometimes you may need cash to pay off a debt, or you may get a slight discount when you purchase an item for cash. It may be cheaper for you to borrow cash for a TV or a car instead of making installment pay-

---

amortization schedule
....
payment plan for repayment of principal and interest

foreclose
....
to take legal action to take possession of a home for failure to meet mortgage payments

long-term consumer credit
....
loans for large or costly purchases

mortgage
....
a loan secured by a home

down payment
....
initial payment on a credit purchase

ELECTRONIC FUND TRANSFERS

While taking a walk, you notice a sale at a sporting goods shop. Just what you have been waiting for! You've been planning to replace your old tennis racket. Today, though, you don't have enough cash with you—and you don't have a credit card or your checkbook, either. However, you do have a debit card.

You pick out a racket and present the debit card to pay for it. The clerk at the store puts your card into a machine—and, at that instant, money from your bank account is transferred to the store's account. There is no paperwork; the transfer is done electronically. This convenient type of transaction is an electronic fund transfer (EFT).

There are several other types of EFTs, too. People can do their banking at automated teller machines, making deposits or picking up cash for dinner and a movie. EFTs may be used for direct deposits of paychecks or for automatic payment of bills.

Federal regulations control EFTs, and they require printed records of these transactions. If you think an error was made in an EFT, your bank (or other financial institution) must investigate. Suppose you lose your EFT card. Can other people use it? Not unless they know your personal identification number (PIN), which you should *never tell anyone*. If someone steals your card and knows your PIN, the amount they can take from your account is limited if you report the loss of your card quickly.

With EFTs, you need to be extra careful about how much you spend, to avoid overdrawing your bank account—but they do make transferring money quick and easy.

---

ments to the seller. A cash loan can often be obtained at a lower interest rate than an installment credit.

When you pay with cash, you obtain ownership of your purchase immediately, but you may have to use your purchase as collateral (security) for a cash loan. This depends on the lender. Goods pledged as collateral become the property of the lender if the debt is not repaid. The best sources of cash loans include bank cards (credit cards), banks, credit unions, savings and loan associations, and consumer finance companies. Pawnshops are a source of small amounts of cash. Never borrow from loan sharks.

Bank Cards. Credit cards issued by banks probably provide the most convenient way of obtaining a cash loan. These cards allow you to receive a cash advance by "charging" it. There is a limit to the amount of cash you may obtain, based on your credit rating and income.

Procedures may vary from bank to bank, but usually you do not have to fill out an application form to get a bank credit card loan. You obtain it from the bank that issued your card. Give your card to a teller or use your ATM card. Indicate how much cash you need and it will be charged to your account.

You may pay back the entire loan the following month and pay only a small "handling charge," or you may pay interest from the day the loan is received. For example, you may have to pay an amount equal to 2 percent of the loan, or you may make monthly payments, just as if you had charged merchandise. If you repay the loan in monthly payments, you will be charged interest on the unpaid balance. Interest rates may

collateral
....
security for a loan

vary (and are often higher than for other loans), so be sure you know the costs before agreeing to the loan.

Banks. Obtaining a bank loan is not as simple as just asking for the money. Banks usually require completion of an application form, and they check credit history carefully. If you can qualify, a bank is a good source for a loan. Because they loan only to applicants with good credit records, banks often charge a lower rate of interest than many other sources.

Most bank loans require collateral, but not always. If you obtain a loan to buy a car, you will almost surely have to pledge the car as collateral.

If you have an excellent credit record, a fairly high income, and are financially sound, you may qualify for a **line of credit**. The bank will agree to loan you whatever money you need, whenever you need it—up to a set amount. If you are approved for a line of credit of $5,000, you could then call the bank when you need to borrow money. They would place it into your account, as long as the total borrowed did not exceed $5,000.

If you anticipate a need for a bank loan, open a savings or checking account where you plan to apply. Banks usually give preference to their own customers. If this isn't possible, your best chance for a bank loan is where your family has an account.

Some people have not established credit records. You may be new in an area or may have never borrowed before. You may be able to get a loan from a bank, anyway—but you will probably need a **cosigner** who does have a good credit record. A cosigner guarantees payment. This person might be a family member or an adult friend who will sign the loan contract with you. Then, if you don't repay the loan, the bank can collect from your cosigner.

Credit Unions. If you belong to a credit union, that is probably the best source of a cash loan. A credit union is a nonprofit organization set up by a group of people with some common bond. It works for their benefit. The group may be employees of one company or members of the same organization. Because the members are associated with one another, less money may be spent checking credit records of loan applicants. Other costs are often lower, too, because officers and committee members often serve without pay. Employers sometimes provide free office space. For these reasons, it is often easy to get a loan at a credit union—and the interest rate is usually lower than you would have to pay elsewhere.

Credit unions usually require collateral for larger loans, but **signature loans** are often available for amounts under $3,000. For a signature loan, no collateral is required. By signing your name, you are promising to pay back the loan on time. To borrow from a credit union, you must be a member.

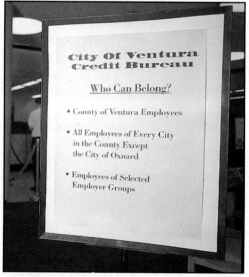

Credit unions usually offer lower interest rates than banks. Why are they able to do this? Do you know anyone who is a member of a credit union?

line of credit

agreement to loan a specified amount of money on demand

signature loans

loans given with no collateral required

cosigner

person guaranteeing payment of a loan

Savings and Loan Associations.
The original purpose of savings and loan associations was to provide money for home loans, but they now make loans for other purposes as well. Regulations vary from state to state, but many of these institutions will provide loans for education and for other personal reasons if your credit is good. If you have a passbook savings account with a savings and loan association, you can probably borrow an amount equal to your deposits. When you need cash for only a few weeks or months, this is sometimes less expensive than withdrawing the money from your passbook account.

Consumer Finance Companies.
Consumer finance companies were formerly called "small loan companies," because their loans were limited to $300, but consumer finance companies can now loan much larger amounts. These companies operate under state law, and the maximum amount they may loan varies from state to state. In California, for example, the amount is unlimited.

Consumer finance companies often make loans to those who can't get a bank loan, and they occasionally make loans that are not repaid. Because of this, they must charge a higher rate of interest than other lending agencies. The average rate often ranges from 18 percent to more than 40 percent on amounts up to $5,000.

Pawnshops. **Pawnshops** are not a major source of loans, but some people borrow small amounts of money from these shops. To do this, a person must leave something of value, such as jewelry or a camera, as collateral. There is no application form to fill out, few questions are asked, and the person gets the money immediately. If the loan is repaid on time, the item left as collateral will be returned. If not, the item is sold, and the pawnbroker will keep the money. The cost of borrowing money from a pawnshop is greater than almost any other source of loans.

Loan Sharks. Sometimes people who feel desperate borrow money from loan sharks. This is a very dangerous thing to do. Loan sharks are people who loan money illegally. A state or federal license is required to operate any type of loan business legally. Some states limit the amount of interest that can be charged, but loan sharks do not have licenses. They want to set their own interest rates. The rates they set are very high, so paying back such a loan is difficult, but loan sharks usually stop at nothing to collect. They may threaten or actually use violence, so never borrow money from a loan shark! There is always a better alternative.

pawnshops
. . . .
businesses that provide loans in exchange for collateral

CONSUMER PROFILE

Ramona just graduated from high school. She has been working at her new job for three months. When she applied at her bank for a car loan, she was denied. She felt discouraged and, assuming she wouldn't qualify, didn't even apply at other places or try other ways of getting the money.

Then a letter came in the mail offering a $2,500 loan through a private loan company. The offer said the loan was pre-approved! When she called to get more information, she discovered that she could get the loan, but that it was at an interest rate of 22 percent!

When she discussed this with her uncle, he advised her not to go near a loan with such a high interest rate. Later, he went with Ramona to a used car dealership. They gave Ramona a loan on the car she wanted and her uncle cosigned for the loan at 10.75 percent interest. It certainly pays to shop around for loans.

Pawnshops require that something of value be left as collateral. The item is returned if the loan is repaid, but the interest on the loan can be high. Do you think borrowing money from a pawnshop is a good idea? Why or why not?

Summary

- There are several types of credit, including service credit, sales credit, and cash loans.

- Short-term credit can be in the form of revolving accounts, installment credit, or credit cards.

- There are basically three types of credit cards—single-purpose, cards for entertainment and travel, and all-purpose.

- Debit cards look like credit cards but, unlike credit cards, automatically deduct the amount of purchase from your checking account.

- Long-term credit usually involves credit on large amounts of money, such as a loan to buy a home.

- A credit union, if you are a member, is probably the best source for a cash loan.

CHAPTER REVIEW
11

E NRICHING YOUR VOCABULARY

Number your paper from 1–20. Beside each number, write the word or phrase that matches that definition. Choose your answer from the following list.

amortization schedule
collateral
cosigner
credit cards
debit cards
defaults
down payment

foreclose
grace period
installment credit
line of credit
long-term consumer credit
mortgage
pawnshops

repossess
revolving account
sales credit
service credit
short-term consumer credit
signature loans

1. Use of service with agreement to pay later
2. Fails to pay in full
3. Period during which interest is not charged
4. Payment plan for repayment of principal and interest
5. Agreement to loan a specified amount of money on demand
6. Businesses that provide loans in exchange for collateral
7. Charge account that allows you to make partial payments and add to balance due up to a specified amount
8. Take the goods back
9. Loan secured by a home
10. Security for a loan

11. Purchase of product with agreement to pay later
12. Contract to purchase a product by paying in equal periodic payments
13. Cards used to charge purchases to an account
14. Cards used to deduct payment from checking account
15. Installment credit, credit card credit, revolving account
16. Loans for large or costly purchases
17. Loan given with no collateral required
18. Person guaranteeing payment of a loan
19. Initial payment on a credit purchase
20. Take legal action to take possession of a home for failure to meet mortgage payments

R EVIEWING WHAT YOU HAVE LEARNED

1. Give two examples of service credit.
2. Explain the three kinds of short-term consumer credit.
3. Explain how credit cards are used.

4. Why do department stores often prefer to issue their own credit cards instead of using all-purpose credit cards?
5. What are the least expensive sources of cash loans?

CHAPTER REVIEW
11

U SING YOUR CRITICAL THINKING SKILLS

1. Craig and Judy Cameron have been married for one year. Recently, they moved from their hometown, Rushville, to the city of Newton. They need a new car, but they do not have enough cash to pay for it. Both Craig and Judy have jobs. There is a credit union where Judy works, but she has not yet joined. They have not established a credit rating and have not opened a bank account in Newton. They have $1,400 in an account in Rushville. There are a bank, a savings and loan, and a finance company in Newton. What should Craig and Judy do to get a loan to buy their car?

A PPLYING WHAT YOU HAVE LEARNED

1. Learn about sources of cash loans in your community, and prepare a chart showing banks, savings and loan associations, a credit union (if you or someone in your family is a member), and other sources. Include the name, address, and telephone number of each source. Then, find out as much as you can about the loan policies of each institution, and show them on your chart, along with the current interest rates for loans.

You will be able to gather much of this information by talking with members of your family and friends who have taken out loans. You will probably have to talk with some bank or savings and loan employees to complete your chart. When this activity is completed, keep the chart for reference. It can save you time and money when you are ready to apply for a cash loan.

CHAPTER 12

Using Credit

OBJECTIVES

After completing this chapter, you will be able to do the following:
1. List the advantages and disadvantages of repaying a loan over a long period of time.
2. List the steps followed to compute the cost of credit.
3. Explain the "Three Cs of Credit."
4. Explain why it is important to pay bills on time.
5. Explain how the Truth in Lending Act is helpful to consumers.
6. List your rights under the Fair Credit Reporting Act.

TERMS

annual percentage rate (APR)	Fair Credit Reporting Act	origination fee
	finance charges	Truth-in-Lending Act
assets	liabilities	
credit contract	net worth	

Almost all types of credit cost something. Costs vary, depending on the source of the loan, how much you borrow, how long you take to repay, and the state of the economy. The economy affects the money supply, which in turn affects prevailing interest rates. When there is a lot of money in savings accounts, interest rates are lower. Some people try to wait until interest rates are low before making major purchases, especially homes.

FIGURING CREDIT COSTS

When figuring the cost of credit, several factors must be considered in addition to the amount borrowed. These are the time allowed for repayment, the interest rate, and the various fees and finance charges.

Time

When obtaining a loan, it's often tempting to spread the payments over as long a period as possible. By doing so, payments are lower, but the total cost is higher—usually much higher than you would guess without computing it. Suppose that you get a loan of $500 at a monthly interest rate of 1½ percent. By making payments of $87.76 (including interest), you can pay it all off in six months. Your total cost for interest will be $26.56. If you want low payments, you can pay $24.96 (including interest) for 24 months, but then you will end up paying $99.04 in interest!

Sometimes, having low monthly payments is worth paying extra interest because high monthly payments cannot be met. In order to make a decision, you will need to know what the extra time for repayment will cost you. When borrowing larger amounts of money, such as for a car, extra time for repayment is more expensive. Figure 12.1

Figure 12.1

....

Notice the difference in "Total Payback in 30 Years" for a loan with 12% interest and a loan with 13% interest. The difference is $15,642! Obviously, it pays to shop around for the best interest rate possible.

Effect of Interest Rate on Cost of $100,000 Loan Repaid in Thirty years

Interest Rate	Monthly Payment	First Year's Interest	Total Payback in 30 Years
12%	$567.02	$6,726.92	$207,367.20
13%	619.47	7,284.92	223,009.20
14%	663.53	7,843.40	238,870.80

Effect of Repayment Period on Cost of $100,000 Loan at Thirteen Percent

Repayment Period	Monthly Payment	First Year's Interest	Total Payback
15 years	$656.08	$7,298.99	$157,459.20
20 years	631.59	7,289.58	189,477.00
30 years	619.47	7,284.92	223,009.20

shows the difference in monthly payments and total payback when making equal monthly payments over 15, 20, and 30 years.

If you repay the $100,000 of the loan over 15 years, you will pay $57,459.20 in interest! You have, in effect, borrowed $157,459.20, but you only get to use $100,000 of it. If you borrow $100,000 at 13 percent APR (annual percentage rate and repay it over 30 years, your total interest will be $123,009.20. You will save $65,550 by paying off the loan in 15 years instead of 30 years. As you can see, you can save a great deal of money by taking as short term a loan as possible.

Interest Rates

During the ten-year period ending in 1994, interest rates charged by banks for car loans declined from a high of about 17 percent to less than 10 percent. This was due to changes in the economy and in the policy of the Federal Reserve Board. On a $7,000 loan of five years, a change in the interest rate from 15 percent to 10 percent decreases the total cost by $1,068. Economic conditions may cause interest rates to increase again before the end of the century.

On larger loans to be repaid over a longer time, small changes in the interest rate make a big difference. For example, on a thirty-year home loan of $100,000, a change in the interest rate from 10 percent to 12 percent increases the total cost by $54,374. If the rate on the same loan were increased to 15 percent, the total cost would go up an additional $84,899.

Fees and Finance Charges

Many lenders charge fees and finance charges in addition to interest

to cover the cost of such things as credit reports, appraisals, and even an origination fee (a fee for starting the paperwork for a loan). These fees are legal and often are a percent of the loan value, but they vary a great deal—so know what you will be charged besides interest for a loan before you sign any papers. Shop around for a loan to make sure you get the best terms available.

Computing the Cost of Credit

Some people spend a great deal of time shopping for the best product at the lowest price, but when they purchase it on credit they don't know how much they are paying for the credit. Their only concern is that they will be able to afford the monthly payments. Certainly, that's important. However, the total cost is even more important. Saving $200 on the price of a car and then paying $400 more than you would have to pay elsewhere for credit doesn't make sense. To compute the cost of credit:

1. Multiply the amount of your monthly payment times the number of months.

2. Add the down payment.

3. Subtract the price of the product if you had paid all cash. If you are obtaining a cash loan, subtract the amount of cash you receive. The difference is the cost of using credit.

ESTABLISHING AND USING CREDIT

If you have never used credit, don't worry—there is nothing mysterious or

origination fee
. . . .
a fee charged for starting the paperwork on a loan

annual percentage rate (APR)
. . . .
the amount credit costs expressed as a yearly percentage

finance charges
. . . .
the amount that credit costs, which must be paid back over the length of a loan

difficult about applying for credit. In most cases, you will have to fill out an application form so that lenders can see how much of a risk they will be taking if they grant credit to you. They estimate this risk by analyzing three factors: character, capacity, and capital—often called the "Three Cs of Credit."

- **Character** is your willingness to pay your bills on time.
- **Capacity** is your ability to pay your bills.
- **Capital** is represented by things of value that you own, such as your car.

You may be asked to pledge some of your capital as collateral. For larger loans, it is usually necessary to provide a statement of your **net worth**. You will need a listing of your **assets**—all the things of value that you own. You must also list your **liabilities**—amounts you owe. The value of your assets minus the total amount owed is your net worth.

Credit Bureau Information

Those to whom you apply for credit may get some information on your character, capacity, and capital from your application form, but they obtain most of their information from a credit bureau, an agency that keeps records of the credit activity of individuals. There are three major credit bureaus in the United States, and most businesses that extend credit belong to a credit bureau. (You will want to be very careful about paying your bills on time. How well you do this will determine whether you will be able to obtain credit in the future.)

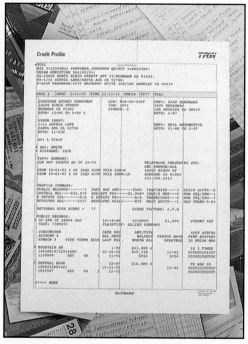

The credit records prepared by credit bureaus often contain errors. If you are denied credit because of something in your credit report, obtain a copy of your credit report. If there is an error on the report, contact the credit bureau issuing the report and have them correct the error.

Government Supervision of Credit

There are several laws that protect the consumer in credit transactions. These laws assure the consumer of a clear understanding of his or her financial obligations and assure a fair reporting of how the obligations are discharged.

For example, The Equal Credit Opportunity Credit Act (1974) prohibits discrimination against a person applying for credit because of age, sex, marital status, religion, race, color, national origin, or the receipt of public assistance. If you are denied credit, you must be notified in writing. Then you have the right to a written explanation of the reason you were denied.

The **Truth-in-Lending Act (1968)** requires lenders to state the interest rate and dollar costs of loans. This requirement applies to banks, savings and loan associations, all credit card issuers, credit unions, consumer finance companies, and many other lenders. Thus, it is easy to know the cost of credit if you read carefully before you sign a contract. You can also compare the credit plans of different lenders.

The **Fair Credit Reporting Act (1970)** gives you the right to see your credit record and to correct errors. If you are denied credit because of a bad credit report, you must be told the name and address of the credit bureau that gave the report. If you request a copy of the report, it will be given to you without charge. (If you haven't been denied credit, you may request a copy of your credit record for a small fee.)

If you find untrue statements in your credit record, give a corrected statement (in writing) to the credit bureau and ask them to check it out. If their reinvestigation shows that you are correct, the credit bureau must correct its records. If you are not satisfied, you may write a statement of 100 words or less correcting their records. Your statement will be attached to the credit

Fair Credit Reporting Act
. . . .
a law passed in 1970 that gives people the right to see their credit record and to correct any errors that may be on it

FEDERAL STUDENT AID

Education after high school can be very costly. The federal government offers several types of financial aid, including grants and loans. Grants are not paid back, but loans must be repaid.

Federal aid can be used for many types of education after high school, including vocational, professional, and technical schools as well as college. Not all schools take part in the federal student aid programs, but more than 6,500 do.

The five main federal programs are:
1. Pell Grants. These grants are awarded to undergraduates. To qualify, students must go to school at least half-time.
2. Supplemental Educational Opportunity Grants. These are also grants to undergraduates. At least half-time enrollment is usually required, but not always.
3. College Work-Study. Jobs may be awarded to both undergraduate and graduate students.
4. National Direct Student Loans. Both undergraduate and graduate students may qualify, and the

loans are made through the schools at low interest. At least half-time enrollment is required to qualify for these loans.
5. Guaranteed Student Loans. These low-interest loans are offered through banks, credit unions, and the like. At least half-time enrollment is required to qualify. Students may be undergraduates or graduates.

To qualify for these federal aid programs, you must be making satisfactory academic progress—and you must show that you have financial need. You do this by reporting financial information about you and your parents, usually based on federal income tax returns.

You can get further information about these federal programs from school counselors and financial aid officers who also may be able to tell you about state and private aid.

bureau's file on you, and it will be included in future reports about your credit record.

If you do not pay some bills on time, and this is reported to the credit bureau, it can remain on file for as long as seven years. If you claim bankruptcy, that information can be listed for ten years.

Qualifying for a Loan

You may not be interested in obtaining a loan now, but the chances are good that you will consider borrowing money within the next few years. To help them make decisions, some lenders give "points" for things they believe indicate character, capacity, and capital. They use this type of scoring in addition to a loan application form and a credit report, and your "score" helps the lender decide whether to grant you credit.

Young people without a work history or credit record sometimes have diffi-

culty establishing credit. You may have already been turned down for credit—or you may be afraid that you will be turned down if you apply. If so, you need to lay some groundwork. A good first step is to establish a checking or savings account (or both) and use it responsibly.

Getting approval for credit is easier after you have been granted credit by another firm, so apply for credit from a store that is looking for young customers. You may be offered an account with limited credit. This means that you may charge only up to a specified amount, perhaps two or three hundred dollars. Charge small amounts for things you would buy even if you did not have the account, and always pay promptly. In a few months, your charge account will show up on your credit record. Then, you can obtain credit more easily when you need it.

Some young people take out small loans and put the money in a savings account. When the payments on the loan are due, they take the money out

Institutions that make loans are able to ask a person applying for a loan for information that is directly related to that person's ability to repay the loan. They may not legally ask questions about such things as family relationships, religious or ethnic background, or whether the person has ever been fired from a job.

of savings to pay the lender. (Usually, additional money must be added for interest.) By showing that they are responsible for paying off small loans, it is easier for young people to get larger loans when needed.

Credit Contracts

If you use credit, you will have to sign a **credit contract**. These are legally binding agreements and usually include the following:

- the total amount charged or loaned
- any down payment or trade-in allowance
- the interest rate you will pay
- any special charges that you must pay
- the total amount you will pay
- the amount and due date of each payment
- the name and address of the creditor

When you sign a credit contract, you are agreeing to everything it says—whether or not you read it—so always read any contract very carefully before you sign it. If there is anything that is not clear to you, ask for an explanation before you sign. Finally, always get a copy of any contract that you sign.

CREDIT DECISIONS

You will be faced with many opportunities to say "Charge it." There are times when credit should be used, but be careful. It's very easy to get into the habit of spending next month's—or next year's–income today.

You must decide for yourself, based on your own spending plan, when to use credit. Before making a credit pur-

chase, always ask yourself this question: "What else can I spend this money on if I don't spend it on this credit purchase?" Your answer may change your decision.

CHECKLIST FOR USING CREDIT

When you do decide to use credit, the following checklist may be helpful:
___ Know the cost of credit before accepting it.
___ Borrow the smallest amount that will enable you to make the purchase you want.
___ Borrow only from a reputable (respected) source.
___ Shop for a low interest rate.
___ Borrow for the shortest period of time possible, as long as you can afford the payments.
___ Pay off what you owe as early as possible if it will save you on interest costs.
___ Read all contracts carefully before signing.

credit contract
....
a legally binding agreement that includes all information pertaining to a loan

Summary

- Credit has a cost. The factors which determine that cost include time for repayment, the interest rate, and any fees and finance charges.
- It is most economical to take as short term a loan as possible.
- A lender examines three factors when evaluating the risk involved in loaning you money: your character or willingness to pay your bills, your capacity or ability to pay your bills, and your capital or actual assets.
- Several laws protect the consumer regarding credit: the Equal Opportunity Credit Act, the Truth-in-Lending Act, and the Fair Credit Reporting Act.
- Reading a credit contract before signing it is essential to protect your consumer rights.

E NRICHING YOUR VOCABULARY

Read the following pairs of sentences. Write the sentence that correctly uses the underlined word or phrase.

1A. The Truth-in-Lending Act prohibits discrimination.

1B. The Truth-in-Lending Act requires lenders to state the interest rate and dollar cost of loans.

2A. The annual percentage rate states the rate of interest.

2B. The annual percentage rate states the length of a loan.

3A. Liabilities are debts.

3B. Liabilities increase net worth.

4A. The Fair Credit Reporting Act requires clear statement of loan costs.

4B. The Fair Credit Reporting Act gives you the right to see and correct your credit record.

5A. Finance charges cover the cost of lending money.

5B. It is not legal for lenders to collect finance charges.

6A. Assets are part of liabilities.

6B. Assets are things of value that you own.

7A. An origination fee is included in interest costs.

7B. An origination fee covers the cost of paperwork.

8A. A credit contract is not legally binding.

8B. A credit contract states the amount of each payment.

9A. Net worth is the difference between assets and liabilities.

9B. Net worth is represented by what you own.

R EVIEWING WHAT YOU HAVE LEARNED

1. What are the advantages and disadvantages of repaying a loan over a long period of time?

2. Explain the "Three Cs of Credit."

3. Why is it important to pay your bills on time?

4. What are your rights under the Fair Credit Reporting Act?

5. What steps are followed to compute the cost of credit?

6. Explain how the Truth-in-Lending Act is helpful to consumers.

USING YOUR CRITICAL THINKING SKILLS

1. Think of your lifestyle in five years. What major purchases are you likely to make? Which ones will you buy on credit? Which will you buy only when you have the cash? Be prepared to give reasons for your decisions.

2. At least one of the "Three Cs of Credit"—character, capacity, and capital—are demonstrated in each of the following situations. Identify the C that is demonstrated in each situation. Be ready to explain your decision.

   a. Maria has saved over $2,000 over the last two years by depositing a percentage of her paycheck each week. She has never received a late notice for any of her bills.

   b. Jerome owns a fast-food restaurant that he inherited from his grandfather.

   c. Ron's take-home pay is $1,500, every two weeks. His current bills for each month total about $1,000.

APPLYING WHAT YOU HAVE LEARNED

1. Review various publications—newspapers, magazines, catalogs, and so on—and cut out advertisements that encourage people to open charge accounts. Share these with the rest of your class, and review what they find. Why do creditors encourage consumers to buy on credit?

2. Identify a purchase someone you know has made by getting a loan from a bank. (This could be a home loan, car loan, etc.) Ask the person about the process he or she went through to get the loan. Share the information you learn with your class.

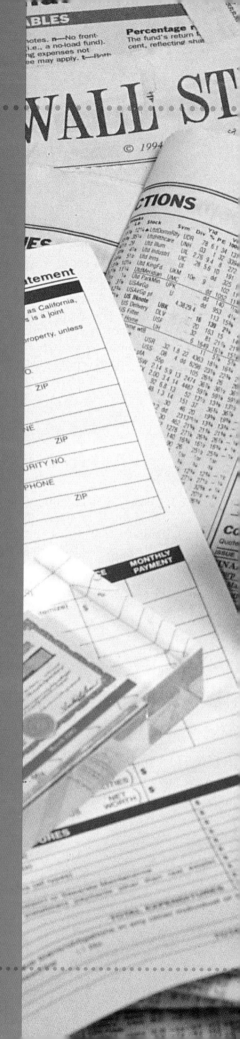

Chapters

According to financial expert Sylvia Porter, *financial security* means different things to different people. But there is a basic blueprint for financial security, which can be applied to any situation.

We can illustrate the process of building financial security as a pyramid. (See Figure 13.1 on page 133.) The foundation of the financial security pyramid is a budget that enables you to meet your basic needs in a timely way.

The next step in the building process is to establish a fund equal to three to six months' income. This protects your budget when unexpected expenses arise.

Then you will need to protect your assets and earning potential. You can do this by purchasing insurance to cover loss of income or assets such as household possessions and an automobile, as well as to cover health care expenses.

After building a financial base with these components, you will be in a position to consider investing some of your earnings. Investments are useful for achieving mid-range and long-range financial goals such as home ownership and retirement.

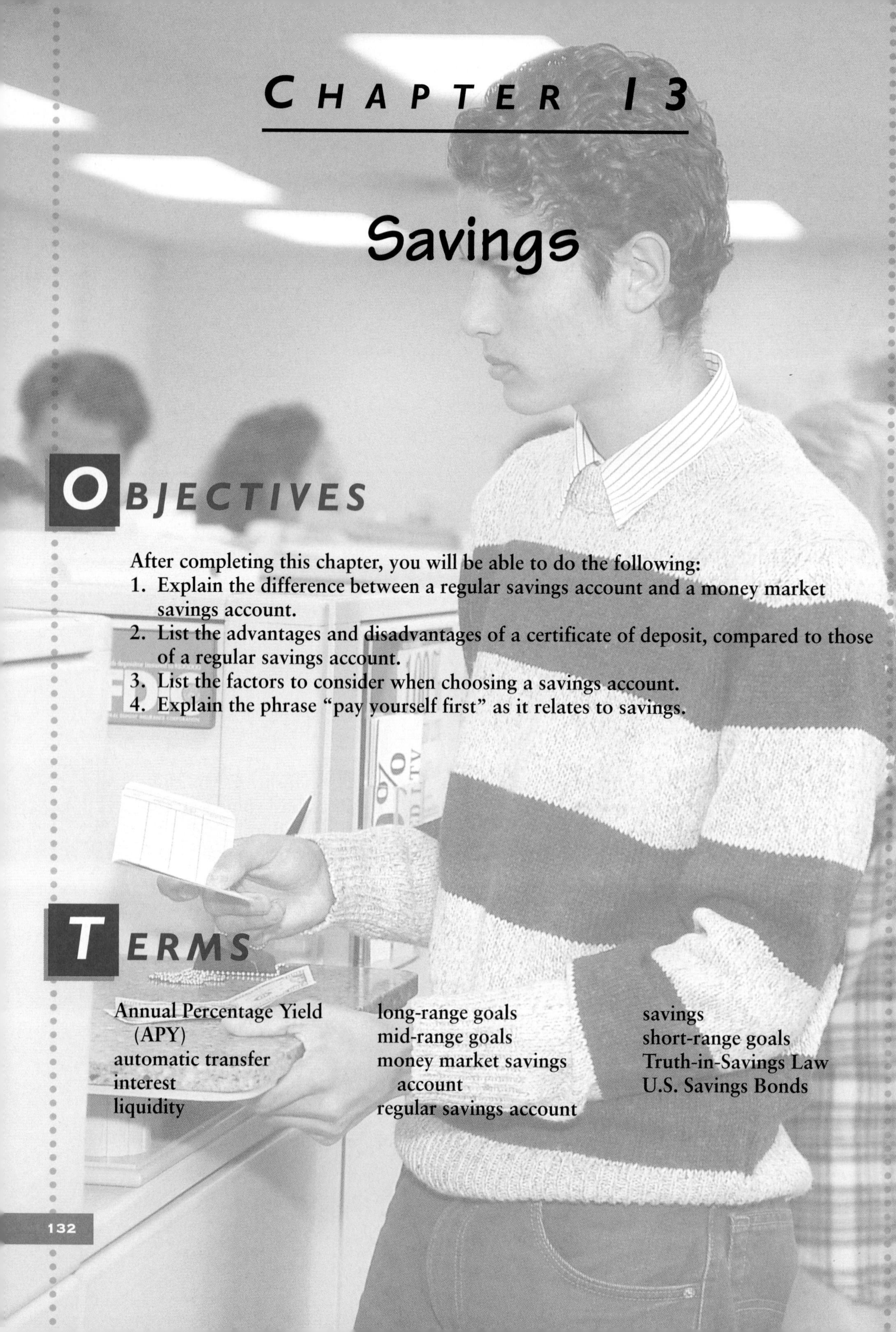

CHAPTER 13

Savings

OBJECTIVES

After completing this chapter, you will be able to do the following:
1. Explain the difference between a regular savings account and a money market savings account.
2. List the advantages and disadvantages of a certificate of deposit, compared to those of a regular savings account.
3. List the factors to consider when choosing a savings account.
4. Explain the phrase "pay yourself first" as it relates to savings.

TERMS

Annual Percentage Yield (APY)
automatic transfer
interest
liquidity

long-range goals
mid-range goals
money market savings account
regular savings account

savings
short-range goals
Truth-in-Savings Law
U.S. Savings Bonds

Saving means putting aside present income to use sometime in the future. You can build and protect your **savings** by placing money in a savings account at a financial institution such as a bank, credit union, or a savings and loan association.

FINANCIAL GOALS

If you have ever saved for weeks or months to buy something you wanted, then you know the good feeling that comes with reaching a goal you have set. A savings account is a very useful tool to help you reach your financial goals.

At first you may think you don't have any financial goals, but think about it. Maybe there is a pair of athletic shoes you've been wanting but couldn't quite afford. Maybe you've been trying to figure out how you can get enough money to pay for the prom or the down payment on a car. Each of these concerns could represent a financial goal.

There are several types of financial goals. Some are **short-range goals**: they can be reached in less than a year. For example, you may want to buy a new swimsuit, tickets to a concert, or have enough to pay for your auto insurance when it comes due in three months.

Some goals require more money, so it takes longer to reach them. These are **mid-range goals**, and take one to five years to achieve. Some possible mid-range goals might be buying a big-screen TV, making the down payment on a new or used car, or paying for your college education. **Long-range goals** require even more money and possibly as long as ten or more years to reach, such as saving the down payment on a house or condo.

savings
. . . .
money put aside in savings accounts or investments for future use

short-range goals
. . . .
financial goals that can be accomplished in less than one year

mid-range goals
. . . .
financial goals that can be reached in one to five years

long-range goals
. . . .
financial goals involving large sums of money and requiring more than five years to complete

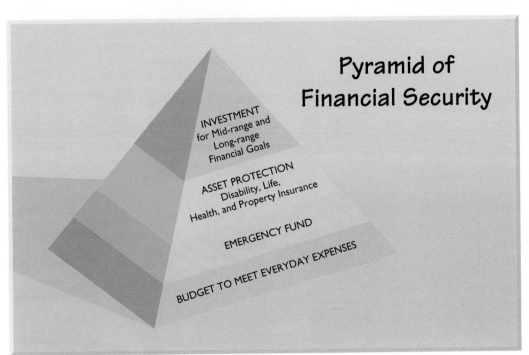

Pyramid of Financial Security

INVESTMENT
for Mid-range and Long-range Financial Goals

ASSET PROTECTION
Disability, Life, Health, and Property Insurance

EMERGENCY FUND

BUDGET TO MEET EVERYDAY EXPENSES

Figure 13.1
. . . .
The different levels of the Pyramid of Financial Security are explained on page 131. On which level of the pyramid are you at this time? What will you need to do to move to the next level?

SAVINGS ACCOUNTS

Savings accounts are an ideal tool for reaching your short-range goals. They can also be used to accumulate a large sum of money to invest for your mid-range or long-range goals.

When you put money in a savings account, it earns `interest`. Interest is money the bank pays you for leaving your deposit in a savings account, and it is calculated as a percentage of the balance in the account. The interest is paid to your account at regular intervals. The bank uses your savings to invest or to lend to borrowers.

TYPES OF SAVINGS ACCOUNTS

There are four basic types of savings accounts: regular savings accounts,

money market savings accounts, certificates of deposit, and U.S. savings bonds. All are available at banks, credit unions, and savings and loan associations.

Regular Savings Accounts

When you think about savings, what probably comes to mind is a `regular savings account`. A regular savings account can be opened with any amount of money, and you can make deposits or withdrawals as often as you wish. This type of account pays a fixed interest rate.

Regular savings accounts may be either *passbook* accounts or *statement accounts*, and they are the same except for the record-keeping system. With a passbook account, the saver receives a passbook to record all account activity. The teller updates the balance in the passbook whenever a deposit or withdrawal is made. For statement accounts, the bank sends a monthly

interest
·········
money that is earned on deposits

regular savings account
·········
a savings account with a fixed interest rate and unrestricted deposits and withdrawals

The interest rate paid on savings accounts varies at different institutions. Before opening an account, do some research to find out what interest rates are paid at different institutions on the type of account you want. Do you currently have a savings account? Are you getting the best interest rate possible?

Tellers are very helpful when you want to make a deposit or withdrawal from your savings account. Many people, however, seldom go into a bank because they prefer to do their banking at the ATM.

report detailing the activity and earnings in the account.

Money Market Savings Accounts

A money market savings account differs from a regular savings account in two ways. These differences involve restrictions on the number of withdrawals and the method of computing interest on the account.

Withdrawals. Money market savings accounts strictly limit the number of withdrawals from the account. In most cases, savers are limited to three withdrawals per month. Otherwise, there is a penalty—which usually involves the loss of all interest for that month.

Interest. Unlike a regular savings account, which pays a fixed interest rate on the balance, money market savings accounts have a very complex interest rate structure. The interest rate varies according to the balance in the account. Most accounts require a minimum balance in order to pay any interest at all. (In some cases, that minimum may be several thousand dollars!)

Certificates of Deposit

A certificate of deposit, often referred to as a "CD," gets its name from the certificate issued to the saver when an account is opened. Unlike opening a regular savings account, to purchase a CD, a saver must deposit a minimum amount (usually $2,500) and agree to leave it on deposit for a specified period of time, usually six months or longer. In exchange for these limitations, CDs earn a higher rate of interest than regular savings accounts.

Interest is paid on a CD only if it is held to maturity (the end of the period you agree to invest your money). The saver forfeits all interest if funds are withdrawn prior to the end of the term. So before investing in a CD, make certain you can live with the time limitation. If not, a regular savings account is probably the best choice for your savings dollars.

Some financial institutions also offer a *flexible CD*, which allows one or more withdrawals during the term without a penalty. Additional deposits can be made anytime during the term. Some flexible CDs even offer the depositor a one-time opportunity to change the interest rate on the account if rates go up during the term.

U.S. Savings Bonds

U.S. Savings Bonds are very useful for saving to reach mid-range financial goals. They are safe, inexpensive, and offer a guaranteed interest rate.

money market savings account
....
a savings account with a variable interest rate, restricted withdrawals, and a required minimum balance

U.S. Savings Bonds
....
an investment vehicle that can be purchased at a discount and held until maturity

INTERACTING WITH TECHNOLOGY

HIGH-TECH BANKING

Americans write an estimated 13 billion checks a year for paying expenses. But in the future this number will probably be greatly reduced. Why?

Personal banking is going home via personal computer. Anyone who has a home computer, software such as *Managing Your Money*, *Quicken*, *CheckFree*, or *Prodigy*, and a modem can pay bills electronically without ever writing a check.

How does this work? The first time a check-paying program is used information such as names, addresses, and account numbers of businesses and creditors who are to be paid, must be entered into the computer. For fixed monthly expenses such as insurance and mortgages, the amounts to be paid are also entered only once. For monthly expenses that change (electric and telephone bills, for example) the amounts must be entered each month. When all of the information is correct, the computer can be directed to start the electronic transfer needed to pay the bills. The funds are transferred electronically from your account to the account of the person or business being paid. It may not be possible to pay some smaller businesses electronically. So, some checks will still have to be written. Some experts predict that in the future, bill paying will be virtually paper-free.

For several years it has been possible to use a computer to do banking from home. Banks have encouraged people to make electronic transactions from the comfort of their den but many people are hesitant to do so. In an attempt to persuade more people to bank from home, some banks have recently introduced screen phones. These devices are combination phones and computers and they allow customers to complete nearly every banking transaction, except getting cash, without ever going to a bank.

Screen phones can be used for checking balances and other transactions that can be conducted on an automatic voice-response phone line. They can also be used for nonbanking services such as reading classified ads in newspapers and buying tickets to the theater.

Different models with more features are being developed. Some of these models allow customers to purchase items and pay bills; and at least one model will have a slot for making transactions by credit card.

The screen phone is not for everyone, however. Unless these are services you will use consistently, it might not be the right thing for you. Some models of screen phones cost several hundred dollars. Others can be rented for less than $10.00 a month. The prices for screen phones may come down in the future though, and become affordable for almost everyone.

Computer banking, screen phone banking, what's next? TV banking? Probably, according to the experts.

Because they are backed by the U.S. Treasury, savings bonds provide excellent security for your savings dollars. They are sold at a 50 percent discount off the face value. This means you can buy a $50 savings bond for $25. Bonds are worth twice the purchase price and pay a guaranteed interest rate if held to maturity, but savings bonds are not redeemable for at least six months after purchase.

If you are saving money for college, consider Series EE savings bonds. The yield on these is not taxable if the money is used for college education. (In order to receive the tax break, a bond holder must be a U.S. resident and at least 24 years old.)

You can purchase savings bonds from most financial institutions, and many employers allow the purchase of savings bonds through regular payroll deductions.

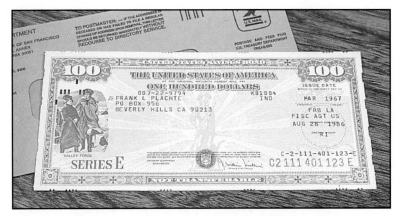

Often, savings bonds can be purchased through your employer. Money for the bonds can be taken from your pay before you receive your paycheck. Check with your employer, or have your parents check with theirs, to see if this type of savings plan is offered.

Shopping for a Savings Account

All savings accounts are not created equal, so it pays to shop around before you choose a place to put your savings. The most important factors to consider are safety, earnings, and liquidity.

Safety

To ensure the safety of your deposits, select a financial institution that has government insurance. If your savings are in an insured account and the financial institution fails, your money will be protected. This is a very important consideration, given the collapse of the savings and loan industry that began in the late 1980s. Usually, insur-

ance information is posted by the financial institution—but you can ask if you are unsure.

Earnings

In a national survey, Consumers Union found large differences in the dollar return paid on various accounts—even within the same city and, surprisingly, even between accounts in the same financial institution. To get the highest return on your savings, you'll want to find out the interest rate, any minimum balance requirements for opening the account or for earning interest, and any fees you will have to pay. (Some accounts even charge consumers a fee to withdraw their own money!)

The **Truth-in-Savings Law** makes it easier for you to comparison-shop for a savings account. The law requires financial institutions to tell you the **Annual Percentage Yield** or the APY, which indicates the actual return on a $100 deposit left for one year. Using this information, you can easily compare savings accounts to get the best return.

Truth-in-Savings Law

. . . . .

requires that financial institutions must state the annual percentage yield of all investments

Annual Percentage Yield (APY)

. . . .

the actual return on $100 invested for one year at a given rate

Liquidity

liquidity
....
a measure of how
accessible money is

Liquidity refers to the accessibility of your money, how quickly and easily you can get cash from the account. There is a relationship between interest and liquidity: The higher the liquidity, the lower the interest rate paid on the account.

If you will need or want to make frequent withdrawals from a savings account, select a regular savings account. This type of account offers high liquidity, so you can get cash from your account quickly, easily, and without cost.

Money market accounts are slightly less liquid because the number of withdrawals is limited. A savings bond cannot be redeemed for at least six months after it is purchased. It can be sold for varying returns after that time, but must be held to maturity to get the full yield. Early withdrawal of a CD results in loss of interest, so it is considered the least liquid of all the savings accounts.

THE PSYCHOLOGY OF SAVING

automatic transfer
....
a method of savings in
which money is taken
from the paycheck and
deposited in a savings
account by the bank

Some people find it easy to save, while others find it almost impossible. What makes the difference? Our attitudes. The following paragraphs explain why some people don't save, suggest where you might find some money in your budget for savings, and tell you how to get started.

Why Some People Don't Save

People give a variety of excuses for not saving money, including ideas such as the ones expressed in the statements below.

"I don't make enough money to save any."

"It's better to buy now rather than save, since prices are going up."

"I can buy what I want, so why save?"

Others plan to start saving at some point in the future, such as:

"When I get a steady job,"

"When I earn more money," or

"When I'm on my own."

All of these are excuses for someone who doesn't want to save money. If we wait until we have extra money to save, most of us will *never save at all*. Generally, we have to make choices. We may choose *not to spend* in the present in order to have more to spend in the future.

Finding the Money to Save

Although people make all kinds of excuses for not saving, it may not be as hard to save as you think. Here are some painless suggestions from a variety of financial advisors:

1. Save something out of every paycheck. A good way to do this is to arrange for an **automatic transfer** from your paycheck to your savings account. If you don't see the money, you probably won't miss it.

2. Don't spend your whole raise. When your pay goes up, save 50 percent of the increase. You won't miss it since you never had it.

3. Make your own lunch. A Big Mac, fries, and a soft drink will set you back as much as five dollars a day. If you take your lunch to school only two days a week, you could save $10 a week, or $40 per month.

4. Give up a bad habit. The cost of smoking, eating candy bars, or buying a soft drink every day on the way home after school can add up—if you put it in your savings account instead of spending it.

5. Use the library instead of buying paperback books. Books from the library don't cost you anything, and you don't have to find a place to store them when you're done reading. CDs and videos may be available for check-out at your local library.

Getting Started: A Step-by-Step Savings Strategy

The hardest part about saving money is getting started. Here are the steps to take, so that you can move closer to reaching your financial goals.

Step 1: Specify what the goal is and exactly how much money you need. For example: I want to buy a compact disc player that costs $225.

Step 2: Decide on the time frame for reaching your goal. Specify the month and year. For example: I want to buy the compact disc player when school is out next June (nine months from now).

Step 3: Figure how much money you will need to save each week (or month) in order to reach your goal. In the example above, you would need to save $25 per month.

Step 4: Identify the best type of savings account for your goal. A regular savings account would work great for our goal in the example above.

Step 5: Begin saving. *Pay yourself first* by putting the specified sum into your savings account at the same time you pay any other bills. Better yet, have

Taking your lunch to school or work rather than buying it is one way to save money. Calculate how much money you could save by taking your lunch everyday.

the money deposited from your paycheck directly into your savings account.

Summary

- Savings accounts are an ideal tool for reaching your short-range financial goals. They can also be used to accumulate a large sum of money to invest for your mid-range or long-range goals.

- There are four basic types of savings accounts: regular savings accounts, certificates of deposit, money market savings accounts, and U.S. savings bonds. All are available at banks, credit unions, and savings and loan associations.

- It pays to comparison-shop when choosing a savings account. The most important factors to consider are: safety, earnings, and liquidity. Use the Annual Percentage Yield to find the highest-paying account.

ENRICHING YOUR VOCABULARY

Write and define each of the following words or phrases on a separate sheet of paper.

Annual Percentage Yield
  (APY)
automatic transfer
interest
liquidity

long-range goals
mid-range goals
money market savings
  account
regular savings account

savings
short-range goals
Truth-in-Savings Law
U.S. Savings Bonds

REVIEWING WHAT YOU HAVE LEARNED

1. Explain the differences between a regular savings account and a money market savings account.

2. What are the advantages and disadvantages of a certificate of deposit, when compared to those of a regular savings account?

3. List the factors to consider when choosing a savings account.

4. When referring to savings, what does it mean to "pay yourself first"?

USING YOUR CRITICAL THINKING SKILLS

1. Define what financial security means to you. Compare your ideas to those of others in your class. Try to understand why the meaning differs among individuals.

2. What is your attitude toward saving money?

Discuss why attitudes differ from one individual to the next.

3. Describe your efforts to save money. Explain what works (for you), what doesn't work, and why.

APPLYING WHAT YOU HAVE LEARNED

1. The text indicates that everyone needs an emergency fund. List the types of financial emergencies that could affect your household's budget. Beside each, estimate the potential cost.

2. List three financial goals you have. For each, indicate the amount of money needed and time frame, then estimate the monthly savings necessary to reach each goal. Evaluate how realistic your goals are.

3. Assume you have $100 to open a savings account. Using information provided under the Truth-in-Savings Law, compare three different accounts. Decide which savings account you would choose and explain why. How do your findings and decision compare to those of others in your class? What conclusions can you draw from this experience?

CHAPTER 14

Insurance for Income Protection

OBJECTIVES

After completing this chapter, you will be able to do the following:
1. Define the concept of "income protection."
2. Name the tools that are potentially available to provide income protection.
3. Explain the primary purpose of buying life insurance.
4. Explain the difference between term and whole life insurance.

TERMS

accidental death
dependents
disability insurance
FICA (Federal Insurance
   Contribution Act)

guaranteed insurability
guaranteed renewability
riders
sick leave

term life insurance
whole life insurance
workers' compensation

One of the most valuable financial assets you have is the ability to earn an income. As you become independent and perhaps take on responsibility for a family, it is important to protect your earning potential.

What would happen if you couldn't work due to an injury or a long-term illness? How would you pay the rent, buy food, or meet your other financial obligations? What if you died unexpectedly? Who would be responsible to pay your debts and provide for your family (if you had one)?

Understandably, young people seldom think about these possibilities, but they can happen! As you are working to establish your financial security, develop a plan to protect your future earning potential.

Several tools are available to you. These include personal savings; employer-provided protection such as sick leave, workers' compensation and group disability insurance; government insurance programs which include Social Security and state disability coverage; and individual disability insurance. Each alternative is discussed in the following pages.

sick leave
....
employers' payment to employees who are unable to work because of illness; it is usually limited to 5 to 10 days per year

workers' compensation
....
income protection provided by some employers that covers both the medical expenses and lost salary due to a job-related illness or accident

PERSONAL SAVINGS

Remember the emergency fund we talked about earlier in this unit? That savings can help get you through times when you can't work due to illness or injury, but most of us don't have enough savings to cover an extended absence from work. Fortunately, there are several other resources to help you manage this risk.

EMPLOYER-SPONSORED INCOME PROTECTION

Sick Leave. Many employers provide paid sick leave to employees who must miss work due to illness or injury. An individual's sick leave is limited to a certain number of days per year (usually five to ten), depending on the job. Even though you can't work, you still get a paycheck.

Workers' Compensation. If you are unable to work due to an injury incurred on the job, you may be eligible to receive workers' compensation payments. Workers' compensation covers both the medical expenses and lost salary due to a job-related illness or accident. Check with your employer to see if you have this type of income protection.

Group Disability Insurance. Some employers offer a small disability insurance policy as a fringe benefit, and some offer employees the option to purchase additional coverage at group rates. This coverage is almost always less expensive than individual disability insurance.

GOVERNMENT-MANDATED SOCIAL INSURANCE

Social Security Disability Insurance. You may think Social Security benefits are only for retirees, but Social

Disabilities can affect people of all ages. In the case of a worker, he will need to have enough insurance coverage to take care of himself and possibly his family while he is unable to work. Has anyone you know been disabled for any length of time? What type of income did they have?

Security also pays disability benefits to eligible workers who experience a long-term or permanent disability.

Under Social Security, a disability is defined as "a severe mental or physical condition that prevents you from working and is expected to last for at least twelve months, or is expected to result in death." Payments start at the sixth full month of disability and continue for as long as the disability lasts.

Eligibility to receive benefits is based on work history (years contributing to the fund). The amount of the benefit depends on the worker's age and past earnings. Under some circumstances, the spouse and/or children of an eligible worker may also receive benefits.

Like all Social Security programs, the disability insurance is funded by mandatory *contributions* from employees and their employers. Each pays an equal amount that is a percentage of the worker's earnings. Employees pay through paycheck deductions, which are identified on pay stubs with the initials FICA (Federal Insurance Contribution Act). Self-employed individuals pay the full amount themselves. (See Figure 14.1 on the next page.)

State Disability Insurance. In addition to Social Security, most states also have a mandated disability insurance program. Employees pay a percentage of each paycheck for the coverage. There is a short waiting period (usually just several weeks) before benefits begin. Payments are limited to a percentage of previous earnings and may last up to twelve months.

INDIVIDUAL DISABILITY INSURANCE

In the case of a disability, you will need 60 percent to 70 percent of your pre-disability income. You don't need

FICA (Federal Insurance Contribution Act)
....
established payroll deductions for the Social Security system

disability insurance
....
insurance that will help cover expenses when a person can't work due to a physical or mental condition

Figure 14.1
....

FICA and SDI are in bold type here to show how the deductions are indicated on a check stub. What do FICA and SDI stand for?

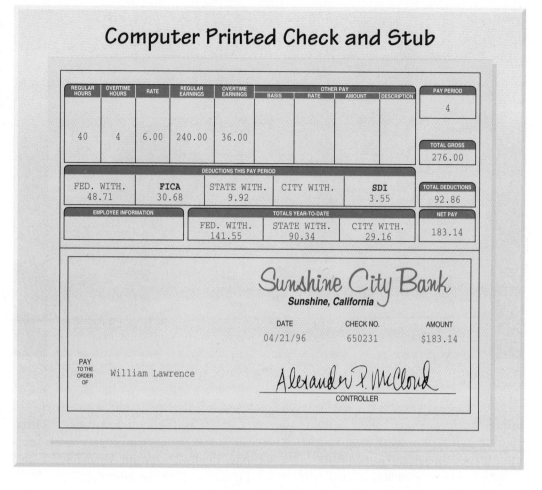

Computer Printed Check and Stub

REGULAR HOURS	OVERTIME HOURS	RATE	REGULAR EARNINGS	OVERTIME EARNINGS	OTHER PAY				PAY PERIOD
					BASIS	RATE	AMOUNT	DESCRIPTION	4
40	4	6.00	240.00	36.00					

TOTAL GROSS
276.00

DEDUCTIONS THIS PAY PERIOD					
FED. WITH. 48.71	**FICA** 30.68	STATE WITH. 9.92	CITY WITH.	**SDI** 3.55	TOTAL DEDUCTIONS 92.86

EMPLOYEE INFORMATION	TOTALS YEAR-TO-DATE			NET PAY
	FED. WITH. 141.55	STATE WITH. 90.34	CITY WITH. 29.16	183.14

Sunshine City Bank
Sunshine, California

DATE	CHECK NO.	AMOUNT
04/21/96	650231	$183.14

PAY TO THE ORDER OF   William Lawrence

Alexander P. McCloud
CONTROLLER

100 percent replacement because some expenses (such as transportation, uniforms, or professional dues) would be eliminated if you could not work.

If you evaluate the resources you would have from all of these sources and find that additional coverage is necessary, you can buy an individual disability policy from an insurance company. This policy, in conjunction with employer-sponsored and government-mandated programs, may replace up to 70 percent of pre-disability income.

Comparison-shop with several insurance companies before buying a disability plan. Consider, besides cost, how long the benefit period lasts (up to age 65 is best), the waiting period before benefits begin, and how the policy defines total and partial disability.

dependents
....
those who rely on your earnings for all or part of their support

LIFE INSURANCE

If you have dependents, you will want to provide for their financial security as well as your own. **Dependents** are those who rely on your earnings for part or all of their support. This might include a spouse, children, and/or an aging parent. In the event that you died, they would continue to need the income that you provided—and you can purchase life insurance to meet this need.

Purpose of Life Insurance

The main reason to buy life insurance is to provide a continuing income

DETERMINING HOW MUCH LIFE INSURANCE YOU NEED

Life insurance salespeople generally recommend buying insurance equal to several times your current yearly income. At best, that is only a very general rule of thumb. It may leave you overinsured or, worse yet, it may leave your survivors with less than enough to meet their needs.

There are six steps you can take to estimate the amount of life insurance to buy. How much you need will be based on the number and age of your dependents, as well as other factors.

Step 1: Calculate how much money your dependents would require to meet current living expenses. This figure will generally be about 75 percent to 80 percent of your current income. Multiply this annual figure by the number of years that income replacement will be needed (until children are grown and spouse retires, assuming he/she has retirement savings).

Step 2: Add the total amount necessary to repay all credit cards and other outstanding debts.

You may also decide to provide money to repay the mortgage on your residence. If so, add the outstanding balance on the home.

Step 3: Estimate the amount that would be needed to cover final medical expenses and funeral costs. This will depend in part on whether or not you have health insurance.

Step 4: Add together the amounts needed for present and future income, debt repayment, and last expenses. This provides a preliminary estimate for the amount of protection a family needs. However, you're still not ready to buy insurance.

Step 5: Assess the resources you already have available to protect your family. This might include emergency savings, employer-provided life insurance, and Social Security benefits. Calculate the total of all these resources.

Step 6: Subtract the total of all available resources (Step 5) from the total amount of protection needed (Step 4). The difference indicates how much life insurance you need. Life insurance needs will change over the family life cycle. Review your coverage periodically to see that your coverage keeps pace with your earnings and the effects of inflation. Always review your coverage when there is a change in family status (marriage, divorce, birth of a child) as well as when you buy or sell your primary residence.

to those you are financially responsible for in case you die and are thus unable to provide for their needs. You can also purchase life insurance to repay outstanding debts and final expenses in the event of your death, relieving your survivors of these obligations.

Sometimes consumers have other reasons for buying life insurance. They may see a particular life insurance policy as a means of financing a child's college education at some point in the future or saving for retirement. Since we deal with investments in Chapter 15, this section will focus only on life insurance as a means of providing income protection for your loved ones.

Who Needs Life Insurance?

Should high school or college students take out life insurance policies on themselves? Perhaps you've been told that it's important to buy insurance while you are young and the price is quite low. Does that mean you should buy insurance now?

In order to decide, you can go back to the stated (primary) purpose of life insurance: protecting the income of those you are responsible for. Do you have anyone depending on your earnings as a major part of their support? If not, you probably don't need life insurance at this point in your life.

Selecting a Life Insurance Policy

When you decide it is time to buy life insurance (although that may seem a long way off right now), it will be helpful to have some basic knowledge about what's out there. The following paragraphs briefly describe the most common types of policies. Most other policies are just variations of these basic types.

Types of Life Insurance Policies

Term Life Insurance. Term life insurance provides benefit payments if the insured dies within a specified peri-

od of time, usually one or more years ("the term"). Annual payments (premiums) may be the same for each year of the term, or they may increase periodically as the insured person reaches specified ages. When the term expires, the insured has the option to renew the policy for an additional term. When premium payments stop, the insurance protection stops. (See Figure 14.2.)

Whole Life Insurance. Whole life insurance may also be referred to as "ordinary" or "straight" life insurance, and it pays benefits whenever the insured dies. Unlike term insurance, the insured owns this policy for an entire lifetime (hence, the name "whole life" insurance). Annual premiums remain the same each year the policy remains in force.

In addition to providing death benefits, a whole life policy also has a *cash value* or savings component. The savings portion of the premium payment earns interest at a guaranteed rate of interest (usually a very low interest rate).

Universal Life Insurance. Universal life insurance is similar to whole life insurance. It pays death benefits when the insured dies and also has a residual cash value. However, instead of a

whole life insurance
....
life insurance that pays benefits whenever the insured dies, and which does not have to be renewed

term life insurance
....
life insurance that provides benefit payments if the insured dies within a specified period of time, usually one or more years ("the term"); the insured has the option of renewing the policy at the end of the term

Figure 14.2
....
Information given in this chart can help you decide what type of insurance would be right for you. Which type of policy typically does not have any cash value?

Comparison of Term, Whole, and Universal Life Insurance

Term	Whole	Universal
• Protection for a specified period of time	• Permanent protection	• Permanent protection
• May be renewable and convertible to whole life insurance	• Fixed premium	• Flexible premium
	• Fixed death benefit	• Flexible death benefit
• Low initial premium	• Fixed cash value	• Cash value reflects premiums paid and market conditions
• Premium rises with each new term	• Earnings generated by the policy are not taxed while the policy is in force	• Earnings generated by the policy are not taxed while the policy is in force
• Typically no cash value		

fixed-rate savings component, a universal life policy incorporates a variable-rate investment component to build the cash value.

Special Purpose Life Insurance Policies. Life insurance policies are also sold to meet specific financial needs. Examples include mortgage life insurance (pays off the mortgage if the insured dies); credit life insurance (pays all outstanding debts if the insured dies); and funeral insurance (pays burial costs for the insured). These policies are very expensive relative to the coverage provided, and they are unnecessary if you already have adequate life insurance.

Major Provisions of a Life Insurance Policy

Life insurance companies offer many **riders** (special features which are optional) in addition to the basic policy. A few of these are worth considering.

A **guaranteed renewability** rider (only for term insurance) ensures that you will be able to renew your insurance when the current term expires, regardless of your present health condition. **Guaranteed insurability** allows you the option to purchase additional life insurance coverage without a physical exam at some specified point in the future.

Skip the **accidental death** benefit. Your dependents will need the same amount of coverage regardless of the cause of your death.

Shopping for Life Insurance

The cost of life insurance is based on your age, sex, heredity, and your general health as determined by a physical exam—and your lifestyle choices such as smoking, drinking, and use of drugs. Other than lifestyle choices, you have little control over these factors.

However, there are several factors under your control that can influence the cost of buying life insurance. Most important are the type of policy you select (term, whole, or universal life) and whether you buy a group or an individual policy. It is also important to shop for the best price and evaluate the financial stability of the insurance company before you buy.

Selecting the Type of Policy. Term life insurance is the least expensive to buy, followed by whole life and universal life insurance. According to Consumers Union, the only way most young adults can afford to buy as much life insurance as they need is to buy term life insurance. When choosing your policy, give priority to buying adequate coverage.

Two Ways to Buy Life Insurance. There are two ways to buy life insurance: a group policy or an individual policy. Group policies may be available through your employer, union, or trade organization. Group policies are less expensive and usually have less stringent health requirements than if the same policy were purchased individually. You may not even have to have a physical examination or provide proof of insurability in order to obtain coverage. (This may change due to the AIDS epidemic.)

Comparison Shopping for the Best Price. It pays to shop around before you buy. A 1993 *Consumer Reports* survey found costs for the same policy varying by as much as 50 percent between companies! Comparison shop with at least three companies to obtain the best price.

Evaluate the Insurance Company. An insurance policy is only as reliable as the company that you buy it from.

riders
......
special features, which are optional, that are added to a basic insurance policy

guaranteed renewability
....
ensures that term insurance can be renewed when the current term expires, regardless of the person's physical condition

guaranteed insurability
....
allows the option to purchase additional life insurance coverage without a physical exam at some specified point in the future

accidental death
....
an unexpected death that happens without intent or possibly through carelessness

Wise consumers compare prices on life insurance policies. It's important to know you're not being overcharged and that the company is reliable and will pay any claims. Do you know anyone whose insurance company has failed to pay a claim?

Check out the company by looking up its rating in *Best's Insurance Report.* Most public libraries subscribe to this annual report, which evaluates the financial stability of most insurance companies.

You know, of course, that an insurance salesperson's chief purpose is to sell the most insurance possible. So be informed and don't allow a salesperson to pressure you into buying more insurance than you need.

Summary

- Your most valuable financial asset is the ability to earn an income. You can protect this asset through a combination of savings, employer-provided protection, disability insurance, Social Security, and state disability coverage.

- The main reason to buy life insurance is to be able to provide a continuing income to your dependents if you die and are unable to provide for their needs. There are three basic types of life insurance policies: term, whole life, and universal life insurance.

- Term life insurance is the least expensive to buy, followed by whole life and universal life insurance. The only way most young adults can afford to buy as much life insurance as they need is to buy term life insurance.

CHAPTER REVIEW
14

ENRICHING YOUR VOCABULARY

Number your paper from 1–11. Read each sentence below. If the sentence is true, write "true" next to that number. If the sentence is false, rewrite it to make a true statement.

1. Workers' compensation is a form of medical and income protection insurance that is provided by some employers.

2. People that employers rely on to get the job done are called dependents.

3. Disability insurance provides income protection if you are fired from a job.

4. An accidental death benefit can be added as a rider to a basic life insurance policy.

5. The premiums on whole life insurance increase as the insured person gets older.

6. Riders are a basic part of insurance policies.

7. Guaranteed insurability is a rider that allows you to purchase additional insurance without a physical exam.

8. Term insurance insures you for the entire term of your life.

9. The Federal Insurance Contribution Act established payroll deductions for our Social Security program.

10. FICA provides sick leave for all employees.

11. Guaranteed renewability is a feature of whole life insurance.

REVIEWING WHAT YOU HAVE LEARNED

1. Define the concept of "income protection."

2. What tools provide income protection? Include those available through personal resources, employers, and the government.

3. According to the text, what is the primary purpose for buying life insurance?

4. Explain the difference between term and whole life insurance.

USING YOUR CRITICAL THINKING SKILLS

1. Why is income protection an important part of financial security? What are some possible threats to one's ability to earn an income?

2. Some financial planners feel that for young adults disability insurance is more important than life insurance. Under what circumstances might this be true? Explain your logic.

APPLYING WHAT YOU HAVE LEARNED

1. Your friend, age 19, received a life insurance application in the mail. She has heard that it is wise to buy insurance when you are young as the cost is low and will not increase. What should your friend consider when deciding whether to buy life insurance now?

CHAPTER 15

Investments

OBJECTIVES

After completing this chapter, you will be able to do the following:
1. Explain the difference between saving and investing.
2. List the advantages (for a beginner) of investing in mutual funds rather than in individual stocks and bonds.
3. Explain the relationship between risk and return on investments.
4. Name two ways you can protect yourself from fraudulent investment schemes.

TERMS

bonds	no-load mutual fund	real estate
investments	prospectus	risk
mutual funds		

Investing is simply using current income to produce income at some point in the future. In other words, investing is putting your money to work for you!

You may be eager to "play the stock market" and to experience the thrills and the riches that come to the successful, or you may think investments are only for the rich. You may prefer to put your money where it's safe, so you can sleep well at night.

There is a middle ground between these extreme points of view. Very few investors make a fortune overnight, but some do build a comfortable sum by carefully and regularly investing over a period of time. And they sleep easier because of it!

SAVING VS. INVESTING

The primary difference between saving and investing is the way in which the two types of accounts change in value over time. Savings accounts earn interest at a specified rate. Investments, on the other hand, change in value according to the economy and the business environment. Saving and investing also differ according to the degree of safety, earnings potential, and liquidity as discussed in the following paragraphs.

Safety

Savings accounts are generally very safe, especially if placed in a government-insured account. All offer protection of the principal (original amount put into savings) and most offer a guaranteed rate of return. Investments, however, all involve some degree of **risk**: the risk of lower-than-expected earnings, or the risk of losing part or even all of the money invested.

Earnings

Investments offer the potential for higher earnings than savings, and the reason is simple. Why would an in-

risk
......
the chance of losing all or part of the money invested

The stock exchange is where stocks are bought, sold, and traded. Many newspapers offer stock information. Locate this part of a newspaper and then find someone to explain to you what all the figures mean.

vestor take any risk if savings and investments earned the same? It wouldn't make sense! So investment companies offer the possibility of higher earnings to those who are willing to take more risks with their money.

Liquidity

Savings accounts are liquid, which means the account can easily be converted to cash with little or no cost. Investments have varying levels of liquidity, but are not as liquid as savings accounts. It costs time and money to convert an investment into cash. Some investments, such as art and antiques, may be particularly difficult to liquidate.

REASONS FOR INVESTING

Investments aren't just for the rich. Many middle-income consumers invest as part of an overall strategy to achieve financial security.

Some consumers use investments to reach mid-range goals, such as the down payment on a house or condo. Investments are a very important tool for achieving long-range financial goals, such as putting a child through college or funding an early retirement.

People also invest to protect their assets against the effects of inflation. When the rate of inflation is high, cash and savings lose some of their buying power, but some investments grow in value as inflation rises.

TYPES OF INVESTMENTS

The array and complexity of investments can be overwhelming. It's help-

ful to have a basic understanding of the most common investment alternatives: stocks, bonds, mutual funds, and real estate. The following paragraphs describe each type of investment and how to buy it.

Stocks

When you buy *stock* you are actually purchasing partial ownership (shares) in a private company. As a *stockholder,* you share in the profits (or losses!) of the company. With some types of stock, you may even share in company decision making by voting at the annual stockholders meeting.

Buying Stocks. You can purchase stocks from a licensed stockbroker (salesperson) who may work independently or be employed by a financial institution, such as a stockbrokerage house, a bank, or an insurance company. Sometimes companies sell their stock directly to the public. In either case, there is a fee for each transaction (purchase or sale of stock).

Risk. The risk of investing in stock varies according to the stock itself and general economic conditions. There is a great potential for growth and earnings over time. However, there is also the risk of low earnings, no earnings, or even a loss of the original money invested (such as when one holds stock in a company that goes bankrupt).

Bonds

Bonds are essentially "IOUs" sold by governments or corporations to raise money. Bonds earn interest, which is paid semiannually. If the bond is held until maturity, the issuing agency will repay the full principal (amount originally invested).

Types of Bonds. There are three types of bonds: treasury bonds, munici-

investments
. . . .
a way of using current income to produce more income at some point in the future

bonds
. . . . . .
interest-earning "IOUs" sold by governments or corporations to raise money

pal bonds, and corporate bonds. Treasury bonds are issued by the federal government. Municipal bonds are issued by city, county, and state governments, and the interest earned is tax-free. Corporate bonds are issued by private companies.

Buying Bonds. Like stocks, bonds are sold by a variety of financial institutions. Most bonds are available for an initial investment of from $1,000 to $3,000.

Risk. While bonds are generally considered to be safer than stocks, they are not risk-free. If the bond is sold or called (repaid early) prior to maturity, the return on the principal may vary greatly. Or, if the issuing agency defaults, the bond can become worthless.

Ratings. Before investing in a municipal or corporate bond, check out its credit rating. The public library will have reports from *Standard and Poor's* and/or *Moody's* financial services, which rate the bonds according to their levels of risk. The least risky bonds earn the highest ratings (AAA or Aaa).

Mutual Funds

A **mutual fund** is an investment tool that pools the money of many small investors into one large "fund." A professional money manager invests the "mutual fund" in a portfolio of many different stocks, bonds, and other investments.

Advantages of Mutual Funds. For beginning investors, mutual funds have several distinct advantages. First, mutual funds offer full-time, professional management of your investment. Second, mutual funds allow you to diversify your risk, since your money is invested in many different investments. Third, you can begin with a small initial investment, sometimes as low as $1,000.

Selecting Mutual Funds. Mutual funds differ according to their investment goal and the types of investments included in the fund's portfolio. Choose a mutual fund based on your financial objectives and the ratings published in various financial magazines.

mutual fund
....
an investment tool that pools the money of many small investors into one large fund

Buying Mutual Funds. Many financial institutions sell mutual funds, and part of your purchase price goes to pay a sales charge or commission. However, it is possible to buy some mutual funds directly from the company without paying a commission. This is known as a no-load mutual fund. For the informed investor, no-load mutual funds are the sensible way to invest, saving commission costs.

Most funds require a minimum investment of about $2,500, but some newer funds waive this requirement if you agree to automatic deposits of at least $50 per month from your savings or checking account.

Real Estate

The term real estate refers to vacant land and structures such as houses, condominiums, or industrial buildings and the land they occupy. Owning a home of your own is the American Dream, and has often been a good investment, too.

But is real estate a sure investment? Sylvia Porter says emphatically, "No!" When you buy a house (or condo), you are first and foremost buying a place to live. Make that your primary consideration in selecting property; the investment potential should be a secondary purpose for you.

Other Investments

Some investors choose to invest in precious metals, such as gold or silver. Others invest in fine art, collectibles, or antique furniture. Get information and expert advice for these investments. Only the very knowledgeable (or the very lucky) investor turns a profit in this type of investment.

PRINCIPLES OF INVESTING

If you know a few basic principles, you will be prepared to invest to

---

no-load mutual fund
. . . .
a mutual fund that can be purchased directly from a company and which has no commission costs

real estate
. . . .
land and any structures built upon it

As with all purchases, it pays to research stocks and bonds before you buy. Some magazines offer ratings of the top stocks or bonds. Should you rely on information from just one magazine? Why or why not?

For people who are knowledgeable and have patience, stamp collecting can be a form of financial investment. Talk with a collector and ask how they became interested in collecting. If you don't know any collectors, many hobby stores have employees who are collectors.

achieve your financial goals. These principles are described in the following paragraphs.

1. **Understand the relationship between risk and return.** On any specific investment there is a direct relationship between risk and return: the higher the risk, the higher the potential return. Low risk means a lower return on your money, but less potential for loss.

2. **Diversify to minimize risk.** We have all heard the old saying, "Don't put all your eggs in one basket." That advice can well be applied to an investment strategy: Don't invest all your money in one stock, one industry, or even one mutual fund. Put your money into a variety of investments to spread the risks you are taking. That way, if one investment goes bad, you won't lose everything.

3. **Choose the right investment for your goals.** No single investment is right for everyone. Set your financial goals and then find investments to help you reach those goals. The "right" investment is based on the amount you have to invest, your personal values, how much risk you are willing to assume, and your stage in the life cycle.

4. **Recognize the benefits of time.** Investments seldom make money overnight or even over several months. When you decide to invest, plan to leave the money for a period of time. Every time you buy or sell an investment, there are transaction charges. Frequent transactions may reduce or even cancel out any earnings on an investment. Holding the investment over time reduces the effect of these costs.

5. **Only invest money you can afford to lose!** The risks associated with investments are real! Not every investor makes money. Some lose money; some even lose all they have put into a particular investment. Consider investing only after you have built a secure financial base as discussed earlier in this unit. Then, only invest money you can afford to lose and still be able to meet your financial commitments.

GETTING STARTED

Many people set investment goals but keep waiting for the right time to get started. The most important step in investing is the first step! Time is the investor's ally. A small sum of money invested over a long time can become a large amount.

Financial advisors suggest starting with a small investment and then investing a consistent amount at regular intervals. The next paragraphs outline how to get started as an investor.

Accumulate Funds to Invest

Most investments require an initial investment of $1,000 to $2,500. You can accumulate funds for this initial amount in a savings account. The money will earn interest while you are waiting to invest. Some stocks and mutual funds now allow an initial purchase as low as $100—if the investor agrees to purchase additional shares through automatic deductions from a savings or checking account. This is worth investigating if you can afford to invest but don't want to wait while you accumulate several thousand dollars to begin.

Identify Your Investment Goals

Investments can be used to achieve a variety of financial goals. Before selecting an investment vehicle, clearly identify what you hope to accomplish. Consider the type of goal and the time frame to determine the appropriate type of investment. You may also want to consider social values in choosing among specific alternatives.

Different Investments for Different Goals. Your goal may be to provide income to supplement your earnings at a time in the future. Some investments offer annual dividends (payment of earnings) while others

only generate income when sold. It's important to know the difference.

Different Investments for Different Time Frames. Your investment choice will also be influenced by when you will need this income. Bonds, for example, have specific maturity dates and you can purchase one that matches your goal. Other investments, such as stocks, should only be considered for long-range goals.

Different Investments for Different Social Causes. Besides investing for financial goals, you can also invest to promote specific social goals. For example, some mutual funds only invest in companies that are environmentally responsible, or that recruit and hire minorities. Other funds avoid investing in companies that make bombs, sell alcohol, or market cigarettes to third world countries. You can put your money where your political beliefs are founded!

Research Investment Alternatives

Once you have set goals and specified a time frame, you are ready to select the specific investments to implement your plan. The choices may seem overwhelming, but there is help available as close as your public library.

Investment Information. Public libraries subscribe to many publications offering investment tips and advice. The *Wall Street Journal* is an excellent resource. There are also many useful investment guides, including one published by Consumers Union and those by well-known financial advisors such as Sylvia Porter, Jane Bryant Quinn, and Andrew Tobias.

Investment Ratings. *Consumer Reports* and *Money* magazine both publish annual ratings of stocks, bonds, and mutual funds. These reports summarize the earnings history of each product, minimum investment requirements, and how to obtain more information.

Investment Advice. If you decide to consult a financial advisor, verify that the individual is licensed by the securities commission of your state. It is also a good idea to check with the local Better Business Bureau to learn if there are unsettled complaints against the advisor. Beware—many "advisors" are merely sales representatives for the products they recommend. The only earning potential these advisors are concerned about is their own!

Obtain the Prospectus for Investments You Are Considering

The **prospectus** is a written description of the philosophy, objectives, earnings, and current financial status of an investment such as a mutual fund. It also gives the investor important information about fees, commissions, and minimum investment requirements. Request a prospectus from the company or a sales representative and read it carefully before investing.

FRAUDULENT INVESTMENT SCHEMES

Fraudulent investment schemes are abundant. Even experienced, well-educated consumers sometimes get taken in. The next paragraphs will help you understand why fraud exists and expose some fraudulent schemes that are often directed toward students. You will also learn how you can avoid fraud.

Why Fraud Exists

Fraud thrives because we all believe (or want to believe) we can get something for nothing. Even well-informed investors get taken in by schemes that play on these fantasies. Some of the "investments" sound good, and we want to be convinced that dreams can come true. Remember, "con men" get their name because they are convincing. They get your "confidence", and then they get your money!

Fraud Directed Toward Students

Work-at-Home Schemes. Among the most popular "investments" are work-at-home schemes offering unlimited earnings for only a few hours of work per week. The advertising makes the work sound easy! All you have to do is send the promoter a fee for information on how to get started.

The promoter makes money by selling information and equipment for doing the job. Typically, the work involves a task such as stuffing envelopes, which the promoter pays for by the piece. In other cases, all you get (for your fee) are written instructions about how to start a home business.

Pyramid Sales Schemes. You may have encountered this plan. It works much like a chain letter. For a small "investment" you get the opportunity to sell a product and recruit others to sell it, too. It is called a pyramid, because each investor recruits others, who in turn recruit others, building a pyramid of salespersons below them. Each recruit pays a percentage of his or her sales to the one who recruited him or her, who also passes on part of the earnings to the one above (all the way to the top of the pyramid).

prospectus
....
a written description of the philosophy, objectives, earnings, and current financial status of an investment such as a mutual fund

The more salespeople you recruit, the more money you make. "Soon (the salesperson tells you), you won't even need to make sales at all. You can just sit back and watch the income flow in from all those (in the pyramid) below you." This sounds really enticing, but typically, the only investors who earn a profit are those few at the very top of the pyramid (the person making this offer to you!).

Ways to Avoid Fraud

The best way to avoid fraud is to use your head. If a deal sounds too good to be true, it probably is. Here are some sales lines you should watch out for:

"This opportunity is only available to a few investors."

"You need to move quickly while the price is still good."

"You can trust me; I'm an expert on these things."

"This price is only good if you buy now."

Protect yourself from fraud. Don't do business with telephone solicitors (those who sell over the telephone) unless you initiate the call. Even then, be very cautious about giving out your credit card number. Watch out for salespeople who discourage questions or try to rush you into making a decision. Investigate before you invest. It's YOUR money!

Summary

- You can use investments to pursue mid-range and long-range financial goals. The most common investments are stocks, bonds, and mutual funds. They can be purchased from most financial institutions, and sometimes directly from the company itself.

- On any specific investment there is a direct relationship between risk and return: The higher the risk, the higher the potential return. Diversify to minimize risk.

- Research before you invest. Public libraries subscribe to many publications offering investment tips and advice.

- Before consulting a financial advisor, verify that the individual is licensed and check with the Better Business Bureau to learn if there are unsettled complaints against the advisor.

- Protect yourself from fraud. If a deal sounds too good to be true, it probably is!

ENRICHING YOUR VOCABULARY

Number your paper from 1 to 7. Write a T if the statement is true or an F if it is false.

1. The purchase of <u>bonds</u> gives you ownership in a company.
2. <u>Investments</u> are more liquid than savings accounts.
3. <u>Mutual funds</u> pool the money of many investors.
4. <u>No-load mutual funds</u> save the investor the cost of commissions.
5. A <u>prospectus</u> is a potential investor.
6. Most people buy <u>real estate</u> as an investment.
7. <u>Risk</u> should always be avoided when selecting an investment.

REVIEWING WHAT YOU HAVE LEARNED

1. What is the difference between saving and investing?
2. List the advantages (for a beginner) of investing in mutual funds rather than in individual stocks and bonds.
3. Explain the relationship between risk and return on investments.
4. How can you protect yourself from fraudulent investment schemes? Suggest at least two ways.

USING YOUR CRITICAL THINKING SKILLS

1. What is your response to the statement: "Real estate is always a good investment"? Do you agree or disagree? Explain why.
2. Many people put off investing their money until "the right time." How will you decide when it is the right time for *you* to begin investing? Explain your answer.

APPLYING WHAT YOU HAVE LEARNED

1. Pick a specific stock, bond, or mutual fund. Find out how to purchase it and the cost. Be sure to ask about any minimum investment requirements. Track the progress of this investment for a month by reading the financial section in your local paper or the *Wall Street Journal*. Report to the class about the changes in value during that time.
2. Watch the news for reports about investment fraud. In each case, think about how consumers could have recognized and avoided the fraud. Discuss this with your class.

UNIT
6

FOOD

CHAPTERS

99¢ lb.

en
Peppers

Red
Bell Peppers

Actually a Green Pepper
Left to Ripen on the Vine
It Has More Sugar so
It's Sweeter and Slightly More Tender

179 lb.

Green

• Approximately 21 ca
• Main Nutrients: Vita
• Serving Suggestions:
  with Parmesan chee
  pearl onions for ma

For centuries, people had to spend most of their time obtaining food for themselves and their families. Today, it is readily available in supermarkets. We spend more money on food than our ancestors did, but we spend less time and energy obtaining it. We have traded one resource (time) for another (money).

CHAPTER 16

Why Do We Eat What We Eat?

OBJECTIVES

After completing this chapter, you will be able to do the following:
1. Describe some general guidelines for eating the right kinds and amounts of food.
2. Explain why caloric needs differ for different people.
3. Explain the best way to lose weight.

TERMS

anorexia nervosa
balanced diet
bulimia
calories
convenience foods

empty calories
Food Guide Pyramid
food habits
nutrients
nutritionists

obesity
Recommended Daily
Allowance (RDA)

Food is important to our physical, mental, and emotional health. Besides meeting the basic need for survival, food often has special meaning. We use it when we celebrate special occasions, it is often given as a reward, and food can provide a feeling of security.

GUIDELINES TO HEALTHY EATING

Nutritionists study food and its effects on the body, and their studies show that a good diet is necessary for good health. The National Academy of Sciences–National Research Council has established the Recommended Daily Allowance (RDA), which is a guide for the amounts of certain items we should eat every day to stay healthy. Amounts vary with our age, sex, size, and physical activity.

The National Academy of Sciences–National Research Council also helped establish general guidelines for healthy eating for all Americans. Follow these general guidelines to help ensure that you are eating the right kind and amount of food:

- Eat a variety of foods. Since 1916, nutritionists have used many different ways of placing foods into groups. In 1992, the U.S. Department of Agriculture introduced a new guide called the Food Guide Pyramid to suggest foods containing the nutrients we need (protein, carbohydrates, vitamins, and minerals). The foods are divided into five groups (bread, cereal, rice, and pasta; vegetables; fruits; milk, yogurt, and cheese; meat, poultry, fish, dry beans, eggs, and nuts). This guide recommends eating large quantities of breads and cereals, vegetables, and fruits. Fats, oils, and sweets are not recognized as a food group and, although

Food Guide Pyramid
....
a guide to daily food choices developed by the U.S. Department of Agriculture

nutrients
....
the items in foods, such as vitamins and minerals, that the body needs to function properly

nutritionists
....
people who study foods and their effects on the body and help develop diets that are necessary for good health

Recommended Daily Allowance (RDA)
....
a guide developed by the National Academy of Sciences–National Research Council, which details the amounts of such things as vitamins and minerals that should be eaten daily to maintain good health

Supermarkets offer a great variety of foods that meet our tastes and nutrition needs. When you go grocery shopping, do you find yourself buying more processed foods or more fresh foods?

included at the top of the pyramid, should be eaten sparingly. (See Figure 16.1 on the next page.)

- Maintain ideal weight.
- Avoid eating too much saturated fat and cholesterol.
- Eat foods with adequate starch and fiber.
- Avoid eating too much sugar.
- Avoid eating too much salt.

Many of the most nutritious foods are not expensive. Studies conducted by the United States Department of Agriculture (USDA) indicate that many people with high incomes are malnourished. Although they have food to eat, it is often not the most nourishing kind of food.

In 1994, The Harvard School of Public Health, along with the World Health Organization European Regional Office, developed another food guide, the Traditional Healthy Mediterranean Diet Pyramid. It is based on the eating habits in Crete, Greece, and southern Italy, regions whose people have low chronic disease rates and high life expectancies. If you were to follow this guide, most of the fat in your diet would come from olive oil. You would eat small portions of yogurt or cheese every day, with helpings of bread and grains, beans and potatoes, and fruits and vegetables. You would also eat modest amounts of fish and poultry. Red meat would be only an occasional treat. (See Figure 16.1.)

WHY DON'T WE ALL EAT THE SAME THINGS?

The amount and type of food that people buy are different in different families. The number, size, sex, and activities of family members influence the foods that are bought. Special diets, personal preferences, methods of entertaining, and the number of meals eaten away from home may determine what we eat. Cultural influences often play a strong role in the foods we learn to like. Cooking ability, storage facilities, and the stores where we shop—as well as the amount of money we have to spend—also influence what we eat.

Physical Need for Food

Food provides our bodies with energy for all of our activities, and we measure the amount of energy food provides in units called calories. Almost everything we consume, except water, provides calories. Some foods give you calories plus nutrients. Other foods are high in calories but provide few nutrients, so these calories are called empty calories or simply "junk" foods.

How many calories you need depends on how much energy your body uses. Generally, older and less active people need fewer calories than younger and more active people—and men usually need more calories than women.

Health Problems Related to Eating. Many health problems are related to eating. For example, people with heart disease are often put on special diets that restrict certain kinds of foods. Other health problems, such as diabetes, can be helped or controlled by following the proper diet. Recent studies have indicated that eating some foods and eliminating others may even help to prevent some serious diseases such as heart disease and cancer. Eating disorders such as anorexia nervosa and bulimia create serious eating problems for some people. Overeating or eating the wrong types of foods can cause a

calories
....
units that measure the amount of energy provided in foods

empty calories
....
a term that describes those foods that are high in calories but low in nutritional value

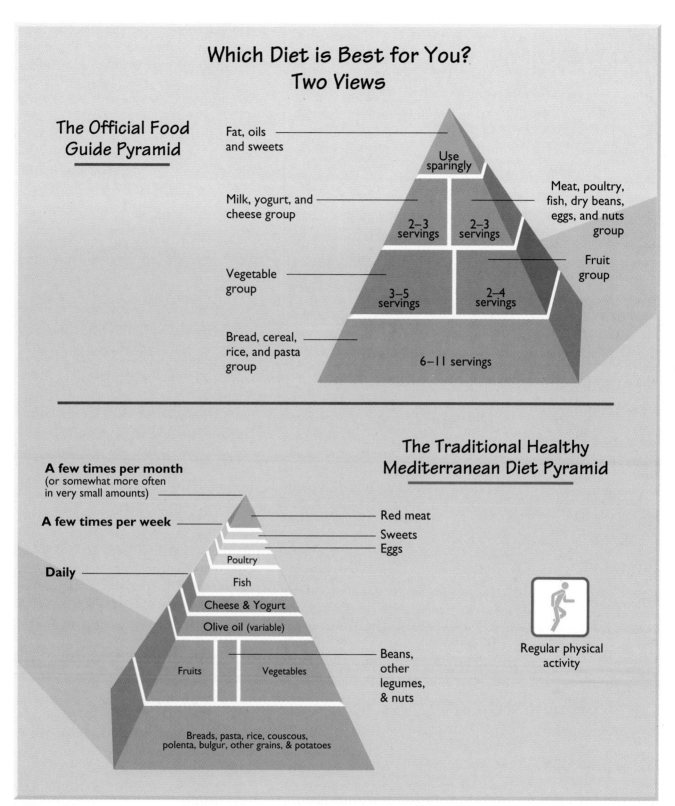

Figure 16.1

Following a food plan such as the Official Food Guide Pyramid or the Traditional Healthy Mediterranean Diet Pyramid not only ensures that you will be getting necessary nutrients, it also helps regulate caloric intake for those who are counting calories. Which plan fits best with your lifestyle?

Casey is sixteen years old, 6'1" tall, and swims on the swim team at school. The team works out for an hour before school and an hour and a half after school. The team competes in regional and statewide swim meets and usually brings home a medal or two. It is common for Casey to eat six eggs, a couple of pieces of bacon, and four or five pieces of toast for breakfast.

Shawn is sixteen years old, 5'6" tall, and spends most of his spare time reading and listening to music. His breakfast often consists of a bowl of cereal.

Both boys are healthy. Although their age and sex are the same, their different eating habits are appropriate to the big difference in their size and physical activity level!

bulimia
....
a dietary problem in which people crave food constantly and so overeat and then cause themselves to vomit before the food can be absorbed by the body

obesity
....
excessive fatness; the condition of being more than 20% over a recommended weight

anorexia nervosa
....
an eating disorder caused by physical and emotional problems, which causes a person to eat very little or not at all in order to lose weight

person to become overweight, which can lead to many problems.

The average American consumes more than 1,500 pounds of food per year. This includes 100 pounds of sugar (which provides only empty calories) and more grams of fat than their bodies need. Calories from heavy intake of fat and sugar (combined with insufficient physical activity) has helped make many Americans excessively fat. Excessive fatness (more than 20 percent over the recommended weight) is called obesity, and it can develop when the number of calories going into the body exceeds the number of calories that the body uses. It normally takes 3,500 calories to produce one pound of body fat. The best way to lose weight is to follow the guidelines for healthy eating and exercise to help use up calories.

Anorexia nervosa is an eating disorder caused by both physical and emotional problems. Some people, usually young women, become so dedicated to a slim figure that they refuse to eat, or eat very little—and they get thinner and thinner. People with anorexia nervosa often see themselves as fat, and some

have actually starved themselves to death. This is a serious disease and requires both medical and psychological attention.

Bulimia is a dietary problem in which people crave food constantly. They overeat—then, before the food can be absorbed by the body, they cause themselves to vomit—and the body never gets adequate nutrition. Bulimia can lead to serious health problems.

Emotional Need for Food

To many people, food means security. We may eat more than we need during a meal because we know we won't be hungry again for awhile. When we respond to an infant's cry by giving food, the infant is learning about security.

Food may cause you to recall past events. For example, food served at holiday functions may bring back pleasant memories of home and family gatherings. Other food may bring back unpleasant memories, and many food prejudices arise this way. For example, being forced to eat when sick can cause children to stop liking foods that are nutritious. The sight or smell of these foods reminds them (consciously or subconsciously) of when they were sick.

Social Need for Food

People often eat in social situations. Groups of students may meet after school and socialize while eating at a local restaurant. Food is often given as a gift. Food may also represent status. For example, in the United States, dining on steak represents higher status than eating a hamburger. Sometimes friends influence what we eat. Most teenagers tend to be snackers; and if your friend is having a snack, you will probably want one too.

ANOREXIA NERVOSA

Richard Simmons is well known from his writing and his TV show. He promotes good nutrition and a healthy diet, but Richard once had dietary problems of his own. He was overweight, tipping the scale at 214 pounds after he finished high school. One day, he got a note from an unknown admirer that said: "Fat people die young—please don't die." Richard's response was extreme as he tried various quack diet schemes. Then he developed symptoms of anorexia nervosa, stopped eating completely, and in two-and-a-half months he lost 112 pounds. He also became ill and had to be hos-

pitalized. He was able to overcome his problems, and he has tried to help other people overcome their problems ever since.

Anorexia nervosa was once thought to be a rare problem, but its frequency is increasing. The main symptom of people with this disorder is that they starve themselves and lose too much weight. They also have related physical and emotional problems. Treatment for anorexia is both psychological and medical, and sometimes the patient's family is involved. Anyone can get advice about treatment by writing the National Association of Anorexia Nervosa and Associated Disorders (see Appendix). A person worried about losing weight should avoid the anorectic's extreme behavior.

Snack Foods. Some snacks are loaded with sugar, salt, and saturated fat but are low in protein, vitamins, and minerals. Avoid this type of snack. Many nutritious foods can be eaten as snacks instead. For example, you may eat fresh fruit and raw vegetables instead of cookies and potato chips.

When eating with friends, it is very easy to choose foods that are not the most nutritious for you, if these are the types of foods that your friends have chosen. However, it is important to choose foods that your body needs, no matter what situation you may be in. What is your favorite food to order when eating with friends?

Small children, the elderly, and teenagers benefit especially from nutritious snacks used to supplement their diets.

Fad Diets. Food fads often influence eating habits. A food fad is a special food or diet that becomes very popular. Many people are looking for a magic diet that will make them healthy, beautiful, and thin quickly and easily.

Food fads develop for many reasons. Some are based on philosophy and culture, others are based on a desire to be different from most people. Some people may think a certain fad diet is a cure-all—but be careful. Fads often are based on false ideas. Some of these fad diets, if followed strictly, can be hazardous to your health—and they may also be expensive.

Avoid fad diets, food fads, and snacks that are not good for you. A balanced diet, with a variety of foods, is the best way to make certain your diet is nutritious. Use the Food Guide Pyramid to help you select a balanced diet. Combine a balanced diet with exercise to lose weight.

Sport Drinks. Fruit juices and some prepared drinks have been used for years to replenish electrolytes (such as sodium, potassium, and magnesium), which are lost in vigorous sports activities. The idea of an energizing *sport drink* really caught on in the 1990s. Two popular sport drinks are All-Sport and Gatorade.

Food Habits. Every consumer has ideas, beliefs, attitudes, and practices related to foods. Consumers usually acquire food habits over a long period of time by being exposed to family beliefs and values. These beliefs and values influence what we consider acceptable food and what we buy and eat, and food habits are difficult to change.

Ethnic groups to which we belong may influence our food habits, too. Eating habits of one ethnic group are usually different from those of another group. For example, a typical meal for Mexican Americans is quite different from a typical meal for Polish Americans or Chinese Americans.

Religion may affect what we consider edible as well. For example, some members of the Jewish and Islamic religions do not believe in eating pork.

food habits

a person's ideas, beliefs, attitudes, and practices that relate to foods

balanced diet

eating habits that include foods that provide the right amounts of protein, carbohydrates, and fat

People who have special diet needs can seek the help of dietitians. Dietitians are specially trained to develop the right diet to meet the person's needs, but the person is responsible to follow the advice of the dietitian. Have you or anyone you know ever gone to a dietitian?

ECONOMIC INFLUENCE ON FOOD BUYING

Wise spending results from good planning, so the first thing to do when setting up a food spending plan is to estimate how much money you have available to spend on food. In the United States, about 13 percent of the average family's income is spent on food. When income is low, a higher percentage of the total income is spent on food. No matter what your income, you must have an adequate diet for good health.

Food Waste

A sad fact is that a lot of food is wasted. On the average, we throw away about 8 percent of the food we buy—about four dollars for every fifty dollars spent on food. Waste occurs when:

- we buy food we don't like
- we buy too much food
- we buy food for a specific use but don't use it

Plan your food purchases carefully to avoid waste. You will save money as well as food.

TECHNOLOGY'S INFLUENCE ON FOOD

Many of the foods in the stores today are **convenience foods**, and they have a large amount of processing or marketing services (packaging and advertising) applied to them. Frozen, microwaveable meals provide a good example of a convenience food. In the 1990s, convenience foods became more popular than ever—with dozens, even hundreds, of choices behind the glass doors of frozen food cases in most supermarkets. Convenience foods taste better than the ones sold some years ago, and many consumers have

The modern technology of frozen foods and microwave ovens has changed the way many Americans cook and eat. Frozen meals can be prepared in a matter of minutes, but convenience foods usually cost more than foods that require preparation. Do you think the extra expense of convenience foods is worth the time saved?

fewer hours at home to prepare daily meals from scratch. More consumers own microwave ovens today, which makes it even faster to prepare convenience foods.

The USDA food consumption survey indicates that more than a third of the amount we spend on food is spent on convenience foods. Generally, lower-income consumers spend a larger percentage of their income on convenience foods than do higher-income consumers.

Usually, increased processing of food leads to higher prices—but not all convenience foods cost more than their fresh-food counterparts. Foods that require a great deal of work for you to prepare or foods that are not always available locally may be less expensive than the fresh food. Frozen orange juice, for example, is usually cheaper to prepare than fresh orange juice.

convenience foods
....
foods, such as those that are frozen or microwaveable, that have a large amount of processing and so are more easily prepared, but which are also more costly

INTERACTING WITH TECHNOLOGY

TECHNOLOGY AND THE FOOD WE EAT

Food is one of our basic needs. The shift from hunting and gathering food to growing food has had an enormous effect on the development of modern societies. Our society relies on an agricultural and distribution system for our food supply. Few members of our society are self-sufficient when it comes to meeting basic food needs. This reliance on an agricultural system frees many members to do other kinds of work, but it also creates problems.

One of these problems is the ability to supply enough food to meet the demands of our society. Technology exists to increase production and to speed up production of many kinds of foods. However, the application of some of this technology is controversial. For example, growth hormones have been developed that can dramatically increase the amount of milk that dairy cows can produce. Some consumer groups object to the use of these hormones out of concern that the hormones will enter the milk supply and be harmful to humans. They are also concerned that the increased demands on the animals will lead to more infections, which will in turn require the use of more drugs such as antibiotics. Animal rights groups object to the use of the hormones on the basis that such treatment of animals is cruel. All of these factors must be weighed and tested before the technology can be used.

The shelf life and safety of our food supply is another area that technology attempts to address. Methods have been developed to expose foods to gamma rays or X rays. These small doses of radiation can destroy bacteria, fungi, and insects that infest food products. Such treatment can slow down the rate at which food spoils and extend the shelf life by one to two weeks. Irradiation can also prevent many instances of serious food poisoning caused by dangerous microorganisms. Much larger doses have the potential to sterilize foods and increase their shelf life to years.

Some researchers are concerned that essential nutrients will be destroyed during irradiation. Other experts worry that irradiation will create harmful compounds in foods. The widespread use of this technology would also increase the amount of radioactive material that must be handled, which is of concern to environmental groups. As savvy consumers we must be prepared to examine both the risks and the benefits of technology in order to make wise choices.

Most often, though, convenience foods are more expensive than fresh foods because part of the work in preparing convenience foods is done before you buy it. When you buy convenience foods, you are paying for someone else to prepare the food for you. By paying more for convenience foods, you save your own time and energy.

Technology has made it possible to manufacture new foods from other natural food resources and chemicals. Margarine was one of the first manufactured foods, and today manufactured foods have become part of our food supply for several reasons:

- There may not be enough natural food, at a reasonable price, to meet the demand. A manufactured product may be plentiful and could be sold more cheaply than the natural food.

- The flavor of the natural product needs to be improved.

- There is a need to prolong the shelf life of the product.

Summary

- Food is important to our physical, mental, and emotional health.

- The Recommended Daily Allowance (RDA) is a guide for the amounts of various nutrients we should eat daily to stay healthy.

- Food provides energy (in units called calories) for all our activities.

- There are many health problems related to eating. These include diabetes, anorexia nervosa, overeating, and bulimia.

- A balanced diet is the best way to be sure your diet is nutritious. Avoid fad diets, food fads, and snacks that are not good for you.

- Good planning can help you have an adequate diet for good health, no matter what your income.

- Convenience foods are more expensive than fresh foods, but take less time and energy to prepare. For many people, the time and energy saved is worth the extra expense.

CHAPTER REVIEW
16

ENRICHING YOUR VOCABULARY

Number your paper from 1–12. Read each sentence below. If the sentence is true, write "true" next to that number. If the sentence is false, rewrite it to make a true statement.

1. Anorexia nervosa is a disorder of the nervous system.
2. A balanced diet includes equal amounts of food from all of the food groups.
3. Bulimia is an eating disorder characterized by overeating and induced vomiting.
4. Calories measure the nutrient value of foods.
5. Convenience foods are foods that are processed for easy preparation.
6. Empty calories provide no energy.
7. The Food Guide Pyramid recommends the quantities of food that should be consumed from five food groups.
8. People's food habits are easily changed.
9. Protein, carbohydrates, vitamins, and minerals are nutrients.
10. Nutritionists are trained to prepare healthy foods.
11. Obesity can be caused by consuming more calories than the body uses.
12. The RDA is a guide for good nutrition.

REVIEWING WHAT YOU HAVE LEARNED

1. Describe some general guidelines for eating the right kinds and amounts of food.
2. Why do the caloric needs differ for different people?
3. What is the best way to lose weight?
4. What are three reasons that manufactured food has become part of our food supply?

USING YOUR CRITICAL THINKING SKILLS

1. Why are American consumers eating more and more convenience foods?
2. Explain why people have an emotional need for food.

APPLYING WHAT YOU HAVE LEARNED

1. Plan some nutritious snacks for a small child, an elderly person, and yourself. Explain why your choices would be good ones.
2. Identify two ethnic groups in your community. How do their food and eating patterns differ? Share what you learn with the class.

CHAPTER 17

Our Food Needs and Wants

OBJECTIVES

After completing this chapter, you will be able to do the following:
1. Name the factors that consumers consider when buying food.
2. List the five major industries involved in supplying our food needs.
3. Describe how our food system is regulated.
4. Describe the procedure you will follow when making a complaint about a food product.

TERMS

fast foods
processor

retailer
transporter

vertical integration
wholesaler

Today, in your local supermarket you can choose among the widest variety of food products ever assembled. Many organizations are working to ensure good, safe, and nutritious foods in the stores. Even so, we all need to be well informed in order to make the right food-buying decisions.

THE FOOD CONSUMER

Values change over time, bringing changes in the way we eat as well as what we eat. Today, the average consumer drinks more than 350 cans of soft drinks per year, and we consume 50 pounds of snack foods per person per year. We want less kitchen work, improved food quality, a greater variety of food, and lower food costs.

How Do Values Influence Food Decisions?

What makes a good buy in foods? Most consumers buy food with the following considerations in mind:

- Does my family like it? Will it look, taste, and smell good to them? People tend to base many food decisions on their cultural heritage. Consider bread, for instance. In the South, cornbread is popular; but in New England, brown bread is more acceptable. A sale on brown bread would be a bargain for one family but not for another.

- Is the food safe and nutritious? Read the labels on products to find out what nutrients they provide and what additives they contain.

- How much will the food cost? Does it fit into the budget? You may have

In the past, people made their own bread out of need. Today, people typically make their own bread for recreation or pleasure, and bread machines have made the task even easier. If you can measure ingredients, you can make bread!

to eat beans on Wednesday in order to eat salmon on Friday.

- Is convenience worth the price? Consumers who prepare homemade meals spend up to five hours per day on food preparation. Those who use convenience foods spend as little as one hour per day preparing food. Eating at restaurants is another choice consumers make regarding convenience and price.

Eating Out. In 1929, Americans ate only 13 percent of their meals outside the home. Sixty five years later, in 1994, the figure was more than 30 percent, and we spent 43 percent of our food budget eating out. The average teenager eats 25 percent of all meals away from home.

More and more people are eating at fast-food restaurants where the food is prepared and served quickly. The average American spends nearly $1,000 a year on **fast foods**, yet the food at

fast foods
....

foods that can be prepared and served quickly, often with little regard for nutritional value

Four Cost Levels for One Week of Food at Home

Age (years)	Thrifty	Low	Moderate	Liberal
Children				
1-2	$19.50	$24.50	$30.25	$35.75
3-5	23.50	29.25	36.25	43.50
6-8	30.00	38.25	47.75	57.25
9-11	37.75	47.75	59.75	71.50
Males				
12-14	40.25	50.75	63.50	75.75
15-19	44.00	56.00	70.00	84.25
20-54	42.50	55.00	69.25	83.25
Over 54	37.75	48.50	60.25	72.00
Females				
12-19	35.50	45.25	56.00	66.75
20-54	34.50	44.25	55.50	65.75
Over 54	31.25	40.00	49.25	58.50
Family of two				
20-54 years	84.75	109.25	136.75	164.00

Figure 17.1

This chart shows estimates of what families might spend weekly on food to eat at home. Costs must be added to find the total cost for a family. For example, if a family's spending habits are in the moderate range and they have one child 3–5 years of age ($36.25), one male age 15–19 ($70.00), one male age 20–54 ($69.25), and one female age 20–54 ($55.50), the total cost for groceries for one week would be around $231.00. How much does your family spend on food each week?

these restaurants is inexpensive compared to other eating places. Even so, most of these foods could be prepared for less money at home. Judging by its popularity, people like fast foods. Many fast-food restaurants have reduced the level of fat in some of their offerings, but most fast foods are high in fat and have few vitamins and minerals. Some of these restaurants have begun offering salads or skinless meats. If you eat at fast-food restaurants often, select foods that will help you eat a balanced diet.

HOW CAN I AFFORD THE COST OF FOOD?

There are many factors to be weighed before purchasing food, but one factor has the most influence over what we choose to buy. This factor is the amount of money we have for food. Stretching the food dollar in today's economy is a challenge.

The United States Department of Agriculture (USDA) has prepared estimates of how much money four different types of families might spend for food. Recent figures are given in Figure 17.1.

The Food Stamp Program uses the Thrifty Plan as a basis for the allotment of food stamp coupons. Food stamps are made available by the government to people with limited incomes, and these stamps can be used in place of money to pay for food.

As consumers, we need to consider the trade-offs surrounding the food budget. Remember, the more food prepared at home, the lower the cost. However, more and more consumers have less and less time for food preparation, and the time and energy savings we get from convenience foods may well be worth the higher cost. You

retailer

in the food industry, the people or companies that sell food to consumers

processor

in the food industry, the people or companies that prepare and package food products

transporter

in the food industry, the people or companies that move food between the other steps of the industry

wholesaler

in the food industry, the people or companies that store the food and make it available to the retailers

must make the food-buying decisions that are right for you.

THE FOOD INDUSTRY

The food industry is one of the largest industries in the United States, with more than $700 billion spent on food and food-related products in 1994. Nearly one-fifth of all workers in the United States are engaged in the food marketing system to meet the consumer demand for healthful, convenient, economical food. Different people are involved at different steps of food marketing:

- The producer grows and harvests the food.
- The **processor** prepares the food products and puts them into packages.
- The **transporter** moves food between the other food industries.

- The **wholesaler** stores the food and makes it available to the retailer.
- The **retailer** sells the food to the consumer.

At each step, the costs of labor, transportation, advertising, and promotion are added—and a profit must be made at each step, too. For example, a retailer will generally make between 1 percent and 2 percent profit. Some foods change hands ten or more times before reaching the grocery shelf. For example, consider the journey a taco shell makes before you can eat it at home:

1. Corn is harvested by a farmer.
2. The corn is hauled to a grain elevator and stored.
3. The corn is shipped to the processor by rail.
4. The corn is transported from a railroad car to the processing plant.
5. The corn is milled and shipped to a taco-mix maker.
6. The mix is shipped to the plant in which taco shells are made and packaged.

In the food industry, the producer grows and harvests the food and the transporter hauls the food between the different steps of the food industry. Why would few steps between the producer and the consumer be important to the consumer?

Processors prepare and package foods for the consumer. Which food items in your supermarket have had little processing? Which have had more processing? What does this do to the price of the product?

vertical integration
....

a situation in which
one group controls all
the steps in the food
marketing system

7. The packaged product is transported to a regional warehouse and stored.

8. The packaged product is shipped to a wholesaler and stored.

9. The packaged product is shipped to a retail outlet.

10. The packaged product is bought by you (an individual consumer) and taken home.

The California Department of Food and Agriculture estimates that sixty cents of every dollar consumers spend on food goes to pay for the packing, shipping, handling, brokering (trading), wholesaling, distributing, and retailing of food.

Who Controls the Food Supply?

Some consumer and farm groups are concerned about the **vertical integration** they see taking place in the food marketing system. Vertical integration occurs when one group controls all the steps in the system. The control ranges from the food producers to the group responsible for disposing of the food wrappings.

As much as 60% of our food money goes to pay for processing and transporting the foods we buy. Check the price of one of your favorite processed foods (cookies, cereal, frozen pizza, etc.). Subtract 60% from the price. What is the actual cost of the food (without the processing)?

The Federal Trade Commission (FTC) estimates that 1 percent of the twenty thousand food-manufacturing firms control 80 percent of the total food manufacturing assets. This allows those firms to influence prices for a number of products.

Who Controls Food Quality?

Who protects our food? Food regulation is a partnership between:

- federal government agencies responsible for food protection
- state and local agencies with inspector or enforcement functions
- research scientists in laboratories and colleges and universities
- the food service industry
- the consumer

Regulation by Government Agencies. Prior to the 1900s, there were no food regulations or laws. Today, the Food and Drug Administration (FDA) and the Department of Health and Human Services, along with the United States Department of Agriculture (USDA), are charged with ensuring the safety of the nation's food supply. Other federal agencies involved include the Environmental Protection Agency (EPA), the Public Health Service, and the Department of Transportation.

The USDA conducts inspections of meat, meat products, poultry, poultry products, eggs, and dairy products for purity. Each processing plant must be registered and is subject to inspection of the premises at all times. Inspectors check to see that the plants are adhering to the federal standards for wholesomeness and sanitation. The USDA also inspects these food products for grade and quality if they are requested to do so.

The FDA regulates all foods except meat, poultry, and milk products. This agency develops standards to regulate the quality and safety of foods, food additives, and colors.

State and county representatives check food establishments on an unannounced schedule. They also expect the industry to do a good job of policing itself.

As consumers, we pay the costs of food regulation through taxes to support the federal agencies. More directly, the cost of complying with food safety regulations is added to the cost of the product on the grocery store shelf, but the result is better, safer products.

Making a Complaint

Sometimes consumers get inferior or defective products. This happens in spite of all the care taken by the food processor and all of the inspecting done by the government. If you get an inferior product, the FDA suggests you follow these procedures:

- Report your complaint promptly. Give your name, address, and telephone number.

CONSUMER PROFILE

Gabe went to his neighborhood supermarket to buy some chicken to fix for dinner. He chose a package of chicken thighs. When he got home and opened the package, it smelled terrible. He checked the date on the package, but it had not expired. He took his receipt and the opened chicken back to the store and spoke with the manager. The manager replaced his package with one that was more fresh.

Gabe kept the label from the bad package and sent it to the company with a copy of his receipt. He wrote a brief letter and described what happened. A few weeks later, Gabe received two coupons in the mail for free packages of chicken.

- State clearly what is wrong.
- Describe the label of the product. Give any code marks that appear on the container.
- Give the name and address of the store where the item was purchased and the date of the purchase.
- Save whatever remains of the product for examination by a doctor or the FDA.
- Save any unopened container of the product bought at the same time.
- If any injury is involved, see a doctor.
- Report the suspect product to the manufacturer, packer, or distributor shown on the label of the product. Also report the product to the store manager where you purchased it.

Summary

- Eating out is very popular in America. Even in restaurants, try to select foods that help you eat a balanced diet.
- The food industry is one of the largest industries in the United States.
- Generally, food goes through many steps before it reaches the consumer. It goes from the producer, to the processor, the transporter, the wholesaler, and the retailer. Each step adds cost.
- Food quality is regulated by a partnership that includes: federal government agencies, state and local agencies, research scientists, the food service industry, and the consumer.
- If you get an inferior product, report it to the manufacturer, packer, or distributor shown on the label of the product. Also report it to the store manager where you bought it.

CHAPTER REVIEW 17

ENRICHING YOUR VOCABULARY

Write each sentence and complete it using one of the following words or phrases.

fast foods   retailer   vertical integration
processor   transporter   wholesaler

1. Food is prepared and packaged for sale by the
2. A food retailer buys most foods from a
3. A trucker is a common food
4. A supermarket is a food

5. Inexpensive restaurant foods that are prepared and served quickly are called
6. Control of all the steps in the food marketing system in order to influence prices is called

REVIEWING WHAT YOU HAVE LEARNED

1. What factors do consumers consider when buying food?
2. Identify the five major industries involved in supplying our food needs.

3. Describe how our food system is regulated.
4. What procedure would you follow when making a complaint about a food product?

USING YOUR CRITICAL THINKING SKILLS

1. Each step in the food marketing system adds to the cost of food. What can be done to reduce the number of steps in order to reduce costs to the consumer?
2. Suppose one soft drink manufacturer controlled the market (set the price) for soft

drinks. Then suppose a competitor became strong. What effect would you expect this to have on the price of soft drinks? Explain.

APPLYING WHAT YOU HAVE LEARNED

1. Figure the cost per serving of hot dogs, bologna, and peanut butter.
2. Compare the cost per serving of four different forms of potatoes: raw potatoes, frozen french

fries, dehydrated mashed potatoes (instant), and potato chips.

CHAPTER 18

Buying Food

OBJECTIVES

After completing this chapter, you will be able to do the following:
1. List the information required on food containers by the Fair Packaging and Labeling Act, including changes made in 1992.
2. List four reasons why nutrition labeling is important.
3. List three reasons why food additives are used.

TERMS

cash-and-carry
chain store
coupons
dehydrated
discount supermarket
expiration date
Fair Packaging and
    Labeling Act
farmer's market
food additives
food cooperatives

generic brands
grades
GRAS (Generally
    Recognized As Safe)
health food stores
house brands
independent store
inspected
national brands
natural foods
nutrition labeling

open dating
pack date
pull date
shelf life
specialty shops
standard of identity
supermarket
unit pricing
universal product code
    (UPC)

dehydrated
....
dried

Fair Packaging and Labeling Act
....
a law specifying what must be on a food label

standard of identity
....
ingredients common to a particular food product such as catsup

In the supermarket today, we may choose from over 10,000 items. There are many factors to consider when making decisions about which foods to buy. We must try to keep within the food budget. Family members come and go at different times. One person wants to lose weight while another one wants to gain. What foods will meet the needs of all?

There are other considerations. Food comes in many forms, such as fresh, frozen, canned, or **dehydrated** (dried). It is sold under many different brand names and varies in cost from one store to the next.

Because such a large portion of our budget is spent on food and we want to get our money's worth, we need to have as much information as possible.

Reading food labels will give the consumer many different types of information about the product. Do you read food labels? Why or why not?

In this section, we will learn to use information to help us understand our food alternatives.

WHAT LABELS TELL US

A great deal of information is given on food packaging and labels, and most of it is easy to understand—but some is not. The government enacted the **Fair Packaging and Labeling Act** in 1966. This act requires that the following be on a label, written in English:

* Name of the product.
* Name and place of business of the processor.
* Net contents by weight, measure, or count.
* Ingredients, listed in order from the greatest in weight to the least. This is not necessary for some common food products. For foods such as catsup and mayonnaise, a **standard of identity** has been established by the FDA. This means the product contains standard ingredients in amounts needed to make it.
* Any additives used in the product to flavor, color, or preserve it.
* Nutritional content of any food for which nutritional claims are made or that have nutrients added to the food.

A new food labeling law, enacted in 1992, requires that the labels provide the percent of Daily Value of particular ingredients. These ingredients are fat, saturated fat, cholesterol, carbohydrates, fiber, and sodium. The law also established standards for the use of the words "fat free," "low fat," "lean," "light," or "cholesterol free" on food labels. The new laws help consumers to choose healthier foods. (See Figure 18.1.)

Nutrition Labeling

Today's consumers have become more interested in the nutritional value of foods. If a processor makes nutritional claims about a product or adds nutrients to it, the FDA requires **nutrition labeling**. This is a list of the kinds and amounts of nutrients contained in the product. All the information on the label applies to a single serving and is listed in the following order:

1. Serving size and number of servings.
2. Number of calories.
3. Protein, carbohydrate, and fat content—given in grams.
4. Percentage of the U.S. Recommended Daily Allowance of protein, vitamin A, vitamin C, thiamin, riboflavin, niacin, calcium, and iron. These must be shown if present; other nutrients may or may not be shown. (See Figure 18.2 on the next page.)

Nutrition labeling is especially helpful to consumers who are on restricted diets; who need to limit sodium, sugar, or fat intake; or who are counting calories. Nutrition labeling is also helpful to consumers who have certain allergies and who may need to avoid allergy-producing substances, such as artificial flavoring or food coloring.

Food Additives

Food additives are substances put into food to beautify, retard spoilage, or improve the nutritional value of food. In 1990, more than half of the food sold contained food additives. Each of us eats more than five pounds of food additives per year.

Over 2,800 different substances are used in foods today. The most popular of these are sugar, salt, corn syrup, pepper, citric acid (from lemons and oranges), baking soda, vegetable colors, and mustard. Look at some food labels. What other substances are listed?

About 700 substances appear on the **GRAS** (Generally Recognized As Safe) list prepared by the Food and Drug Administration (FDA). These substances

nutrition labeling

a listing of the kinds and quantities of nutrients in a product

food additives

substances added to foods to enhance appearance, nutritional value, or shelf life

GRAS (Generally Recognized As Safe)

a list of food substances tested and proved to be safe by the Food and Drug Administration

Definitions of Food Label Terms

fat free —contains half a gram or less of fat per serving

low fat —contains 3 grams or less of fat per serving

lean —contains not more than 10 grams of fat, not more than 4 grams of saturated fat and less than 95 milligrams of cholesterol per serving

light —there are three meanings, a product needs to meet only one:
1. a serving provides one-third fewer calories or half the fat of the regular product;
2. a serving of a low-calorie, low-fat food provides half the sodium normally present;
3. the product is light in color and texture

cholesterol free —contains no cholesterol or a trivial amount

Figure 18.1

The government has recently established standards for use of some words commonly found on food labels. Now when consumers see these words on food labels, they know what the words mean.

Figure 18.2

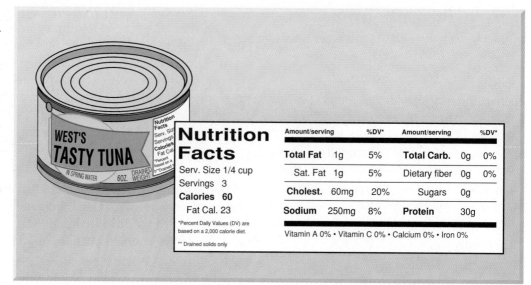

The percentages of
nutrients listed on a
Nutrition Fact Panel
are based on a 2,000
calorie diet. What
percentage of a 2,000
calorie diet does one
serving of this tuna
fulfill for sodium? For
total fat? What is the
size of one serving of
this tuna? How many
servings in a can?

national brands

brands of food that are
available nationwide

natural foods

foods that do not
contain additives or
have excessive
processing

house brands

private-label items
found only in one chain
of supermarkets

shelf life

the length of time a
product can be safely
stored

have been tested and proved to be safe.
Food processors can add these to food
without obtaining approval from the
federal government, which monitors
the use of food additives in our foods.

Not all people favor the use of food
additives, particularly chemical additives. Some consumers feel additives
are used unnecessarily, and that certain
additives may cause allergic reactions
in some people.

Consumers who wish to avoid additives and excessive processing are buying **natural foods**. There are no
government regulations regarding the
standards for labeling foods as "natural," so consumers need to be sure they
understand what they are buying. Generally, natural foods have a shorter
shelf life than processed foods. Shelf

life is the length of time the foods can
be stored. A natural food may cost up
to one-and-a-half times as much as a
similar product that has been
processed, usually because the supply is
limited and it has a shorter shelf life.

Brand Labels

National brands are sold across the
country in many different stores, and
they are heavily advertised. They are
generally more expensive than other
foods of the same type, but they tend
to be consistent in quality.

House brands are sometimes called
"private labels." These are products
found only in one chain of supermarkets. (All "Market M" stores carry
"Market M" canned and frozen

*Natural foods usually
cost more than foods
that are processed
regularly. Have you
ever purchased
natural foods? Why?
Did you feel they
were worth the extra
money you had to
spend?*

LABELING FOR SPECIAL NEEDS

Helen Ortega cannot tolerate sodium so she cannot eat most processed foods. For years, she has bought only those labeled as low sodium or reduced sodium. Unfortunately, low-sodium products are often more expensive to buy than regular products because they must be specially processed.

Most of Helen's food must be prepared from basic substances. She can't eat in most fast-food restaurants—and in other restaurants, she requests that no salt be used. Listing sodium content on nutrition labels, as required by the 1992 labeling law, makes it easier for Helen to find food she can eat safely.

foods.) The quality of these products is usually the same or close to the quality of the national brand products. In fact, they are often produced by national companies and packaged under the store's label. The products generally cost a little less.

Generic brands list no copyrighted brand name—only the name of the product is given. Generic products cost less than national brand products, but the nutritional value is generally the same. The quality may not be as good, though. For example, generic peaches may be chopped up into less uniform pieces than national brand peaches. If you are going to cut up the peaches to use them in a salad, the generic peaches might be the best buy. If appearance is important, you might want to buy the national brand product. Because needs are different, our selections will also be different.

Open Dating

Consumers are concerned with the freshness of a product, so many food processors put dates on their packages. This is called open dating. These dates tell the consumer and the store owner when a product has passed its peak of perfection or should no longer be used.

There are three ways products can be dated. The pack date tells us the day the food was manufactured, processed, or packaged. A pull date may also be listed. This is the last day a store

Dairy products typically have an expiration date after which the product will probably not be fit for use. It's important to check the dates on dairy products carefully, many times stores do not remove products after their expiration date has passed. Have you ever purchased a dairy product that was spoiled? What did you do?

generic brands
....
products with no brand names

open dating
....
date placed on a product that indicates peak performance or use

pack date
....
the date a food was processed and packaged

pull date
....
the last date a food can be offered for sale but not the last day it can be eaten

Glossary Terms (left margin)

expiration date

last date a food product is acceptable for intended use

grades

quality ratings given to meat, eggs, and dairy products by the U.S. Department of Agriculture (USDA)

inspected

checked to ensure proper labeling and wholesomeness

universal product code (UPC)

electronic label that identifies the processor, package contents, and price of a product

---

should offer the food for sale but not the last day it can be eaten. The **expiration date** is the last day the food may be acceptable for intended use. For example, milk may begin to sour after the given date.

Grading and Inspecting

About half of all the money we spend on food is spent on meat, eggs, and dairy products. These products are available in various **grades**, or quality ratings, given by the United States Department of Agriculture (USDA). The higher the grade, the better the quality and the more expensive the product. A higher grade does not tell you anything about the nutritional value of the food.

Foods such as meat and poultry are **inspected**. This is different from grading. "Inspected" means that the food has been checked to ensure proper labeling and wholesomeness. Meat-packing plants and raw meats are inspected for sanitation and contamination. Grading and most inspecting are voluntary, but inspection of meat and poultry is required.

Meats are graded by the U.S. Department of Agriculture. The grades you will probably see at your supermarket are prime, choice, and good. Prime is the highest or best ranking, while a ranking of good usually means the meat has less fat and is less tender.

METRICS ON LABELS

Nutrition labels use metric units, with amounts given in grams instead of ounces because grams are smaller units of measure. Many ingredients in foods are present in small amounts. The following key will help you:

1 pound (lb.) = 454 grams (g)
1 ounce (oz.) = 28 grams (g)
1 gram (g) = 1000 milligrams (mg)
1 milligram (mg) = 100 micrograms (mcg)
1 quart (qt.) = .95 Liter (l)

Universal Product Code

You have probably noticed a pattern of black and white lines on food packages. This is a **universal product code (UPC)**, and it identifies the food processor and what the package contains. A scanner at the supermarket "reads" the code and records the price on a tape. The UPC checkout system is faster than the older systems, and it eliminates the marking of individual foods in the store. It can make comparison shopping a little more difficult, so check printouts carefully for accuracy.

DETERMINING THE BEST FOOD BUY

Compare prices to determine the best food buy. To do this, you need to know:
- the price per unit (ounce, liter, pound, etc.)

Making Consumer Decisions

House brand products usually cost a little less than national brands and are of the same quality. Generic products generally cost less than house brands or name-brand products, but the quality and flavor may also be inferior.

In an effort to save money on her grocery bill, Renata decided to look for house brands and generic products for some items on her shopping list. Her list included sugar, coffee, hamburger, tomatoes, cooking oil, bread, salt, cheese, canned tuna fish, mayonnaise, butter, peanut butter, and milk.

She decided that, if her store had them, she should buy generic or house brand sugar, cooking oil, salt, cheese, tuna fish, and butter. She had favorite brands, however, of coffee, bread, mayonnaise, and peanut butter and didn't want to give those up.

Which foods would you be interested in replacing with generic or house brand products? Which ones would you not be interested in replacing? Is it worth the savings to you? How much do you think you would save? What are some other ways to save money on your grocery bill?

- the number of servings the unit provides

Unit pricing provides the cost of food per unit, and it helps us compare costs for different sizes of packages. It is usually found on tags on the shelf beneath the product. If the unit price is not given, you can calculate it by dividing the cost by the number of units. Suppose a 48 oz. bottle of apple juice is priced at $2.16. Divide $2.16 by 48 to get the unit price of $.045 per ounce.

The number of servings per unit enables you to determine the cost per serving. Chicken may cost less per pound (unit cost) than ground meat, but bones make up part of the chicken's weight. Since the bones are not eaten, there is waste. This means that you can get more servings from a pound of ground meat than you can from a pound of chicken, so the cost per serving for the ground meat may be less.

Checking for Quality

You will need to be an alert shopper to ensure that you are getting the highest quality food for your money. Bulging cans, broken seals on packages, and torn inner liners are bad signs—indicating the food may be stale or even spoiled. (Never purchase or eat these foods.) Foods such as milk should be refrigerated and cold when purchased. Frozen foods should be frozen solid. The color of food is a good clue to its freshness, too. Some private or independent stores buy food from local farmers to help assure its freshness and quality.

Deciding on Quantity

Some food purchase decisions are more important than others and will have a greater effect on our budgets. For example, suppose you are trying to make a decision between two cereal box sizes—a decision that won't cost a great deal of money. However, if you buy a quarter or half of beef and put it in a freezer, you are investing several hundred dollars. You may want to seek more information and spend more time selecting the expensive items.

unit pricing
....
the cost of food per unit of measurement

Remember that buying in large quantities is not always the best buy. Check the unit pricing to be sure the larger size offers the best value—if so, ask yourself if you have room to store the food, and if you will use all of it. Then decide whether the large size is the best buy.

Deciding Where to Shop

Shop around for a store that best meets your needs. Look for the lowest prices in local markets on items that you buy frequently. If prices are much lower at a market way across town, you may want to make that trip perhaps once a month to stock up on certain items. Be sure to consider how much gasoline it would take to drive across town to another store. Sometimes it's even worth paying a price that is considerably higher for one or two items at a so-called convenience store when you are really in a hurry.

Supermarkets. The supermarket has become an important part of the shopping center of today. Most supermarkets follow the cash-and-carry policy on merchandising. There are usually no charge accounts or delivery services. Customers pay "cash" (or by check, debit card, or bank card) and "carry" the food away themselves. These stores buy and operate in large volume and minimize operating expense with self-service. Over 80 percent of all food sales are made in supermarkets.

Chain Stores. A chain store is one of several stores under common ownership and management. Chain stores buy in large quantities to provide real savings to the customer, and they are usually cash-and-carry stores.

Independent Stores. An independent store is owned and operated by an individual or group of individuals. This kind of store buys in relatively small quantities, but it may stock hard-to-get food items that cannot be purchased at other stores. Credit and delivery service are sometimes available at independent stores, too.

Specialty Shops. specialty shops. These carry only certain products such as meat, fish, baked goods, candy, or fruits and vegetables. Delicatessens and food sections in department stores are examples of specialty shops. They may be independently owned or part of a chain and usually offer more service than the larger chain stores or supermarkets.

Health Food Stores. Health food stores sell "organic" foods—that is, foods grown without use of artificial fertilizers or chemicals such as pesticides. Processed foods sometimes are also called "organic" if they are made

A farmer's market (see page 190) is a direct point of sale between the producer and the consumer. We know that the processors and transporters who handle food between the producer and consumer add cost to the price of the food. If this is so, would you expect the prices at a farmer's market to be higher or lower than prices in a supermarket? Why?

specialty shops
....
stores that offer only certain products

health food stores
....
stores that sell natural foods—foods grown without the use of artificial fertilizers or other chemicals

supermarket
....
a type of large volume food store which accounts for 80 percent of food sales

cash-and-carry
....
a store policy that allows the customers to pay for a product and take it with them

chain store
....
one of several stores under common ownership

independent store
....
a store owned and operated by an individual or a group of individuals

CHECKLIST FOR BUYING FOOD

When you buy food, follow these guidelines:

___ To obtain the best food value, plan your meals before you go shopping. If possible, plan menus for a week at a time.

___ Make a list of the items that you have used or that will need to be purchased.

___ Avoid impulse buying. Except for substitutions, don't vary from your list.

___ Know the regular prices of the items that you shop for. Then you can determine whether the advertised specials are really bargains.

___ Take advantage of unit pricing. Make price comparisons by figuring the costs per serving. This is more important than the price on the package, so if you can't do the quick arithmetic, take a small calculator with you.

___ Compare costs of foods that are similar in nutritional value. Prices may vary widely for products with similar nutritional value.

___ Buy foods in large quantities if the unit price is less, you have storage space, and your family likes the foods.

___ Don't shop when you are hungry.

___ Take advantage of foods in season. Know when these products will be good buys.

___ Buy the quality that is best for the use you have planned for a product. Mushroom pieces may work just as well as whole mushrooms on a pizza, and they cost less than whole or sliced mushrooms.

___ Buy foods in the physical condition that is best for your needs. For example, foods you will use right away can be purchased fresh. Foods that must be stored may be bought frozen, dried, or in cans.

___ Read labels. Recognize manufacturers' brand names. Become familiar with the quality of the products they sell.

___ Clip and use coupons for items you plan to use.

___ Consider private-label products. Store brands may be similar to national brands but are less expensive. This may be simply because distribution and advertising costs are lower.

___ Handle merchandise carefully. Ruining a package costs a store money. So does taking something out of a refrigerated case and not putting it back. These costs are passed on to all consumers.

___ Watch the scales when your food is weighed and the cash register when you check out.

___ Separate non-food items from food items to find out what you are really spending for food. About twenty-five cents of every dollar spent in a grocery store goes for such items as health and beauty aids, pet food, and detergents.

___ Store foods properly when you get home.

___ Prepare foods correctly. Improper cooking can destroy most of the nutritional value of foods.

___ Plan to use leftovers.

Fresh produce bought at supermarkets may not contain additives, but it may have a residue caused by pesticides on its surface. So it is important to wash produce carefully before preparing and eating it.

wide a selection of produce or fresh meats, vegetables, and dairy products as other supermarkets. Some don't accept coupons, and it may be necessary to buy a membership in order to shop in these stores. They are also usually less conveniently located, so the savings must be enough to offset the disadvantages of shopping in such a store.

from products grown in this way and do not contain artificial additives. In the 1990s, consumers spent over three billion dollars each year on organic foods. These foods are often higher-priced than foods in supermarkets—and they may not keep as long during storage.

Farmer's Markets. The **farmer's market** sells food directly from the farmer to the customer. This is one way the city dweller can obtain fresh produce directly from the producer.

Food Cooperatives. Some groups have formed **food cooperatives** in order to buy in large quantities and sell at prices lower than other food stores. There are over 7,000 food cooperatives in the United States.

Discount Supermarkets. The **discount supermarket** is a store that sells food at reduced prices. These warehouse or "box stores" generally carry 400 to 1,000 items. Most don't have as

PROMOTING FOOD PRODUCTS

The success or failure of products depends in large part on how they are advertised and marketed, and this is especially true for new products. Food industries spend over $500 million each year to research and develop new products, and they market almost 9,000 new food items each year. That is about 24 new items a day, but only about 500 of the 9,000 new items survive.

Advertising helps inform consumers about products, and companies spend a great deal of money on advertising in hopes it will pay off by increasing sales. Three cereal companies alone spend about $50 million annually to advertise their new products. Cola drink companies annually spend more than $100 million.

Advertising costs make products more expensive. About three and a half cents of every dollar spent on food goes to help pay for advertising and promotion. One out of every five commercials on TV is for food or drink.

Advertisements by private businesses may help you find bargains, but sometimes advertisements for specials lead you to stores in which all other products are higher priced. Remember, too, that specials are good buys only if you need the items.

Displays and packaging are parts of advertising. Attractive food displays make it hard to resist buying foods, and advertisers know that we are attracted by see-through colorful packages. Studies show that during each visit to a grocery store, the average consumer buys three more items than planned.

The food industry also spends about three billion dollars each year on coupons and special promotions. Coupons are special certificates good for money off regular prices. Coupons help introduce us to new products, but they are valuable only if we *need* and *plan* to use the products being offered.

You find coupons in newspapers, magazines, and inside product packages. Some companies offer coupons or cash refunds by mail. For example, a company might state that if you send in two proofs of purchase of a certain product, the company will send you fifty cents. Read product packages and printed ads to find such offers. Many newspapers include informational articles, as a service for consumers, about special offers and other ways to save money.

Summary

- The labels on food packaging provide a great deal of information.

- The FDA requires nutrition labeling—a list of the kinds and amounts of nutrients contained in the product.

- You need to be an alert and informed shopper in order to get the highest-quality food for your money.

- Shop around for the food store that best meets your needs. Depending on what's available in your area, you can choose from supermarkets, chain stores, independent stores, specialty shops, health food stores, farmer's markets, food cooperatives, and discount supermarkets.

- A few tips for getting the best value for your food shopping dollar: plan your meals before you go shopping; avoid impulse buying; don't shop when you're hungry; take advantage of foods in season; clip and use coupons for items you plan to use; plan to use leftovers.

coupons
....
certificates good for money off regular prices

E NRICHING YOUR VOCABULARY

Number your paper from 1–29. Beside each number write the word or phrase that matches that definition. Choose your answers from the following list.

cash-and-carry
chain store
coupons
dehydrated
discount supermarket
expiration date
Fair Packaging
    and Labeling Act
farmer's market
food additives
food cooperatives

generic brands
grades
GRAS (Generally Recognized
    As Safe)
health food stores
house brands
independent store
inspected
national brands
natural foods
nutrition labeling

open dating
pack date
pull date
shelf life
specialty shops
standard of identity
supermarket
unit pricing
universal product code (UPC)

1. dried
2. labels available nationally
3. label identifying processor and package contents
4. groups established for buying food in large quantities
5. certificates good for money off regular prices
6. ingredients common to a particular food product
7. a list of food substances tested for safety
8. cost of food per unit of measurement
9. pay for product and take it with you
10. direct point of sale between customer and farmer
11. last date a food product is acceptable for intended use
12. private labels
13. quality ratings of USDA
14. foods without additives or excessive processing

15. length of time product can be safely stored
16. large-volume food store accounting for 80 percent of food sales
17. warehouse supermarket
18. substances added to foods to enhance appearance, nutritional value, or shelf life
19. one of several stores under common ownership
20. list of kinds and quantities of nutrients in a product
21. product with no brand name
22. date of peak performance or use
23. checked to ensure proper labeling and wholesomeness
24. store owned and operated by individuals
25. law specifying what must be on a food label
26. last date a food may be offered for sale
27. a store that sells natural foods
28. date a food was processed and packaged
29. stores that offer only certain food products

CHAPTER REVIEW
18

REVIEWING WHAT YOU HAVE LEARNED

1. List the information that is required on food containers by the Fair Packaging and Labeling Act. What changes were made in the law in 1992?

2. Give four reasons why nutrition labeling is important.

3. Most foods are cheaper when bought in large quantities. Why shouldn't this be done in all cases? Give examples.

4. List three reasons why food additives are used.

USING YOUR CRITICAL THINKING SKILLS

1. In what types of stores do you and other members of your family shop? Discuss your reasons for shopping in these stores.

2. Compare your shopping experiences with those of other members of your class. (For example, perhaps you found that certain food products could be bought more cheaply in one store than they could in another. Why?)

APPLYING WHAT YOU HAVE LEARNED

1. Go to a grocery store. Work together in pairs or small groups. Compare generic, store brands, and brand-name products for cost and quality.

   Make a list. Write down the name of a food product (such as green beans). Then, write the most you can spend and the least you can spend for the product. (Be sure the containers you compare hold the same amounts.) Compare the quality of the cheaper and the more expensive products.

   Compare at least five different types of food products. Total your recorded prices. Can you save money and still buy quality products? Share your results with your classmates.

2. Make a list of the grocery items needed for your household for the following week. Then go through the grocery ads in your local newspaper to find the best price for each item on your list. Finally, decide which store (or stores) will be the best choice for your grocery shopping this week.

UNIT

7

CLOTHING

CHAPTERS

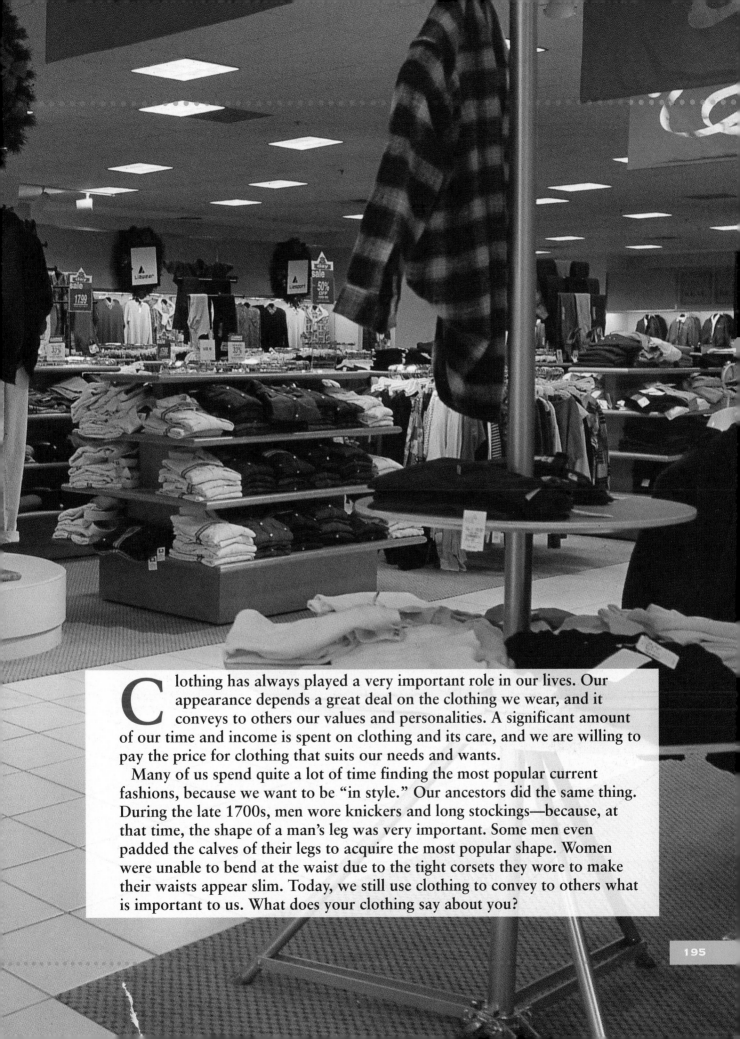

Clothing has always played a very important role in our lives. Our appearance depends a great deal on the clothing we wear, and it conveys to others our values and personalities. A significant amount of our time and income is spent on clothing and its care, and we are willing to pay the price for clothing that suits our needs and wants.

Many of us spend quite a lot of time finding the most popular current fashions, because we want to be "in style." Our ancestors did the same thing. During the late 1700s, men wore knickers and long stockings—because, at that time, the shape of a man's leg was very important. Some men even padded the calves of their legs to acquire the most popular shape. Women were unable to bend at the waist due to the tight corsets they wore to make their waists appear slim. Today, we still use clothing to convey to others what is important to us. What does your clothing say about you?

CHAPTER 19

Influences on What We Wear

OBJECTIVES

After completing this chapter, you will be able to do the following:
1. Explain the major influences on clothing decisions.
2. List five factors that affect our choice of clothing.
3. List four physical influences on our choice of clothing.

TERMS

imports   natural fibers   synthetic fibers

Clothing serves many purposes, so we must plan clothing purchases according to the purpose the clothing is to serve. The final selection of specific items may be influenced by many factors, including the following:

- physical
- psychological and social
- economic
- technological
- cultural and ethnic

PHYSICAL INFLUENCES

Physically, we want to be comfortable no matter where we are or what we are doing. When selecting clothing, we consider the temperature of our surroundings and the length of exposure to the environment. Brief exposure

The social influences on what we wear can be very strong. Sometimes we want to look like everyone else, and sometimes we don't. What has the strongest influence on what you wear?

to hot or cold temperatures requires different clothing than lengthy exposure to temperature extremes. We also consider such factors as humidity, windchill, and exposure to sunlight. Our body's physical condition and the level of our activity influence our clothing choices, too. All of these factors influence how we feel and how we dress.

Some clothing is used for protection, such as the special-purpose garments often worn on the job. Steel-toed boots, designed to protect feet from sharp objects, and special suits, designed to protect workers from chemicals and radiation, are examples of protective clothing. Simple rain gear and wide-brimmed hats are other examples of clothing that are designed to provide protection.

The number of layers of clothing, the color of the clothing, and its fiber content affect how comfortable we are. Some people are allergic to fibers such as wool; others react to dyes or finish materials placed on fabrics. Soaps, detergents, and fabric-softening agents may also cause skin irritations.

Personal Considerations

Since we do not all look alike, we need to understand ourselves and make consumer decisions accordingly. We want to buy clothing that will help us present ourselves in the very best way.

At different stages of life, people have different clothing needs. Children require clothing that is comfortable, safe, durable, and easy to care for. They should be able to move freely and be comfortable. Most teens need clothing suitable for active lifestyles, but peer influences (the need to "fit in") and popular styles play an important role in clothing selection during these years. As we learn more about ourselves, we

Making Consumer Decisions

Justin wore the perfect jeans, the perfect shirt, the perfect sweater draped over his shoulder in just the right way. Justin always looked as if he just stepped out of a magazine. The way he dressed and looked, he could have been a movie or TV star.

Many of the guys tried to look and act like him, but Renny stayed away from him. Renny thought that any guy who looked like that must be a snob. "He probably isn't interested in anything but his looks," Renny thought.

In chemistry class, the teacher assigned pairs to work together on the lab assignments. Justin and Renny were paired together and Renny dreaded it. As the two worked together during the class, they got to know each other. It turned out that Justin wasn't such a bad guy! In fact, he wasn't anything like what Renny had expected. He was friendly and helpful, and the two of them became friends. In fact, they discovered that they had some of the same interests. They both enjoyed dirt bikes and started riding together on weekends. Renny's impressions of Justin had sure been wrong!

What would you think of someone who looked like Justin? How important is "first impression" to you? What first impression do you think you would make based on what you're wearing? Have you ever had the experience of discovering that your impression of someone was wrong?

make more decisions about what we like and what clothing looks best on us.

Some elderly people have difficulty putting on clothing, so they need clothing that is easy to put on and take off. This means front openings, and zippers instead of buttons. People with certain types of physical handicaps have similar problems. Properly designed clothing helps elderly and handicapped people to maintain their independence.

Type of Activity

Clothing should be suited to the activities in which we participate. If we plan to jog, for example, we wear athletic shoes, not high-platform heels. If we plan to work on the car, we wear old clothing, not the clothing we would wear to dinner in a nice restaurant. Our clothing should be suitable for the occasion.

Safety

Clothing should be safe. The Consumer Product Safety Commission establishes and enforces federal safety standards for clothing and other consumer products. This commission is an agency of the U.S. government, and it prepares reports on the number of accidents in which product design is a factor. For example, it reports annually on the number of deaths due to bathrobes with long, drooping sleeves that have been ignited while the consumer is cooking. The Consumer Product Safety Commission is discussed further in the next chapter.

Even clothing that is well designed can be a safety problem if it does not fit well. For example, wearing shoes that are too big may cause you to trip. Clothing may be made especially to protect us from harm, too, such as the special clothing designed to protect the body during various sports activities.

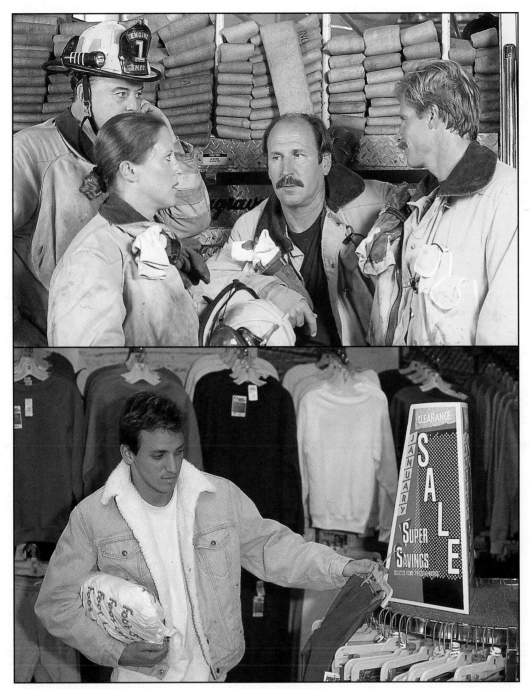

Protective clothing comes in many forms. The protective gear the firefighters are wearing is obvious. What protective clothing is being worn by the person in the bottom photo?

Protection from the Elements

Clothing is used to keep us warm in winter or cool in summer. The length of time we can be outdoors, whether working or playing, depends on how well our clothing is able to keep the body from overheating or from getting too cold. The charts in Figure 19.1 on the next page explain how clothing can be used to keep the body comfortable.

Buying Clothes

Dress to Keep Warm

Select clothing that fits loosely.

Select clothing that has tight-fitting necks and wrists to keep body heat from escaping.

Wear several layers of lightweight clothing to trap air between the layers for additional insulation.

Wear dark-colored clothes out-of-doors to absorb the heat from the sun.

Wear thick-soled shoes with linings for additional warmth.

Wear mittens instead of gloves for better insulation.

Wear a hat or scarf to prevent heat loss from the head.

Do not wear so many clothes as to cause sweating. A wet garment loses its insulating ability.

Dress to Keep Cool

Avoid tight-fitting clothing that restricts airflow.

Clothing should have large openings around neck, arms, and legs.

Avoid lined garments.

Wear a minimal number of layers of clothing.

Wear light-colored clothing to reflect the heat of the sun.

Wear open shoes or lightweight shoes and socks.

Wear a hat to protect head from sun.

Avoid scarves, belts or anything that traps body heat.

Figure 19.1
. . . .

Whether you will buy clothes to keep warm or to keep cool depends on the area in which you live. Think about the area in which you live. Do you need more warm-weather clothing or more cool-weather clothing? Which type of clothing is more expensive to buy in your area?

PSYCHOLOGICAL AND SOCIAL INFLUENCES

Besides offering physical protection, our clothing gives others clues about our personalities. Clothing says something about our likes and dislikes—even what social groups we belong to—and it is also a way of gaining recognition from others.

The First Impression

First impressions are very important in our competitive society. The marketplace is filled with items that are packaged to make a good first impression. The wrapping is the first thing consumers see, and an unattractive wrapper around a product could mean that the product will not be sold.

Our clothing is one of the first things people see when they look at us, so we want to make good first impressions—especially in competitive situations. For example, when you are looking for a job, the first impression you make needs to be a good one. Clothing often makes the difference between a good impression and a bad impression.

Besides clothing, the things we notice first about a person are visual: age, sex, and physical appearance. Depending on who we are, we use nonverbal communication about 90 percent of the time and the spoken word only about 10 percent of the time. Obviously, our appearance speaks very loudly about us.

Often our jobs require that we dress in a certain way. Think about your clothing likes and dislikes. Would you be comfortable in a job that gave you little freedom to dress as you like?

Your Personality

Clothing should match the personality of the wearer. For example, notice how, on TV, the clothing a performer wears helps us understand the character being portrayed. The same principle applies to each of us. What you wear is an extension of yourself.

Examine your wardrobe. What does it say about your personality? What does it tell others about how well you manage money, how concerned you are about detail, and which values are most important to you?

Group Identification

During adolescence, it seems especially important to be like our friends and peers—this is a time when we don't want to look or seem different from others in our age group. Most of us copy the clothing of the groups to which we want to belong. Classmates, older brothers and sisters, popular movie stars, teen fashion models, and athletes are often models for our clothing choices. We tend to select clothing to meet *others' expectations* rather

than our own. Often our choices are not based on our likes and dislikes, how the clothing makes us look, or its cost. The main purpose is to be accepted by the group to which we want to belong.

People who dress alike are generally approving of each other and may be critical of those who dress differently. Many adult consumers continue to dress like their fellow workers. For example, if you work in an office, and everyone there wears a blue suit, you will probably wear one too. If you work on a construction site, and all the other workers wear green coveralls, you, too, will probably wear green coveralls. Members of certain groups are expected to dress alike. For example, in some hospitals and doctor's offices a nurse is expected to wear a white uniform.

Dressing for the Occasion

Clothing can be classified as formal, casual, businesslike, feminine, masculine, and so on. When we are not dressed to fit our personalities or the situations we're in, people may question us or be confused by the "signals" our clothing is sending. A bank clerk dressed in feathers and sequins would appear out of place and not dressed for the occasion, so we might not want to leave our money in that bank.

Dressing for Status

Clothing goes wherever we go—and wherever we are, it can display economic and social status. For example, in the 1800s, English businessmen wore high, tight, white collars, even though this did not allow them to move their heads or breathe very well. The white collar signaled the status of an office worker. These workers did not have to do hard, dirty physical labor. The term "white-collar worker" is a result of this type of clothing. Today, the dark business suit, white shirt or blouse, and briefcase indicate the business executive.

Clothing is also used to indicate rank in our society. For example, a judge wears a robe in court.

Economic status can be shown or implied by clothing. Some people may wear designer fashions, gold jewelry, and furs to give the impression of wealth. Wearing the right labels or styles can be an important symbol of economic status among teenagers.

ECONOMIC INFLUENCES

In the middle 1990s, spending for clothing and shoes averaged just over $1,500 per person per year. This figure includes the amount spent for the care and purchase of these items and is an increase from previous years' figures.

Some of the increase is due to inflation, some to increased purchases.

Buying clothing beyond basic needs is considered discretionary spending. In recent years, the average family has been spending 5 percent to 6 percent of its budget on clothing.

Where Does the Money Go?

The family clothing dollar is divided among clothing, footwear, and care services including laundry and dry cleaning. The amount of money your family needs for clothing depends in part on where you live. Residents of Florida may need to spend less on clothing than those in Minnesota, because Florida has a warmer and more stable climate.

The fastest-growing clothing market is active sportswear. This includes clothes for swimming, tennis, golf, aerobic workout, and running. More people are participating in these activities in the 1990s, and they wear sportswear when they're not active, too. Many people have decided that they like sportswear because it's more comfortable than traditional styles, such as those worn in business offices. This is especially true of shoes. Even in fashionable Manhattan (downtown New York City), many women (when they aren't meeting the public) wear tennis or walking shoes in stores and offices. Many who do meet the public wear leather dress shoes, but put on tennis shoes when they go out for lunch.

Effects of Importing Clothing

A lot of the clothing sold in the United States comes from other countries, and these clothing **imports** influence prices. Labor costs in other countries

imports
....
products sold in the United States that come from other countries

INTERACTING WITH TECHNOLOGY

SNEAKER WARS

Torsion technology, integrated digital pressure gauge, graphite construction composite roll bar, . . . Are we talking about space shuttles or sneakers? Interestingly, these terms come from the new sneaker technology that is taking over the world of athletic footwear.

Low-tech sneakers typically have a leather or canvas upper stitched to a simple outsole. High-tech sneakers, on the other hand, don't have just an upper stitched to a sole. They have such things as multiple air chambers with pumps, honeycomb structures, and 3-D rebound systems.

What does all of this mean? It means more comfort, durability, and stability in sneakers and it also means higher prices. Most high-tech sneakers sell for anywhere from $100 to $200. Because of the potential money involved, sneaker companies are trying to develop the right technology that will sell their shoes.

Nike had the first major advance in sneaker support systems with their Air technology, introduced in 1979. This system features gas-filled chambers that contain different levels of air pressure to ensure comfort and fit.

Reebok's cushioning system uses a honeycomb structure called Hexalite. This system does not use gas or air. The Hexalite, which is used in the heel and forefoot, works like a shock absorber. Reebok also has Pump technology. In the past, this has allowed for a custom fit in the upper part of the shoe, but Reebok is working on ways to use the pump idea in the cushioning of the foot.

Adidas has Tubular technology. This system uses a pressure gauge to set different levels of pressure throughout the heel and foot areas of the sneaker.

Technology developed by the military for use in Vietnam is being used by L.A. Gear to cushion shoes. A material called Donzis Flak is a compressed foam that both cushions and adds stability to the shoe.

Comfort and fit are also being addressed by sneaker suppliers. Many are developing air conditioning systems for their shoes. Several sneaker manufacturers use a material called CoolMax to line their shoes. CoolMax improves ventilation in the shoes.

Material such as neoprene and spandex are being used by some companies to ensure a snug fit for their shoe.

Shopping for sneakers is becoming almost as confusing as shopping for a car. So, because of the potential cost involved, consumers should spend more time researching the right sneaker, for the right activity, at the right price.

are often lower than labor costs in the United States, so imported clothing tends to cost less than clothing made in the United States.

For example, shoe imports have more than doubled in recent years—now more than half of all the shoes sold in the United States are imported. This includes 41 percent of all men's footwear, 65 percent of all women's footwear, and 77 percent of all athletic shoes.

TECHNOLOG-ICAL INFLUENCES

Historically, textiles were made in the home by spinning fibers into thread or yarn and weaving the threads or knitting the yarn into fabric. Then clothing was made from the fabric. Raw products used included plant fibers, such as flax (for linen) and cotton, and animal fibers, such as wool and silk. These are called natural fibers . Animal furs and skins were also used to make clothing.

In the eighteenth and nineteenth centuries, new spinning and weaving machines were developed. The process of making fabrics and clothes was transferred from the home to the factory. Natural fibers were used until the early 1900s—then the first synthetic fiber, rayon, was developed. Rayon was followed in 1920 by acetate, and, since 1930, many new textile fibers have been invented. More recently, new and different types of fabrics and finishes have been placed on the market.

Today, we use many synthetic fibers for our clothing and textiles. Cloth made of synthetic fibers is generally less expensive and more durable than cloth made of natural fibers, and it is easy to care for and usually resists wrinkling. Even so, natural fibers of cotton and wool are still popular with many consumers. Some people prefer to wear these natural fibers because they absorb moisture and thus allow the skin to "breathe."

natural fibers
....
plant fibers such as flax and cotton; and animal fibers such as wool and silk

synthetic fibers
....
fibers made using chemicals

CULTURAL AND ETHNIC INFLUENCES

The type of clothing people wear may keep a group of people separate from the rest of society, or clothing can do just the opposite. It can make people appear more like those around them. Most people coming to the United States soon begin to dress like the people they live near. When clothing is similar, it may be difficult to tell by appearance that someone is from another country.

Most likely the only time you would see Native Americans in their native dress is during a special ceremony or demonstration. Do you have any clothing that shows your ethnic background? If so, at what times do you wear it?

Some ethnic groups have chosen not to change their clothing customs, saying they want to preserve their heritage through their dress. But most people in the United States dress in their ethnic costumes only for special parties or at holidays.

In some regions of the United States, our culture has influenced what we wear. In Milwaukee, some older women wear white scarves, tied around their heads, a style reminiscent of the women's German heritage. Sometimes, regional clothing styles become fashionable throughout the country, such as the cowboy hats and boots that have been popular in the Southwest for many years.

Clothing Related to Sex Roles

In most cultures, men and women wear different types of clothing—but as cultures change, clothing reflects these changes. As the differences in the traditional roles for men and women diminish, so do clothing differences. Today, men and women in the United States have more freedom to dress as they like. Women are free to wear pants and tailored suits, just as men are free to wear bright colors and jewelry.

Some designers say that in the future there will be little if any difference in the clothing worn by men and women. Already there are *unisex* clothing shops, and unisex costumes can be seen in TV and movie stories about the space age.

Deciding What Matters Most

Our income, occupation, social status, and family influence our clothing decisions. The climate in which we live and the way we spend our leisure time influence clothing decisions, too. We expect our clothing to keep us warm and make us more attractive. It should help us feel a part of our social group as well as portray our individuality. Clothing also provides for artistic presentation of ourselves to our world.

A person with strong aesthetic values will probably choose clothing that has an interesting design, texture, and pleasing color. A person with strong economic values may show more interest in the construction and durability of garments.

Often, we feel that we *need* a particular type of clothing when, in reality, we only *desire* it. For example, what type of clothing do we buy to keep us warm in a cold climate? The answer to that question could be very different for different people. One person might buy twenty-five dollars' worth of insulated underwear, and another may purchase a hundred-dollar angora sweater. In this case, the sweater consumer wants something in addition to basic warmth. Appearance, status, and income may all influence the decision. Whichever clothing is chosen, the need to keep warm is the most influential factor in this consumer decision.

Summary

- Our clothing conveys information to others about our values and our personalities.
- Some factors that influence our clothing choices are: physical, psychological, social, economic, technological, cultural and ethnic.
- Our clothing is one of the first things people see when they look at us. It often makes the difference between a good impression or a bad impression.

CHAPTER REVIEW
19

ENRICHING YOUR VOCABULARY

Read the following pairs of sentences. Write the sentence that correctly uses the underlined word or phrase.

1A. U.S. shoe manufacturers import their products to other countries.

1B. Imports are a large part of the U.S. clothing industry.

2A. Linen is made from the natural fibers of flax.

2B. Natural fibers are manufactured products.

3A. Clothing made from synthetic fibers allows the skin to "breathe."

3B. Polyester and rayon are examples of fabrics made from synthetic fibers.

REVIEWING WHAT YOU HAVE LEARNED

1. Explain the four physical influences on clothing decisions.

2. List five factors that affect our choice of clothing.

USING YOUR CRITICAL THINKING SKILLS

1. Elaine is starting her first full-time job next week, following graduation. She doesn't know what kind of clothes she should wear. Among the following, what is the least helpful source of information for her? Why?

   • a formal dress code in the company employee's handbook

   • a current high-fashion magazine

   • what she sees others wearing in the office

   • what her supervisor is wearing

2. We can often tell much about a person by observing the clothing he or she wears. Under what circumstances might these observations be misleading?

APPLYING WHAT YOU HAVE LEARNED

1. Cut out five pictures of people from a newspaper or magazine and tell how the clothing they are wearing helps to identify their jobs or ways of life.

2. List three articles of clothing that were imported. For each item, tell the country from which it comes, the purchase price, the material from which the clothing is made, and the type of care it requires. Compare your information with that gathered by your classmates.

CHAPTER 20

Considerations in Buying Clothes

OBJECTIVES

After you complete this chapter, you will be able to do the following:
1. List six sources of information you might consult before buying clothing.
2. Name the two basic types of clothing stores.
3. Describe five U.S. Government consumer protection regulations for labeling.

TERMS

bargains
care labels
comparison shopping
Consumer Product
  Safety Act

flame-retardant
Flammable Fabrics Act
Fur Products Labeling Act
manufacturer overruns
seconds

Textile Fiber Products
  Identification Act
trade-off
Wool Products
  Labeling Act

Once you decide what you want your clothing to say, you are ready to examine the alternatives concerning what, when, and where to buy. Too often, consumers buy clothing on impulse. Individual pieces of clothing are not usually a major purchase, so we generally spend less time comparing clothing alternatives than we do before making a more expensive purchase. You will get the best value from your clothing if you develop a plan, then make sure the items you purchase fit that plan.

WHAT DO WE NEED TO KNOW ABOUT CLOTHING?

comparison shopping
· · · · · · · · · ·
checking several sources for prices and quality of an item to determine the best buy

Seven out of ten shoppers are *habit shoppers*. They buy the same items and the same brands over and over again, and they appear to give little attention to how or why they shop as they do. To be a knowledgeable consumer, you need to gather information about clothing possibilities and make the best decisions you can.

How do we obtain information about clothing that we are considering buying? Advertisements for the clothing may tell us something about it, but labels and tags on the clothing tell us even more. Helpful and knowledgeable salespeople, magazines and buyers' guides, bulletins from the Better Business Bureau, and local consumer or government agencies can help. (These and related sources are discussed in Chapter 4.) Some knowledge of fabrics

and clothing construction is also useful, and careful inspection is necessary on our part.

Clothing Advertisements

Advertising can make us aware of what clothing is for sale. It attempts to create a desire for particular clothing or for certain brand-name products. We must evaluate the types of advertisements closely to determine if they are presenting worthwhile and helpful information. (Advertising is discussed in detail in Chapter 2.)

In general, the higher priced the clothing, the less information will be presented about it in advertisements. Ads for medium- and low-cost clothing generally provide detailed pictures and information about the garments. Advertisers assume that the consumer who has to watch where dollars go also wants to know more about the products.

Comparison Shopping

Comparison shopping takes time, but for major clothing purchases, you may get better quality and save money by taking time to compare. For example, a winter coat or a special suit may need to last for more than one year. Clothing of this type might be available in different stores at prices that could vary by fifty dollars or more. Other purchases, such as inexpensive jewelry, are less important—and the money saved may not be worth the time to do lengthy comparison shopping.

Some consumers place a high value on their personal time, so they don't often travel from one store to another to compare prices. They feel their time is worth more than the money they could save by comparison shopping.

Labeling for Consumer Protection

When you go to the store to buy clothing, fabric, or other textile items for your home, read the labels. They will tell you who manufactured the garment or fabric, what it is made of, and how to care for it. If the product was made in another country, the name of the country must be given.

Regulations for Labeling

Congress has passed several laws to protect the consumer against deceptive labeling. Laws also ensure that the label provides consumers with the information they need. However, you must read the label if you are to benefit from this legislation.

Wool Products Labeling Act. The **Wool Products Labeling Act** became law in 1938 and was amended in 1965. It requires fabrics and textile products containing wool to be labeled. The amount and kind of wool must be identified. If blends (more than one type of fabric) are involved, the proportion of wool must be listed. For example, a suit label might read "65% polyester and 35% wool."

Fur Products Labeling Act. The **Fur Products Labeling Act** became effective in 1952. This law requires furriers to show on a label the type of animal fur, whether the fur is imported, and the country of origin. The law also requires labels to say if the fur has been dyed or colored and if the garment is made of scraps of fur.

Textile Fiber Products Identification Act. In 1958, the **Textile Fiber Products Identification Act** became law. This legislation was designed to protect consumers against misbranding and false advertising of fiber content of textile products. It defines twenty-one generic terms to be used in the labeling of textiles. The tag, label, or stamp on the fabric must carry the name of the manufacturer of the product. Imported

Fur Products Labeling Act
. . . .
legislation that sets standards for the labeling of items of clothing made from animal fur

Textile Fiber Products Identification Act
. . . .
legislation that regulates the labeling of fiber content of textile products

Wool Products Labeling Act
. . . .
legislation that requires a sweater to be labeled cashmere, mohair, etc.

READ THE LABELS!

County extension agents can give consumers good advice about buying and using products for the home.

One day, extension agent Nancy Nelson received a box in the mail containing three shirts—all with big holes in them. Fred Johnson had sent the shirts. He had already been back to the store where he bought them, demanding a refund, but the storekeeper told him there was nothing wrong with the shirts. She said they had been washed improperly. Fred wanted an unbiased second opinion from the extension agent.

After some testing, Nancy concluded that the holes were produced when chlorine bleach was poured directly on the shirts. Labels inside the shirt contained the warning, "Do not wash in chlorine bleach." The label on the bleach bottle said, "Do not pour directly on clothing." But Fred had not followed the directions, so he had washed the shirts improperly. The storekeeper was right.

---

care labels

··············

laundering or cleaning instructions that must be permanently attached to textile products

Flammable Fabrics Act

··············

legislation that regulates the use of textiles that are likely to burn

Consumer Product Safety Act

··············

legislation that establishes the Consumer Product Safety Commission, which enforces the Flammable Fabrics Act

flame-retardant

··············

resistant to burning or likely to burn at a reduced rate

items must list the country where the product was made.

Care Labeling Rules. Since 1972, the Federal Trade Commission (FTC) has required manufacturers to attach care labels permanently to the textile products they produce—and these labels must provide consumers with clear instructions for care. Fabric sold by the yard must also have labels available for consumers when they buy the fabric.

There is still much discussion about labels. One question is what information they should contain, and another is how much help the manufacturer should be required to give the consumer regarding the care of the fabric.

Flammable Fabrics Act. More than 250,000 consumers are injured each year due to flammable fabrics, with children and older people frequent victims of fires. Fiber content as well as construction of the fabric or garment determines how quickly it will burn. Loose, sheer fabrics, or garments with a pile, such as fuzzy sleepers, will burn more quickly than materials that are smooth and tightly woven.

In 1953, Congress passed the **Flammable Fabrics Act**. It was amended in 1967 to cover not only flammable materials, but some interior furnishings as well. In 1972, the **Consumer Product Safety Act** was passed and the Consumer Product Safety Commission was established. This commission has responsibility for enforcing the Flammable Fabrics Labeling Act.

Early attempts to reduce the burning rate relied on finishes that were sprayed on the fabrics, but these finishes did not last and caused allergic reactions for some consumers. Now, special **flame-retardant** fibers and fabric construction techniques are being used, and these reduce the burning rate of some fabrics. Flame-retardant fab-

rics are used to make pajamas, robes, and children's sleepwear.

The cost of research has made flame-retardant fabrics more expensive than most other fabrics. Flame-retardant clothing often costs about 50 percent more than non-flame-retardant clothing, and these fabrics must be cared for properly to ensure that the flame retardancy is maintained. Labels usually indicate that the garment should not be washed in phosphate-free detergent and that you should not use soap or hot water.

Cost of Protection

The legislation passed concerning clothing and textiles is designed to protect consumers against hazardous materials or false claims by manufacturers. It helps us to know what we are getting for our money, but some industry spokespersons claim that the benefits of this legislation are not worth the increased cost of products. They say it limits the variety of products available to consumers.

Consumers must also decide if they prefer to protect endangered species, such as the leopard, or if they want to be able to wear a leopard coat. It is difficult to do both.

Are the lives that may be saved worth the extra cost of flame-retardant fabrics? By making our wishes known to industry and to Congress, we can influence how much protection is provided. Generally, consumers are willing to spend a little extra money for additional protection.

Importing Clothing and Fabrics

There is a lot of debate today about just how protective the U.S. Government should be regarding imported clothing and fabrics. Some U.S. manufacturers feel the government should restrict foreign clothing and textiles coming into the country. These manufacturers cite the importation of textiles and apparel as a major cause of economic hard times.

In many countries, the cost of producing textiles and apparel is lower than it is in the United States. Because of this, products we import can often be sold for less than products we produce.

Today, one-third of all the garments sold in the United States are imported. Over half of the sweaters are made in foreign countries, amounting to more than twenty-five billion dollars a year. In recent years, foreign imports have taken increasingly larger shares of markets for blouses, coats, shirts, and sweaters.

In order to reduce costs, some companies in the United States send cut garments to countries where wages are lower, mainly to Mexico and other Latin American countries. The garments are sewn, finished, and shipped back to the United States for sale.

The textile and apparel industries are two of the largest employers in this country. They employ over 2.2 million people, and 48 percent of the textile labor force and 82 percent of the apparel labor force are women. Most of these workers have limited education and few skills, and many are immigrants. They work in over 24,000 plants in the United States, mostly in rural areas. If these workers lose their jobs, they may have difficulty finding other work.

trade-off
....
an exchange of one thing for another

Effect on Consumers

As consumers, we often save money by buying imported clothing and textiles, and these low prices have forced many U.S. companies to lower their costs in order to compete with the foreign manufacturers. Once again, the consumer must decide which part of a **trade-off** is more important. Do you prefer to pay low prices for imported clothing? Or are you willing to pay more for clothing produced in the United States in order to help keep this country's workers employed?

WHERE SHOULD WE GO TO BUY CLOTHING?

Many different types of stores sell clothing. Why are there so many? It is largely because each type of store is trying to attract a particular kind of consumer.

Boutiques and department stores offer something for just about everybody. Prices will vary greatly in these types of stores, so it pays to comparison shop. Do you prefer shopping in boutiques, department stores, or some other type of store?

Many aspects of a store are important to the consumer. One aspect is the store's location. Some people prefer a suburban location, others prefer shopping downtown. Another important aspect of a store is its appearance, including the window displays. The store's personnel and its method of billing are also important to the consumer. The people you see shopping in a store and the quality of the clothing will also have an effect on the type of store you choose.

Types of Stores

Today's clothing stores tend to be one of two basic types:

- mass consumption stores
- unique stores

The mass consumption store tries to provide clothing for people of all ages, with a wide range of prices. The unique store tries to do just the opposite, appealing to only a very select or narrow group of consumers.

Department Stores. Fifty-nine percent of all sales in department stores are clothing and shoe sales. More clothing purchases are made in department stores than anywhere else.

A department store may be part of a chain of stores, or it may be individually owned. Department stores supply their customers with many services, including knowledgeable salespeople. Generally, department stores offer a wide variety of clothing at all price ranges. They rely upon their reputation and service to keep customers coming back.

Specialty Stores. Specialty stores are unique stores that cater to very special clientele, who are interested in the particular items they have to sell. They tend to carry a limited selection of items, and may specialize in dresses, shoes, or hats.

Stores for "tall men" or "for petites only" cater to customers with special sizing needs. Shops like these are a growing segment of the clothing industry. They have a special image and carry their themes through logos and their advertisements.

Boutiques. Boutiques are specialty stores that concentrate on fashionable gifts, accessories, and clothing. Merchandise ranges from inexpensive to very costly, one-of-a-kind garments. Consumers who are very interested in fashion are attracted to this type of store. Consumers between fourteen and thirty-four years of age, typically with high clothing expenses, tend to shop here.

Discount Stores. Discount stores generally sell clothing at lower prices than the department or specialty stores, but discount stores provide less service and fewer frills. Labels may have been removed from name-brand clothing, and return policies may be limited. These stores operate on high volume and self-service. A wide variety of consumers use discount stores.

CONSUMER PROFILE

Last year a discount clothing store had a clearance sale. Franny sorted through the racks of clothing and found a name-brand skirt that originally sold for $36 and was now on sale for only $6. She tried it on and it fit. Although it was a rather unusual style and in a color that didn't really go with anything she had, she couldn't pass up such a bargain. Six dollars for a name-brand skirt!

Now, a year later, she finds she has worn that skirt only one time. Franny realizes now that she should have thought about more than the price. How much of a bargain is it if the item only hangs in your closet?

Outlet malls are very popular in some areas. With careful shopping, it is possible to get good buys at outlet stores. Don't assume that outlet stores offer the best buys, however, because this may not be the case. It's still important to compare!

manufacturer overruns
....
excess production from the maker or producer

seconds
....
damaged or flawed clothing

Factory Outlets. Factory outlets sell damaged clothing or **manufacturer overruns** (excess production) directly from the factory. They also sell clothes from the previous season and samples. (The damaged or flawed clothing is marked **"seconds"** or "irregular." Before buying, examine these items carefully for flaws.) Sometimes clothes that are usually expensive can be purchased from this type of store for a reasonable price. See if a factory outlet is located in your community. Entire "outlet malls" are developing in some areas.

Secondhand Stores. Used clothing that is no longer of value to the original owner is sold in secondhand stores (often on consignment). Generally, the clothing is still in style and in good repair.

Mail-Order Buying. Mail-order buying is popular with people who don't like traveling to stores or who are confined to their homes. Many people who work during regular shopping hours also shop from catalogs.

A wide variety of clothing items can be obtained by mail, ranging from inexpensive goods to high-fashion items or one-of-a-kind clothes. Of course, you cannot try on the catalog clothing before you order it. Large catalogs from major companies, such as Spiegel, provide charts to help you determine the correct size.

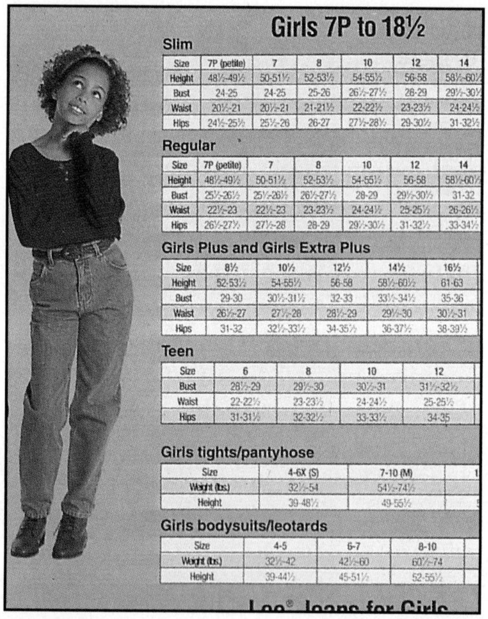

Girls 7P to 18½

Slim

Size	7P (petite)	7	8	10	12	14
Height	48½-49½	50-51½	52-53½	54-55½	56-58	58½-60½
Bust	24-25	24-25	25-26	26½-27½	28-29	29½-30½
Waist	20½-21	20½-21	21-21½	22-22½	23-23½	24-24½
Hips	24½-25½	25½-26	26-27	27½-28½	29-30½	31-32½

Regular

Size	7P (petite)	7	8	10	12	14
Height	48½-49½	50-51½	52-53½	54-55½	56-58	58½-60½
Bust	25½-26½	25½-26½	26½-27½	28-29	29½-30½	31-32
Waist	22½-23	22½-23	23-23½	24-24½	25-25½	26-26½
Hips	26½-27½	27½-28	28-29	29½-30½	31-32½	33-34½

Girls Plus and Girls Extra Plus

Size	8½	10½	12½	14½	16½
Height	52-53½	54-55½	56-58	58½-60½	61-63
Bust	29-30	30½-31½	32-33	33½-34½	35-36
Waist	26½-27	27½-28	28½-29	29½-30	30½-31
Hips	31-32	32½-33½	34-35½	36-37½	38-39½

Teen

Size	6	8	10	12
Bust	28½-29	29½-30	30½-31	31½-32½
Waist	22-22½	23-23½	24-24½	25-25½
Hips	31-31½	32-32½	33-33½	34-35

Girls tights/pantyhose

Size	4-6X (S)	7-10 (M)	
Weight (lbs.)	32½-54	54½-74½	
Height	39-48½	49-55½	

Girls bodysuits/leotards

Size	4-5	6-7	8-10
Weight (lbs.)	32½-42	42½-60	60½-74
Height	39-44½	45-51½	52-55½

Lee® Jeans for Girls

Catalogs often supply a size chart to help customers order the correct size clothing. Use a tape measure to measure yourself to determine which size or sizes on this chart would best fit you.

When ordering from catalogs, judging fabric, color, or quality from photographs is often difficult. If you order from a catalog, check to see if a shipping and handling charge will be added to your order. Knowing how long you will have to wait for your order is helpful.

Other Sources. Not all clothing purchases are made in stores or from catalogs. Popular sources of buying clothing in some areas of the country include flea markets, garage sales, swap meets, and church bazaars. Often, used or even new clothing can be bought at extremely low prices through these channels. There is, of course, no return policy, and the seller may not be around the next day in case a defect is discovered—so you must shop with care.

Another problem with buying from these sources is the likelihood of impulse buying. Consumers faced with racks of **"bargains"** (good buys) are more likely to buy something impulsively—for instance, what they think they will wear when they lose twenty pounds. This may not be a bargain, and it is likely to show up in your own garage sale at a later date.

Summary

- It is important to gather information about possible clothing purchases before you buy. That way you will make the best buying decisions.

- Sources of information about clothing items include: advertisements, labels on the clothing, salespeople, magazines and buyers' guides, bulletins from the Better Business Bureau, and local consumer or government agencies.

CHECKLIST FOR CHOOSING A PLACE TO SHOP

Before you choose a store, ask yourself each of these questions:
- ___ Is the store in a convenient location?
- ___ Are the clerks knowledgeable?
- ___ Does the store stock clothing that is appropriate for my age and style preferences (current, fashionable, conservative)?
- ___ Does the store provide good facilities (such as good lighting, adequate dressing rooms, sufficient mirrors)?
- ___ Does the store stock clothing within my price range?
- ___ Does the store handle dependable merchandise?
- ___ Does the store have a good reputation?
- ___ Does the store have a good return policy?
- ___ Have you or others been satisfied with previous purchases at the store?
- ___ Does the store provide needed services (such as layaway, shopping bags, gift boxes and wrapping, delivery service, special ordering, charge accounts)?

- There are laws about clothing labels that protect the consumer and insure that labels contain certain kinds of information.

- Imported clothing and fabric is generally less expensive than that made in America. However, it is controversial in that importing reduces the number of jobs available for American workers in the clothing and textile industry.

- There are many different types of stores where it is possible to buy clothing. Generally, clothing stores are oriented either toward mass consumption (a wide variety of clothing for people of all ages) or toward a unique or select group of customers.

bargains
....
good buys

ENRICHING YOUR VOCABULARY

Read the following pairs of sentences. Write the sentence that correctly uses the underlined word or phrase.

bargains
care labels
comparison shopping
Consumer Product Safety Act
flame-retardant

Flammable Fabrics Act
Fur Products Labeling Act
manufacturer overruns
seconds

Textile Fiber Products
  Identification Act
trade-off
Wool Products Labeling Act

1A. A purchase must meet a need and be well priced in order to be a bargain.

1B. A sale purchase is always a bargain.

2A. Care labels attached to textile products guarantee that these products can be cleaned of all stains.

2B. Permanently attached care labels provide laundering or cleaning instructions for textile products.

3A. Comparison shopping helps the consumer to find bargains.

3B. Advertised prices discourage comparison shopping.

4A. The Consumer Products Safety Act established the Consumer Product Safety Commission.

4B. The Consumer Products Safety Act protects the consumer against poor quality workmanship.

5A. Flame-retardant textiles will not burn.

5B. Flame-retardant textiles are treated to resist burning.

6A. The Flammable Fabrics Act bans the use of all textiles that burn.

6B. The Flammable Fabrics Act regulates the use of textiles that are likely to burn.

7A. The Fur Products Labeling Act requires that labels on fur products state if the product is made of scraps.

7B. The Fur Products Labeling Act requires that fur garments have permanently attached care labels.

8A. Manufacturer overruns are flawed products.

8B. Manufacturer overruns are often sold at reduced prices.

9A. The flaws found in seconds are often very insignificant.

9B. Garments purchased in used clothing stores are called seconds.

10A. The Textile Fiber Products Identification Act regulates the labeling of the fiber content of textile products.

10B. According to the Textile Products Identification Act, all garments must be flame-retardant.

11A. Some customers feel that a higher price is an acceptable trade-off for good service.

11B. You may trade-off clothing at a secondhand store.

12A. The Wool Products Labeling Act requires that labels on wool products indicate if the wool is imported.

12B. The Wool Products Labeling Act requires that labels on wool products state the proportion of wool in the fabric.

Chapter Review
20

Reviewing What You Have Learned

1. List six sources of information you might consult before buying clothing.
2. What are the two basic types of clothing stores?
3. Describe five U.S. Government consumer protection regulations for labeling.

Using Your Critical Thinking Skills

1. Bobby Simms stopped at the dry cleaners to pick up an order his father had taken there the previous week. Protective coverings had been placed over the cleaned garments. Bobby paid the bill and took the garments home.

   The next morning, when Bobby's father was getting ready for work, he found that all the buttons on his suit had melted into the fabric. The suit was ruined.

   On his way to work, Mr. Simms stopped by the cleaners to ask what had happened and what the cleaners planned to do about the suit. The cleaners refused to do anything, saying they were not at fault, that it was the manufacturer's fault.

   Mr. Simms wrote to the manufacturer and explained the problem. The manufacturer said the label on the suit specified, "Wash only, do not dry clean." Therefore, the manufacturer would not take responsibility for damage and would not replace the suit. Who do you think is at fault? Why?

Applying What You Have Learned

1. Collect newspaper ads for clothing. Compare the information provided from various stores.
2. Examine labels in various articles of clothing. For each article you examine, list the article and the information provided on the labels. Is needed information missing? If so, mention this also. If the article of clothing is new, list information provided on hang tags.

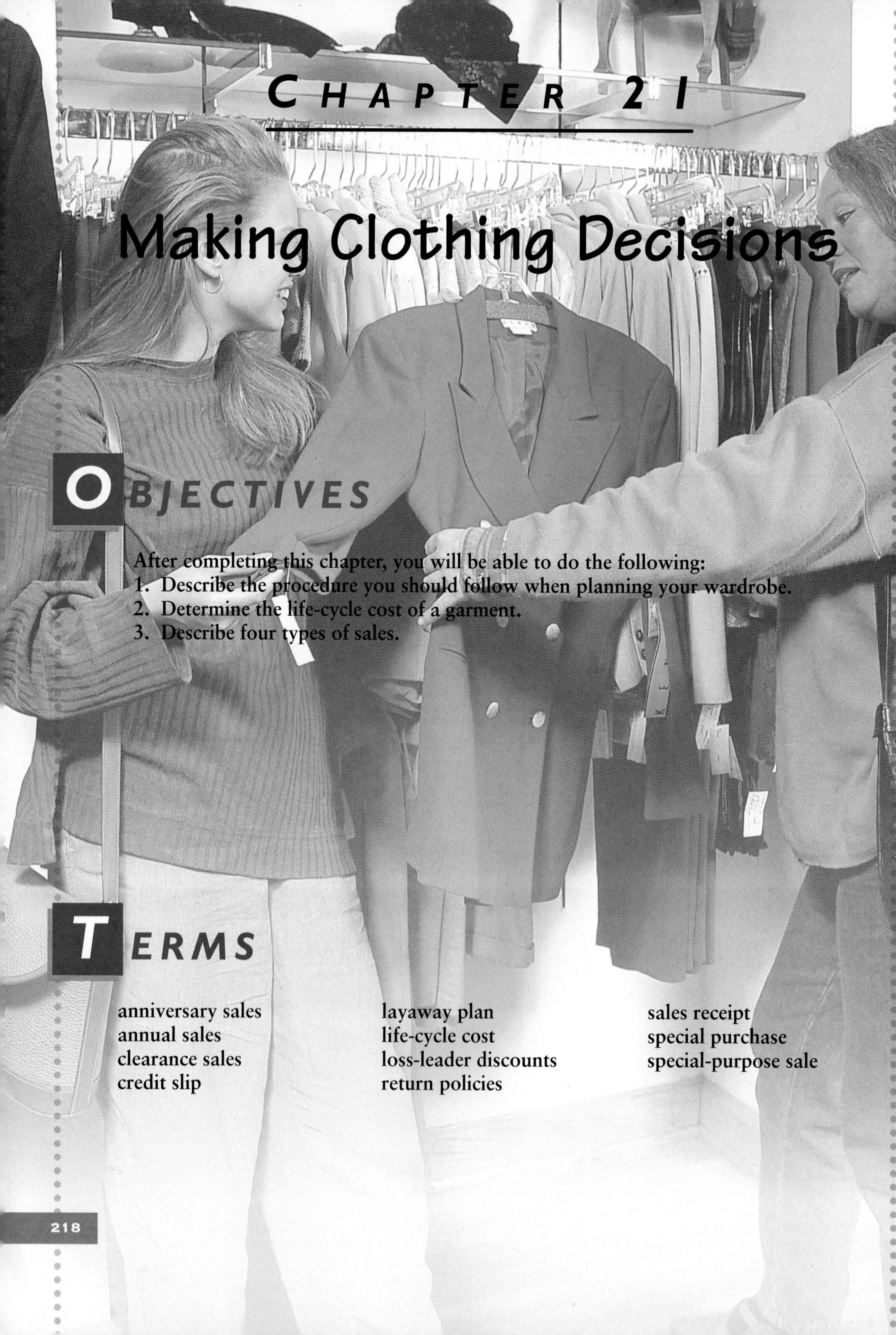

CHAPTER 21

Making Clothing Decisions

OBJECTIVES

After completing this chapter, you will be able to do the following:
1. Describe the procedure you should follow when planning your wardrobe.
2. Determine the life-cycle cost of a garment.
3. Describe four types of sales.

TERMS

anniversary sales
annual sales
clearance sales
credit slip

layaway plan
life-cycle cost
loss-leader discounts
return policies

sales receipt
special purchase
special-purpose sale

A useful, attractive wardrobe doesn't just happen. And it need not be expensive. By planning carefully and by shopping around, you can develop a wardrobe that reflects your values and the way of life you prefer.

PLANNING YOUR WARDROBE

A large wardrobe isn't always a good wardrobe—some people have closets full of clothing they don't wear. To develop a good wardrobe, you must set a goal. Then, to achieve your goal, you need to examine:

- what you have
- what you need
- how to make the best use of your resources
- condition of the garment

Each of us is different, and each of our clothing wardrobes will be different. There is no "right" number of shirts, sweaters, or suits. The supply will depend on your needs, interests, values, and lifestyle.

Keep in mind as you plan your wardrobe that you will need space to store your clothes and accessories. Proper storage will keep them neater and cleaner, and you will spend less time taking care of your clothing. (See Figure 21.1.)

Evaluating Your Present Wardrobe

Examine all of the clothing you own. You can probably divide your clothing into several groups:

- clothes you wear often
- clothes you wear occasionally
- clothes that need something done to them before you can wear them again

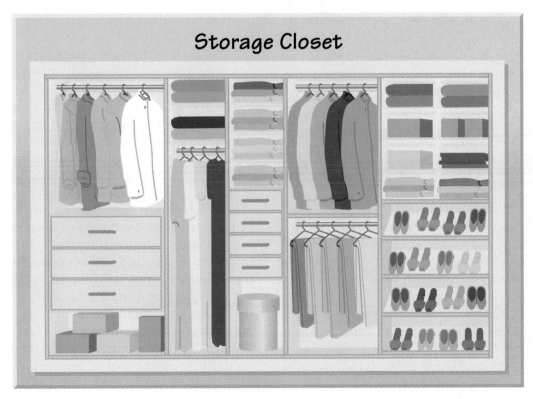

Storage Closet

Figure 21.1
....
Closet storage systems can be purchased or built into your closet for a more efficient use of space. However, these can be quite expensive. Inexpensive cardboard storage boxes and shelves can be used for the same purpose at a fraction of the cost.

Examining your clothing periodically is a good way to determine what you need and what you don't need. Many organizations will accept used clothing that you don't need and distribute it to the needy. Have you checked your closet recently? What clothing items (that you don't wear) might someone else find useful?

life-cycle cost
· · · · · · · · · · · · · · · ·
the money it costs to take care of an item (cleaning, repair, etc.)

• clothes that you have not worn for more than a year

Group your shoes and other accessories in the same way, then ask yourself why you have not worn some of these items. What is wrong with them? Can you repair or alter them to fit your needs? If not, you might consider giving them to a family member, a friend, a secondhand shop, or a charity. You might even sell them yourself at a garage sale or flea market. Look at what is left, and repair or clean those items that need it.

Completing Your Wardrobe

Make a chart to help you identify your wardrobe needs. Write down the items you feel you should buy or sew to make your wardrobe complete, keeping in mind the activities you do regularly. When you have identified your needs, you will be ready to make the best use of any sales and bargains you see. Don't invest a great deal of money in items not on your list. They are not likely to become important parts of your wardrobe.

As your values and activities change, your wardrobe will change with them. A new job or college may require different clothing. Try to look ahead and save money if you will be needing major changes or additions to your wardrobe.

Saving Money on Clothing

If you have done a good job of planning your wardrobe, you can be well dressed on a reasonable budget. For example, you can shop wisely at sales or at discount stores.

You may save money by making your own clothing, although prices of many fabrics have increased. In a recent year, Americans spent five billion dollars on fabric, patterns, notions (such as ribbons and buttons), and sewing machines. People sew for several reasons. Primarily, they enjoy it and feel it saves money. Sewing also gives them a better fit and provides a greater variety in their clothing. You need to consider whether the time spent sewing is worth the money you would save by not buying ready-to-wear clothing.

When buying clothing, consider the total **life-cycle cost** of a garment as well as the initial cost. The extra money it may require to take care of a low-cost item may make it more expensive in the long run.

BUYING CLOTHING

Planning your wardrobe will enable you to take advantage of sales. Whenever you pick up the newspaper or listen to the radio, there is sure to be some mention of clothing sales. Some of these sales are worthwhile, but others are not.

Types of Sales

If you use caution, considerable savings can be realized during sales. There are several types of sales.

Clearance Sales. Clearance sales offer the biggest price reductions. These are usually held in January and February (after the holidays) or at the end of various seasons, and you can often get really good buys. For example, there may be a reduction of fifty percent off the price of a swimsuit at the end of the summer season. Summer sales start after the Fourth of July, and reductions continue through Labor Day. The selection, however, may grow increasingly limited as certain sizes are sold out quickly.

Annual Sales. Annual sales generally reduce regular stock, but not drastically. These sales are mainly held to get you into the store. Advertisements push loss-leader discounts, special prices on regular items that many consumers would find desirable. For example, a store may sell monogrammed sweaters at a special price. The store would make little profit or even take a loss, but people buying the loss-leader sweater may buy a skirt or slacks to go with it, and these would be sold at the

Great savings can be had at sales, if the consumer shops wisely. Have you ever bought a clothing item on sale and then found that you didn't wear it? Why didn't you wear it?

regular prices. Some sale items sold at annual sales are special purchases (or specials). These may not be full quality.

Annual sales are good if you buy in quantities. Underwear and hosiery bought by the box or package are generally less expensive during this type of sale.

Special-Purpose Sales. When the retailer obtains a good buy from a wholesaler, a special-purpose sale may be held. But products may be flawed or below standard, so inspect the merchandise carefully. Then decide whether the area of quality that may be missing is important to you.

Anniversary Sales. Anniversary sales are generally used to stimulate business during slack periods. There is actually little money to be saved.

Shopping Considerations

A bargain in clothing is only good if you or your family will use it. The item should fit into your planned wardrobe. A purple sweater may be on sale, but it is no bargain if you buy it and then have nothing to wear with it.

clearance sales
....
sales usually held in January and February, which offer the biggest price reductions

annual sales
....
sales that push loss-leader discounts and special purchases, but don't usually reduce stock drastically

loss-leader discounts
....
special prices on regular items that many customers would find desirable

special purchase
....
items, which might not be full quality, purchased especially for a sale

special-purpose sale
....
a sale held when a retailer gets a good buy from a wholesaler; products may be flawed or below standard

anniversary sales
....
sales, which actually offer little savings, that are used to stimulate sales during slack or slow periods

sales receipt
....
the ticket that verifies where an item was purchased and the price

layaway plan
....
a convenience offered by some stores that allows customers to make a small down payment, which will hold an item until it can be paid for in full

return policies
....
store rules, which must be posted, about items that are returned

credit slip
....
a ticket issued by stores that do not give money for returned items; it can be used to make a purchase in the store at a later date

Quality is always an important consideration. Each garment must be judged individually. Check to see if the material is good and if the garment is well-made.

Consider how long you will be able to use the item. A winter coat bought at the end of the season may be a good buy, but what if you are not able to wear it next year? Many teenagers grow very quickly. A coat that fits at the end of one season may be too small before it is time to wear it the following winter. Styles change, too, and you may not *want* to wear a coat that is no longer in style.

Clothing Gifts

Unless you know exactly what a person wants and can use, clothing may not be the best gift. For example, your grandparents may like to purchase clothing for you, but they may not know what you need or the style that you like. They may buy the wrong size, or they may not know how a garment will fit with your wardrobe. If you buy a clothing gift, be sure to buy it at a store that will allow you to return it.

Return Policies

Return policies vary from store to store—so when you buy, ask if the item is returnable. And be sure you understand the terms of the return policy. Underwear, swimsuits, and personalized items are generally not returnable, but stores are required to post their return policies somewhere for customers to see.

Some stores are willing to provide return services, others are not. In many cases, you may return items only for other merchandise or for a credit slip. A **credit slip** allows you to obtain other merchandise at a later time.

Always keep your **sales receipt** from a purchase, as it verifies that you bought the item at a certain store. If merchandise you bought is defective, you will have the receipt to show when you purchased it. Return defective items as soon as possible.

When returning merchandise, be polite and as helpful as you can in providing information to a store. If you do not get satisfaction, contact the manager or owner of the store. If you still need help, try the Better Business Bureau or your local consumer protection agency—their numbers are in your telephone directory.

Cash or Credit

More and more consumers are using credit cards to buy clothing. This enables consumers to buy when they need specific items and to take advantage of sales, and it provides a record in case merchandise is returned. However, overuse of consumer credit is a problem for consumers who do not manage their credit well. Advantages and disadvantages of credit are discussed in Chapter 10.

The **layaway plan** is available in some stores. This plan allows you to make a small down payment that will hold the clothing you want until you can pay the full purchase price.

Summary

- Careful planning can produce a useful and attractive wardrobe. Planning includes a look at what you have, what you need, and how to make the most of your resources.

- In addition to planning, shopping at sales and discount stores can help you develop an attractive wardrobe on a reasonable budget.

CHAPTER REVIEW
21

ENRICHING YOUR VOCABULARY

Number your paper from 1–11. Read each sentence below. If the sentence is true, write "true" next to that number. If the sentence is false, rewrite it to make a true statement.

1. The total life-cycle cost of a garment includes the cost of caring for the item.
2. Anniversary sales are scheduled to clear out end-of-season merchandise.
3. Special-purpose sales are a way of passing on good buys from the wholesaler to the consumer.
4. All stores limit return services to credit slips.
5. A sales receipt may be used to purchase merchandise at a later date.
6. Annual sales offer the biggest price reductions.
7. Return policies are standardized throughout the garment industry.
8. Special purchases may not be full quality.
9. Clearance sales are held at the end of seasons.
10. A layaway plan is another name for a charge account.
11. Stores may realize large profits on loss-leader discounts.

REVIEWING WHAT YOU HAVE LEARNED

1. Describe the procedure you should follow when planning your wardrobe.
2. Sue bought a silk dress for eighty dollars. It had to be dry-cleaned each time she wore it. Dry cleaning cost four dollars per cleaning. Sue figures she wore the dress thirty times. What was its life-cycle cost? What was its cost per wearing?
3. Describe four types of sales.

USING YOUR CRITICAL THINKING SKILLS

1. A local clothing store is planning a going-out-of-business clearance sale. Do you think this sale is likely to be a good place to find bargains? What problems might you encounter?

APPLYING WHAT YOU HAVE LEARNED

1. Give an example from your neighborhood or town for different types of stores (discount, department, specialty, etc). Find out and describe their return policies.
2. For your own use, evaluate your present wardrobe. List items you need to complete your wardrobe.

TRANSPORTATION

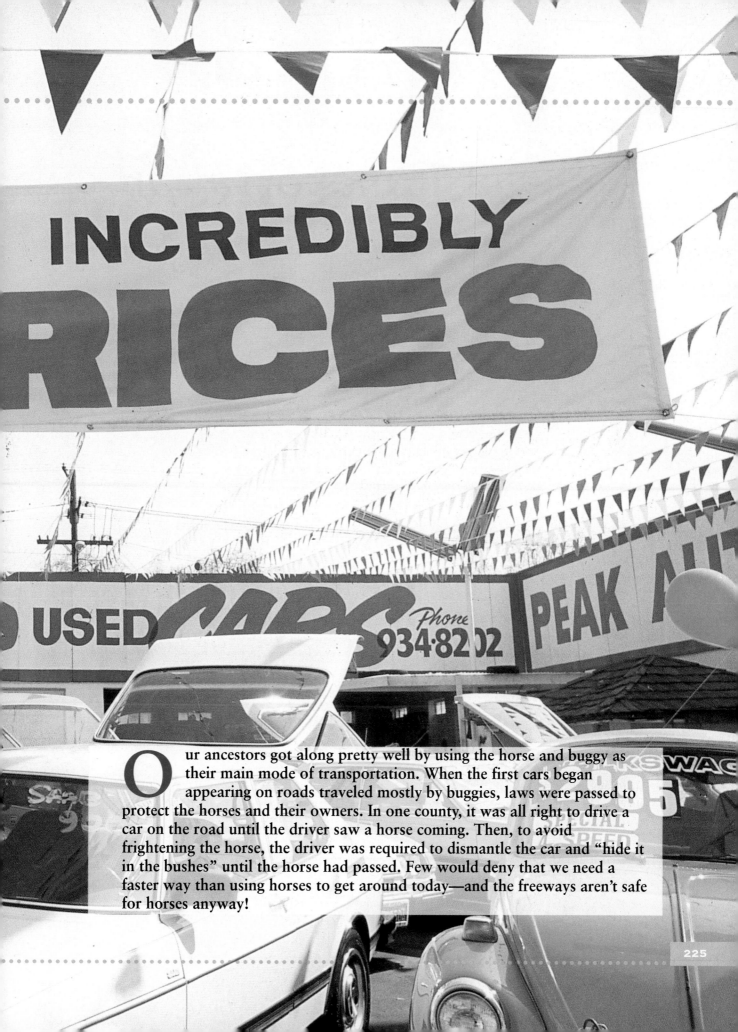

INCREDIBLY RICES

USED CARS Phone 934-8202 PEAK AUT

Our ancestors got along pretty well by using the horse and buggy as their main mode of transportation. When the first cars began appearing on roads traveled mostly by buggies, laws were passed to protect the horses and their owners. In one county, it was all right to drive a car on the road until the driver saw a horse coming. Then, to avoid frightening the horse, the driver was required to dismantle the car and "hide it in the bushes" until the horse had passed. Few would deny that we need a faster way than using horses to get around today—and the freeways aren't safe for horses anyway!

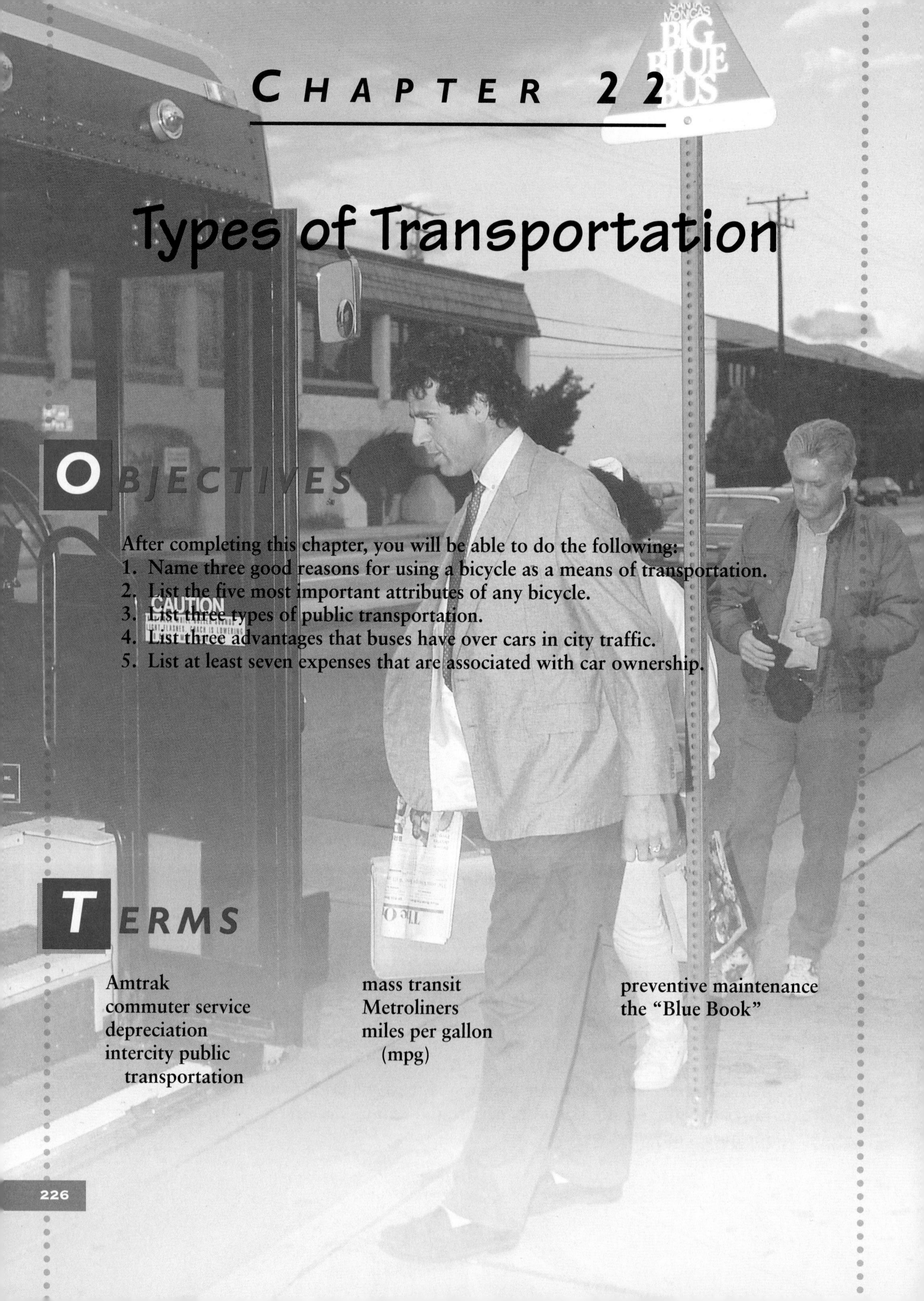

CHAPTER 22

Types of Transportation

OBJECTIVES

After completing this chapter, you will be able to do the following:
1. Name three good reasons for using a bicycle as a means of transportation.
2. List the five most important attributes of any bicycle.
3. List three types of public transportation.
4. List three advantages that buses have over cars in city traffic.
5. List at least seven expenses that are associated with car ownership.

TERMS

Amtrak
commuter service
depreciation
intercity public
   transportation

mass transit
Metroliners
miles per gallon
   (mpg)

preventive maintenance
the "Blue Book"

Do you live where you can walk to school, to work, to all the shopping areas you need to visit, and to the entertainment you enjoy? Walking, of course, is the cheapest way to get from one place to another. It's also one of the healthiest forms of exercise. So, whenever we can, it benefits both our health and our pocketbook to walk instead of ride. Unfortunately, few of us live close to all the places we need (and want) to go. We cannot depend solely on our legs to take us places, so some type of mechanical transportation is a real need for almost everyone.

PUBLIC TRANSPORTA-TION

Public transportation is organized passenger service that is available to everyone. There are three types of public transportation service:

- urban
- intercity
- overseas

Urban Service

In large urban areas, local public transportation is called **mass transit**. Similar public transportation between cities and their suburbs or between nearby cities is called **commuter service**.

Buses are most often used for mass transit. Nearly a thousand cities in the United States have transit systems, and most use only buses. Many offer special rates that make it possible to get to work, to shopping areas, and to recreational areas for less than it would cost to drive a car. Cities favor buses over cars because more people can be

Buses provide inexpensive transportation within and between cities. Do you use the bus system in your town? Why or why not?

moved in less street space and because fewer parking spaces must be provided. Some cities have reserved certain traffic lanes for buses only, which speeds up bus transportation. Bus usage is flexible. If needs change, bus routes can be altered with little expense.

Some major cities offer above ground or subway train service. Have you ever ridden in this type of vehicle? Would you use a service like this regularly if it was available to you?

mass transit
....
local public transportation in large urban areas

commuter service
....
public transportation between cities and their suburbs or nearby cities

Most of the world's largest cities offer rail service, and nine U.S. cities offer both surface and subway rail lines. Many other cities have a type of transit system that uses light rail vehicles, electrically powered railroad cars that run on tracks at street level. Power is provided by an overhead trolley wire or by an electrified third rail.

Trains provide commuter service in most areas. In fact, commuters make up about three-fourths of all train passengers in the United States.

Intercity Service

Most intercity public transportation is provided by buses, trains, and airplanes. Bus service between cities has improved in recent years. Intercity buses have restrooms, and many of these buses have reclining seats and individual reading lights. Some buses even offer refreshments. Most intercity buses are quite comfortable, and bus travel is somewhat less expensive than going by train—and much less expensive than flying.

Trains in the United States are operated by Amtrak, the National Railroad Passenger Corporation, which is subsidized by the federal government. Trains use less energy per passenger-mile than planes, buses, or cars. Unfor-

tunately, much of the railroad track in the U.S. is badly worn, and replacing railroad track is very costly—so there are many parts of the country that do not have intercity train service.

However, eighty-mile-per-hour intercity passenger trains, called Metroliners, have traveled the 225-mile route between New York City and Washington, D.C., for years. In 1993, the X-2000, a train that can reach speeds up to 155 miles per hour, began passenger service over this route. In the first run, some passengers said they had trouble keeping their balance as they walked along the aisles—but they were quite happy to make the trip in two hours and fifteen minutes—forty minutes faster than the older Metroliners. There are 26 Metroliners on the rails between New York City and Washington, D.C., and, if there is sufficient passenger demand, all may be replaced with the new X-2000 high-speed trains.

The 155-mile-per-hour X-2000 is a big step forward in American train travel. Other plans have been proposed to build even higher-speed trains, like the ones found in Europe and Japan that run at speeds of two hundred miles per hour or faster. Because of Americans' travel habits, developers worry that these expensive projects might not pay off—so these high-tech trains do not seem to be in America's near future.

Airplanes carry a larger share of intercity passengers than either buses or trains, and this is especially true for longer trips. The chief advantage of planes over buses and trains is speed. Jet planes fly ten times as fast as buses and most trains can travel, and they don't have to stop for traffic lights. Planes lose this speed advantage in short flights because airports are generally located on the outskirts of cities. So getting to and from airports can take nearly as long as making short intercity flights.

Amtrak provides passenger train service between many cities in the United States. Many commuters use the train to travel to and from work. Do you know anyone who commutes to work by train? How long do they ride the train each day?

Overseas Service

Since the late 1950s, most overseas passengers have traveled by plane. The supersonic Concorde flies between New York and Paris or London in less than four hours, but a ticket may cost four to six times the price of an economy fare on a DC-10.

A few ocean liners are still in operation, but they take four days to cross the Atlantic and usually cost more than a Concorde flight. Those aboard ocean liners take this form of transportation mainly because they want to enjoy a cruise.

Transportation as a means of "getting away" on your vacation is discussed further in Chapter 40, "Applying Consumer Principles to Recreation."

PRIVATE TRANSPORTA-TION

The chief form of private transportation in the United States today is the automobile, which will be discussed in great detail. Many other forms of private transportation may be considered that are generally more economical. Will one of these suit your needs?

Bicycles

Most of us learn to ride a bicycle while still in elementary school, and many people ride bikes to high school and college classes. Now, more adults are riding bikes. Bicycling is good exercise, it doesn't cause pollution, and it's a lot less expensive than driving a car.

Will a bicycle serve your transportation needs? If so, you will need to decide which type of bicycle is best for

Bicycles offer inexpensive transportation and good exercise at the same time. Many cities have bicycle lanes on their main streets to provide a safer place for bicyclists to ride. Does your city provide bicycle lanes on any streets?

you. The least expensive bikes have only one speed and large tires, but they often weigh more than fifty pounds and riding one for more than a few blocks is very tiring. Lighter-weight bikes called *road bikes* come in three-, five-, ten-, fifteen-, and even eighteen-speed models. The five-speed bikes are only produced by a few companies and may not be available in your area. The fifteen- and eighteen-speed bikes are usually very expensive and are used mostly for racing. The three- and ten-speed bikes are popular models for both transportation and recreation. Rugged-style mountain bikes have become the fastest-selling type of bicycle in the U.S. Their sturdy frames, larger tires, and powerful brakes make them ideal for riding in rough terrain. A cross between these popular mountain bikes and the more efficient road bikes is becoming popular for transportation and recreation. You may find them in stores as *hybrid*, *crossbreed*, or *fitness* bikes.(See Figure 22.1 on the next page.)

Comparing Bicycles. A three-speed bike can be a reliable form of

Figure 22.1
Hybrid bikes combine the best features of both mountain bikes and road bikes. These bikes are comfortable and easy to ride. Visit a bicycle shop in your area for a close-up look at a hybrid bike.

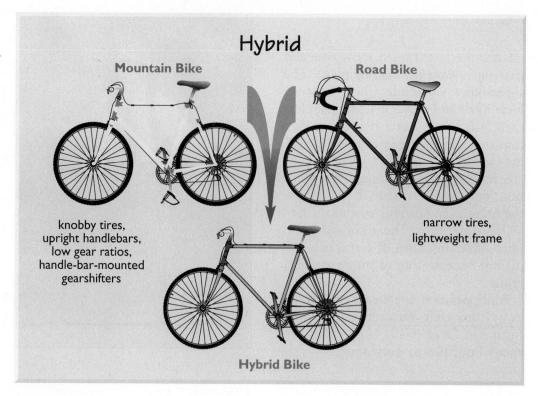

Hybrid

Mountain Bike

Road Bike

knobby tires, upright handlebars, low gear ratios, handle-bar-mounted gearshifters

narrow tires, lightweight frame

Hybrid Bike

transportation, and it isn't as expensive as a ten-speed model. Some people prefer the larger, more comfortable seat and upright handlebars that are typical of three-speed bikes. The shifting mechanisms of three-speed bikes are usually more rugged and require less maintenance than those of ten-speed models.

If you decide to get a three-speed bike, get one with gearing that fits your physical strength and condition. A three-speed with 45-60-80 gearing is about right for most people. It has an easy-pedaling low gear to get started or climb slight hills, a low-medium gear, and a high gear that is useful on level ground. If you are strong and in good physical condition, you will be able to ride faster on a bike with higher gearing (up to 54-72-96). A three-speed bike is not recommended for riding over a lot of hills.

The ten-speed models are more expensive than the three-speeds, but ten-speeds are easier to pedal—especially going uphill. They are usually lighter in weight, yet stronger. Many have dropped, racing-style handlebars and a narrow racing-style seat; however, the newer hybrid bikes usually have straight or upright handlebars.

A forward-leaning position is normal when riding a ten-speed bike. If you want the versatility of ten-speeds, but you prefer sitting upright, you may be interested in one of the new hybrid bikes. These bikes have light frames; narrow, knobby tires; wider seats; and upright handlebars. The gear shifters are mounted on the handlebars, which makes changing gears easier.

Shopping for a Bicycle. The most important qualities of any bicycle are:

- easy pedaling
- precise, predictable handling
- good brakes
- correct size
- overall quality

The best way to find out whether a bicycle suits you is to take a test ride. Check a bike's handling by riding in a pattern of slow, gentle turns, progressing to faster turns. Try the brakes. A slight squeeze should gently slow the bike, and a gradual increase in pressure on the brake lever should bring the bike to a smooth stop. Many stores will not let you test-ride their bicycles. If they do, be careful that you don't crash—or you will have to pay for damages.

When you buy a bike, get one that fits you. The fit is determined by the frame size, which is the distance from the axis of the pedal crank to the top of the seat tube. This distance most often ranges between nineteen and twenty-three inches.

A closed-frame bike has a horizontal top bar. When choosing a road bike, you should be able to straddle the bar with both feet on the ground and still have an inch between your body and the bar. Proper fit on a hybrid bike is about two inches' clearance; on a mountain bike, about three inches. An open-frame bike has no top bar. A frame size that is nine or ten inches less than your inseam is about right.

Price is often an indication of quality in bicycles—but check your local library for back issues of *Consumer Reports* magazine, and read the results of their tests on bicycles. Other magazines, too, may have informative articles about bicycles. Finally, compare warranties of bikes you are considering.

More than 85 million Americans ride bicycles, and the rise in popularity of bicycle riding has brought an increase in bicycle-related injuries. Bicycle helmets reduce the risk of serious head injury by 85 percent. Buy a helmet that meets the safety standards of the American National Standards Institute (ANSI) or the Snell Memorial Foundation. You can buy helmets meeting these standards at bicycle shops and

CONSUMER PROFILE

Will was an avid bike rider. He rode all around town and spent most weekends in long-distance bike rides sponsored by various organizations. He belonged to a local bicycle club, read bike magazines, and spent a great deal of money on the newest high-tech bicycle gear. He was definitely an experienced rider.

One Sunday, Will hopped on his bike to go get the Sunday paper. As he started out, he realized that his bike helmet was in the house. He didn't want to go to the trouble of going back to get it. Besides, as an experienced rider, he felt he was "safe" for this short ride to the store. As he turned the corner, however, a truck failed to stop at a stop sign and hit him head-on. He suffered extensive head and neck injuries. He spent weeks in the hospital and the next six months in a brace. The doctors said, without doubt, that Will's injuries would have been less severe if he had been wearing his helmet. Even an experienced rider can make a costly mistake.

some department and discount stores. According to the *Journal of the American Medical Association*, if all bicyclists wore helmets, a head injury

A helmet should be a basic piece of a bicyclist's gear. The price of a helmet now could save a lot of expense and pain later. It's not a sign of weakness to wear a helmet. Even professional bicyclists wear helmets because they know what's smart!

would be prevented every four minutes! Because many accidents occur near home, always wear a helmet, even on short trips.

Mopeds

For short-distance commuting (five miles or less), the moped (motorized bicycle) may be a convenient form of transportation. You can keep mopeds running for pennies a day, and maintenance is minimal. Generally, insurance for mopeds is less expensive than for other types of vehicles.

If you live in a warm climate, you can ride a moped year-round. Even riding in cold weather is tolerable if you wear a high-quality biker suit, but snow and freezing rain make riding a moped dangerous.

Parking is sometimes a problem. If it costs as much to park your moped as it does to ride the bus, there's not much point in buying a moped to ride to work. If you have to get on an interstate highway, forget the moped. Riding a moped on an interstate highway is against the law and also dangerous.

If most of your commuting is within five miles, over fairly level terrain, and if you don't have to pay for parking, a moped can be a money-saving convenience. If you're interested in a moped, check back issues of *Popular Mechanix* for articles on what to look for and how to get the best buy.

Motorcycles

Many people today use motorcycles for transportation. There are many sizes and types of motorcycles, or "bikes," as they are often called. Some are large and heavy, others are small and light. Lightweight bikes should be ridden only around town or away from fast-moving traffic.

The cost of motorcycles varies greatly. Prices range from about one thousand to about twelve thousand dollars, depending on the size and make of the bike and its accessories. Motorcycles are economical to use, and many will travel fifty or more miles per gallon of gas.

Insurance costs vary. Because the accident rate for motorcycles is high, owners often must pay large premiums. Premiums also depend on the type of bike and the type and amount of insurance.

Most motorcycles can reach speeds between fifty and eighty miles per hour. Since there is little or no external protection, riding a motorcycle can be dangerous. Because drivers of other vehicles often have difficulty seeing motorcycles, the likelihood of having a serious accident while riding a motorcycle is much greater than if you are driving a car—so motorcycle riders need to be especially alert.

If you ride a motorcycle, *always wear protective gear*. A safety visor or eye

Motorcycles can be a form of inexpensive and fun transportation, but they can also be dangerous and have high insurance costs. Much thought and research needs to be done before purchasing a motorcycle. Talk with someone you know who owns and rides a motorcycle. Would they recommend a motorcycle for someone like you?

goggles will protect your vision. Wearing a helmet may save your life in an accident, and it may be required by law in your state. Heavy clothing, gloves, and boots will help protect you in case of a minor accident.

Safety features on a motorcycle are especially important. A rear-view mirror helps you stay aware of other traffic at all times, and a roll bar provides some protection in a spill. A windshield helps keep dirt and insects away from your face or safety visor.

THE AUTOMOBILE

Are you satisfied with your present mode of transportation to school, to work, and around town? If your transportation needs can be met conveniently *without* owning a car, you will save yourself a lot of problems. A car is expensive—and the expenses don't stop with the purchase price. Expenses include finance charges (interest), insurance, operating costs (gas and oil), routine maintenance, taxes, license and inspection renewals, and repairs. These expenses almost always total more than the owner expects.

People buy cars to satisfy transportation needs or just for convenience, and most of us eventually buy cars. Nearly 90 percent of all American families own at least one. For the same type of car, whether new or used, some families pay a much higher price than other families. This happens simply because some people don't know how to shop for cars. And many people buy cars that don't really satisfy them, then lose money by trading in their cars within a short time.

If you are considering the purchase of a car, you have several decisions to make:

- whether buying a car is best for you
- whether to buy a new car or used car
- the type of car you want
- the specific car you will buy

Then, there will be decisions on financing, insurance, and maintenance.

Automobiles have changed greatly over the years. There were few choices with early automobiles. Today, however, it's nearly impossible to keep up with all the different makes and models. What is your idea of the ideal car?

Considering Need and Cost

Would you like to own a car? Many people automatically say *yes*, but weigh your need (or want) against the cost of ownership. Is there any other mode of transportation that will satisfy your real needs? Or does going to school, work, or shopping require a car? Would a car really be a satisfying convenience? Be honest with yourself—if a car would be a convenience instead of a necessity, admit it. Many young people feel a car provides added status and peer approval. If you want one very much and can afford the cost, that's reason enough to buy a car. Decide whether you can afford a car by estimating the cost of car ownership for the type of car you want. Of course, you may decide later that you prefer a much different type of car. In the meantime, though, you will have learned a good deal about the cost of car ownership.

Selecting the Type of Automobile

The type and size car you will buy depends on the driving you will do. A small two-seater or two-door compact model should do nicely if most of your driving will be around town with seldom more than one other passenger. Many of these models are quite economical, too. If you plan to do a fair amount of highway driving, you may prefer a heavier car to get a smoother ride.

If you will often have more than one passenger, a small car would be crowded. If you frequently have back-seat passengers, a four-door model will be more convenient for all the passengers than a two-door model.

Even in this first stage of selecting a type of car, consider your general price range. If you know you want a new, expensive model—and you have the money—there's little point in considering cheaper cars. If your cash and income are limited, why waste time considering a car beyond your reach?

Estimating Ownership Costs

When you have a fair idea of the type and size car you would like, pick one or two models. Then, research the cost of ownership.

Purchase Price. There are several ways to learn how much a particular model will cost. Read the classified ads in your local newspaper to get a general idea of the going prices for used cars. Stop at several used-car lots to see the overall condition of the cars that are being advertised. The prices on most used cars are not firm, so they can usually be purchased for 5 percent to 10 percent less than the asking price. If you talk to dealers, don't let yourself be persuaded to buy on the spot. At this point, you are only gathering information to help you decide *whether* to shop for a car. (Even when you *are* shopping to buy, always allow time to get away and think about the deal.) Another source of average prices for used cars is *The Kelly Auto Market Report* (the "Blue Book"). Banks, credit unions, and car dealers have copies, and your local library probably has one, too.

New cars must have the suggested retail prices listed on window stickers. By shopping around, you may buy most new cars for about 10 percent less than the sticker price. When you have determined the average price of one or two cars that interest you, write down the price of each, including sales tax.

the "Blue Book"
....
The Kelly Auto Market Report, which lists average prices for used cars

INTERACTING WITH TECHNOLOGY

IS A "BATMOBILE" OR "SUPERCAR" IN YOUR FUTURE?

It is not likely that you will be driving around in a car like that of the well-known cartoon character Batman, but an electric or battery powered vehicle could well be part of your future. Some cities are already using electric-powered shuttles for mass transit. Technology also exists for the production of cars driven by fuel cells or batteries. New Generation Vehicles, or supercars, that offer dramatically increased fuel efficiency, are under study throughout the automobile industry.

Most designs call for cars equipped with batteries that provide power for 50 to 90 miles before the battery must be recharged. Another system calls for the development of special battery-exchange stations. You could drive into one of these stations and in a few minutes your used battery would be automatically exchanged for a fully charged one. You would pay for the number of miles on the used battery much the way you now pay for the number of gallons of gas you use.

Obviously, driving a car with a range of 50 to 90 miles between refuelings will change consumer driving habits. Many researchers feel these cars will be ideally suited for the needs of urban errands and commuting. They offer tremendous benefits in terms of cleaning up the smog-filled air of large cities. Electric cars are extremely quiet, and the use of such cars would remove the noise of thousands of gas-powered engines from our cities, providing us with much quieter living and working environments.

In addition to improving the environment, these new designs include special features such as road guidance systems that direct you to the best route for your destination. Some of them feature timing elements that allow the car's heating and cooling systems to come on automatically, thus allowing you to always step into a comfortable vehicle. Others have mirrors that automatically adjust to compensate for glare and alarms that call the police with your location.

As auto makers test-market new designs, your role as a consumer will play a vital part in determining the success of these vehicles. If enough people choose to drive a "batmobile" or "supercar," mass production is likely.

Finance Costs. If you have saved enough money to pay cash for a car, you won't have to figure finance costs. Otherwise, subtract the amount you have saved for a down payment from your estimated purchase price, and the amount left will have to be financed. In 1992, finance charges on auto purchases averaged $750 for the year.

You may select a bank, credit union, or finance company for borrowing the money to buy your car. To get an idea of the monthly payments, call or stop by one or two of these places and ask for an estimate of the cost of a loan for one to five years. If you cannot get an estimate, ask for the current interest rate on auto loans—then multiply that rate times the amount you would need to finance to get the finance cost for one year. Then multiply the results times the years you will need the money. Divide this amount by two. Add the result to the amount you are borrowing. Finally, divide the total by the number of months that you will be making payments (assuming you would be making monthly payments).

This simple way of figuring will not show the exact amount you would have to pay, but it provides a quick estimate. Write down your estimated monthly payment.

Insurance Costs. For an estimate of your car insurance costs for one year, you will need to call several insurance companies. If other family members own cars, it may be less expensive to insure with the same company that insures their cars. Tell the agent the make and model car you are considering, your age, and say whether you are eligible for a "good student" discount. For the purpose of the estimate, ask for the agent's recommendation on coverage. This usually prompts a conversation in which you will learn some basics about car insurance. (Details of car insurance will be discussed in Chapter 23.) Write down your one-year estimate for car insurance (refer to Figure 22.2 below). In 1992, the cost of car insurance averaged $795 per year.

Taxes. Car taxes vary from state to state. Sales tax on the price of a new car purchased from a dealer is already included under the purchase price. All states require licensing of cars, and some states tax cars separately as personal property. Call the local agency that issues license plates to learn the cost of licensing your car. Check with other family members or your teacher about any other taxes that must be paid on cars in your state. Write down the amount you estimate for license plates and any other required taxes.

Estimated Cost of Car Ownership

Purchase Price	$7,500
Down Payment	-$1,500
To be Financed	$6,000
Finance Costs	$1,260
To be Repaid	$7,260
Other Costs (yearly)	
Insurance	$700
License Plates	$120
Maintenance	$1,200
Gasoline	$780
Miscellaneous	$350
Total	$3,150
Monthly "other costs"	$262.50
Monthly Finance Payment	$201.67
Total Estimated Monthly Cost	**$464.17**

Figure 22.2
....
It pays to sit down and figure the monthly costs of owning a car before purchasing one. You might also talk with some car owners you know. Did they realize all of the costs related to owning a car before they purchased theirs?

Maintenance Costs. The costs for maintenance include **preventive maintenance** and repairs, and these costs are likely to be more than you would guess. Preventive maintenance is service done to keep a car running well, to "prevent" major problems. Preventive maintenance includes tune-ups, oil changes, and replacement of the battery and tires as needed. Even with preventive maintenance, some repairs may be needed.

The average maintenance cost in 1992 was estimated to be $1,320 for the year, about $110 a month. This estimate was based on driving ten thousand miles during the year. However, the average annual mileage in this country is now fifteen thousand miles per year. If you expect to drive more or less than ten thousand miles a year, increase or lower your estimate accordingly. (Many young drivers underestimate the miles they will drive per year when they own their own cars.) You might change the oil or tune up the engine yourself. If so, maintenance costs will be somewhat less—but if you are considering a car more than three years old, costs may be higher than this. Write down your estimate for one year's maintenance.

Fuel Cost. The cost of gasoline for one year will depend on the number of miles you drive, the number of **miles per gallon (mpg)** your car delivers, and the type of gasoline your car requires. The cost will also depend somewhat on where you buy gasoline. Gas prices vary, even for the same brands. The cost for driving 15,000 miles a year ranged from $390 to $2,167 in 1992.

Divide the number of miles you expect to drive by the average mpg for your type of car. (The mpg will vary with the type of driving.) Then multiply the result by the price per gallon. Write down the estimated cost for gasoline for one year.

Miscellaneous Expenses. There will be additional costs that are totally unexpected, but you will want to in-

preventive maintenance
....
service done to keep a car or other vehicle running well

miles per gallon
....
the number of miles driven divided by the amount of fuel used

Regular maintenance can keep a car running better and longer. It can help with fuel efficiency, which saves money, and it can guard against future problems. Find out from a car dealer what kind of preventive maintenance they recommend.

MAKING CONSUMER DECISIONS

Brad is a recent high school graduate. He has just moved into a nice apartment with a friend and has a new job with a graphic design firm. The apartment is close to the downtown area where his new job is located.

Brad has been into bike riding for some time and has a good-quality street bike. It would be easy for him to walk or ride his bike to work. The local public buses have adequate routes. Between the buses and his bike, he could probably get just about anywhere he needed to in town. *However*, most of Brad's friends have cars, and he is concerned about what to do when he takes someone out on a date: Use the bus? Walk? So Brad is considering buying a car.

From the financial standpoint, he would have to go to a bank to apply for a car loan. Without any credit history, he would probably have to ask his parents to cosign for the loan. He would probably have to ask his parents to loan him the down payment too. The income from his new job would cover the payments, although that is money he could well save for other things he'd like to buy. He would really like to save up and get a stereo for his new apartment, for example.

What must Brad consider in his decision? Has he considered all the expenses? What are the disadvantages and advantages if Brad buys a car now? What are the disadvantages and advantages of waiting? What would you do?

---

clude an estimate of various other expenses. These may include parking fees and tolls, accessories you might want to add to your car, and the cost of a can of oil now and then. Write down your estimate for these costs.

Figuring the Cost of Ownership. Divide all yearly estimates by twelve to get the monthly cost for each type of expense. Then, add up all the monthly costs to see how much you will have to pay each month if you decide to buy a car. **Depreciation**—the declining value due to the age of a car—is not included in these estimates.

Based on your estimate of costs and your income, you can decide whether you can afford to buy a car. Your income may not be quite enough to buy the type of car you selected, so you may want to estimate the cost of owning a less expensive type. If you expect

your income to increase in a few months or a year or so, then you may want to wait awhile before you buy a car.

Summary

- There are three types of public transportation service: urban, intercity, and overseas.

- Urban public transportation is usually provided by buses; intercity transportation is usually by bus, train, or airplane; and overseas transportation is usually by airplane.

- Bicycles are a popular form of private transportation. They provide good exercise, don't cause pollution, and are much less expensive than driving cars.

depreciation
....
the declining value of a car, boat, or other vehicle, due to age

Used cars can provide good private transportation. However, great care must be taken to be sure the used car is actually a wise purchase. Chapter 23 provides a number of guidelines for buying a used car.

- When shopping for the right bicycle, be sure to take a test ride. Look for these qualities: easy pedaling, precise handling, good brakes, correct size, overall quality.

- Wearing a bicycle helmet reduces the risk of a serious head injury by 85 percent.

- Mopeds are a convenient form of private transportation. They are very inexpensive to run, maintain, and insure.

- Motorcycles are a popular form of private transportation. They vary in size and type, but all are economical to use.

- Automobiles are clearly the most popular form of private transportation. They can be expensive to buy, maintain, and insure.

- When selecting the type and size of car you want to buy, consider the type of driving you do and the number of passengers you usually have.

- Before you buy a car, research the cost of ownership. This includes: the purchase price, finance costs, insurance costs, taxes, maintenance costs, fuel costs, and miscellaneous expenses.

CHAPTER REVIEW
22

ENRICHING YOUR VOCABULARY

Read the following pairs of sentences. Write the sentence that correctly uses the underlined word or phrase.

Amtrak
commuter service
depreciation
intercity public transportation

mass transit
Metroliners
miles per gallon
(mpg)

preventive maintenance
the "Blue Book"

1A. Amtrak provides rail service between cities.

2B. Amtrak provides local transportation service.

2A. Metroliners are underground mass transit carriers.

2B. Metroliners are high-speed trains that run between New York City and Washington, D.C.

3A. Commuter service helps to keep an automobile running well.

3B. Commuter service transports people between a city and its suburbs.

4A. The loss in value of a car due to age is called depreciation.

4B. Finance costs are based on a car's depreciation.

5A. Intercity public transportation provides service within a city's limits.

5B. Intercity public transportation provides service between cities.

6A. City buses are a common form of mass transit.

6B. Airlines provide mass transit for travelers.

7A. MPG is a measure of the miles driven to the fuel used.

7B. The "Blue Book" computes the mpg for your automobile.

8A. A tune-up is a form of preventive maintenance.

8B. Preventive maintenance tends to prevent optimum performance of a vehicle.

9A. The "Blue Book" is a source of average used-car prices.

9B. The "Blue Book" provides a guide to preventive maintenance costs.

REVIEWING WHAT YOU HAVE LEARNED

1. Give three good reasons for using a bicycle as a means of transportation.

2. What are the five most important attributes of any bicycle?

3. What are the three types of public transportation?

4. What are three advantages that buses have over cars in city traffic?

5. Give seven expenses that are associated with car ownership.

CHAPTER REVIEW
22

USING YOUR CRITICAL THINKING SKILLS

1. The city of Transportania has a problem—the public bus system is losing money. Many people ride the buses, but most of them travel at reduced rates. Most riders are below the age of eighteen or above the age of sixty-five. Citizens of the community hold different views:

   - Some want to consider other types of public or private transportation.

   - Some want to do away with all public transportation to save the city money.

   - Others want to save the bus system by raising fares and cutting back on maintenance.

   - Still others want to maintain a quality bus system with reasonable fares by raising taxes.

   Discuss the pros and cons of each view. Can the problem be solved another way? What do you think should be done to best meet the needs of the community?

APPLYING WHAT YOU HAVE LEARNED

1. Research the purchase of a vehicle other than a car (such as a bicycle or moped). Tell what features you would look for, the purchase price, and any other facts that could help you make a decision.

CHAPTER 23

Buying Personal Transportation

OBJECTIVES

After completing this chapter, you will be able to do the following:
1. Name three library sources of information that are helpful when shopping for a car.
2. Explain why some drivers prefer buying used cars rather than new ones.
3. Name five places where you may locate a good used car.
4. Explain why you should test-drive a car before you buy it.
5. Name three types of automobile insurance everyone should purchase and explain why.

TERMS

collision insurance
comprehensive insurance
deductible clause
liability insurance
medical payments
  insurance

no-fault insurance
rating territories
test drive
title

trade-in
uninsured motorist
  insurance

Sooner or later, most of us decide we want the independence of personal transportation. If we must travel more than a few miles at a time, then we need more than a bicycle or a moped. Those who like to camp or need to haul things may prefer vans and pickup trucks. There are general guidelines we can use that are helpful for buying a vehicle, whether we choose a car, van, or a truck. To simplify our discussion, we'll call all of these vehicles cars.

SHOPPING FOR A CAR

If you decide that you do want to buy a car, review the type of car that will best fit your needs, then do some research on various makes and models. The research will prevent you from shopping for a car that is a bad buy at any price.

The U.S. Department of Transportation publishes several guides that are helpful. "*A Gas Mileage Guide*" is published yearly. Another publication, "*Cost of Owning and Operating Automobiles,*" is published about every three years. Your library may have these publications or can tell you how to obtain them.

If you are interested in a new car, read *Consumer Reports* and issues of other magazines which include test results on the cars that interest you. *Popular Mechanix*, *Motor Trend*, and *Car and Driver* all conduct tests on new cars. *Consumer Reports* magazines (January through April issues) are especially helpful, as they include maintenance records of most models of used cars. All of these publications are probably available in your local public library.

You may decide on one particular make and model of car, or you may pick two or three models and look for the best buy among them. If you are shopping for a new car, you should be

There are many magazines that contain information that can help you when car shopping. Many of these magazines should be available at your local library. Wise consumers will give the time and effort needed to research a purchase as important as a car. Talk to someone you know who has purchased a car. What kind of research did they do before making the purchase?

able to pick the options (accessories) that you want. If you are shopping for a used car, your choice of accessories may be limited.

Many people prefer to buy new cars. These people can usually get exactly the car that suits their needs or wants. Some drivers prefer buying used cars, and there are two main reasons for this. First, used cars are cheaper. Due to depreciation, the price of a car usually drops thousands of dollars by the time it is two years old. Second, some drivers feel that by the time a car is a year or two old, the original owner will have taken care of most of the car's "bugs."

test drive
....
driving a vehicle to evaluate its performance

SHOPPING FOR A USED CAR

Buying a used car is an exciting adventure for most first-time buyers. *Consumer Reports Annual Buying Guide* publishes a list of best buys in used cars that is very helpful. With careful shopping, you may find an excellent car at a bargain price, but there is also the chance that you will buy a car that's *no bargain at any price*. The average used-car buyer seldom inspects a car closely enough to find all the flaws. Many buyers don't even take a **test drive**, except for a quick spin around the block. This kind of shopping leads to a lot of wisdom *after the purchase*.

Where Should You Look?

When you have in mind the type of car you want to buy (and perhaps the make and model), check on its availability from several sources, including the following:

- private sales from individuals
- new-car dealers (trade-ins)
- used-car dealers
- banks and finance companies (repossessions)
- rental-car agencies (annual update of stock)

Private Sales. The best buys in used cars are often advertised in local newspapers by private individuals, but you must know what you're doing and be very selective.

The best indication of a good car is very low mileage. Watch the classified ads for several months, and you will probably find several low-mileage cars of the model you want. Many of these cars, up to three years old, are still under warranty (or extended warranty). If you find one, ask if the warranty can be transferred to you. If you can get one of these cars for a fair price, the car will likely prove an excellent buy. About 40 percent of all used cars are sold by the individual owners who advertise in local newspapers.

Used cars are available from many sources. Some sources may be more reliable than others, so it is important to check out the car carefully before you buy.

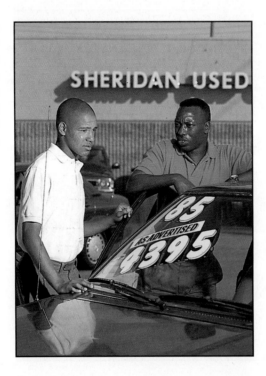

New-Car Dealers. Another source of good used cars is the used-car lot of a reputable new-car dealer. About 42 percent of all used cars are sold by new-car dealers. Many dealers offer to the public only the best of their customers' used-car **trade-ins**. (Trade-ins that are in poor condition and good trade-ins that do not sell in a reasonable time may be sold to wholesalers. The wholesalers often sell them to used-car dealers.)

New-car dealers make more profit on their new-car sales than on their used-car sales, but they know that satisfying you in your purchase of a used car may bring you back later to buy a new one. Many of these dealers have their trade-ins checked over by their service departments. Serious mechanical problems are often corrected before a new-car dealer offers a used car for sale. Where this is done, prices may be increased to pay for the service.

Cars that are less than four years old are warranted by many new-car dealers. If you are considering a warranted car, read the warranty before you buy.

Used-Car Dealers. The lowest-priced cars are often advertised by used-car dealers, and their cars tend to be older models or cars with high mileage. Many are trade-ins that new-car dealers did not want on their own used-car lots or could not sell.

Used-car dealers seldom have their own repair services. Sometimes they have their cars checked and repaired by other garages—but if they don't, you could buy a car that needs mechanical work right away. Then you would have to take your car elsewhere for service and repair. Some dealers have been in business for years, and many take pride in making fair deals, so it is possible to buy a good car from a used-car dealer. Nearly 18 percent of all used cars are sold by dealers who sell only used cars.

CHECKLIST FOR BUYING A CAR

When considering the purchase of a car, ask yourself the following questions:

____ Do I really need a car for transportation? If not, why do I want one?

____ What type of car would satisfy me?

____ Can I afford to buy this type of car? If not, would I be satisfied with the type of car that I can afford?

____ Have I checked all likely sources for the type of car I am looking for?

____ Have I thoroughly examined the car (or several cars) that I am considering? Have I had a mechanic check it over?

____ Am I satisfied that I can buy the car for a reasonable price?

____ Is there a warranty on this car?

____ If financing is needed, have I checked all likely sources and found the one that is best for me?

____ Have I checked with several insurance companies and found one that will insure this car at a reasonable price that I can afford?

Banks and Finance Companies. Cars that have been repossessed are sometimes sold by banks and finance companies. These cars have been taken back from owners who could not make their loan payments.

Repossessed cars are usually advertised in local newspapers, and sometimes you can buy one of these cars by paying off the amount due on the loan. Sealed bids are often required. In that case, you write down the amount you are willing to pay, place it in a sealed envelope, and mail or take it to the seller's office. A deposit is often required. When the bids are opened, the car goes to the highest bidder. Deposits are returned to unsuccessful bidders.

Rental-Car Agencies. Some rental-car agencies buy new cars every year and advertise their one-year-old models through newspaper ads. These cars usually have been driven a lot of miles

trade-in
....
an item, often a vehicle, that is applied toward the purchase of another item of the same type

It can save money later if you have a used car checked by a mechanic before buying it. The car may have hidden problems that won't show up for months. At that time it would probably be too late to take the car back to the dealer. Ask your friends or family if they know of anyone who had mechanical trouble with a used car shortly after they bought it. What did they do?

in a short time, but they are generally well maintained. Some of these cars have a written warranty.

What Should You Look For?

Thoroughly examine any car that you might consider buying. Spend as much time as it takes to determine the car's condition, because this can save you a lot of time and money later on.

Check the Outside. Start your check with the outside. Stand at least ten feet behind the car and see if it's level. If it isn't, there may be a weak or broken spring. Walk slowly around the car, looking for evidence of an accident (dents, faint ripples along the sides, and paint that doesn't match). Check the condition of all the glass (windows, headlights, taillights, backup lights). Push down hard on each corner of the car several times and then let go. If the car continues to bounce, it probably needs new shock absorbers.

Check Under the Car. Look under the car for breaks or excessive rusting in the frame. These are signs of weakness and are expensive to repair. Look for signs of oil or transmission fluid leakage on the ground. Look for leakage around the shock absorbers. Check the tires, and notice if there is leakage of brake fluid on the inside walls of the tires or wheels. Look over the muffler and tailpipe for holes.

Check Under the Hood and in the Trunk. Open the hood and check the condition of the water hoses and fan belts. Look for signs of leakage around the carburetor, oil filter, water hoses, and valve covers. Pull the oil dipstick to see how dirty the oil is. Then rub a drop of oil between your fingers to check for grit. Compare the mileage on the odometer with the mileage on the lubrication sticker. (The sticker should be on the door edge or under the hood.) Subtract to see how many miles the car was driven after the last oil change—this may be a clue to how well the previous owner maintained the car. (If the owner changed the oil, there will probably not be a sticker.) Check the battery to see if it's cracked or corroded. If the car has an automatic transmission, check the transmission dipstick. If the fluid smells burned or looks brown, the transmission probably needs major repairs.

Open the trunk and check the spare tire. If the spare is worn unevenly, there may be something wrong with the front end of the car. (Sometimes, a front tire is exchanged with the spare to hide the problem.) Check to see that there is a jack and that it is in workable condition.

Check Inside the Car. Open and close each door without slamming. If you find one that doesn't close well, it may be sprung (bent out of shape). Adjusting a door that is sprung is almost impossible.

Get inside the car. Examine the upholstery, carpeting, and seat belts. Check the accelerator and brake pedals. If there is a clutch pedal, check it, too. New pedals may mean the old ones were worn out. Excessive wear inside the car indicates wear all over. Does the steering wheel show a lot of wear? Turn it from side to side. It should turn only a few inches before moving the wheels. Too much free play may mean that expensive repairs are needed. Press down on the brake pedal and hold it for a full minute. If it sinks down, there is probably a leak in the hydraulic system.

Turn on the ignition. Check the lights, windshield wipers, and warning lights on the dashboard. If you have a friend with you, have him or her check all the lights from the outside while you turn them on—or ask the salesperson to turn on the lights while you check them. Turn on the radio and check how well it receives your favorite stations.

Go for a Test Drive. If you like the car, take it for a test drive—and don't limit yourself to once around the block. Drive it in town and on the highway, listening for vibrations in the steering that might indicate front-end problems.

If the car has an automatic transmission, notice if it shifts smoothly. If it sounds or feels rough, it may need expensive repairs. If it has a manual transmission, is there excessive play, grabbing, or rattling of the clutch? Drive at different speeds, and listen for vibrations or unusual noises in the engine, transmission, rear end, and wheels.

When safe to do so, step down on the gas. Does the car have all the pep you would expect from this type of car? If it's sluggish, it may need a valve job or an overhaul.

Find a straight, level road with light traffic to test the brakes. Accelerate to about forty-five miles per hour, then brake. Do this three times. The car should stop quickly without pulling to either side. Some cars will stop well a couple of times, but they will pull to one side or require more foot pressure after the brakes are warm.

While driving in stop-and-go city traffic, try the air conditioner. Does it cause the car to overheat? If it does, the cooling system will need repairs. Turn on the heater to see if it puts out enough warm air.

After you return, let the engine idle. Open the hood again and listen for vibrations or noises that may indicate a badly tuned engine or bad valves. Get back in the car and race the engine. Blue smoke coming from the exhaust is an indication of an "oil burner."

CONSUMER PROFILE

When shopping for a used car, Lisa went to new-car dealers, used-car dealers, contacted an auto rental agency, and looked in the classified ads of the newspaper. After spending four or five weekends looking at various cars, Lisa got discouraged and impatient.

The next car she saw was beautiful, clean, appeared to be well cared for, and was offered at a good price. The seller provided all receipts of past repair and maintenance work, and seemed very trustworthy. She liked the way it drove and looked, so Lisa bought the car. She trusted the seller, so she did not have it checked out by a mechanic. Relieved that her search was over, she was happy to have such a pretty car.

Within months, however, mechanical problems developed. She discovered, through *Consumer Reports* magazine, that this make of car has a very poor repair record. In less than a year, major mechanical problems appeared and she had to sell the car at a loss. She certainly regretted having been so impatient. She should have researched this car before she bought it, and she definitely wished she had checked it out with a mechanic!

Check with a Mechanic. If you are considering a car for sale by the owner, ask if you may see the service and repair bills. These will show how often the car has had oil changes and what kinds of repairs have been made. Write down the name of the garage where the car has been serviced, then stop by and see the mechanic. Ask about the general condition of the car and about problems that the mechanic has observed.

You may wish to have your own mechanic check the car before you buy it. Paying a mechanic forty or fifty dollars to check it over is far better than buying a car that needs hundreds or even thousands of dollars' worth of repairs. With the car on a hoist, it is easy to check the frame for damage or to discover fluid leaks. Ask for a check of the engine compression—low or uneven compression is a sure sign of future engine repairs. If you noticed anything unusual in your test drive, mention it to the mechanic.

In many cities, diagnostic centers specialize in finding all kinds of potential problems in cars. If repairs are needed, get a written estimate of the cost. Then, if you're still interested in buying the car, try to get the dealer (or owner) to deduct at least part of the cost of repairs.

Get a Clear Title. Make sure you will get a clear title before you buy. The title is a document that shows you legally own the car. Some buyers get stuck with a car that's about to be repossessed or one that's stolen. If the seller says he or she will get the title for you later, wait until it arrives before agreeing to buy the car.

When Not to Buy

Don't buy a car at night, unless you have examined it during the day, when you could check it out thoroughly.

Don't buy a car when it's raining, unless you have checked it over when it was dry. Even cars with bad paint jobs look good when wet. Don't buy if you are refused a test drive with you at the wheel. Don't buy if you aren't permitted to have your own mechanic check the car. Don't buy if you're refused another test drive after promised repairs have been done.

Getting the Best Price

When you've found a car that satisfies you, ask the dealer for the lowest price. Whatever the answer, he or she will almost always take even less—so you can save money by bargaining. Make the lowest offer you think might be accepted—then, if it isn't, you can always offer more.

Used-Car Warranties

Warranties on used cars, when offered, differ from dealer to dealer. Some warranties provide for all parts and labor for thirty to ninety days. Others pay half the cost of repairs for a certain period of time. If you receive a warranty and you suspect something is wrong with your car, take the car back right away. If it's not repaired to your satisfaction, keep taking the car back until it's done right. Don't accept an excuse like: "You don't have an appointment, bring your car back next week." The mechanic may be ill next week. And the following week, your warranty may run out.

Some states require motor vehicle inspections. If the dealer guarantees that a car will "pass inspection," get it in writing.

title
. . . . .
a document that shows legal ownership

SHOPPING FOR A NEW CAR

A new car will cost you more money than a used one, but shopping for a new one will be faster and easier. If you are willing to wait a month or two, you can get a new car with exactly the options you want. This is recommended, since there is little point in paying for extras that you don't care about. If you already know the type of car you want to buy, look over and drive a car like it. Dealers usually have "demonstrator" cars just for this purpose.

New Car Warranties

One of the advantages of buying a new car is that you will receive a warranty covering most major repairs for several years or until you have driven the car a specified number of miles. Terms of new car warranties vary considerably between car manufacturers and sometimes even between models. Usually, the warranty covers all parts and labor for major repairs for 2 years or 24,000 miles. Some cars are warranted for 5 years or 50,000 miles. You can buy an extended warranty for additional years and miles, but those who have studied the costs and benefits of extended warranties feel that they are usually priced higher than the cost of expected repairs. A good time to check the terms of the warranty is when you begin shopping for a new car.

Finding the Best Bargain

Decide on exactly the make, model, color, and options you want, then refer to one of the paperback books that list wholesale prices. Check *Edmund's New Car Prices* for American cars or *Foreign Car Prices* for imports. Your public library probably has copies of these books. Armed with this information, ask the dealer for the lowest price. As with a used car, you can almost always buy a new car for even less than the stated "lowest price." Most dealers are satisfied if they make $500 to $1,500 profit on a new car.

If You Have a Trade-in

If this is your first car purchase, you won't have to worry about getting a fair price for your old car. If you do have a car to trade, it's often best *not* to trade it in on your new one. Instead, sell your old car through an advertisement in your local newspaper. This will usually net you more than trading in your old car on the new one, and selling it yourself makes bargaining for your new car a lot simpler.

FINANCING A CAR

The least expensive way to buy a car is to pay all cash—then you won't have to pay any interest or loan fees. If you can't afford to pay cash (most car buyers can't), you will have to borrow some money. You will probably be able to borrow up to 70 percent or 80 percent of the selling price of the car, so you should have about 20 percent or 30 percent of the selling price saved for a down payment before you go looking for a car. If you have an older car to trade in or sell, it may serve as your down payment.

Many dealers are willing to arrange financing for you. This saves some time, but it may cost more than if you arranged financing on your own. (Sources of cash loans are discussed in Chapter 11.)

The best sources for a cash loan to buy a car are probably banks, savings and loan associations, and credit unions. If this is your first big loan, you may be required to have a cosigner. If you don't qualify for a loan through these sources, then check with a consumer finance company. A loan through a finance company will probably cost you more money in finance charges and interest.

Wherever you obtain a loan, arrange for the highest monthly payment you can afford. This will pay off the loan in the shortest time possible and hold down the cost of the loan. If you arrange for low payments over a longer period of time, you might want to save money by paying off the loan early—but this may not work. Some loan contracts call for payment of all finance charges even if the loan is paid off early. You can avoid this problem with a statement in the loan contract. The contract would need to allow reduction of finance charges if you prepay your loan.

BUYING INSURANCE

When you test-drive a car, the dealer or former owner has insurance on it. When you buy a car, you need your own insurance before you drive it home. If you finance a car, the bank or loan company will probably require insurance to protect its money in case the car is badly damaged. In many states, car insurance is a legal requirement. Even if it isn't, you will need insurance for your own protection. For example, a lawsuit resulting from an accident could be decided against you and cost you hundreds of thousands of dollars to be paid out over a period of years.

Types of Car Insurance

Did you get estimates of insurance costs before deciding whether you could afford to buy a car? If so, you are already somewhat familiar with the

There are many types of car insurance available, and an insurance agent may try to sell you more insurance than you actually need or want. You should know what types of insurance are required and what additional types of insurance you want before going to an agent's office. As with any purchase, research before the purchase can save you money.

kinds of insurance you will need. There are five basic types of car insurance:

- liability
- medical payments
- uninsured motorist
- comprehensive
- collision

All drivers should have liability, medical payments, and uninsured motorist insurance. You may wish to consider the other types of insurance as well.

Liability Insurance. Costs resulting from bodily injury and property damage to others are covered by **liability insurance**. The amount of coverage, in dollars, is often stated separately for each. Bodily injury insurance pays if your car injures or kills someone else. Many companies recommend coverage of $100,000 per injured person, with a maximum per accident of $300,000. Damage to property (usually another car) is usually less costly. Coverage of $50,000 is generally considered adequate for property damage insurance.

Liability insurance protects you whether you are driving or someone else is driving your car with your permission. You are also protected while driving someone else's car with the owner's permission. This protection covers the cost of claims or lawsuits brought against you, including the cost of an attorney to represent you in court. The cost of damage to your own car is not covered by liability insurance.

Medical Payments Insurance. Certain medical costs for you and your immediate family are covered by **medical payments insurance**. It covers injuries suffered while riding in your car or in someone else's car. It covers you if you are hit by another car while walking and it covers guests injured while riding in your car. The insurance company will pay these medical costs, up to the maximum amount stated in

When an accident occurs, the insurance company's adjuster will determine whether the company will pay to have the car fixed, or whether the car should be "totaled" (demolished) because the repairs would be too costly. If a car is totaled, the insurance company will pay toward a replacement vehicle.

your insurance, regardless of who caused the accident.

Uninsured (or Underinsured) Motorist Insurance. You and your immediate family are covered by **uninsured motorists insurance** against injury by a hit-and-run driver or a driver who has no insurance. You and your family are covered while in your own car, someone else's car, or while walking. Guests injured in your car are also covered. The insurance company will pay just as if it carried the insurance for the unknown or uninsured motorist. Recent estimates suggest that as many as 25 percent to 30 percent of drivers do not carry car insurance, so

liability insurance
· · · · · · · · · · · · · · · · · · · ·
insurance that covers costs resulting from bodily injury and property damage to others

medical payments insurance
· · · · · · · · · · · · ·
insurance that covers injuries suffered while riding in your own car or someone else's; it also covers guests riding in your car

uninsured motorists insurance
· · · · · · · · · · · · ·
insurance coverage against injury by a hit-and-run driver or a driver who has no insurance

uninsured motorist insurance is an important option to consider when purchasing insurance.

Comprehensive Insurance. If your car is damaged by fire, flood, earthquake, hurricane, hail, or collision with an animal, comprehensive insurance covers the losses. It also covers losses if your car is stolen. Damage by vandals and from many other causes is covered as well, but comprehensive insurance does not cover damage due to a collision with another vehicle.

Collision Insurance. The cost of repairing your car if it is damaged in an accident with another vehicle is covered by collision insurance. This insurance also covers repair costs if you run into some other object. It usually pays off only when the damage is not the fault of someone else.

Since even slight damage is expensive to repair, complete coverage is very expensive. To keep premiums at a reasonable rate, most policies include a deductible clause. In case of damage, you would then have to pay the repair costs up to the deductible amount. (The deductible amount is often $100, $200, or $300.) The insurance company would pay the rest.

Collecting from your insurance company for damages to your car will probably affect your premium, and renewing your policy the following year will probably cost you more. Many insurance companies "reward" those who don't have accidents that cost the companies money by not raising their rates.

No-Fault Insurance

Following an accident, the cost of repairing vehicles or other property is estimated by a car-body repair shop or an insurance claim adjuster. Repairs are usually made for the amount esti-

mated, but the amount that should be paid for personal injury is not as easy to determine. Besides the cost of medical expenses, injured parties often make claims for money for permanent injury. Deciding how much should be paid to a person who has lost an arm or an eye in an accident is not easy, and claims are also made for "pain and suffering." Settling these matters can take time.

Expensive claims for personal injury are often decided in court by a jury, which determines the amount that must be paid for damages. Juries sometimes award very high sums to victims, and these large payments increase the cost of insurance for all of us.

Sometimes a personal-injury claim is decided out of court—but even then the injured party cannot collect until there is agreement on who was "at fault" (who caused the accident). This, too, can take months. The injured person may not be able to work, yet medical bills must be paid. Thus, some states have passed laws approving no-fault insurance.

With no-fault insurance, the driver's own insurance company pays for his or her accident costs no matter who caused the accident. Medical bills are paid promptly. If the person cannot work, the lost income is also paid. No-fault policies pay on the basis of need.

Insurance Rates

Insurance rates are based on risk, which is the chance of losing something. An insurance company has greater risk when there is a greater chance of an accident—and the greater the risk to an insurance company, the higher the rates it charges.

In setting rates, companies keep track of accidents so they can know which groups of people are more likely to have them. Most companies base their

comprehensive insurance

insurance that covers the cost to repair a vehicle that is damaged by fire, flood, earthquake, hurricane, hail, a collision with an animal; it also covers the loss of a stolen vehicle

collision insurance

insurance that covers the cost of repairing a vehicle if it is damaged in an accident with another vehicle or if it runs into another object

deductible clause

a part of an insurance policy that tells how much the owner must pay toward damage or replacement of a vehicle (the deductible) before the insurance company will pay

no-fault insurance

insurance in which the driver's own insurance company pays for his or her accident costs no matter who caused the accident

rates on territory, coverage, driver classification, and the age and type of car. For example, a driver over thirty, living in a rural area and driving an older car, may pay under $200 yearly. An unmarried man under twenty-five, living in a large city and driving an expensive sports car, may pay more than $1,000 for the same coverage.

Rating Territories. Each state is divided into **rating territories**. A person is more likely to have an accident in city traffic than in the suburbs, so insurance rates are higher in cities. Those who live in rural areas are least likely to have an accident, so rates there are lowest.

Coverage. The greater the coverage, the higher the rate. A liability policy with $300,000 coverage will cost more than one with $100,000 coverage. A full-coverage collision policy will cost more than one with a deductible clause.

Driver Classification. Your age, sex, marital status, how much you drive, and your driving record are also considered in setting rates. Unmarried males under twenty-five have the highest accident rate, so insurance rates are highest for this group. Unmarried females under twenty-five are rated as the second-highest-risk group. If your driving is limited to a certain number of miles per week, rates are somewhat less. A record of several moving violations (such as speeding) increases rates greatly, and some companies cancel the insurance on anyone receiving three citations (tickets) in a three-year period.

Many companies have lower rates for people who have had behind-the-wheel driver training or for people who are nonsmokers. Some companies reduce rates for students with good grades. Statistics show that good students have fewer accidents.

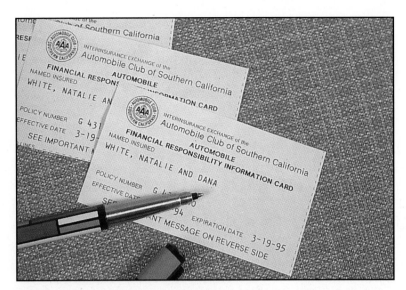

All states require that drivers be able to show proof that they can pay for any damages they might cause if they are involved in an auto accident. Most people carry insurance for this purpose. Ask someone you know to show you their proof-of-insurance card.

Age and Type of Car. Collision and comprehensive insurance rates are higher for newer cars and for cars that are more expensive to repair. Rates are also higher for sports cars than for sedans because sports cars are involved in accidents more often.

Motorcycle Insurance

Motorcycle insurance is similar to car insurance, but motorcycle insurance often has more restrictions. Policies vary greatly from company to company, and not all policies cover passengers. If you need motorcycle insurance, check with as many companies as possible.

Financial Responsibility Laws

Some drivers do not carry vehicle insurance, but all states have laws that require insurance or proof of financial responsibility in case of an accident.

rating territories
....
areas that states are divided into, by which insurance rates are determined

Almost all drivers elect to buy insurance, even if they have cash on hand to pay out the hundreds of thousands of dollars sometimes awarded as a result of an accident.

Summary

- When shopping for a car, be sure to research various makes and models. The public library has several publications that are helpful.

- Buying a used car is much cheaper than buying a new one. However, you may not find your exact choice of accessories.

- *Consumer Reports Annual Buying Guide* publishes a helpful list of best buys in used cars.

- There are a number of sources for used cars: private sales from individuals, new-car dealers, used-car dealers, banks and finance companies, and rental-car agencies.

- Thoroughly examine any used car you might consider buying. Take it for a test drive and have a mechanic check the car.

- One advantage of buying a new car is that you get a warranty that covers major repairs for several years.

- You can almost always buy a new car for less than the dealer's stated "lowest price."

- If you are going to finance your car purchase, you should have at least 20 percent to 30 percent of the selling price for a down payment.

- With a loan, choose the highest monthly payment you can afford. This will reduce the overall cost of the loan.

- It is important to have car insurance for your own protection.

- There are five basic types of car insurance: liability, medical payments, uninsured motorist, comprehensive, and collision. All drivers should have liability, medical payments, and uninsured motorist insurance.

- Insurance rates vary. These are based on: rating territory, extent of coverage, driver classification, and age and type of car.

CHAPTER REVIEW
23

ENRICHING YOUR VOCABULARY

Number your paper from 1–11. Read each sentence below. If the sentence is true, write "true" next to that number. If the sentence is false, rewrite it to make a true statement.

1. No-fault insurance protects you against ever being found at fault in an accident.

2. Before you can qualify for car insurance, you must complete a test drive.

3. Collision insurance protects against the cost of damage caused by hitting another car or object.

4. Cities are divided into rating territories for insurance purposes.

5. Liability insurance protects you against the cost of damage you may cause to others.

6. A large deductible clause increases insurance premiums.

7. Comprehensive insurance protects against losses incurred by theft.

8. Uninsured motorist insurance pays for damage caused by a driver with no license.

9. A car that is applied toward the purchase price of another car is called a trade-in.

10. A title is the same as a warranty.

11. Medical payments insurance pays for injury to anyone who is a passenger in your car.

REVIEWING WHAT YOU HAVE LEARNED

1. Name three library sources of information that are helpful when shopping for a car.

2. Name five places where you may locate a good used car.

3. Why should you test-drive a car before you buy it?

4. Which three types of insurance should all drivers purchase? Why?

USING YOUR CRITICAL THINKING SKILLS

1. To buy the car you want, you must borrow $2,000. If you want two years to repay the loan and the interest rate is 12 percent, about how much will it cost to borrow the money?

2. Why are insurance rates higher for younger people than for people in their thirties, forties, fifties, and older? Do you think this is fair? Why or why not?

APPLYING WHAT YOU HAVE LEARNED

1. Study the classified section of the newspaper to determine the approximate value of the car of your choice. Then, visit several used-car lots to check the conditions of cars within your price range.

2. Call or visit several insurance agencies to determine the approximate cost for car insurance.

CHAPTER 24

Transportation—Care, Economy, and Safety

OBJECTIVES

After completing this chapter, you will be able to do the following:
1. Name the three most important factors in selecting tires.
2. List eight things that you can do to improve your gas mileage.
3. Estimate the cost of maintenance per month, based on the number of miles per year that you drive.
4. Estimate the amount that you will pay for gasoline each month, based on the average mpg, expected miles driven per year, and average cost per gallon.

TERMS

lemon law   tread   vacuum gauge
traction

Driving home in the car you have chosen is a happy experience, but will you continue to be happy and satisfied with your choice? This depends a great deal on how you care for your car and on how economical your car is to drive. Find out how to care for your car properly and learn to drive it economically and safely. These practices are just as important as making a good choice of which car to buy.

CARE AND ECONOMY

All vehicles need repair now and then, but regular maintenance makes major repairs less likely. Every new car comes with an owner's manual that provides information about the car and how to care for it properly. Follow the regular maintenance schedule outlined in the manual, and you will save money in the long run by keeping repair bills down and by saving gas. Regular maintenance is money well spent, regardless of the type of vehicle.

Choosing a Repair Garage

If you buy a new car, you will probably get the best service by having it maintained and repaired in the dealer's garage. For a used car bought from a new-car dealer, the dealer's garage is also likely to give you good service. If you buy from an individual, ask where the car has been serviced—and ask whether the owner was satisfied with that garage's maintenance and repair service. Members of your own family or family friends are other good sources of information on garages with good reputations.

When Your Car Needs Repairs

When your car needs repairs, make an appointment and allow the garage enough time to do the repairs properly. If you take your car in late in the day or if you say you need it by noon, some mechanics will hurry the job. They may not be as thorough and careful as they would be otherwise.

Taking Your Car to a Mechanic.
Working in, around, and under cars is often a dirty job. Place an old towel on the front seat and you may avoid getting grease on your upholstery.

At many garages, cars are checked in by service managers. If possible, though, talk with the mechanic who will actually be working on your car.

Unless you know for sure what's wrong with your car, just describe the symptoms. Then leave the diagnosis to the mechanic. If you drive in and ask for a new alternator, it's likely that you'll get one, even if reattaching a loose wire would have solved the problem!

Leaving Your Car.
Before you leave your car, write down the odometer reading (mileage). If the mechanic takes your car for a road check, it won't add many miles—but some garages occasionally use customers' cars to pick up parts or make deliveries. When you pick up your car, the odometer should not show a figure much higher than before. If it does, ask why.

If you keep valuable items in your car, remove them before leaving the car at a garage. Don't even leave any valuables in the glove compartment or trunk. Garage owners often post a sign saying, "Not responsible for items left in cars." In a garage, many people come and go daily. If you remove valuable items, other customers and garage employees will not be tempted to take

If you buy a new car you will get a schedule that tells when you car needs regular maintenance. If you don't have a maintenance schedule, talk to a mechanic you trust about when your car should be checked for different things. Regular maintenance now can save big repair bills later.

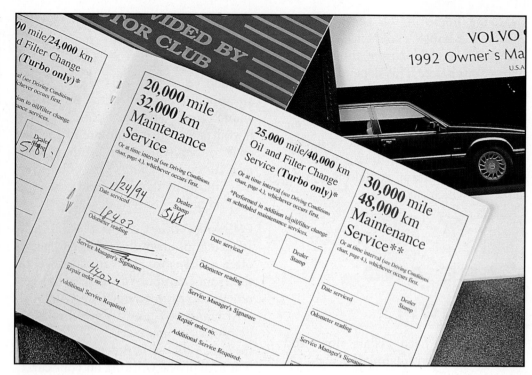

them. It would be hard to prove that a loss occurred while the car was in the garage.

The only keys you should leave at a garage are your car keys. Have an extra set made for this purpose. Attach a tag with your name on it. This will make it easier for garage employees to match your car with your keys—or to find your keys if they are mixed in with others. Make certain that the garage has a safe place for keeping the keys before and after your car is repaired. Otherwise, a casual thief could walk by and pick them up.

Getting Your Car Back. When you return for your car, look it over carefully. Sometimes a car gets a dent while in the garage. If you drive away and then return with a dent, you may have a hard time convincing the mechanic that the dent happened there. When you do drive away from the garage, notice whether the original problems have been solved. If they haven't been, drive right back and point out the problems to the mechanic or service manager.

You may have to make another appointment and bring the car back later, but at least you won't be charged for something that was not corrected.

New Car Lemon Laws

When you buy a new car, you expect it to run well for a long time, but sometimes this doesn't happen. Once in awhile, a person buys a new car that seems to have one problem after another—or the same problem over and over. These problem cars, which have left a bad taste in the mouths of owners, are known as *lemons*. Most states have **lemon laws** that provide some relief for the customers who buy these new cars. These laws vary from state to state, but most define a lemon as a new car, truck, or van that has been in the shop at least four times for the same repair or is out of service for a total of 30 days during the first year.

If you think your new car is a lemon, you can learn the details of your state's lemon law from your local consumer

lemon law
....
a law that varies from state to state, but which usually defines a *lemon* as a new car, truck, or van that has been in the garage at least four times for the same repair or is out of service for a total of 30 days during the first year

protection office or your state attorney general's office (c/o your state capitol).

Buying Tires

Even if you take good care of your car, some parts do wear out. Some things, like spark plugs, batteries, and tires must be replaced periodically. The most expensive replacements are tires—and good tires are essential for safe driving, so replace tires that have any deep cracks or cuts. Tires with less than one-sixteenth of an inch of tread should be replaced too.

When you buy tires, select according to your needs. Will you be hauling extra-heavy loads? If so, you will want to buy heavy-duty tires. Will much of your driving be in snow? Then you would need snow tires. Snow tires are designed to "bite into" snow, and they improve traction (holding power). However, these tires have less traction than regular tires on wet pavement because less of the snow tire's surface touches the driving surface. Even if you don't need special tires, there are other considerations.

Factors in Selecting Tires. The three most important factors in selecting tires are:

• tread wear

• traction

• resistance to heat buildup

Of course, everyone wants to get as much wear from tires as possible. Generally, thicker tread gives longer wear, but thick tread tends to heat up at highway speeds, sometimes causing a tire to come apart. Good traction means being able to stop quickly even on a wet pavement. Thicker tread provides quicker stops.

The National Highway Traffic Safety Administration sets testing requirements for passenger tires. The ratings for tread wear, traction, and temperature appear on the sidewall of all tires, as follows:

• Tread wear—if the tread is expected to last thirty thousand miles, the tire

tread
....
the part of a tire that makes contact with the ground

traction
....
friction or holding power

Tread wear is one of the three most important factors to consider when buying tires. Traction and resistance to heat buildup are the other two factors. Check the tires on your family car. What ratings for tread, traction, and resistance to heat buildup appear on the tires? (See this page and the next for explanations of what the ratings mean.)

CHECKLIST FOR INSPECTING YOUR CAR

You can check some important parts of your car quickly and easily yourself. Take a few minutes each month to make sure your car is in good condition by checking each of the following:

___ Engine oil—if you need more, add the same grade that is already in the engine.

___ Belts—make sure they are not loose, frayed, or cracked.

___ Hoses—squeeze them to make sure they are not too soft, which means they might be ready to split.

___ Air filter—replace this when it is dirty and before it becomes clogged.

___ Radiator coolant—make sure that there is enough and that it is not rusty. Don't open any cap when the engine is hot.

___ Battery water—clean off any corrosion at the posts and check for enough fluid. Don't get corrosion or fluid on your hands or clothing.

___ Other fluids—check fluid levels for automatic transmission, power steering, brake master cylinder, and windshield washer.

___ Tires—check the inflation pressure of all tires, including the spare, and check for wear.

___ Wheels and shock absorbers—check the inside of the wheels for brake fluid leakage. Check the shocks for leaks.

___ Lights—check the headlights (low and high beams), turn signals (front and rear), and taillights.

___ Wipers—with some fluid on the windshield, check for streaking, missed spots, or chattering.

___ Leaks on the pavement—note the colors: black or brown for engine oil or rear axle fluid, usually reddish for automatic transmission fluid, greenish for antifreeze.

___ Exhaust system—shake the tailpipe when it's cool to check that it is firmly attached.

is given a tread wear rating of 100. A tire rated at 150 should provide 50 percent longer tread wear, or about forty-five thousand miles.

- Traction—according to the tire's ability to stop on wet pavement, it is rated A (best), B, or C (worst).

- Temperature—samples of each kind of tire are run at high speeds in a hot testing lab. Those that are most resistant to heat buildup are given a rating of A. Those that get hot and break down at highway speeds are rated C.

Types of Tire Construction. There are three basic types of tire construction:

- bias
- belted-bias
- radial

Bias tires are made with layers of fabric laid on the bias (diagonally). Belted-bias tires are similarly constructed but also have one or more layers laid around the tire as a belt. The fabric in radial tires is laid in a radial pattern, across the circumference. A radial tire also has one or more belts laid around it.

Radial tires are the most expensive type you can buy, but they generally provide better gas mileage because they have less road resistance than regular bias tires. They also have longer tread wear and permit better handling. Belted-bias tires are better than regular bias tires, but are not as good as radial tires.

For best performance and safety, all tires on your car should have the same type of construction. If this is not possible, then the two tires on the front should be of the same type, and the two on the rear should be of the same type.

Driving for Economy

The average driver uses about 800 gallons of gasoline each year. Because the cost of gasoline has increased greatly in recent years, many drivers are learning to drive for better economy. Many have attended economy-driving school, and what they have learned has helped them improve their car's mileage from 20 percent to 30 percent. A savings of 20 percent is 160 gallons of gasoline each year. Multiply that by the price per gallon you pay, and you will see how much can be saved by learning to drive for economy. This savings can be achieved by following proper car maintenance and driving techniques.

Checking Your Driving Techniques. If your car has a vacuum gauge, you will always know if your driving techniques are saving gas. (When the vacuum is high, fuel use is low.) A vacuum gauge can pay for itself in two or three months in gas savings. Vacuum gauges are available at most auto accessory stores, and they shouldn't take more than an hour to install.

"First-Aid" Supplies for Your Car

You don't have to be a mechanic to fix many of the little things that can go wrong with your car. The following items have been found to be among the most useful in emergencies. You can keep some of these items in your glove compartment:

- spare fuses for the electrical system
- a good flashlight
- a pocketknife
- an ice scraper for winter driving
- the name, address, and phone number of a mechanic or friend to call in an emergency

Keep these items in your trunk:

- a spare tire (with air in it)
- a fire extinguisher
- a first-aid kit
- a jack and a lug wrench for changing tires

- flares (stored where children can't easily get to them) or reflective day/night devices

Other useful items are:

- a fire department-approved empty can (never carry gasoline in the trunk) for carrying gasoline if you run out of gas

vacuum gauge
....
a device on some vehicles that indicates when fuel use is high or low

CHECKLIST FOR DRIVING ECONOMY

The following tips for gas-saving maintenance and driving really work. Try them all, and see how many added miles you can get from a tank of gas.

Maintenance
____ Keep your car properly tuned.
____ Inflate tires to the correct pressure. Check them when they are cold.
____ Keep the air filter clean.
____ Keep the fan belt tightened.
____ Use radial tires to improve mileage.

Driving
____ On the highway, drive at a steady speed between fifty and fifty-five miles per hour.
____ Keep the windows closed when driving over forty miles per hour. Open windows cause wind resistance, and that uses more gas.
____ Look ahead to traffic lights. If a light is red, take your foot off the accelerator and coast to a stop. Avoid using the brakes when you can. When the light turns green, accelerate smoothly.
____ Whenever you stop for more than a minute, turn off the ignition and restart the engine when you're ready to go. Of course, you will have to decide whether it would be difficult to restart in very hot or cold weather.
____ When starting your car in cold weather, don't let it sit still to warm up for more than a minute.
____ Fast, erratic ("jack-rabbit") starts waste gas, but so do very slow takeoffs. A medium-fast start is most economical. Accelerate slowly on gravel, sand, and on snowy, icy, or rain-slick roads.
____ Accelerate slightly before starting up a hill. Don't try to gain speed going up. Once over the top, let up on the gas pedal and let gravity help carry you down the other side.
____ Don't cut in and out of traffic.

There are many practical items that should be kept in your car to be used in case of an emergency. Many of those items are shown here. Emergency kits containing these items can be purchased at auto supply stores and many discount department stores. What items are kept in the trunk of your family's car?

- a small toolbox (in the corner of the trunk) containing pliers, screwdrivers, an adjustable wrench, tape, wire, and some rags

- one or two cans of engine oil

- battery jumper cables

- an aerosol can for inflating tires or a tire pump

- a plastic sheet for changing a tire in the rain, or for placing on the ground if you need to get under the car to check something

Summary

- There are many things you can do yourself to keep your car in good condition. Take your car to a reputable mechanic for needed repairs.

- The three most important factors in selecting tires are: tread wear, traction, and resistance to heat buildup.

- There are three basic types of tire construction: bias, belted-bias, and radial.

CHAPTER REVIEW
24

ENRICHING YOUR VOCABULARY

Read the following pairs of sentences. Write the sentence that correctly uses the underlined word or phrase.

1A. The depth of the <u>tread</u> on a tire is one measure of a tire's safety.

1B. Radial tires do not have <u>tread</u>.

2A. A <u>vacuum gauge</u> is a handy tool for cleaning out the interior of a car.

2B. A <u>vacuum gauge</u> is helpful in determining how efficiently you are using fuel.

3A. <u>Lemon laws</u> protect buyers of new cars that have excessively high repair rates.

3B. <u>Lemon laws</u> protect buyers of used cars.

4A. Snow tires have good <u>traction</u> on snow and poor traction on wet pavement.

4B. <u>Traction</u> is a measure of how well a tire will wear.

REVIEWING WHAT YOU HAVE LEARNED

1. What are the three most important factors in selecting tires?

2. What are eight things you can do to improve your gasoline mileage?

USING YOUR CRITICAL THINKING SKILLS

1. How will you choose a garage for having your car repaired? What factors must be considered? What are some possible sources of information?

2. Consider that the average cost of car maintenance is $1,320 per year, based on ten thousand miles of driving. If you expect to drive eleven thousand miles per year, how much should you set aside for maintenance each month?

3. Suppose that your car delivers 22 mpg. You expect to drive eleven thousand miles per year. You pay an average of $1.60 per gallon for gas. How much, on the average, will you pay for gasoline each month?

APPLYING WHAT YOU HAVE LEARNED

1. Follow the suggestions made in this chapter to estimate the cost per month of owning the car of your choice.

2. Using research and your imagination, describe what future transportation will be like. Give reasons wherever possible.

UNIT

9

HOUSING

CHAPTERS

E arly American settlers built single-room cabins using wood from the forests. In the cabin, a family would cook, eat, sleep, and entertain. Today, most of our housing is more elaborate, and we have many more types of housing to choose from—so we must make decisions about the style of housing we want. We also need to decide where to live and whether to buy or rent. These decisions are important because housing takes as much as one-third to one-half of our income. This chapter will help you understand better how to make your housing decisions.

What is Housing?

OBJECTIVES

After completing this chapter, you will be able to do the following:
1. List five reasons why we need housing.
2. Name the four main groups of values that determine housing decisions.
3. Explain how the stages in the family life cycle affect the choice of housing units.

TERMS

family	household	housing unit
family life cycle	housing	

Housing is available in many styles. Condominiums, apartments, and houses are the most common types of housing. Take a survey in your class to find how many students live in condominiums, apartments, houses, or other types of housing.

Housing may be of any shape or size. Your idea of housing may be a large apartment building or a small house for a single family. For the Pueblo Indians, housing was once a cliff dwelling carved into the side of a mountain. For the Masai tribe in Africa, housing is one large, round hut surrounded by several small huts—the women live in the small huts, and the men live in the large hut. In each of these cases, housing is a structure that provides protection from the weather, a place where people live, work, and play together. It is also a place for privacy.

People occupy housing either singly or in groups as families or households. According to the federal government's definition, a **family** is two or more persons who are related by blood or marriage and live together. A **household** is any person or group of persons living together in a housing unit. All families are considered households, but all

housing
· · · · · · · · ·
shelter or lodging provided for people

family
· · · · · · · ·
two or more persons who are related by blood or marriage and who often live together

household
· · · · · · · · ·
any person or group of persons living together in a housing unit

households are not families. For example, a single person living in an apartment is considered to be a household but not a family.

As we discuss the needs and costs of housing, keep in mind that many different types of buildings will be called housing or housing units. A building with twenty apartments contains twenty housing units. A housing unit is a part of a structure or a whole structure in which one or more people live together.

housing unit
....
part of a structure or an entire structure in which one or more people live

WHY IS HOUSING NEEDED?

Housing meets the most basic human needs and may meet all of the five basic human needs described by Maslow. (See Chapter 2.) These are the needs for:

- survival
- safety and security
- social belonging
- self-esteem
- self-actualization

You will recall that these needs are hierarchical. That is, each level of need must be met before the next level of need can be fully met.

Meeting the Need for Survival

The need for survival is the most basic need. Everyone must have food, clothing, and shelter in order to survive. Housing provides shelter.

By providing shelter, housing keeps people protected and increases the likelihood that they will stay alive. Depending on the climate, housing protects people from rain, snow, sun, and wind. Protection is provided in different ways. For example, houses in New England usually have steeply sloping roofs that enable the snow to slide off in the winter. In the southwestern United States, thick concrete or adobe walls often provide protection from the hot sun.

To maintain good health, housing must also allow light and fresh air inside. Over 100 years ago in England, city houses were built very close together. Some of these houses had no windows—and since no light or fresh air could enter, many people became ill.

Meeting the Need for Safety

Security (safety) is the second most basic human need. Historically, housing protected people from animals and from invaders. During the Middle Ages, high, outer walls or deep, water-filled ditches called moats were sometimes used to make homes safe. Today, people still need protection; and many housing units use lighting, locks, and sometimes even fences and alarms for safety.

Meeting Social Needs

Housing provides a place for members of a family or household to meet social needs, to work and play together, to interact. The amount of space in a house affects our relationships with other members of the family or household. In a large housing unit, each person has more privacy. There is space for people to pursue their own interests as well as work and play together. Different rooms can be used for different activities. In a very small housing unit, however, there is less privacy. Sleeping quarters may have to be shared. Each room may have to serve several purposes.

Think about it. If you live in a small housing unit now, imagine how your life would be different in a large housing unit. If you live in a large housing unit now, imagine how your life would be different in a very small housing unit.

The size and location of housing units also influence how we behave. In open country, families can raise chickens without affecting neighbors, but families that live in city apartments must be more considerate of their neighbors. For example, the volume on a stereo may need to be kept low so that the sound will not disturb neighbors.

Meeting the Need for Self-Esteem

Generally, people like to live in houses that make them feel good, that they can be proud of. A house that does these things meets the need for self esteem or status. Outside appearance is important. As you approach your house from the street, does it make you feel good and proud to live there? If not, is there something about its appearance that you could improve?

Housing can be a reflection of how we feel about certain things. What about this house tells you that the owners are concerned about the environment and saving money? Take a look around your neighborhood. What types of things are reflected in the housing?

Meeting the Need for Self-Actualization

Housing provides a place for self-expression because housing can be personalized. It can provide space for hobbies and other self-development activities that meet the highest level of housing need. Some examples include a photo darkroom in one's home that provides a place for creative expression; a music room for improving music skills, composition, and even concerts; a writer's study where ideas for books are born and manuscripts polished. For a student, a desk in the bedroom makes it easier to study—which in turn leads to better understanding, better grades—and makes the student feel better about himself or herself.

VALUES IN HOUSING

There is no formula for a house that meets all needs, because each family member tends to want or need different things, and each family is different from every other family. To help you make decisions, rely on your own values. You will recall from Chapter 2 that values are things you consider important, things you believe in. They help establish your course of action. We all hold many values, and some-

Having a place at home where you can pursue hobbies can help meet your need for self-actualization. What hobbies do you have? Is there a place at home where you can work on your hobbies?

times we must choose one value over another. This can be difficult.

Values influence each decision made, even when we are not aware of them. Studies show that the following four main groups of values influence people in their choices of housing:

- economy-oriented values
- family-oriented values
- aesthetic-oriented values
- prestige-oriented values

Economy-Oriented Values

Some decisions are made to minimize costs. Many people give up a level of appearance, quality, and efficiency if doing so saves money. You might ask the following questions when selecting housing:

- How much does it cost?
- What are the utility bills?
- What is the resale value of this house?
- Will the house be costly to maintain?
- What will I need to spend for adequate furnishings?

Family-Oriented Values

Some decisions are made for the well-being of the family. Safety, security, and the amount and division of space within the house are important. The housing should enable each member of the household to have privacy and space enough to pursue individual activities. You might ask questions such as:

- Is the house located away from busy traffic intersections?

- Is there room for family activities?
- Is there space to entertain groups?
- Is there privacy for each family member?
- Will the school system provide a good education for the children?

Aesthetic-Oriented Values

Some decisions are made based on appearance. The beauty of the design and how well the housing fits the surroundings are concerns of many people. You might ask questions such as:

- Does the house add beauty to its surroundings?
- Do the surroundings add beauty to the house?
- Is the house well designed and well maintained?
- Is the floor plan usable and pleasing?

Prestige-Oriented Values

Decisions may be based on the status and recognition people can gain from housing. Some people want expensive, visible features, such as fancy siding or a swimming pool. They want people to know by the appearance of their home that they have succeeded financially. Questions reflecting these values include:

- What are the neighbors' occupations?
- Does the house have the latest appliances?
- Is the house custom built?
- Does the location suggest success?

Which types of values, economy-, family-, aesthetic-, or prestige-oriented, do you think are most important to the people who live in the neighborhood pictured here? Why do you think this?

Values change as individuals and families change and grow. Overall, however, financial resources are the most important factor in determining housing decisions.

THE FAMILY LIFE CYCLE

Family life moves through various stages, and these stages make up the **family life cycle**. As a family moves through the different stages in the life cycle, different things are considered important and necessary in housing. These changes cause families to move or alter their housing. For example, a single person or a young couple may find apartment living very comfortable. A family with children may prefer a single family housing unit that provides more space and outdoor areas. Older, retired individuals may no longer need so much space and may be unable to

maintain yards or to do needed repairs. Family resources also change over time, and these changes may require a change in housing.

Summary

- Decisions about housing are important decisions. Housing takes as much as one-third to one-half of our income.

- Housing may meet some or all of the five basic human needs described by Maslow: survival, safety and security, social belonging, self-esteem, and self-actualization.

- People choose housing based on four main types of values: economy-oriented, family-oriented, aesthetic-oriented, and prestige-oriented.

Families with schoolchildren and families with adolescents are just two of the many stages of the family life cycle. Is it possible for a family to be at more than one stage at the same time? At what stage is your family?

CHAPTER REVIEW
25

Enriching Your Vocabulary

Number your paper from 1–5. Read each sentence below. If the sentence is true, write "true" next to that number. If the sentence is false, rewrite it to make a true statement.

1. The U.S. government defines a <u>family</u> as a household.

2. A single person or a group of persons living together constitutes a <u>household</u>.

3. <u>Housing</u> meets a basic human need.

4. Huts, houses, and apartments are all examples of <u>housing units</u>.

5. The <u>family life cycle</u> refers to the fact that most American families move several times during a lifetime.

Reviewing What You Have Learned

1. List five reasons why we need housing.

2. What are five economy-oriented questions that you might ask when selecting housing?

3. What are five family-oriented questions that you might ask when selecting housing?

4. What are four aesthetic-oriented questions that you might ask when selecting housing?

5. What are four prestige-oriented questions that you might ask when selecting housing?

6. How do the stages in the family life cycle affect the choice of housing units?

Using Your Critical Thinking Skills

1. Which values in housing are especially important to you and your classmates now? Why?

2. Which values do you think will be important to you at later stages in your lives? Why?

Applying What You Have Learned

1. From magazines, cut pictures of houses to illustrate different types of values. Tell what features of the houses reflect the values.

2. Survey your classmates and determine which type of housing structure they prefer. Make a list of their reasons.

CHAPTER 26

Examining Housing Alternatives

OBJECTIVES

After completing this chapter, you will be able to do the following:
1. List the two basic types of housing structures.
2. List one advantage and one disadvantage for each type of structure.
3. Name three reasons why many people prefer to rent housing.
4. Explain and describe the trend toward buying condominiums rather than renting or buying a house.

TERMS

condominium	lease	multifamily housing unit
cooperative	location	security deposit
energy efficient	maintenance fee	single-family housing unit
Home Owners Warranty	mobile home	subsidy
(HOW)	modular house	tenant

Each year, the demand for housing units increases. This is due primarily to the number of households being formed. Many new households are composed of single individuals because people are remaining single longer, divorcing more often, and living longer. The country as a whole has been unable to meet the increased demand for housing.

When looking for housing, you probably will not find a "perfect house." You may have to give up one desired feature in order to obtain another that you consider more important.

One factor in making housing decisions is important to everyone, and that is **location**. Before considering features and prices, consider the location of the property. Find out as much as possible about the neighborhood and community by talking with neighbors, shopkeepers, and school and church officials. Try to learn whether there are any hazardous waste dumps or unpleasant odors in the area. Find out whether there are high levels of noise, such as from a nearby airport. An undesirable location can make the most ideal housing unit unacceptable.

IDENTIFYING HOUSING ALTERNATIVES

What are the housing alternatives? The Figure 26.1 is a decision-making model for housing consumers. It shows the alternatives possible for each decision to be made. One decision leads to another until satisfactory housing is

location
....
neighborhood or community in which a housing unit is situated

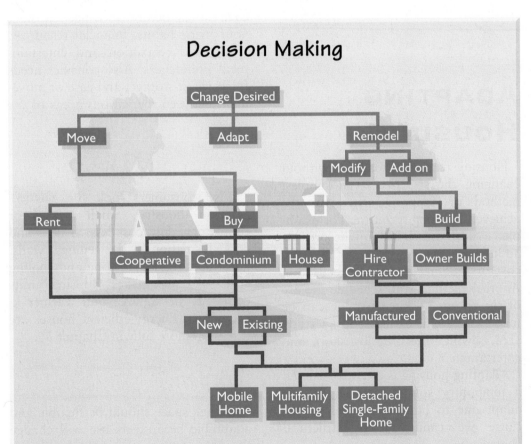

Figure 26.1
....
There are many alternatives to choose from when deciding on housing. The first consideration, however, is finances. Be sure the choice you make—moving, adapting, or remodeling—fits within your budget.

obtained. In the rest of this chapter, we will examine each part of the model from the viewpoint of the consumer so that you will be able to make wise consumer decisions about housing.

The average American family moves once every five years, often due to changes in family composition. For example, a baby may be born or a child may grow up and move away from home. Sometimes people move because of a new job, or the company they work for may transfer them. Sometimes they acquire more money to spend on housing and simply want a larger or more satisfying home. Any of these reasons could cause people to seek different housing.

Once the decision is made to change housing, there are three alternatives from which to choose:

- Adapt
- Remodel
- Move

ADAPTING HOUSING

Housing can be adapted without changing the structure. The simplest method of adapting space can be achieved by using furniture. For example, a new hide-a-bed might provide additional sleeping space without the cost of building a separate bedroom. Another method is to schedule the use of the rooms. A kitchen table can be made to serve as eating space, a study area, sewing room, hobby shop, and entertainment area.

Adapting housing is often considered a temporary solution. Generally, we adapt due to limited finances or because we cannot make structural changes.

REMODELING HOUSING

Remodeling involves structural changes, such as adding a bedroom or a bathroom. Doing this is usually expensive. It often involves changing or adding to electrical, plumbing, or heating systems—and these changes can be especially costly. As a general rule, the cost of remodeling should be no more than half the cost of a new house. The checklist on the next page will help you decide whether you should remodel.

DECIDING TO MOVE

Twenty percent of all families move each year. Before moving, consider your living habits, financial resources, work, and relaxation and entertainment preferences. Also consider needs for privacy, storage, and ease of movement between the various areas of the house.

Energy and Housing

Wise consumers look for energy-efficient housing. Small houses or rooms generally cost less to heat and cool. Insulation in the ceilings, walls, and floors reduces heating and cooling costs—and it makes housing units cooler in the summer and warmer in the winter. Energy-efficient houses are discussed more fully in Chapter 36.

Storage

Storage space should be flexible and adaptable because its use will change throughout the stages in the family life cycle. As a general rule, about 10 percent of the total square footage of a house or apartment is needed for storage. Where the space is located and how it is used are really more important than how much space you have.

Items should be stored according to how often they are used as well as where they are used. Store together items that are used in the same place. For example, cleaning equipment and supplies may be stored in the same area.

Try to locate storage at convenient heights and within easy reach and sight of the person who will be using it most. For example, children take better care of their clothing if they are able to reach the rod on which their clothes hang. Proper storage helps you keep your house or room neat, and maintenance takes less time.

TYPES OF HOUSING

What type of housing will you choose? When seeking housing, this must be one of your first decisions. There are three major types of housing structures:

- detached single-family housing units (house)
- multifamily units (apartment building, townhouse, condominium)
- mobile homes (factory-built housing that can be moved)

Single-Family Housing

Occupants of single-family dwellings claim that **single-family housing units** provide more living and storage space—and more privacy and freedom. Throughout the 1970s and 1980s, an average of 1.2 million single-family housing units were built each year.

Since 1990, the number has dropped to about 800,000 new units each year. Although increased unemployment and a general economic decline in the early 1990s reduced the demand for new housing, the number of new housing units is far below the demand in normal years.

Why aren't new houses built for everyone who needs or wants one? Local restrictions may limit construction. These concern land use, lot size,

single-family housing unit
....
a house

CHECKLIST FOR REMODELING

Remodeling a house or apartment can be very expensive. The costs can be especially high if any of the following areas present problems. Check these areas before remodeling:

Exterior
____ Are the walls straight? Bulges may be signs of a weak structure.
____ Will water drain away from the foundation? Is there any decay near the foundation?
____ Is the structure free of termites and rodents?
____ Is the roof sound? It should be intact, and it should not sag.
____ Are chimney and vents strong and unbroken?
____ Are the siding and trim firmly attached and free of decay and damage?

Interior
____ Do windows and doors move freely?
____ Is the woodwork solid?
____ Are the floors straight? Sags may indicate weak supports.
____ Are all room surfaces smooth and dry? Spots may be signs of water leaks.
____ Is the fireplace solid? Is it properly vented?
____ Is the plumbing system in good condition? Will it need to be expanded?
____ Is the electrical system adequate? Does it meet regulations? Does it provide enough electricity?
____ Do the heating and air-conditioning systems work well? Will they need to be replaced soon? Do they have enough capacity for any added areas? Are they energy efficient?

Multifamily housing allows many people to live in a relatively small area. What are some advantages of living in multifamily housing? What are some disadvantages?

and minimum floor space in a housing unit. Some communities also attempt to limit growth for environmental reasons, such as limited water supply or concern about pollution and population density. Economic factors contribute to the shortage too. These factors include limited money for mortgages, high interest rates, and unemployment.

Multifamily Housing

Multifamily housing provides homes for a large number of people in a relatively small area. They include apartment buildings, cooperatives, and condominium complexes. As land prices and the population increase, we are likely to see more **multifamily housing units**.

Mobile Homes

Mobile homes are built and furnished in factories, using assembly-line techniques much like those used to make automobiles. Once it is connected to water, fuel, and electrical lines, a mobile home is ready for use.

A mobile home generally comes equipped with a cooking range, refrigerator, and all the furniture and basic accessories needed to "move right in." Nothing further needs to be purchased. This is one reason that senior citizens and young couples, as well as many lower-income families, find a mobile home such an acceptable housing alternative.

Mobile homes account for the majority of all the new homes selling for less than $70,000. Over 50 percent of these homes are located in mobile home parks. Lot rentals range from $40 per month to more than $500 per month. The price generally depends on the services available. Services may include garbage pickup, laundry and recreational facilities, or special programs. The amount of space also determines the rental price.

multifamily housing unit
....
a structure, such as an apartment, a condominium, or a cooperative, that provides housing for a large number of people in a relatively small area

mobile home
....
factory-built housing that can be moved

HOUSING CONSTRUCTION

Building a new house takes time and some knowledge of construction methods and materials. Most often, it requires the services of an architect, housing designer, and/or contractor-builder.

Methods of Construction

Housing units are constructed by two methods. When the conventional construction method is used, all pieces of the structure are put together on the site. When the manufactured method is used, all or part of the housing is built in a factory—then the structure is placed on a foundation on the site.

Manufacturing large sections of a structure decreases building costs. Less time is needed for on-site construction, and the use of centralized manufacturing facilities can reduce the total building time. One form of manufactured housing is the **modular house**, with entire rooms put together at a manufacturing plant or yard and then shipped to the site. Another form of manufactured housing is the most common type, the mobile home.

RENTING VERSUS BUYING

For the same quality and space, is it better to rent or buy? The processes of renting and buying are very similar. Renters should use the same care in selecting their housing as buyers. In either case, we must decide what we consider important in housing and set priorities. Then we must determine how much we can afford to pay for housing.

Many times, factors other than economics are important when selecting your housing. Cost is an important consideration, but it is not the only one. The average family spends 25 percent to 35 percent of its total income (before taxes) for housing.

Renting Housing

Over one-third of all Americans choose to rent rather than buy. Most of these renters are single individuals, young married couples, or retirees. Renting provides some advantages over owning a home. For example, renters are able to change housing more quickly than owners, they know what their monthly expenses will be, and they have no hidden repair expenses and no responsibility for maintaining the housing unit. The reasons given most frequently for renting rather than buying are:

- I have no long-term commitment.
- I prefer to invest money in other ways.
- I want to be on my own.
- I do not like to mow grass and paint.
- I lack the down payment needed to purchase housing.
- I do not want the responsibilities of ownership.

The Cost of Renting. Monthly rental costs are often related to the size and location of the rental unit and may cover extras such as air conditioning, a swimming pool, and parking. Rent may or may not include utilities. Deposits are often required and may include a security deposit, a pet deposit, and a fee for subletting an apartment.

modular house
....
housing unit constructed of rooms that have been built in a factory and shipped to a location for final assembly

INTERACTING WITH TECHNOLOGY

BUILDING GREEN HOMES

Architects are combining technology and thorough knowledge of building sites to design homes that are "green," or environmentally friendly. This trend is known as sustainable architecture and takes into account how the structures we build today will affect the planet and future generations.

Technology is developing a wide range of new building materials. Many of these materials are made from products that are currently piling up in landfills. Crushed glass is being used in foundation and landscaping materials. Rubber pavers are being produced from old tires. Junked cars are providing material for steel roofs, and plastic soda bottles are being recycled into carpeting. Even recycled newspapers are showing up as insulation in new houses.

Sustainable architecture also relies on renewable energy sources to power new homes. Some homes are equipped with special solar panels that generate enough electricity to run heating and ventilation systems or to operate household appliances. Other homes come equipped with windmills for generating electricity. These homes are also connected to local power sources. When they need more electricity, they draw from the local source. When they produce excess electricity, they may store it in batteries or sell it to the local utility company.

Solar panels are also being used to heat large tanks of water. These storage tanks then provide water for showers, laundry, and home-heating systems.

Energy conservation is another major emphasis in new home designs. Specially glazed windows reduce heat loss and heat gain by as much as 50 percent with no change in the amount of light coming into a home. Such high-tech improvements are impressive, but energy conservation is also being achieved in new home construction through some low-tech methods. Special attention is being given to sun and wind conditions of a site before deciding where to locate a home. Even such simple approaches as taking advantage of shading from trees is a part of the design process of sustainable architecture.

Special features in new home designs contribute to creating a better living environment. Windows are available that screen out much of the unpleasant street noise. Special sensor devices regulate the ventilation systems to reduce harmful levels of carbon dioxide or other air pollutants. New flooring, wallcovering, and paint products that are free from substances that release toxic fumes are being used more frequently. Changing lifestyles and changing environmental concerns will continue to influence the homes we build.

In addition, expenses might include a renter's policy for insuring personal possessions against theft, fire, flood, and wind.

The following points are especially helpful for securing the best in rental housing:

- Read the lease or rental agreement carefully. The **lease** is a legal document which states the responsibilities of the property owner and the **tenant**. It identifies the property being rented and the length of time for which it is rented. The lease sets the dollar amount of the rent, and it lists special restrictions such as "no cats or dogs" and details such as who pays for the utilities. Make sure you understand the lease before you sign. Leases may be for any time period but usually are for six months or a year.

  A rental agreement is often simpler than a lease. Rental agreements usually run "month-to-month," so that you may continue renting if you pay the rent each month—but you can move any time after giving a month's notice.

- Inspect the house or apartment before you take possession. Document any conditions that could create a problem later. You may lose your **security deposit**, usually equal to one month's rent, if the property owner thinks you caused damage.

- Complete an itemized checklist of items in the apartment and previous damages done. Sign this checklist before moving in—and ask the manager to sign it too. (The checklist on the next page gives several important points you will want to consider.)

- Discuss any problems with the property owner as soon as possible.

- Be familiar with laws that protect renters. A local tenants' organization or the housing code department can assist you. Call the city hall or check the telephone directory for listings.

Lease Clauses

Clauses in a rental lease can be very confusing, and they could cost you money if you fail to take the time to read the lease before signing it. Here is an example:

Security Deposit. The $200 Security Deposit is to be applied against damage to any part of the premises leased hereby, **including the common** areas, or to the furnishings therein, unpaid utility bills, unpaid rent, late-payment charges, cleaning expenses, attorney fees, court costs, or any other costs or losses related to the

lease
......
legal document stating the responsibilities of property owners and tenants

tenant
....
renter

security deposit
....
money a renter pays in advance to cover possible damages to a rental housing unit

CHECKLIST FOR APARTMENT RENTERS

Check an apartment thoroughly before you rent it. Because you may not have much time to look at an apartment before renting, you may want to bring a checklist like this one with you. That way, you will remember to look for many of the important features.

____ Is the apartment clean?
____ Do the heating and air-conditioning systems work properly?
____ Are doors and windows in good shape? Do they lock securely?
____ Is the electrical system adequate and safe?
____ Are the kitchen and bathroom facilities in good condition?
____ Are there adequate phone connections?
____ Are good laundry facilities available?
____ Are walls, floors, and ceilings clean and in good condition?
____ Which services and utilities are included in the rent? Which ones are not?
____ Are the neighbors quiet?
____ Is the outside of the building well maintained and well lighted?
____ Is the floor plan of the apartment convenient?
____ Is there adequate room for parking?
____ If you have your own furniture, will it fit in the apartment? If furniture is provided, is it in good condition?
____ Are the trash-disposal facilities convenient?
____ Does the manager live in the building?

subsidy
....
money furnished by the government to help pay some cost

aforesaid apartment and premises **regardless of which of the Tenants allegedly** causes the loss, unless the damage is paid for prior to the end of this lease. Owner expressly agrees to itemize all deductions from the Security Deposit. When there is no such damage or loss, the Security Deposit shall be refunded to Tenant within thirty (30) days after expiration of this lease term.

The boldface portion of this lease is important, and you should object to this particular wording. Common areas include hallways, basements, laundry rooms, and other public areas. In many states, your liability for these areas may be limited. You may not be liable for damage to common areas unless you committed the damage yourself or you signed a lease with a clause like this.

Government Subsidies. Because housing accounts for the largest part of a family's monthly expenses, it is sometimes difficult for low-income families to obtain suitable housing. The Brady family is a good example. Ellen Brady is a divorced mother, with two small preschoolers, who works as a clerk in a grocery store. After she pays for child care, transportation to work, and food, she has less than $100 per month available for a housing payment. She needs help.

Since 1965, the federal government has provided **subsidies** (grants of money) to low-income households to help them reduce their monthly housing costs. In general, these government programs involve payment of part of the family's rent by the government. There are approximately three million units of multifamily subsidized housing in the United States.

The amount paid by the government depends on the income of the family and the number of children in the family. If the monthly apartment rent is $400, the renter would pay no more than 25 percent of the monthly rent—in this case, $100. The government would subsidize or pay the remainder of the rent, $300. When a family becomes capable of paying the entire rent, they no longer qualify for the rent supplement program. There are also special programs that assist the elderly with their housing costs.

At one time, part of the "American dream" was to own your own home. Many people still have this dream, but many others don't want the problems that come with ownership. Would you prefer to own your own home or to rent from someone else? Why?

Buying Housing

The majority of Americans choose to buy their housing rather than rent, and those who buy like the security and stability of home ownership. They expect to stay in one location for a long period of time, and most of them make improvements to their housing. Home buyers have enough money for a down payment, and they consider owning a home a good investment.

For the most part, housing has increased in value from one year to another. The 1970s and early 1980s produced large gains in the value of housing. After some losses in value during the early 1990s, the average home value is predicted to increase at least until the end of this century. Long-term increases in value have made home ownership a good investment. Home ownership also provides a tax benefit to the owners.

The Costs of Buying. The first question to ask yourself in deciding whether to buy housing is "Can I afford it?" If you fail to meet your monthly payments, you may damage your future credit rating and possibly lose the house. In 1994, the median price for a single-family home in the United States was over $104,000—but prices vary a great deal from one area to another.

Sometimes you may have to spend more than you would like for housing. In that case, you will be forced to examine the rest of your budget to determine what you can do without. If you have other debts, such as car payments or credit card balances, you cannot afford to pay as much for your housing. If you have money saved, you can afford to pay more.

LOCATING HOUSING

Once you figure how much you can afford to spend for housing, you can begin your search. You will want to find a house that is in good condition and conveniently located to work, schools, and shopping areas. You may want to be near public transportation. The checklist for home buyers on this page will help.

Contact local real estate personnel who know the community. Drive around town. Talk to your friends. Ask your employer to help you identify housing for sale.

Home Owners Warranty (HOW)

guarantee on a new home

CHECKLIST FOR HOME BUYERS

If you are thinking of buying a particular house, you will want to learn as much about it as you can. The following features are good things to check before deciding to buy.

___ Is the location desirable? What facilities are nearby? Homeowners may want nearby shopping, public transportation, schools, churches, or recreation.

___ Are good public services available at reasonable cost? These include water and sewer systems, garbage collection, and street maintenance.

___ Are other utilities available? Consider electricity, gas, telephone, and cable TV.

___ Is the construction sound? On the outside, check walls, roof and chimney, and the foundation. On the inside, check ceilings, walls, and floors.

___ Is the house energy efficient? Check the furnace, water heater, and air conditioning. Does the house have storm windows and doors? Is it well insulated? How much will the utilities cost?

___ Will the house be safe and secure? Does it have outside lighting? Are handrails present where needed? Consider routes for escaping from fires. Check for good locks on doors and windows.

___ Is the layout of the rooms desirable? Consider traffic patterns and privacy.

___ Does the house have extras, such as a fireplace, patio, or garage?

___ Are there any special problems? A house may look good, but it may still have basic flaws. Check for: termites, rotting wood, warps in outside or inside surfaces, faulty wiring or plumbing, roof leaks, basement moisture, poor furnace.

New Housing

Buying a housing unit that is already built is faster, of course, than building a new one. We can see the finished product and move in as soon as we make the necessary financial arrangements, but many people prefer new houses. Purchasing a new house allows the buyer to make choices regarding the features of the house.

Before buying a new house, check the reputation of the builder and the guarantees that come with most new houses today. The guarantees are builders' insurance policies to cover any defects. The most often used of these home warranties is the **Home Owners Warranty (HOW)**, sponsored by the National Home Builders Association. It backs the housing unit for one year against defects in both materials and work quality. Some of the housing's systems, such as plumbing, are covered for up to nine years.

Used Housing

Two out of three buyers select a used home. An older home often provides up to 50 percent more space for the same dollars as a new home. The trees and shrubs, patio, fences, drapes, and carpeting may be included with a used home. However, look for cracks in the foundation, watermarks in the basement, and the presence of termites—any of these will cause serious problems later.

The special home-buyer's checklist will be a useful tool in making a good decision about a house. A contractor or local community housing association can take a look at the house if you are unsure of its value. It may also be wise to hire an independent home inspector for a report before buying a used home. Some sellers purchase insurance to cover defects on their homes, so consider asking the seller for such a policy.

Condominiums and Cooperatives

What should you do if you don't want to rent or buy a house? Many people are choosing to buy a **condominium** or **cooperative**—apartments or apartment buildings owned by the people who live in them.

Housing economists predict that, by the turn of the century, more than 50 percent of the U.S. population will live in condominiums. An increasing number of Americans cannot pay the price for a single-family detached housing unit, but they can afford a condominium or cooperative. In addition to a lower price, some other advantages are better use of land, modular construction techniques, and less maintenance.

Today there are more retirees and more single-person and single-parent households than ever before, and this has resulted in an increased interest in condominiums. In 1994, nearly one-third of all households were single individuals. Why the keen interest in condominiums and cooperatives rather than rental apartments? Housing arrangements such as condominiums preserve part of the dream of "owning your own home." A condominium is usually a privately owned apartment or row house. The term condominium refers to a way of purchasing housing rather than a method of construction or a type of structure.

In a condominium, people own individual apartment units. The owners may sell or lease to others as they please. They also own shares of all the common areas. These areas include hallways, parking areas, yards, recreational areas, garages, and elevators. Owners must pay a **maintenance fee**

condominium

a multiple housing structure in which owners purchase individual units and shares of the common areas

cooperative

a multiple housing structure in which owners purchase shares of the entire building

maintenance fee

money charged by condominium associations for the upkeep of common areas

For those people who want to buy a home, but can't afford a single-family house, a condominium or cooperative might supply the answer. These types of housing typically cost less than single-family housing. What are some other advantages to living in a condominium or cooperative?

each month to help maintain the common areas of the condominium.

Cooperative is also a method of purchasing, not a type of structure. In a cooperative, people purchase shares in the entire building and are allowed to live in one of the units of the building. Individuals do not own their apartments. Cooperatives are generally more selective than condominiums in their memberships. People living in the building must approve new members. Cooperatives also have tighter building control than condominiums, and rules about almost any aspect of the structure or its use are much more strict.

Summary

- Each year, the demand for housing units increases. In general, the nation has been unable to keep up with this demand.
- Location is a major factor that is important to everyone when making housing decisions.
- The average American family moves once every five years, often because of changes in the family makeup.
- When changing housing, there are three main options: adapt the house you have, remodel, or move.
- There are three major types of housing structures: detached single-family units, multifamily units, and mobile homes.
- There are two methods for constructing housing: the conventional method (all pieces of the structure are assembled at the site) and the manufactured method (part or all of the structure is built and preassembled in a factory).
- There are some advantages to renting rather than buying. More than one-third of Americans rent their housing.
- Be sure to check an apartment thoroughly before you rent it. Take time to read and understand the lease agreement before you sign it.
- Buying a house is a major investment and should be researched thoroughly. It is a good idea to get professional advice and assistance.
- Condominiums have some advantages: a lower price, better use of land, modular construction techniques, and less maintenance.

E NRICHING YOUR VOCABULARY

Read the following pairs of sentences. Write the sentence that correctly uses the underlined word or phrase.

condominium
cooperative
energy efficient
Home Owners Warranty
   (HOW)

lease
location
maintenance fee
mobile home
modular house

multifamily housing unit
security deposit
single-family housing unit
subsidy
tenant

1A. A condominium is an individually owned unit of a multiple housing structure.

1B. A condominium is a single-family housing unit.

2A. A cooperative is a structure that is built cooperatively by the owners.

2B. A multiple housing unit in which owners purchase shares of the entire building is called a cooperative.

3A. A home that uses low amounts of electricity or fuel for heating, cooling, etc. is energy efficient.

3B. A Home Owners Warranty guarantees that a home is energy efficient.

4A. A Home Owners Warranty is a guarantee on a new home.

4B. A security deposit pays for a Home Owners Warranty.

5A. A lease spells out the terms of a HOW.

5B. A lease is a legal document stating the rental terms between property owners and tenants.

6A. Location is an important consideration in choosing housing.

6B. The location of most homes can be changed.

7A. The maintenance fee is the amount charged for rent.

7B. A maintenance fee is the money charged by condominium associations for the upkeep of common areas.

8A. A mobile home is assembled on the site.

8B. A mobile home can be moved from one location to another.

9A. Modular houses are constructed of rooms that are built in a factory and shipped to a site for final assembly.

9B. A modular house is a housing unit in which rooms are owned by the tenants.

10A. Mobile homes are multifamily housing units.

10B. Apartments, condominiums, and cooperatives are multifamily housing units.

11A. A security deposit pays for the insurance on a home.

11B. A security deposit is often collected from renters to cover potential damages.

12A. A house is a single-family housing unit.

12.B Cooperatives are single-family housing units.

13A. A housing subsidy is a fee charged to all renters.

13B. The government provides a housing subsidy for individuals who qualify.

14A. A tenant is a property owner.

14B. A tenant rents a housing unit.

CHAPTER REVIEW
26

1. What are the two basic types of housing structures?

2. List one advantage and one disadvantage for each type of structure listed in number 1.

3. Give at least three reasons why many people prefer to rent housing.

4. Explain and describe the trend toward buying condominiums rather than renting or buying a house. How are these three options different?

U SING YOUR CRITICAL THINKING SKILLS

1. How can housing be adapted as a family moves through the family life cycle?

2. Do you feel it is better to buy a used housing unit rather than a new one? Discuss the advantages and disadvantages of each.

A PPLYING WHAT YOU HAVE LEARNED

1. Discuss with your family the five most important things they would look for in a new housing unit. Compare your list with those of your classmates.

2. List the five electrical appliances you feel you absolutely must have when you move into your own apartment. Compare your list with lists prepared by your classmates.

CHAPTER 27

Investing in a Home

OBJECTIVES

After completing this chapter, you will be able to do the following:

1. List the four factors that affect the amount of a monthly mortgage payment.
2. Explain the methods of financing housing that are available besides the conventional loan.
3. List the steps you can take to help ensure that moving is a successful experience.
4. Determine how much money per year you should allow for maintenance and repairs.

TERMS

basic coverage
broad coverage
buying on contract
fixed-rate mortgage

foreclosure
principal
start-up costs
special coverage

term
variable-rate mortgage

Buying a housing unit is a process that takes a long time. If you are a buyer, you will probably follow these steps:

1. Identify housing needs.
2. Become familiar with types of financing.
3. Become familiar with the housing market in a community.
4. Seek the help of real estate agents and other professionals.
5. Find an acceptable unit and negotiate its price.
6. Arrange for financing the property.
7. Sign the contract for sale.
8. Transfer ownership of the property.

FINANCING YOUR HOUSING

When they purchase housing, most people have to borrow money in the form of a mortgage, which is a loan on real estate housing property. The buyer's credit rating and personal references are important in securing a home loan. Savings and loan associations, banks, mortgage corporations, and individuals are common sources for obtaining housing loans. When you are ready to buy a home, ask at least two or three different lenders for their current interest rates before deciding where to borrow. Ask what other fees you will be charged for the loan, then compare the total cost of the loan, including interest and loan fees, to help you choose the best lender.

There are four factors that will affect the amount of the monthly payment of a housing mortgage:

- price
- down payment
- interest rate (fixed or adjustable)
- length of term

Price

The price of a house will largely determine how much you have to borrow. Your total monthly housing costs will include your mortgage, taxes, and insurance costs—which together add up to about three-fourths of one percent of the value of the housing unit. Utilities and maintenance add up to about one-third percent, depending on the age and condition of the housing.

Down Payment

The down payment is the cash needed in order to obtain a mortgage, and it will usually vary between 10 percent and 30 percent of the purchase price of the housing. Generally, the larger the down payment, the better. The less money you have to borrow, the less your payments will be, and you will pay less interest. (See Chapter 12 for more about interest rates.)

Borrowing money for the first time can be a very frightening experience. The larger the sum being borrowed, the more frightening the experience can be. Fortunately, the people loaning the money are usually very helpful. They will answer any questions you might have. Be sure you understand everything about the loan, and never *sign anything without reading and understanding it.*

How can you obtain the money necessary for the down payment? One way is to live "spartan-style." This means buying the least that you can live on and saving every cent you can. If your household has two incomes, live on one and save the other. Resist vacations and installment buying. Keep food, clothing, and entertainment purchases to a minimum. Live in a low-cost housing unit.

Another way is to work off the down payment with the owners of the property by painting, cleaning, and making repairs. Sometimes owners will loan you the down payment in order to sell the housing unit, but this would require a personal loan to be paid back later.

Interest Rate

The interest rate is a percentage charge on the amount that you borrow. Various factors influence interest rates, as discussed in Chapter 7. In the early 1980s, long-term, fixed rates most often ranged from 12 percent to 20 percent. In the early 1990s, these rates were much lower—often around 6 percent to 7 percent—but then they began to rise again. Interest rates always vary among lending institutions.

Term

The **term** of the mortgage is the length of time for which you borrow the money. Today, that generally varies from fifteen to thirty years. The chart on this page illustrates how interest rate and term affect your monthly housing payment.

FIXED-RATE MORTGAGE

In the past, about 80 percent of all home buyers used the **fixed-rate mortgage**. A mortgage is a contract between the buyer and the lender.

The money borrowed is called the **principal**. With a fixed-rate mortgage, monthly payments are planned so that they will be the same each month for the lifetime of the loan. The major portion of the monthly payment during the first several years goes for interest charges.

Fixed-rate mortgages are usually available to anyone who can qualify. You need a good credit record, a steady job, and money for the down payment. Generally, the lender will not loan more than 80 percent of the cost of the housing, so the amount of cash needed for the down payment is usually equal to 20 percent of the cost. When the amount of money available to finance homes is limited, lending institutions may offer variations of the conventional mortgage.

OTHER TYPES OF MORTGAGES

One variation of the fixed-rate loan allows the interest rate and/or term of the mortgage to change periodically. These loans are called **variable-rate mortgages** (vrm). There are also graduated-payment mortgages (gpm), flexible mortgages, and mortgages with large payments due at the end of the term.

Monthly payments on a vrm may rise in an unpredictable manner, since interest rates are related to U.S. Treasury Notes and other variables. You may

fixed-rate mortgage

a loan in which the rate of interest and payment remain the same over the lifetime of the loan

principal

money borrowed

variable-rate mortgage

a loan in which the interest rate and/or terms may be changed periodically

term

the length of time for which money is borrowed

foreclosure
....
the event in which the buyer is unable to make monthly housing payments, which may allow the lender to take possession of the property

buying on contract
....
an arrangement in which the seller holds the title to the property while the buyer makes the monthly payments to the seller

also be required to renegotiate your loan after a period of time to a higher interest rate. Some buyers prefer these kinds of mortgages because the interest rates for the first few years are usually lower than the interest rates on fixed-rate mortgages. This helps some buyers to afford the home. It is also an attractive mortgage for buyers who do not intend to keep the home for a long period of time.

Buying on contract is an arrangement in which the seller holds the title to the property while the buyer makes the monthly payments to the seller. There is no third-party loan involved. Usually, a buyer can purchase housing with less cash on contract than by conventional methods.

Before obtaining financing, examine several loan possibilities. People at lending institutions will explain the unique features of various types of loans.

Guaranteed or Insured Mortgages

A small percent of homes purchased use either a Federal Housing Administration (FHA)-insured loan, Veterans Administration (VA)-guaranteed loan, or a Farmers Home Administration (FmHA)-insured loan. Each of these special mortgages assures the lender that if the buyer should default, the government agency will pay the lender. Not all people qualify for a VA, FHA, or FmHA mortgage. For example, to obtain a VA loan, you must have been a member of the U.S. armed services. Check with a lending institution to see if you qualify for one of these special mortgages.

Foreclosure and Prepayment of Mortgages

Circumstances such as prolonged ill health or a labor strike may make a buyer unable to meet monthly housing payments. When this happens, the lender may be able to take the property. This action is called foreclosure. If payment cannot be made, the buyer should contact the lender to work out an acceptable repayment plan. This notice will usually delay foreclosure.

Check to see if you can prepay the mortgage. Being ahead on payments may save embarrassment or foreclosure if you cannot make your payment at the regular time. Paying ahead on the mortgage also saves on the amount of interest paid. The borrower pays off the mortgage in a shorter period of time than scheduled in the original contract.

INSURING HOUSING

Once the housing is yours, whether you rented it or bought it, there is a need to protect the investment with insurance. Housing units and their contents need protection from fire, storm, and theft.

Homeowner's insurance and property insurance can help protect an investment in housing. If you are renting, you may want to carry renter's insurance. The contents of your dwelling will not be replaced by the property owner if they are destroyed by fire, wind, flood, or other perils.

The cost of insurance varies but is usually based on what it would cost to

Homeowner Policies: Kinds of Losses Covered

Basic Coverage

1. fire or lightning
2. windstorm or hail
3. explosion
4. riot or civil commotion
5. damage caused by aircraft
6. damage caused by vehicles
7. smoke
8. vandalism and malicious mischief
9. theft
10. breakage of glass or safety glazing material that is part of a building and damage caused by that breakage
11. volcanic eruption

Broad Coverage

12. falling objects
13. weight of ice, snow, or sleet
14. accidental discharge, or overflow of water or steam from within a plumbing, heating, or air-conditioning, or automatic fire-protective sprinkler system, or from a household appliance
15. sudden and accidental tearing apart, cracking, burning, or bulging of a steam or hot-water heating system, an air-conditioning or automatic fire-protective system
16. freezing of a plumbing, heating, air-conditioning, or automatic fire-protective sprinkler system, or of a household appliance
17. sudden and accidental damage from artificially generated electrical currents (does not include loss to a tube, transistor, or similar electronic component)

Special Coverage

all perils except flood, earthquake, war, nuclear accident, and others specified in the policy

Figure 27.1
....
Some of the insurance options listed here wouldn't be needed in some areas of the United States. Can you name them? Which type of coverage do you think would cost more—basic, broad, or special coverage? Why do you think this?

basic coverage
....

homeowners' insurance that protects the home against 11 perils stated in the policy

broad coverage
....

homeowners' insurance that protects the home against 17 perils stated in the policy

special coverage
....

homeowners' insurance that protects the home against all perils with the exception of those that are specifically named in the policy

replace a home in a particular area and the type of coverage desired. The purchaser must decide whether to buy **basic, broad**, or **special coverage**. (See Figure 27.1.)

MOVING DAY

As was mentioned earlier, typical Americans move at least once every five years due to changes in occupation, economic status, or because of family separations. A successful moving day depends on advance preparations, such as planning how you will pack items and the order in which you pack certain things. Children should be encouraged to help with the packing of some of their personal things. This will help them accept their new home more readily.

Mail address cards to magazines, newspapers, friends, and firms where you have charge accounts. Cancel or transfer the telephone, electricity, car license, and water. Plan to carry the title to your car, your checkbook, automobile and health insurance cards, credit cards, and other important records, such as bank and medical records.

When moving a long distance, it is helpful to subscribe to the newspaper in the new area. The library and the chamber of commerce are good sources of information on the history and tourist attractions in the area. Having some information about your new location will help to make the move more comfortable.

Making Consumer Decisions

Lisa has made a study of home-buying. She has learned what to look for in terms of construction, energy efficiency, safety features, financing, and other factors. She has consulted with real estate people and other professionals to get the best advice. After a long search, Lisa finally found a house that met most of her needs.

Lisa's parents gave her the down payment—but even with that, the monthly payments would be high. Her house payment, together with her normal monthly bills, would take most of her paycheck. Some of her friends told her to "Go for it." But Lisa had done her homework, and knew that there would be added costs to owning a home. What about the increased utility bills in the winter? What about the property tax? Insurance? Unexpected maintenance or repair expenses?

Lisa decided not to buy the house. The additional costs were too much of a gamble for her. She bought a condominium instead, at a lower cost than the house and with maintenance fees that were predictable and steady.

What would you have done in Lisa's position? What other kinds of expenses would Lisa have encountered if she'd bought the house? What advantages would the house have offered? What advantages might the condo offer?

Hire a Mover or Do It Yourself

A moving company may be hired to do the packing, loading, unloading, and unpacking. Hiring a mover is more expensive than doing it all yourself, but it's convenient. You can lower the cost of moving by doing the packing yourself, but you will be responsible if something is broken or damaged.

Ask for recommendations from friends or your employer, then get estimates from two or three moving companies. Select a reputable, reliable mover to assure that your belongings arrive on time and in good condition. Check with the Better Business Bureau before signing a contract with any mover. Ask about the mover's liability insurance in case of damage to your property while it is being moved.

Upon arrival at the new house, have cash or a cashier's check ready for pay-ment. Some movers will not unload the truck until payment is made. Check the weight of the load and the condition of the goods as they are delivered. Take pictures if necessary. Note any damage and mark it on the bill. You have nine months to file a claim for damage.

Two-thirds of all moves are do-it-yourself moves with help from friends or family. Many do-it-yourself movers borrow or rent a truck or trailer.

ESTABLISHING YOUR FIRST HOME

If this is the first move out of your parents' house and into an apartment of your own, be prepared to pay for a number of **start-up costs**. These costs are in addition to the cost of transport-

start-up costs

. . . .

costs that must be paid by those who move into a house or apartment; costs may include deposits that must be made to utility companies

ing belongings. Generally, there are deposits to make to the utility companies before they will connect the water, gas, electricity, and telephone. These can run as high as $300 in some areas of the country—and they are in addition to the deposit required for the apartment.

Although the apartment may have a range and refrigerator, you will still need some common kitchen items: cookware, glasses, dishes, appliances, flatware, and other utensils. These items may cost between $200 and $300. Another $100 will be needed to stock the pantry with such basic things as catsup, napkins, salt and pepper, sugar, and other food staples. Cleaning supplies and personal supplies can cost an additional $100.

In some areas, you may be able to rent an apartment for as little as $300 per month. But in other areas of the country, you may have to pay more than $1,000 per month. Check prices in your area.

About 5 percent of average take-home pay will cover the utility costs. An additional 3 percent will be needed for monthly telephone charges.

Furnishing Your First Home

Unless you rent a furnished apartment, you need to beg, borrow, or buy some basic furnishings and appliances. Some young people furnish their apartments with "oldies-but-goodies" from junk shops, family discards, and garage sales.

In addition to the basic furnishings, you will need to invest in some appliances. Generally, you will need to know the following for each appliance:

- What will the appliance do? Can it perform more than one task?

- How frequently will you use it? You may want to pay a little more for an appliance that will be used daily, versus one that will seldom be used.

- Where can you store the appliance? In some apartments, there is limited storage space. If you do not like clutter, you may want to think again before buying.

- Is the appliance easy to handle and easy to clean?

- What special features does it offer? Can you wash it easily, use it at the table, remove the cord?

MAINTENANCE AND REPAIRS

In 1994, Americans spent more than $60 billion on housing maintenance and improvements. Almost 25 percent

It doesn't have to cost a lot to furnish your home. Often, good furniture deals can be had at garage sales and from ads in the newspaper. If you don't want to spend a lot of money on furniture, do some careful shopping. You might be surprised at the furnishings you can acquire with very little money.

FIRE SAFETY

The Garcia family lives in a single-story home. One night, they are awakened by a loud tone. They see smoke entering their bedrooms, and, according to their plan for such an emergency, they quickly leave through the bedroom windows. They meet outside to make sure all four of them are safe. At a neighbor's home, they phone the fire department.

The Garcias were awakened by a smoke detector, a device that sounds an alarm when smoke is in the air. Smoke detectors are strongly recommended for any housing unit. One detector should be near the sleeping area (in many states this is required), but more detectors give added protection.

Fire extinguishers are also helpful, but only for small fires. The best extinguishers for the home are labeled ABC, and they will put out most types of small fires. Fire extinguishers should be located near escape routes.

Learn how to use and maintain safety equipment before you need it—and make plans for emergencies, particularly for children and people with special needs. Like the Garcias, you can be safe with good plans and good equipment.

of the yearly expenditures for owner-occupied, single-family homes is spent on maintenance and repairs. The average outlay for maintenance on a single-family home was over $1,000 per year.

You can learn to do many maintenance and repair tasks yourself. Workshops on how to paint and wallpaper, carpet, or install new floors are often offered by retail stores. A few simple tools and some time and energy will enable you to save on maintenance costs. A good paintbrush, stapler, ruler, scissors, hammer, screwdriver, and pliers—plus lots of glue, nails, and screws—should prepare you to handle many household repairs.

Summary

- Most people have to borrow money (mortgage) when buying a house.

- Four factors affect the amount of the monthly payment on a housing mortgage: the price, the down payment, the interest rate, and the length of term.

- Moving from one house to another is a big undertaking. Hiring a moving company to do the work is expensive but convenient; most people do it themselves.

- When moving into a new home, be prepared to pay for a number of start-up costs.

CHAPTER REVIEW
27

E NRICHING YOUR VOCABULARY

Use the following words or phrases to complete the sentences below. Write the completed sentences on a separate sheet of paper. (Not all words are used.)

basic coverage	foreclosure	term
broad coverage	principal	variable-rate mortgage
buying on contract	start-up costs	
fixed-rate mortgage	special coverage	

1. A mortgage generally varies from a fifteen- to a thirty-year

2. Fees paid to utility companies for connecting services are part of

3. It is possible for the interest rate to increase or decrease on a

4. Failure to make payments on a mortgage may cause a property to be put into

5. Mortgage payments generally include payment of interest and

6. The rate of interest and the payment remain the same over the life of a

7. A homeowner's loss due to fire or windstorm is covered by

8. A homeowner's loss due to falling objects or faulty plumbing is covered by

R EVIEWING WHAT YOU HAVE LEARNED

1. List the four factors that affect the amount of a monthly mortgage payment.

2. What methods of financing housing are available in addition to the conventional loan?

3. What steps can you take to help ensure that moving is a successful experience?

4. If you live in a house worth $100,000, how much money per year should you allow for maintenance and repairs?

5. Approximately what percentage of take home pay goes to pay for utility costs?

U SING YOUR CRITICAL THINKING SKILLS

1. Why is it important for both owners and renters to carry insurance on their property?

2. Why should you investigate a moving company before hiring it?

A PPLYING WHAT YOU HAVE LEARNED

1. Using research and your imagination, describe what future housing will be like. Give reasons wherever possible. Draw illustrations of some of your ideas.

UNIT
10

FURNITURE, APPLIANCES, AND ELECTRONICS

CHAPTERS

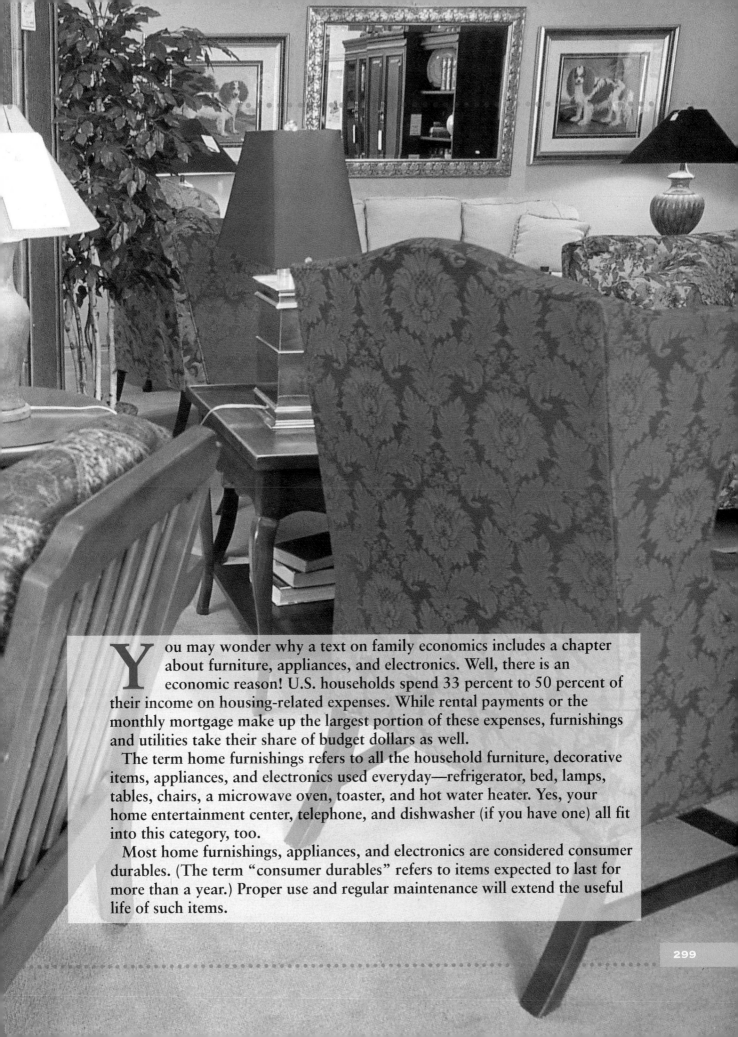

You may wonder why a text on family economics includes a chapter about furniture, appliances, and electronics. Well, there is an economic reason! U.S. households spend 33 percent to 50 percent of their income on housing-related expenses. While rental payments or the monthly mortgage make up the largest portion of these expenses, furnishings and utilities take their share of budget dollars as well.

The term home furnishings refers to all the household furniture, decorative items, appliances, and electronics used everyday—refrigerator, bed, lamps, tables, chairs, a microwave oven, toaster, and hot water heater. Yes, your home entertainment center, telephone, and dishwasher (if you have one) all fit into this category, too.

Most home furnishings, appliances, and electronics are considered consumer durables. (The term "consumer durables" refers to items expected to last for more than a year.) Proper use and regular maintenance will extend the useful life of such items.

Furnishing a Place to Live

OBJECTIVES

After completing this chapter, you will be able to do the following:
1. Explain the four steps in furnishing a home.
2. Name the factors you should consider when deciding whether to purchase home furnishings on credit.

TERMS

accessories
analogous color scheme
complementary color
  scheme
eclectic decorating

in-home consultation
life expectancy (of
  household equipment)
master plan
monochromatic color
  scheme

multipurpose furnishings
personal style
prioritize

Being independent and having a place of your own is an exciting prospect. Maybe you'll start out in the college dorm or rent a room in someone's house. Perhaps you'll get an apartment with a friend. In most cases, you'll be responsible for furnishing the room or apartment yourself. Even in a furnished apartment, you'll probably want to add some personal touches that make it "home."

STEPS IN FURNISHING A HOME

Where do you start? Whether you are furnishing a room, an apartment, or an entire house, the same principles

Moving can be a very exciting experience. The more planning you do in advance of the move, the more easily the move should go and the more time you should have to enjoy the process. Have you ever moved? What kind of advance planning did you do?

apply. First, assess what you have and identify what you need. Next, determine how much you can afford to spend. Then comes the fun part: developing and implementing a plan to make a home—wherever you live! The following pages outline the process and offer suggestions for creating your own style.

Step 1: Identify Your Needs

Walk into a home furnishings department or store, and you may suddenly have lots of "needs"! The merchandising strategy is designed to motivate you to buy—not just one item, but all the coordinating pieces and **accessories** (nonessential, usually decorative items) displayed in the showroom. What catches your interest in the showroom may not be what you need. It's well worth the time and energy to develop a plan before you shop.

Assess the Furnishings You Have. The first step in developing a furnishing plan is to assess what furniture, appliances, and electronic equipment you already have. Maybe you'll have the good fortune to start out with some furniture, such as a bed or bookshelves, loaned to you by family and friends. Perhaps you've already acquired some items on your own. A rented room may come with basic furnishings: a bed, table, and chairs. Even an unfurnished apartment may have the basic appliances such as refrigerator/freezer and range. If not, these items must go on your list of furnishing needs. (It may be desirable to find an apartment that includes these appliances, since they are expensive to buy and difficult to move.)

Identify the Furnishings You Need. The next step is to identify what fur-

accessories
· · · · · · · · · · · · ·
items such as throw rugs, pillows, or plants that are not essential but add beauty

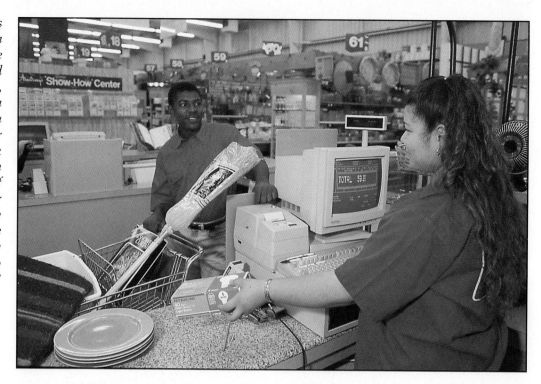

Buying furnishings for a new home can be very time consuming and expensive. Here, too, advance planning can help ensure that you don't overspend your time or money. Think about the things you would want to buy if you moved into your own place. Which items would be necessary and which would be nice to have?

nishings you need. This might include basic items such as a lamp, desk, refrigerator, or window coverings. Don't forget those everyday items: dishes, flatware, towels, or a shower curtain.

At this point, be sure to consider all the activities you will carry out at home: eating, sleeping, personal hygiene, studying, watching television, listening to music, or socializing with friends. Do you have the essential furnishings or equipment for each activity that is a regular part of your life? If not, these items should also go on your list of needs.

Consider Other Furnishings You'd Like to Have. Now is a good time to consider additional items you would like to supplement your needs. Maybe you want a new bedspread or comforter, a stand for your television and VCR, or decorative items, such as framed prints or houseplants. Put these items on your list for future consideration.

Step 2: Determine What You Can Spend

How much money do you have to spend on furnishings? Do you have credit? If so, should you use credit to purchase furniture and equipment? These are important questions to answer before you begin to make purchase decisions.

Initial Costs May Surprise You! There are a lot of expenses involved in moving into and furnishing a place to live. There are the obvious costs of any furniture or appliances you must rent or buy. Other costs are not so obvious. Even small purchases such as cleaning supplies, paper goods, a laundry basket, and trash cans add up quickly (not to mention the costs of purchasing a telephone, answering machine, or TV remote control!).

Generally, it's a good idea to save money for the initial expenses of setting up your own place. You can plan for these costs before you move out, by opening a special savings account for home furnishings and making regular deposits to the account.

Should You Buy on Credit? "Easy credit!" "Ninety days same as cash!" "No down payment and no interest charges for six months!" Do these advertising phrases sound familiar? Should you buy home furnishings on credit? Can you save money by buying on credit? If you can't afford to buy what you need and want now, should you use credit?

As you implement your plan, you'll need to make some decisions about how to pay for your purchases. Consider these factors before you decide to use credit. First, can you afford the monthly payments? If you have a steady job and can fit the payments into your budget, credit might be an option. Second, how long will you use the equipment? A good rule of thumb

is to buy on credit *only* if the item will outlive the credit payments. You don't want to be stuck with payments on a futon when it is too worn to be useful. Finally, figure out the total cost of buying the item on credit. After looking at the cost, you may decide to postpone the purchase until you can pay cash.

When credit is easy to get, it's tempting to spend a lot. Sometimes consumers use credit to buy more than they can comfortably afford. Make this decision thoughtfully. "Easy credit" may be difficult to repay (especially if the purchase was impulsive and not really a part of your overall plan).

Plan for Future Furnishing Needs. Even after you settle into your new room, dorm, or apartment, you'll probably want (or perhaps need) to acquire other household equipment, furnishings or decorative items. It's a good idea to budget a monthly amount for these costs. If you don't spend the full budgeted amount each month, it can

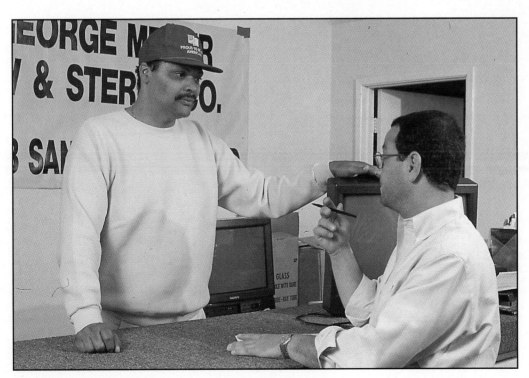

Even if you buy the "best" products on the market, things can go wrong and repairs may be necessary. Repairs can be very expensive. In fact, it is often less expensive to replace an item than it is to repair the item. Have you ever taken an item to a repair shop? Do you feel you were treated fairly?

be accumulated (ideally in a savings account) for larger purchases in the future.

Save for Repairs. Knowing the life expectancy of household and personal care appliances will help you budget for equipment repair and replacement. Information about life expectancy is available from manufacturers.

Consumer specialists recommend budgeting a regular amount each month for repairs. If the funds are placed in a savings account that earns interest, you'll have enough to pay for repairs as needed. Any remaining money in this account could go toward replacing the equipment when necessary.

Step 3: Develop a Furnishing Plan

Most of us don't have unlimited money to spend, so it makes sense to develop a master plan, a furnishing plan that can be implemented in stages. Your master plan should begin with a list of the needs and wants identified in Step 1.

Set Priorities. Next, prioritize your needs by listing them from most important to least important. It may help to divide the items on your list into three categories: essential, important, and desirable.

The essentials are items you must have, such as bedding or a refrigerator. Any furnishings that you need but could temporarily live without should be placed in the "important" category. You may be able to borrow these furnishings, or you may be able to devise a substitute. An example would be using the kitchen table for a desk. Everything else on your list goes into the third category.

Plan to purchase the essential items first. Then, buy the important items.

Before you are ready to buy furnishings for your home, it is important to spend some time "window shopping," (shopping with no intention of buying at that time). Window shopping will help you decide the styles you want and it will also help you know if the styles you want will fit within your budget.

Choose your furnishings carefully and with thought given to the future. If you choose contemporary styles today, you may not like those same furnishings in a few years when they are no longer in style. At that time, however, you may not have the money to replace the items. What styles do you prefer? Do you think these are styles you will like in the future?

Remember, you can add or delete items on the list as well as reevaluate your priorities as needed.

Identify Your Style. Implementing a furnishing plan in stages has design advantages as well as monetary advantages. Even if you have a lot of money, it's not a bad idea to begin slowly. If you purchase one item at a time and live with it for a while, you learn what you like and can develop your own personal style—which reflects your own choices in color, furniture types, and decorating schemes.

Just as clothing styles change from year to year, so do home furnishing styles. There are fashion colors in home furnishings, too. Sixties interiors used "psychedelic" colors, tie-dyed fabrics, and casual furnishings. Earth tones and shag carpeting were popular in the seventies. The eighties ushered in country living, cast in tones of Wedge-wood blue and rose. Ethnic designs and traditional furnishings in jewel-toned fabrics found their way into nineties interiors.

As you develop a furnishing plan, take time to find out what colors, types of furnishings, and decorating schemes you like best. Look through books and magazines to see what catches your eye. Browse through furniture displays to get a sense of what you like. Enjoy developing your own personal style.

Gather Information. Before you decide what to buy, identify the criteria and price range for each purchase. You can get this information from consumer publications, advertising, home decorating publications, and knowledgeable salespersons. (In every case, ask yourself how each potential purchase fits into your overall plan. If it doesn't, reconsider your decision to buy.)

personal style
....
your own preferences in color, furniture types, and decorating schemes

Figure 28.1
. . . .

Developing a floor plan for placement of your furnishings can be a very fun and helpful experience. A floor plan will allow you to "rearrange" your furnishings without actually moving them. When you have things arranged on paper just the way you want them, then you can actually move the furnishings. Develop a floor plan for your room or home. How many different arrangements can you create?

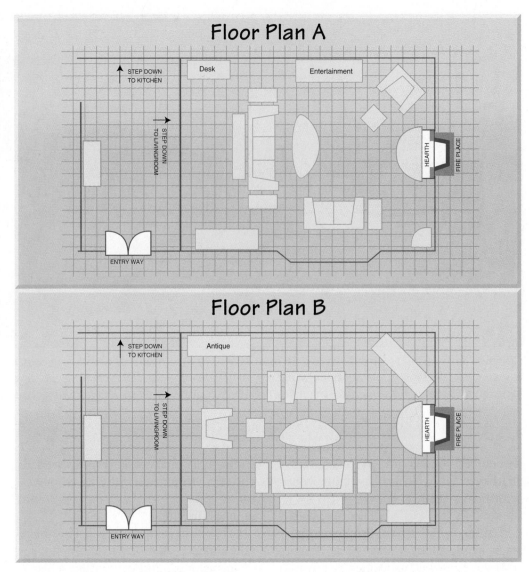

Start a file of decorating ideas related to your master plan. Collect photos, drawings, brochures, catalogs, and fabric samples that catch your interest. Also, be sure to include information and color samples for furnishings you already own. (This will be a great help, for example, when shopping for a chair to match your print sofa.)

Now is also a good time to measure the dimensions of your rooms and the size of all furniture. Using this information, you can plot a floor plan by drawing on a sheet of paper where each piece of furniture will be placed.

Then you won't end up with the "perfect" chair that ends up being too big for the room it's supposed to go in! Put this information on graph paper and save it for future reference. (See Figure 28.1.)

Create a Plan. There are many places to get ideas for a furnishing plan. Among the possible inspirations are a favorite color scheme, a special piece of furniture, or one's own personal interests.

You can build a color scheme around one, two, or three favorite colors. You might use a painting or the upholstery

FURNISHING YOUR HOME

If you've followed the first three steps suggested in the text, you're ready to begin implementing the plan. Following are some suggestions to help you stay on track and keep your budget intact.

Remember that furnishing your home (room, apartment, condo, etc.) is a process. Everything doesn't have to be done at once. Keep your priorities in mind (although you may periodically revise them) and enjoy the journey!

1. If you are starting from scratch, resist the temptation to buy many items just "to fill up the room." Keep in mind your master plan and priorities. A simple (even sparse) look can be pleasant and sophisticated. A few houseplants or inexpensive accessories such as throw pillows or rugs can provide warmth and charm. (Be careful, though—many "inexpensive" items can add up to a lot of money!)

2. Consider home furnishings as an investment. The relatively large purchase price means the furnishing should (ideally) result in many years of use and enjoyment. Begin by carefully selecting one or two well-made, well-designed items that can provide a focus for future acquisitions.

3. Only buy furnishings you *really* like. It's a false economy to purchase something that you don't like, just to save money. A low price can't make up for furnishings that are the wrong color, size, or style. Remember, you're going to live with your choice—most likely for a number of years! A "bargain" is not a good deal unless you like it *and* it fits into your overall plan.

4. Consider **multipurpose furnishings**, items that can serve more than one purpose. Perhaps you can choose a kitchen table that doubles as a desk; a bookcase that also serves as an end table; a sleeper sofa that provides accommodations for overnight guests; or director's chairs that can be moved from room to room or even used outdoors. Multi-use pieces provide flexibility and can

save you money, since fewer purchases are necessary.

5. Impulse buying can ruin your furnishing plan *and* your budget. Before buying, ask yourself a few questions related to your master furnishing plan. Is it the right color? The right style? The right size? The right scale to fit with your other furnishings? If you're uncertain, find out! Most stores will loan fabric samples and provide detailed information on dimensions. Some offer complimentary **in-home consultations** (decorator advice) for major purchases; other stores charge for this service, so be sure to ask.

6. If you're short on money, you can substitute time for money. Comparison shopping pays off in lower prices (and sometimes greater consumer satisfaction). Don't be afraid to bargain or to ask the salesperson when the item you want will go on sale and wait to purchase it then. (Most stores have regularly scheduled sales throughout the year.) If you have the time and inclination, you can learn how to paint, refinish, or otherwise renew used furnishings and appliances.

7. Color is an effective decorating tool that won't blow your budget. Paint a room or an old piece of furniture to update it and add vitality to your environment. Accent or create a focal point in a room by accessorizing with carefully selected, colorful items. Accessories don't need to be expensive. Rearrange decorative items you already own or try shopping at flea markets, estate sales, and art stores. Then add your own creativity and imagination—they're free, and the results may impress you!

multipurpose furnishings
....
items, such as a sleeper sofa, that can serve more than one purpose

in-home consultation
....
decorating advice given by a decorator who comes to the home

Figure 28.2
··············

These drawings show the different looks that can be created by monochromatic and complementary color schemes. Look at the furnishings in your home. What color scheme, if any, do they fall into? What color scheme do you prefer?

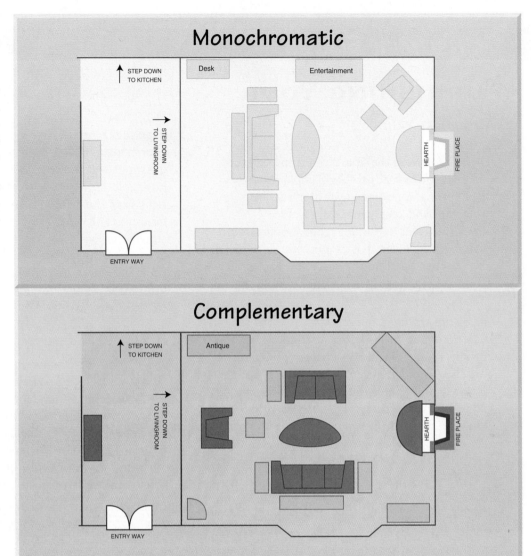

complementary color scheme
··················

a color scheme that brings together contrasting colors such as purple and yellow or blue and orange for a visually stimulating environment

monochromatic color scheme
··················

a color scheme that uses several shades of one color to provide a unified and sophisticated interior

analogous color scheme
··········

a color scheme that uses two or more related colors to create a naturalistic and comfortable environment

fabric on your furniture to guide you in choosing colors. There are three basic types of color schemes. In all cases, there should be one dominant color, with the others used as secondary or accent colors. (See Figure 28.2.)

• A **monochromatic color scheme** uses several shades of one color to provide a unified and sophisticated interior.

• An **analogous color scheme** utilizes two or more related colors (colors that are adjacent on the color wheel), such as green, blue, and purple, to create a naturalistic and comfortable environment.

• **Complementary color schemes** bring together contrasting colors, such as purple and yellow, for a visually stimulating environment.

Another possibility is to build your plan around a special piece of furniture such as an antique bed or a sleek, contemporary entertainment center. Let the unique character of this item guide you in selecting other furnishings, choosing a color scheme, and creating your own style. A distinctive art item or accessory can also establish the foundation for your home furnishing plan.

You may even create a furnishing plan by focusing on your interests, such as sports, playing an instrument, or nature photography. Inspiration may come from a collection of old movie posters, a handmade quilt, or sea shells collected on vacation. This is a great way to personalize your room or apartment. An added benefit is that it can be inexpensive, since you are using what you already own. This approach may reduce your storage needs, since frequently used items can be displayed rather than stowed away.

Step 4: Implement Your Plan

This is the fun part! Start slowly and keep your overall plan in mind when making any purchase decision. If an item doesn't fit into your plan, don't buy it!

It's not necessary to buy a whole room of furniture at one time (a bedroom "set," for example). In fact, the trend today is toward **eclectic decorating**: combining a variety of styles in the same room. This is often more interesting than a room where every piece matches, and it doesn't require a large initial investment!

See the Consumer Focus "Furnishing Your Home" on page 307 for additional suggestions about creative and inexpensive ways to implement your plan. You can probably add some ideas of your own!

Summary

- The ideal home furnishing plan is based on one's needs, budget, lifestyle, and decorating preferences.
- The first step in creating a furnishing plan is to assess the furnishings you have and then analyze your home activities to see if additional furnishings are required.
- Establishing a home furnishing budget is the next step in creating your plan.
- Many consumers find it useful to open a savings account and save regularly for future purchases.
- You can begin to identify your preferences and develop your own personal style by reading magazines, browsing in home furnishing stores, and observing the elements you are drawn to.
- Since most people cannot afford to furnish their entire home at one time, it makes sense to prioritize your needs and implement the plan in stages.

eclectic decorating
....
a trend in decorating that combines a variety of styles in the same room

ENRICHING YOUR VOCABULARY

Number your paper from 1–11. Read each sentence below. If the sentence is true, write "true" next to that number. If the sentence is false, rewrite it to make a true statement.

1. A room decorated with varying shades of white, cream, and tan is an example of a monochromatic color scheme.

2. Furniture, appliances, decorative items, and electronics are all considered accessories.

3. Multipurpose furnishings is a term used to describe used furniture.

4. Prioritize means to list from most important to least important.

5. A complementary color scheme uses colors that are next to each other on the color wheel.

6. An analogous color scheme creates a visually stimulating environment.

7. Personal style can be seen in an individual's choice of color and furniture types.

8. A master plan allows you to furnish your home in stages.

9. All furnishing stores provide free in-home consultations.

10. Eclectic decorating combines a variety of styles.

11. The life expectancy for all appliances is six years.

REVIEWING WHAT YOU HAVE LEARNED

1. Explain the first step in developing a home furnishing plan.

2. What factors should you consider when deciding whether or not to purchase home furnishings on credit?

USING YOUR CRITICAL THINKING

1. Do you think it is beneficial to develop a master furnishing plan? Why or why not?

Discuss your ideas with someone who holds the opposite point of view.

APPLYING WHAT YOU HAVE LEARNED

1. Design a bedroom furnishing plan according to the steps outlined in the text. Be sure to do the following:

    a. Develop a color scheme and decorating plan.

    b. Shop for the essential elements to learn about the prices and alternatives.

    c. Prioritize the purchases and plan how you will implement the plan.

    d. Use graph paper to arrange purchases to scale, using your own bedroom dimensions.

    e. Write a summary about what you learned in the process.

CHAPTER 29

Selecting Furniture, Appliances, and Electronics

OBJECTIVES

After completing this chapter, you will be able to do the following:

1. Name at least three factors to consider when buying case goods made of wood.
2. Explain the importance of reliability when choosing appliances.
3. Explain how to compare the energy efficiency of refrigerators made by different manufacturers.
4. Explain the meaning of an Underwriter's Laboratory Seal on an electric appliance.

TERMS

case goods	function	traditional style
compatibility	modern style	upholstered furniture
durability	product recall	veneer
energy efficiency	reliability	wood products
Energy Guide	technology	

Furniture and home furnishings are available in all shapes, sizes, colors, styles, and price ranges. With so much to choose from, how can you identify quality? Is price a good indicator? What about the brand or manufacturer's name? Does a warranty indicate a product is well designed and made of durable materials? In each case the answer is "not necessarily."

FACTORS TO CONSIDER

Neither price, brand name, nor the presence of a manufacturer's warranty is a reliable indicator of quality. Expensive furniture is not always high quality. Likewise, a budget price does not indicate inferior quality. However, many brand-name manufacturers offer warranties against flaws, and budget manufacturers usually do not. Prices are strongly affected by brand name—which is based on advertising, not ob-

jective fact. Advertising is designed to make you *believe* there is a relationship between a certain brand name and quality! A warranty simply provides consumer protection if a product problem occurs. A product without a warranty will probably sell for less, but may be of equal or even better quality than a product that has a warranty.

Selecting Furniture

To get the best buy for your furnishing dollars, learn how to identify quality design and construction. The following paragraphs suggest basic factors to consider, along with specific guidelines for choosing case goods, upholstered furniture, and furniture made of wood, metal or plastic.

Basic Considerations. There are three basic considerations when selecting *any* type of furniture: style, function, and durability. These are discussed in the following paragraphs. (Later in this section we'll discuss how to select appliances and electronic equipment.)

Shopping for furniture can be overwhelming. It will take some time for you to recognize the styles you prefer, the quality you are looking for, and the prices you can afford. Make a list of furniture items you would like to purchase. Take your list to a local furniture store and look at these items keeping in mind your style preferences, quality, and price.

UNIT 10 FURNITURE, APPLIANCES, AND ELECTRONICS

Style refers to the general character or personality of furnishings. The two broad categories of furniture styles are traditional and modern. **Traditional style** reflects the styles of old, usually with at least some carving of wood pieces. **Modern style** has clean lines. However, in-depth knowledge about interior design is not required to create a pleasing home environment. Within these two categories, there are as many decorating styles as there are individuals.

Begin to identify or cultivate a decorating style by collecting ideas from magazines and observing the styles you are naturally drawn to as you shop, watch television, or observe the homes of others. What styles appeal to you? Modern and high-tech? Country and cozy? Or traditional and graceful? Maybe you prefer the clean lines and serenity of Japanese-style furnishings, the warmth of the Southwestern look, or the energy of contemporary styling.

Analyze your preferences, looking for a common thread that can be used to weave your own style. Look for balance and a pleasing line in any items you select. Good design is available in all price ranges. (So is poor design!)

Function is as important as style in furniture selection. According to an old saying, "form should follow function." This means the design (form) of an object should be secondary to and enhance its usefulness. For example, a well-designed chair should be comfortable and sturdy as well as attractive. A chair that does not adequately provide seating can never be considered well designed.

In other words, a well-designed piece of furniture will also be functional. A bed must be comfortable for sleeping. A lamp must provide adequate illumination. An entertainment center should hold all necessary equipment and easily fit into the available space.

Durability is a relative term, and needs for durability will be affected by household size and composition. Furnishings that a single person with no children finds durable might not be appropriate for a family with small children or a couple with three pampered (indoor) dogs.

If small children and/or pets are present, selecting furnishings constructed of strong, easy-to-clean materials can reduce conflict and increase family harmony. Large households will naturally have more wear and tear on furnishings and may want to choose solid furniture styles and heavy upholstery fabrics.

Choose durability according to the intended use of the item. Some furniture receives heavy use; therefore, durability is very important. An example is a sofa used for watching TV and taking naps. Durability is less important for decorative items and infrequently used furniture, such as the bed in a guest room.

Types of Furniture. Furniture can be classified into three categories: case goods, upholstered furniture, and other. Shopping is simplified when you know how to identify quality in each category.

Case goods describes furniture items with no upholstered parts. Examples are tables, bookshelves, and storage chests. Wood is the most popular material, but case goods are also constructed of plastic, metal, or woven materials such as bamboo. When selecting wooden case goods, consider the appropriateness of the materials, the finish on the furniture, and the construction of joints and moving parts.

Wooden case goods are made of solid wood, veneer, wood products or some combination of these. Solid wood requires special care and can be very heavy. Usually solid wood is used in combination with **veneer**, which is a

durability
....
the anticipated length of service without repair

traditional style
....
furnishings with classic lines that often include wood carving

modern style
....
having clean, simple lines

function
....
the intended use of an item

case goods
....
wood, plastic, metal, or woven furniture items that have no upholstered parts

veneer
....
a thin panel of hardwood laminated to a core of plywood or pressed board

Refinishing a piece of furniture can be a very rewarding experience. It can also be very time consuming and messy. Have you ever refinished a piece of furniture? If not, talk with someone who has. Would they recommend the experience?

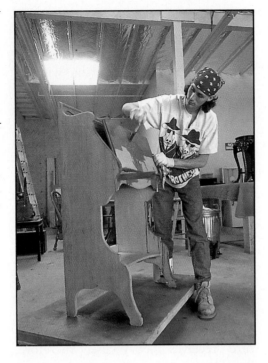

wood products
....
plywood or pressed wood

upholstered furniture
....
furniture covered with padding and fabric

reliability
....
resistance to wear

panel (or panels) of hardwood laminated to a core of plywood or pressed board (**wood products**). The advantage of veneer is an attractive but lightweight product that can be used by itself or in combination with solid wood. Veneer construction is used in all price ranges.

If you want new furniture but can't afford it, consider unfinished or unassembled furniture. It is new, and it costs less than finished furniture. But you have to do the finishing work.

Upholstered furniture is covered with padding and fabric, and it is more difficult to shop for because you can't see the construction under the upholstery. Some furniture stores provide models showing the construction. If not, check the label or product brochures for construction information.

Look for pieces built of hardwood frames and upholstered with a durable fabric. (Avoid fabric with loose weaves and metallic threads, as they will soon show wear.) The fabric should be attached without wrinkles and the corners should be smooth. A stain-

resistant treatment can be sprayed on most fabrics, and it is usually worthwhile.

Reupholstering a worn piece of furniture is very expensive. Consider this option only if the furniture construction and style warrant the investment. Some consumers purchase slipcovers to cover worn upholstery or change the look of the item.

Other furniture constructed of plastic, metal, or wicker, offers quality at affordable prices. Look for good design and good workmanship (such as no rough edges that will snag clothing), just as you would with any furniture.

Selecting Appliances

Most U.S. households own or rent a variety of major appliances. These include a refrigerator, range, a microwave oven as well as a conventional oven, one or more televisions, and, in many cases, a washer and dryer and a dishwasher.

In addition, most also have several small kitchen appliances such as a toaster, blender, coffeepot, or rice cooker. Before buying, consider the amount and type of storage you have available. Most apartments have a very limited amount, so multiuse appliances such as a toaster oven or crockpot (which can be used as a rice cooker) may be the most practical.

Although you will spend more time and money shopping for major appliances, the same basic considerations apply to selecting small appliances. These include product reliability, energy efficiency, consumer safety, and the warranty (if one is available). In addition, consider ease in use and cleaning of small appliances.

Product Reliability. A recent survey by Consumers Union reported that, "Each year, millions of household products break—and consumers throw out millions of TV sets, toasters, and other hardware." Appliances that don't work and need frequent repairs are expensive and frustrating to own.

A reliable product is one that consistently operates properly and seldom needs repairs. According to *Consumer Reports,* some brands are more reliable than others and you can increase your chances of getting a reliable appliance by using the magazine's recommendations. These recommendations are based on repair histories and independent laboratory tests.

For equipment that you will use frequently over a long period of time, choose a brand with above-average reliability. You'll save yourself the expense and hassles of frequent repairs.

Energy Efficiency. After repairs, the cost of energy is the most important factor affecting equipment-operating costs. Long after paying the purchase price for an appliance, you'll still be paying operating costs. You can save a lot of money over the lifetime of an appliance by purchasing an energy-efficient model. Of course, the more energy a product consumes, the more significant the savings on energy costs.

To compare the energy costs of different makes and models of an appliance, look for the yellow **Energy Guide** required on all new appliances. This tells you about the relative energy efficiency of a particular model and gives the estimated annual operating costs.

Safety. Appliance safety is an important consideration, particularly in households that include young children or elderly members. Consumer publications offer tips for selecting safe appliances.

Product design affects the safety of an appliance (or any other consumer product). For example, a range with controls on a panel behind the burners may pose a fire hazard. One could easily burn an arm or even catch clothing on fire when reaching for the controls. Consumer publications can identify de-

Energy Guide
. . . .
a label required on all new appliances that tells the relative energy efficiency of a particular model and gives the estimated annual operating costs

energy efficiency
. . . .
the ratio of energy consumption to use

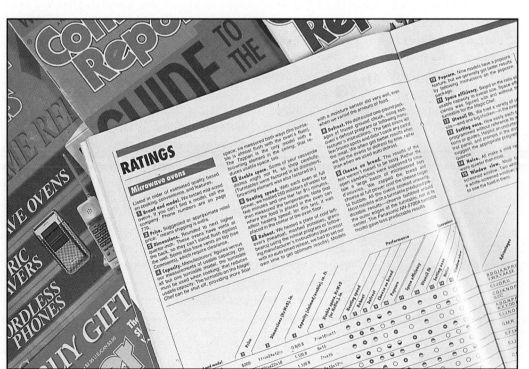

Many consumer magazines give ratings on various furnishings. Before you buy, check in a consumer magazine to find how it rates the item you're going to buy. You may find that the item would not be worth your money!

INTERACTING WITH TECHNOLOGY

A NEW GENERATION OF SMART APPLIANCES

Would you like to be able to freeze ice cubes in just five minutes, or cook in an oven that automatically turns off when the food is properly cooked? You may soon be able to do such things. New household appliances are being designed that will be more energy-efficient and will employ new sensor technology to help do the job better.

Have you ever missed an important phone call because you were using a vacuum cleaner or hair dryer? Systems are being tested that link household appliances together to avoid such problems. A ring of the doorbell or telephone causes noisy appliances to turn off so you can hear the bell.

Have you ever been uncomfortable in a shower as you tried to adjust the temperature? Future faucets will allow you to program water temperature and flow so that you step into a shower that is just right every time.

Sensor devices are being tested in vacuum cleaners that decrease suction when the carpet is clean and in washing machines that turn off when the rinse water is clear. Future heating systems will be able to adjust to the number of people in a room, their locations, and their level of activity to ensure a comfortable environment at all times. Gas furnaces are being designed that produce their own electricity so that they will continue to operate during power outages.

Extensive research is going into designing new refrigerators for home use. These new appliances will look very similar to the refrigerators of today, but they will be much more energy-efficient and free of chlorofluorocarbons (CFCs), which destroy the earth's ozone layer.

These improvements will be achieved through a combination of new advances. Some of the refrigerators will be equipped with vacuum insulation panels that will remove much of the oxygen from the interior of the box. This will allow foods to be stored for longer periods of time at warmer temperatures. Other designs will include sensors that only defrost the freezer when necessary rather than at regular intervals.

As research continues, we will continue to benefit from designs that have not yet even been considered. Perhaps you will come up with an idea for a new design. Our responsibility as consumers is to select products that serve us well and that also protect our environment.

sign features to look for and point out those that are dangerous and to be avoided.

The materials used to construct an appliance can also affect its safety. Look for appropriate use of materials, such as insulated casings on heating appliances and sturdy, and securely fastened handles on a coffeepot.

Underwriters' Laboratories (UL) certifies the safety of electrical appliances. A UL seal indicates that the appliance (or some components of it) have been tested and met the safety standards of Underwriters Laboratories. Gas appliances are certified for safety by the American Gas Association (AGA). Both certification programs are optional (for manufacturers), so a product without a safety seal is not necessarily unsafe, only untested.

Some appliances have added safety features, which may increase the purchase price. An example is a curling iron that automatically shuts off if not used after thirty minutes. In some cases, such features are well worth the additional cost.

The Consumer Product Safety Commission (CPSC) regulates consumer appliances and electronics, giving special attention to items used by infants and children (such as baby furniture). If the agency discovers a safety problem, it may issue a warning or recall items that have already been sold. Both warnings and recalls are published in *Consumer Reports* magazine. A **product recall** notifies the consumer to return, repair, or discard an unsafe item. Among the household appliances recalled in 1993 were dishwashers, garage door openers, hair dryers, smoke detectors, fans, and electric mixers.

Warranty. Comparison shopping should include comparison of warranty coverage on products under consideration. Find out whether or not there is a product warranty and what coverage it provides. The presence of a warranty does not mean the product is better than a similar one without a warranty, but it does offer protection against the costs of repairing or replacing a faulty product.

product recall
....
a notice to consumers to return, repair, or discard an unsafe item

Many times a problem is found with a product after it is already on the market and in many homes. When this happens, the manufacturer will issue a recall telling consumers to return, repair, or discard the item. Consumer magazines will list products that have been recalled by the manufacturer. Have you ever purchased an item that was recalled?

A warranty is a legal contract, but not all warranties are created equal! In Chapter 30 we will discuss how to read and evaluate a warranty, as well as the pros and cons of buying a service contract.

Selecting Electronic Equipment

In many ways, the process of selecting electronic equipment is similar to buying appliances or any other consumer durable. There are, however, several additional factors to consider when buying products such as videocassette recorders (VCRs), tape decks, stereos and stereo components, camcorders, and compact-disc players (CDs). When shopping for electronics, one should understand the relationship between technology and price and clearly identify desirable product features.

Technology and Prices. The high-tech nature of most electronic products sets them apart from other home furnishings. Product features are numerous, and shopping requires a very high level of knowledge—more than many salespeople have (*Consumer Reports*, March 1993).

When a **technology** (science applied to produce a new type of product) is new, prices are high. For example, in early 1994, a Home THX sound system designed and licensed by Lucasfilm cost $8,000 to $10,000 (installed) and was out of reach for most people.

On the other hand, as technology is refined and standardized, subsequent models of a particular type of equipment are less expensive and have greater reliability. VCRs are a good example. In writing about home theater equipment, *Consumer Reports* described VCRs as "mature" products characterized by falling prices. Just a few years ago, wireless remote and on-

More and more electronic equipment is on the market each day. Items that were new and unproven (and very expensive) a few years ago are commonplace today. Waiting a few years for the price to come down on an item you want can make the item very affordable. What new electronic equipment would you be interested in buying?

screen programming were only available on deluxe-model VCRs. Now these features are standard on VCRs priced as low as $189.

Your decisions about technology will depend on your values and resources. If you want to have the newest features on your sound system to impress your friends, you'll pay a premium for the privilege. If you only want to enjoy rented videos, then an inexpensive VCR may be just what you need.

Product Features. Each new product introduction brings a multitude of new options to choose from. When buying a VCR, one may choose from many useful and some not-so-useful product features. These include auto channel-set, auto head-cleaning, auto tracking, bilingual display, cable-channel capacity (up to 181 channels), childproof lock, front-panel A/V inputs, head count, index search, jog-shuttle control, center or mid-mount chassis, power backup, Quasi S-VHS playback, and quick-start transport.

Simplify the process of shopping for electronics by identifying which product features are essential to have. Consumer publications offer detailed information about the quality and usefulness of the features available on specific products, often by brand and model number.

There's no sense in paying extra for features that you can't understand or won't use. More features mean more potential problems. Choose carefully and don't be swayed by a "dazzling" display or a high-pressure salesperson.

Other Considerations. When buying computers and home entertainment equipment, check for compatibility—how well it goes with what you already have. Think about your future needs as well. Can you add additional components if you want to? Buying an expandable system may save money in the long run.

As with buying appliances, choose a product with above-average reliability. Also consider the availability of a warranty and access to repair services.

Summary

- When selecting furniture one should consider style, function, and durability.

- Before buying an appliance it is important to evaluate product reliability, energy efficiency, consumer safety, and the warranty coverage.

- There is an inverse relationship between price and technology in electronics. Prices are highest and reliability is lowest when a technology is first available. Later, as the technology becomes standardized, prices decrease and reliability increases.

- You can reduce repair hassles by choosing an appliance that is rated above average in reliability.

- Save on repair costs by selecting an appliance or electronic product with a manufacturer's warranty.

compatibility

having the ability to work with other components; how well an item will go with other items

E NRICHING YOUR VOCABULARY

Number your paper from 1–11. Beside each number write the word or phrase that matches that definition. Choose your answers from the following list. (Not all words are used.)

case goods	function	traditional style
compatibility	modern style	upholstered furniture
durability	product recall	veneer
energy efficiency	reliability	wood products
Energy Guide	technology	

1. Science applied to consumer products
2. Plywood or pressed wood
3. Wood, plastic, metal, or woven furniture items with no upholstered parts
4. The ratio of energy consumption to use
5. Intended use
6. Notice to consumers to return, repair, or discard an unsafe item
7. Having the ability to work with other components
8. Appliance labels indicating energy use and estimated operating costs
9. Anticipated length of service without repair
10. Resistance to wear
11. Thin panel of hardwood laminated to wood products

R EVIEWING WHAT YOU HAVE LEARNED

1. Name at least three factors to consider when buying case goods made of wood.
2. Why is reliability an important consideration when choosing appliances?
3. How can a shopper compare the energy efficiency of refrigerators made by different manufacturers?
4. What does an Underwriters' Laboratories Seal on an electric appliance mean?

U SING YOUR CRITICAL THINKING SKILLS

1. A salesperson states that durability is the most important criterion when selecting furniture. Do you agree or disagree? Explain your perspective.
2. Would you expect to spend more or less for electronics equipment in the future? Explain your perspective.

A PPLYING WHAT YOU HAVE LEARNED

1. Go to the public library and find consumer information about an electronic product that you might want to buy. Read at least one article about that product. Report to the class about the source you used, the type of information you found, and what you learned.

CHAPTER 30

Shopping for Home Furnishings and Equipment

OBJECTIVES

After completing this chapter, you will be able to do the following:

1. Explain the purpose of preshopping and list the steps in the preshopping process.
2. Name a consumer publication you could consult to compare the reliability of various brands of compact-disc players.
3. Explain the relationship between price and quality in home furnishings, equipment, and electronics.
4. Explain the difference between a regular sale and a special-purchase sale.
5. List the advantages and disadvantages of buying used furniture.
6. Explain the difference between full and limited warranties that both last for three years.
7. Explain the difference between a manufacturer's warranty and a service contract (extended warranty).

TERMS

biased information
Consumer Reports
Consumer's Research
deferred-payment plan
extended warranty

floor sample
full warranty
going-out-of-business sale
limited warranty
month-to-month rental
    agreement

on-site repair service
preshopping
rent-to-own option
service contract

Shopping for furniture, appliances, and electronics is fun! However, the process can also be overwhelming. The choices seem limitless—and so do the costs! You may feel pressured because you are spending a lot of money and you'll be living with your decision for a number of years.

PRESHOPPING

You can increase your chances of making a satisfying choice by **preshopping** before you buy home furnishings (or any other major consumer item). Preshopping helps you make a rational decision rather than an emotional decision based on sales pressure or the influences of the shopping environment.

Preshopping involves two steps. The first step is to get objective information about the item you will be buying. Learn how to identify quality materials and workmanship, the costs and benefits of product features you may want, and the expected price range for your purchase.

The second step involves making preliminary decisions *before* you actually go shopping—and before the sales pressure is on! Decide what product and features will best meet your needs and maybe even the brand and model you prefer, so that you enter the marketplace as a knowledgeable consumer.

Sources of Consumer Information

Consumer information is available from many sources. Two of the most useful sources are *Consumer Reports* and *Consumer's Research* magazines. Both publish annual buying guides with name-brand ratings for a variety of consumer products. They are available at any public library.

Other sources of consumer information include special-interest publications or magazines, government publications, and consumer hotlines; and information provided by manufacturers on labels, in product brochures, and in advertising. Friends, relatives, and salespersons can also offer helpful information.

Biased Information. Always evaluate the potential biases of any consumer information. For example, *Consumer Reports* generally places a high priority on product safety in its ratings. However, for a given purchase, price may be more important to you than safety. Salespeople are often very knowledgeable, but their recommendations may be influenced by sales quotas and potential commissions. Friends

Do your homework! You probably don't like to hear that phrase. It's important, however, to do your homework before you shop for home furnishings. Read all the information you can about the items you're looking for before making a purchase, it could save you money and time later.

and relatives may base their advice on limited product experience rather than objective information. Product ratings in magazines may be influenced by the advertisers who support the publication. Knowing the source's perspective can assist you in evaluating the usefulness of the information.

Current Information. Also consider whether the information is up-to-date. This is particularly important with information about electronic equipment, which may change rapidly due to changing technology.

Preliminary Decision Making

After gathering information about your planned purchase, you should be able to make at least three decisions before you shop. First, determine your needs and wants. Identify which product features are essential and which would be desirable. Decide on the level of quality and materials that are acceptable to you.

Second, establish a budget for the purchase. If you know what the basic price range is, you'll recognize a good buy when you see it.

Third, decide on a payment method. The alternatives are: cash, credit, or a deferred-payment plan. Your choice will affect the total cost of the purchase as well as where you shop for the purchase. Cash is the least expensive option. All stores accept cash and some even offer a discount for payment by cash. Credit is another possible option. Assuming you have credit and can afford to use it, a "rule of thumb" is that the useful life of credit purchases should outlast the payment period. If not, it's better to wait until you have cash. Furniture and electronics stores may also offer a variety of **deferred-payment plans** that allow you to buy

now and pay later, on layaway, or a "90 days same as cash" plan.

SHOPPING FOR HOME FURNISHINGS

Many things must be considered when shopping for home furnishings. Some things to consider are whether to buy new or used furniture, whether to rent furnishings, warranties offered, caring for equipment, and safety procedures. The following pages will provide you with information on these and other topics that will help make your shopping for home furnishings a positive experience.

Types of Stores

There are many outlets for purchasing both new and used home furnishings, equipment, and appliances. Each type of store offers its own combination of pricing, services, and product selection.

Specialty Stores. As the name implies, these outlets "specialize" in a particular type of product such as consumer electronics, appliances, or outdoor furniture. Such stores employ knowledgeable sales personnel who can answer technical questions about the product. They also offer a large selection of makes and models in one location. Specialty stores may offer **on-site repair services** and they are sometimes more willing to accept returns.

Department Stores. Department stores offer a more limited selection of specific types of items but a wider assortment of home furnishings. These stores tend to be service-oriented, since they hope to earn your repeat business.

on-site repair service
....
repair services located in the store where a purchase is made

deferred-payment plan
.....
an arrangement that allows consumers to buy now and pay later, use a layaway plan, or use a "90 days same as cash" plan

If you're handy with tools, you can save money by buying merchandise that is still in the original shipping crate and assembling it yourself. Have you ever purchased merchandise this way? How did you feel about assembling it?

Warehouse Stores. Warehouse stores rely on low prices to attract consumers. They generally have a very limited selection of a particular type of item (televisions, for example), but offer very competitive prices. Typically, these stores offer minimal service and no frills.

Mail-Order Stores. Convenience is the hallmark of mail-order shopping. You can shop for name-brand stereo components, designer furniture, or discounted linens—all from the comfort of your own home.

When shopping by mail, retain copies of all receipts in case there is a problem with the order. Be sure to include shipping costs when comparing the price to similar merchandise from other sources. Before ordering, review the company's return policy.

Unfinished Furniture Stores. Another alternative is to buy unfinished furniture and add your own finishing touches. If you have the necessary skills or are willing to learn them, this can be a way to save money on wood furnishings. Unfinished furniture is not cheap, but it can be a good value.

Shopping Strategies

Informed consumers have a great advantage in the marketplace: They know what they want and they know a good buy when they see it! In fact, they often know more about their purchase than the salespeople! They are not swayed or misled by exaggerated sales pitches. Here are some suggestions to help you in the process of comparison shopping.

Avoid Impulse Buying. Impulse buying can wreck your furnishing plan as well as your budget. The wrong color, size, or style of furniture selected in haste will *never be right*. Choose carefully to find furnishings you can live with. Furnishings that don't fit into your overall plan are not a bargain at any price!

Learn How to Identify Quality. Price is not always an indicator of quality. Look for good construction, appropriate use of materials, reliability (for equipment and appliances), easy maintenance, and a good warranty with easily accessible repair services.

Ask for a Discount When Paying Cash. Retailers pay your credit card company up to 5 percent on credit card purchases you make. If you plan to pay cash, it is sometimes possible to negotiate a 3 percent to 4 percent discount (and the merchant will still make more than on a credit transaction). Don't be afraid to ask; you might be surprised at the answer!

Know How to Spot a "Real" Sale. Just because an item is "on sale" doesn't mean that you are getting the best price—or even a reduced price. It helps to understand what different terms mean. Some frequently used terms are identified below.

- **Regular Sales:** Many stores offer sales on their regular merchandise. Usually this takes the form of a discount off the regular price of merchandise sold at that store. Prices go back to the original level when the sale ends. Furniture, appliance, and electronics stores schedule regular sales at planned intervals throughout the year. A careful consumer can time purchases to coincide with regular sales.

- **Clearance Sales:** Retailers offer clearance sales on their regular merchandise to make room for new goods. You can find clearance sales when a manufacturer brings out a new model to replace an older model of the same item, such as a television set. Seasonal and fashion items are often offered at clearance sales (near the end of the relevant season). An end-of-the-season clearance sale might include furnishings such as holiday decorations, patio furniture, or bed linens. Clearance sales offer very good prices on first-quality merchandise. Selection may be limited.

- **Special Purchase Sales:** Unlike regular and clearance sales, special purchase sales do not feature regular store merchandise. As the name implies, merchandise is specially purchased and priced for the sale. The quality may not be as high as the quality of the store's regular merchandise. However, if an item suits your needs, style, and pocketbook, it may be a good buy.

- **Going-Out-of-Business Sales:** The Council of Better Business Bureaus warns consumers to watch out

going-out-of-business sale

a sale that may or may not be legitimate, but which indicates that a business will not be open for returns (or anything else) after the sale is over

Retailers offer sales many times throughout the year to draw customers into the store. It is especially important to check sale merchandise carefully, it may turn out that the item is not a bargain at all! Have you ever purchased a sale item that did not meet your expectations? What did you do?

when you see this type of sale! The store may not have any intention of going out of business (especially if bargain-hungry shoppers keep taking their bait!). If you do decide to shop these sales, comparison-shop just as you would for any other purchase. Make your selections carefully; there won't be an opportunity for refunds or returns.

- **Other Sales:** Retailers occasionally offer sales featuring particular types of goods. **Floor samples** are items that have been displayed in a retail store. They may be soiled or slightly damaged, or the store may simply be selling them to make room for newer items. Electronics stores sometimes offer a discount on *opened merchandise*. This is usually a new item that has been returned to the store, but which cannot be sold as new because the packaging is damaged or missing. If you buy, be sure that all parts are in the package. When a manufacturer produces too many of a particular item, first-quality goods may be discounted and sold as *factory overruns*. Slightly imperfect goods are sold as *factory seconds* (rather than first-quality). In most cases, the imperfections in seconds are only cosmetic and may not be noticeable to a casual observer. If, however, the imperfection affects the serviceability of the item, then it will be sold as *damaged merchandise*.

Buying Used Furniture, Appliances, and Electronics

Another alternative for furnishing your home is to buy used furniture, equipment, and electronics. While you may not always find the latest colors and styles in home furnishings or cutting-edge technology in electronics, you can find good quality at affordable prices. You may also find some real treasures!

Sources for Used Furnishings. The place to begin your search is in the classified advertisements of your local newspaper. Many neighborhoods also publish flyers or maintain community bulletin boards where individuals advertise items for sale. Other good sources are garage sales, flea markets, appliance stores selling rebuilt or reconditioned equipment, used-furniture stores, and rental-furniture companies that periodically sell their inventory in order to replace it with something newer.

Advantages of Buying Used Furnishings. The main advantage of buying used furnishings is cost: Used equipment costs much less than new equipment. Some people also enjoy the process of shopping for used furnishings and derive satisfaction from "reclaiming" and restoring life to a useful item. Often, the original owners have simply grown tired of these items and want to update their furnishings.

Disadvantages of Buying Used Furnishings. The primary disadvantage of buying used furniture is the time investment required to find what you want. Aside from shopping in used-furniture stores, there is no central place where you can go for comparison shopping, and at any given time, the selection is limited. Used furnishings seldom come with warranties, and the merchandise cannot be returned or exchanged. Let the buyer beware!

Renting Furnishings and Equipment

When you move out on your own, you may first live in a furnished room

Fleamarkets and garage sales can be sources of good used furniture buys. It's necessary, however, to check the furniture carefully. It probably won't be possible to return the item if you find a problem with it. Have you ever shopped at a fleamarket or garage sale?

or apartment. If you rent an unfurnished place, however, you may find it necessary to rent some basic furnishings (such as a bed or refrigerator) or even entire rooms of furniture. There are several advantages to renting home furnishings rather than buying them.

Renting Can Be Inexpensive. If you don't have any furnishings at all, renting can enable you obtain the basics (a bed, desk or table, clothing storage chests, and seating) for a low initial cost. If the monthly rental fee fits into your budget, renting can be an affordable way to get started (especially if you share the costs with roommates).

Renting Is Convenient. Simply go to the rental company, select what you want, sign a contract, and pay the security deposit. Then the furnishings will be delivered to your home. You pay a fixed monthly fee for the period of the agreement. A **month-to-month rental agreement** allows you (or the rental company) to change or cancel the contract on thirty days' notice. A lease (usually for six months or longer) offers you a guaranteed price for a specified period of time. You may have to pay the full cost even if you do not keep the furnishings for the full length of time agreed to in the lease.

Renting Can Help You Decide What to Buy. Renting also gives you the opportunity to identify your needs and discover your own style before making a major investment in home furnishings. It allows you time to save for exactly what you want, rather than purchasing something just to get by.

Renting Offers Flexibility. Renting may also be advantageous if you plan to live somewhere for only a limited time, such as during your first year of college. You also avoid the hassles of moving that come with owning your own furniture!

Renting Can Lead to Ownership. Some furniture companies offer a **"rent-to-own" option**. By agreement, all rental payments go toward the purchase price of the furniture. This

month-to-month rental agreement
....
a contract that allows the renter or rental company to change or cancel the contract on thirty days' notice

rent-to-own option
....
an agreement by which all rental payments go toward the purchase price of a piece of furniture

full warranty
· · · · · · · · · · · · · ·
an agreement that covers all repair or replacement costs (parts, labor, shipping) during the warranty period

limited warranty
· · · · · · · · · · · · · ·
a written guarantee that covers only the costs specified in the contract

service contract
· · · · · · · · · · · · · ·
an agreement by which the consumer prepays for repairs of an item purchased; repair insurance

extended warranty
· · · · · · · · · · · · · ·
an agreement that allows the buyer of a product to pay a fee to have the product's warranty extended for a longer period of time; a service contract

sounds good, but there are some drawbacks to this method for acquiring furniture. There is a relatively small selection available from the rental company, and the price is much higher than if the furnishings were purchased from other sources.

Manufacturer's Warranty

The manufacturer's warranty (if there is one) provides you with financial protection against the cost of repairs. If a product is faulty, the problems will usually show up during the early months or years of ownership, which coincide with the warranty period. If so, all or most of the repair costs will be paid by the manufacturer.

The store can show you a copy of the product warranty before you buy the product. Read it carefully to answer three important questions:

1. What type of warranty is offered?

 • A **full warranty** covers all repair costs (during the warranty period), including: parts, labor,

and even shipping if the item must be returned to the manufacturer for repairs. If the item cannot be repaired, the warranty provides a replacement at no cost to the consumer.

 • A **limited warranty** covers only the costs specified in the written warranty contract. For example, the warranty on a VCR may specify that it pays for parts, but not for labor costs. If you purchase a product with a limited warranty, be sure you understand the limitations of the warranty coverage.

2. How long is the warranty period?

 • It may cover any period of time, from thirty days to five years or more. The warranty duration may vary among similar products and it is worth comparing to find the best buy.

3. Who will perform any necessary repairs?

 • Can you take your product to any repair service, or must it be returned to the seller or manufacturer? How convenient or easy will that be? (It's much easier to take a VCR in for repairs than a washing machine!)

Service Contracts and Extended Warranties. A **service contract** is essentially "repair insurance." The consumer pre-pays for repairs with the purchase of a service contract. If the equipment doesn't need repairs during the time period specified in the contract, then the money is forfeited (as with any other type of insurance).

At the time you purchase home appliances or electronics, you will have the option to buy a service contract or an **extended warranty**. (The two are basically the same.) But should you buy it? Is it a good investment?

Retailers encourage customers to buy extended warranties or service contracts for the products they have purchased. There are advantages and disadvantages, though, that need to be considered before purchasing an extended warranty or service contract.

The major benefit of owning a service contract or extended warranty is that there will be no unexpected repair bills during the contract period. This can provide peace of mind, particularly if unexpected repairs would affect your ability to meet your regular expenses.

On the other hand, a service contract covers equipment when it is new—and when it is unlikely to need repairs. Service contracts may also overlap the warranty period and you certainly don't need double insurance coverage for the unlikely event that you'll need repairs while the equipment is new! Remember, equipment repairs are most likely to occur as the equipment gets older. (Service contracts aren't available then!)

Don't be surprised when you get the "hard sell" on a service contract. Service contracts are extremely profitable for retailers (who make sometimes as much as 70 percent profit, according to Consumers Union!). However, only 12 percent to 20 percent of consumers ever use them! *Consumer Reports* magazine suggests buying a service contract *only* if you cannot save for repairs.

How can you get the best service from home appliances and electronics? Begin by purchasing a product that is reliable and comes with a manufacturer's warranty.

After carefully shopping for the right equipment or appliance, you will probably use it for a number of years. Here are some steps you can take to increase your satisfaction and reduce the problems associated with owning consumer durables.

Set Up a Record-Keeping System

File your receipt, warranty information, and owner's manual or maintenance booklet for future reference. It is not necessary to return the warranty registration card in order to obtain coverage. However, if you do, the manufacturer can notify you of any product problems or recalls.

Keep receipts for all repairs (even those under warranty). Be sure the bill indicates the specific problem and includes an itemized list of work completed.

Learn How to Use and Care for Your Equipment

Read the owner's manual so that you know how to properly use and care for your new appliance. Only use an appliance for its intended purpose. In order to preserve the warranty coverage, you must service the product according to the manufacturer's instructions. However, the warranty cannot require you to use a specific brand-name product for the servicing (Comet cleanser, for example).

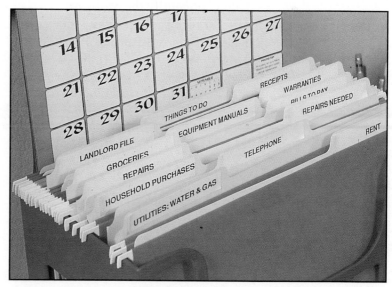

A filing system such as this can make it easy to keep track of your receipts, warranties, and owner's manuals. How do you keep track of these items?

Observe Safety Procedures with Electrical Equipment

Don't operate an electrical appliance with wet hands. To unplug an appliance, grasp the plug firmly. Pulling the cord weakens the connection with the plug and could lead to shorts or even a fire. Periodically check all electrical cords for damage and repair if necessary.

If you use an extension cord, it should be the same size (or larger) than the appliance cord. Avoid using an extension cord with heating appliances, such as a toaster or coffeemaker. Never run an electric cord under a rug.

Follow Manufacturer Instructions for Repairs

If an appliance doesn't work, first check to be sure it is plugged in and turned on. (You'd be surprised how often this is the "problem"!) Then, read the owner's manual. It may include a trouble-shooting checklist to help you identify the problem.

If problems occur while the equipment is under warranty, follow the procedures specified in the warranty contract. Be sure to contact the manufacturer *before* the warranty expires.

Anticipate and Plan for the Cost of Repairs

Generally, few repairs are needed in the early years of owning a consumer durable. However, even the best, most reliable electronic equipment and appliances will eventually need repairs. If you don't plan for these expenses, they can wreck your budget. A good strategy is to buy a product with a warranty *and* save regularly in order to pay for repairs as they occur.

Summary

- Use preshopping to assist in rational decision making and resist sales pressure and the influences of the shopping environment.

- Two useful sources of consumer information are *Consumer Reports* and *Consumer's Research* magazines. Both publish annual buying guides with name-brand ratings.

- Price is not an accurate indicator of quality. Look for good construction, appropriate use of materials, reliability (for equipment and appliances), easy maintenance, and a good warranty. Just because an item is "on sale" doesn't mean that you are getting the best price—or even a reduced price. It helps to understand the terminology used to describe various types of sales.

- All warranties are not the same! Carefully evaluate a warranty to learn whether it is a full or limited warranty, the duration of coverage, and procedures for obtaining repairs.

- Don't buy a service contract or extended warranty, unless you can't save for repairs and an unexpected repair bill would keep you from meeting your budgeted commitments.

CHAPTER REVIEW
30

ENRICHING YOUR VOCABULARY

Number your paper from 1–12. Read each sentence below. If the sentence is true, write "true" next to that number. If the sentence is false, rewrite it to make a true statement.

1. A service contract is included in a full warranty.
2. A full warranty covers all repair costs during the specified period.
3. *Consumer Reports* and *Consumer's Research* magazines publish annual home-shopping catalogs.
4. A month-to-month rental agreement can be canceled with 30 days' notice.
5. Sometimes a deferred-payment plan allows you to pay no interest for a specified period.
6. Consumers should disregard biased information when making a decision to buy a product.
7. An extended warranty is a service contract.
8. A going-out-of-business sale may not be a legitimate sale.
9. Stores are not allowed to sell floor samples.
10. Flea markets generally offer on-site repair service.
11. With a rent-to-own option, all payments go toward the purchase of the product.
12. A limited warranty provides full coverage.

REVIEWING WHAT YOU HAVE LEARNED

1. What is the purpose of preshopping? List the steps in the preshopping process.
2. Name a consumer publication you could consult to compare the reliability of various brands of compact-disc players.
3. Explain the difference between a regular sale and a special-purchase sale.
4. Compare the advantages and disadvantages of buying used furniture.
5. What is the difference between a manufacturer's warranty and a service contract (extended warranty)?

USING YOUR CRITICAL THINKING SKILLS

1. Your friend says that if a manufacturer offers a warranty on a VCR, that means the product is high quality. How would you reply to this statement?

APPLYING WHAT YOU HAVE LEARNED

1. Comparison shop for an electronic product at three different types of stores. Report to class what you learned, where you would make the purchase, and why. Discuss the differences in sales practices, service, and price at the stores you visited.

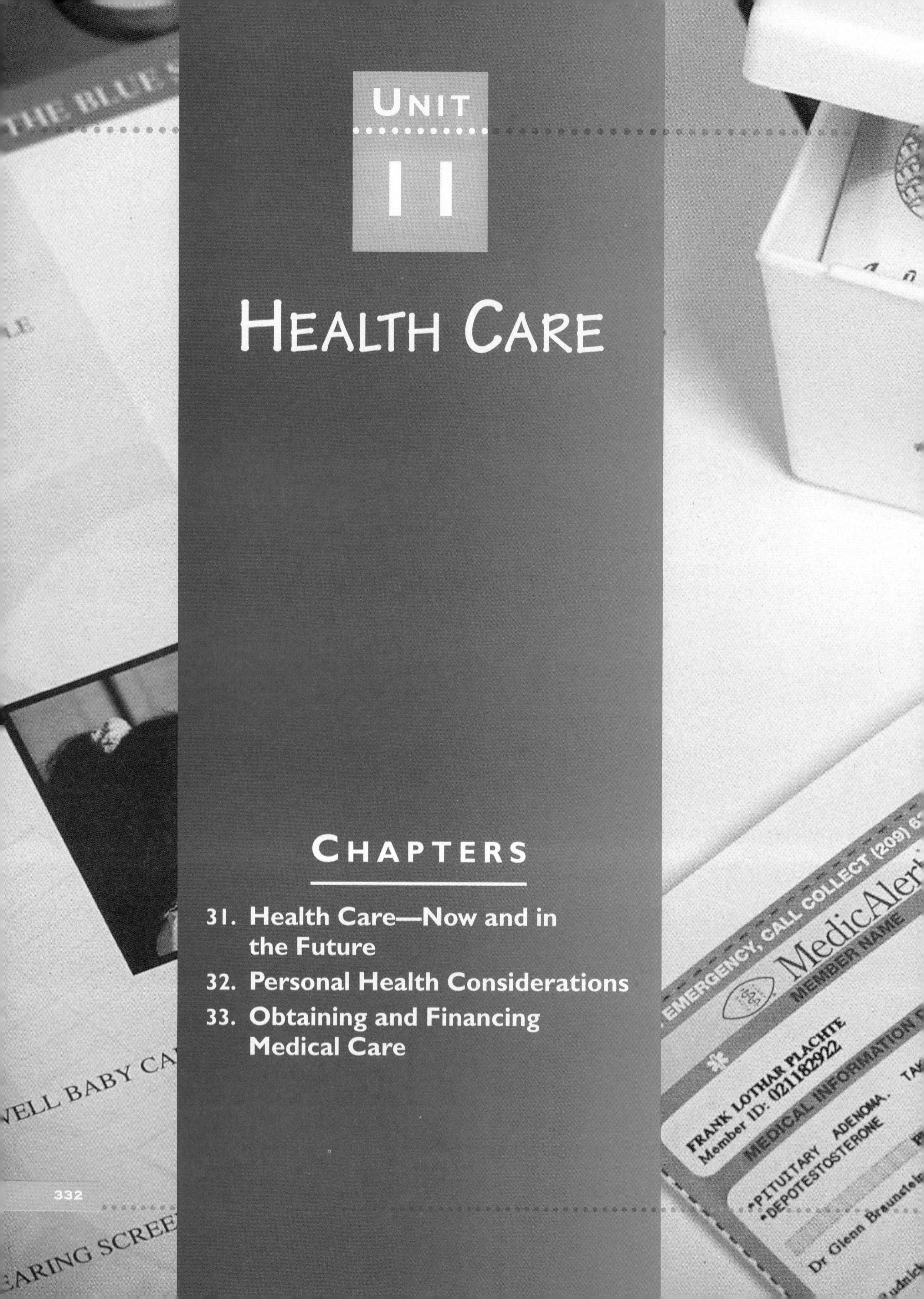

UNIT 11

HEALTH CARE

CHAPTERS

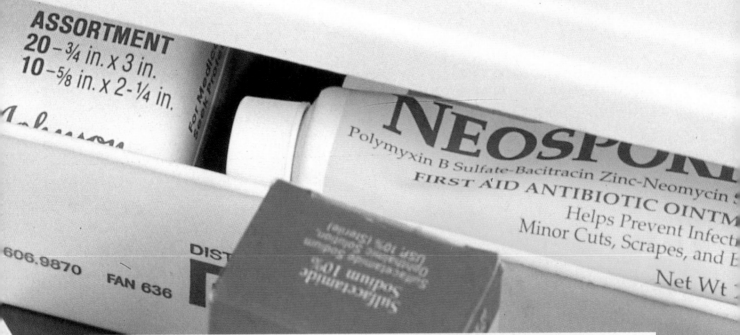

The best health care in the history of the world is available in the United States. Unfortunately, health care costs have risen faster than just about anything else, so there are some who cannot afford this quality health care and who do not have adequate health insurance.

In the years following World War II, Americans came to believe that good health care was a right, something they should receive whenever they needed it. It seems somehow different from buying a car or TV, things you get only if you can afford them. This feeling that we ought to have good health care on demand leads one to the illusion that health care is free, but someone has to pay, and it's us—and we don't like that, either. So our ideal health care system is logically impossible. We do know *what it should do*:

- provide complete health insurance for everyone;
- allow complete freedom to choose our doctors, and for our doctors to choose the best treatments;
- control the costs so that neither families, businesses, nor government will go bankrupt by soaring health spending.

Unfortunately, no health care system can fully achieve all of these goals. Complete coverage with complete freedom of choice would make costs uncontrollable. We can control health care costs only if some treatments are not covered by insurance.

Most political observers expect that Congress will eventually pass a national health care package. However, it may take years to fully implement a national health care program.

CHAPTER 31

Health Care—Now and in the Future

OBJECTIVES

After completing this chapter, you will be able to do the following:
1. Explain why penicillin is called the miracle drug.
2. Name and explain how the two types of activities involved in preventive medicine help prevent disease.
3. List four agencies or organizations that are fighting medical quackery.
4. Describe advertising techniques of quacks.

TERMS

communicable diseases
diagnosis
epidemics

holistic medicine
immunization program

preventive medicine
quacks

Health care has changed a great deal over the years, becoming more scientific and effective. As consumers, we should know about the modern types of medical care that are available—and we need to be on guard against useless medical treatments that some people offer.

IMPROVEMENT IN HEALTH CARE

All areas of health care have improved at an increasing rate in recent years. With the notable exception of AIDS, which is discussed in detail later, we no longer suffer massive epidemics of communicable diseases as in the past. Epidemics have been eliminated through sanitary living conditions and vaccines that produce immunity to disease.

During the 1700s, smallpox killed sixty million people in Europe. But a vaccine against smallpox was developed, and a worldwide immunization program provided vaccinations for children. As a result, the disease has been nearly wiped out. In the United States, vaccination against smallpox is no longer routine.

Poliomyelitis (polio) reached epidemic proportions in the 1950s, but it is rarely seen now. Giant steps have been taken against cancer and heart disease and research continues in these areas.

To understand how far health care has come, consider the account of the treatment of King Charles II of England in the Consumer Focus below. It is taken from the writings of Dr. Scarburgh, one of a dozen doctors who "treated" the king.

Major advances have also been made in drug therapy. Penicillin, called the "miracle drug" because it is effective against many kinds of bacterial infections, was first used in 1943. Penicillin is still widely used in addition to many other antibiotics.

immunization program

a system of administering vaccinations, which are doses of medicine that stimulate the immune system to help fight off infectious diseases

epidemic

an illness that spreads quickly through a population and affects a large number of people

communicable diseases

illnesses that can be transferred from person to person

CONSUMER FOCUS

KING CHARLES II DIES

On Monday, February 2, 1685, the king was being shaved. About eight o'clock, he fell to the floor, unconscious.

Medical treatment began with bleeding a pint of blood from the king's right arm. When this did not revive him, another half-pint of blood was taken, but he remained unconscious. Then his head was shaved and a blister raised on his scalp. This didn't help, so a sneezing powder was given to strengthen his brain. More blood was taken.

Potions were administered. Melon seeds, slippery elm, black cherry water, and extract of flowers of lime, lily of the valley, peony, and dissolved pearls were forced down the unconscious king's throat. Next came nutmeg, quinine, cloves, and gentian root.

By morning, his serene majesty's strength seemed exhausted. The whole assembly of doctors lost hope and became despondent. Still, so as not to appear to fail in doing their duty in any detail, they brought into play the most active cordial. This last dose of medicine was a mixture of Raleigh's antidote, pearl julep, and ammonia.

The king died a few days later without rallying.

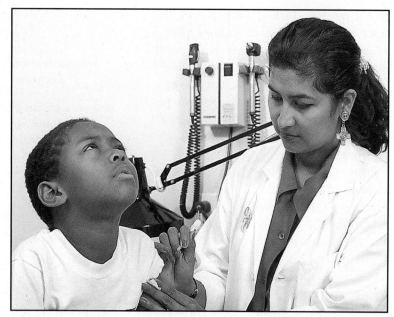

Unless you are very unique, at some time during your lifetime you will need the services of a medical professional. Fortunately, medical care is constantly improving and qualified doctors are available in all areas of the United States. Do you have a doctor you see when you need medical attention?

HEALTH CARE TODAY

diagnosis
....

identification of the presence of a particular illness as well as the cause of that illness

preventive medicine
....

care taken to stop or reduce the risk of disease; this can include a change in diet, exercise, and screening tests

The health care of Americans in the 1990s benefits from both improved processes and new areas of specialized training for personnel in preventive medicine, diagnosis, and treatment.

Preventive Medicine

Preventive medicine includes all kinds of activities aimed at the prevention or early detection of disease. Primary prevention consists of changing one's personal environment to reduce the risk of a disease. For example, a person concerned about respiratory problems may give up smoking.

Secondary prevention detects disease by the use of screening tests that check for diseases before symptoms appear. A simple skin test for tuberculosis is an example of this type of screening. In business, doctors or nurses are employed by many companies to monitor the health of employees. For example, the exposure of employees to certain chemicals is watched carefully.

Diagnosis

Diagnosis is identifying the presence of a particular condition as well as the cause of that condition. There have been incredible advances in diagnostics in recent years, including the computerized axial tomography (CAT) scanner, which has revolutionized the diagnosis of tumors. This machine can find the exact location of a tumor anywhere in the body.

X rays have long been used to look inside the body, but too many X rays can be harmful. Ultrasound and fiber optics are other ways of "looking into" the body, and neither of these requires X-radiation. Ultrasound uses sound waves. Fiber optics uses light-conducting fibers and a light source to look into the body.

Some diseases are hereditary—passed from generation to generation. Muscular dystrophy is an example. Genetic research improves diagnosis of hereditary diseases by predicting the likelihood of acquiring the disease.

Treatment

Improved surgical techniques and more effective medications are becoming available constantly. Laser (light beam) surgery and cryosurgery (extreme cold) are examples. These are now used extensively for repair of detached retinas (the light-receptive film in the back of the eye). Radioactive "seeds" are implanted in some tumors as a treatment for cancers. Constant infusion of insulin is available to diabetics. The insulin is not injected. Instead, it is released as needed by a pump implanted in the person's chest.

Personnel

The education of health care personnel has improved in recent years too. As science has revealed more complexities of disease, doctors have continued their studies beyond medical school. New areas of special study include nuclear medicine and geriatrics (treatment of the diseases of aging). Other new areas are child psychiatry, emergency medicine, family practice, and sports medicine. Training programs for nurses, therapists, and other health care personnel continue to be upgraded as well.

MEDICAL QUACKERY

Some people who claim to be doctors or medical specialists are not what they represent themselves to be, but are, instead, only trying to take others' money by deceiving people who are ill. People who make untrue claims that they can cure illnesses are known as quacks.

It's easy to understand how quacks could prosper in the early days of medicine, before much was known in the field of science. Have we become too knowledgeable now to be ripped off by quacks? Hardly. In the 1990s, quacks are robbing us of about four billion dollars a year!

Many state and federal laws protect us from those who prey upon the sick. The Food and Drug Administration (FDA) and the Federal Trade Commission (FTC) have controlled quackery to some extent. So have the National Better Business Bureau and the American Medical Association (AMA). The United States Post Office has done its part to control medical fraud (trickery) through the mail, but putting quacks out of business is not easy. Former patients are seldom willing to testify in court against the quack because they don't want it known that they were victimized.

How to Recognize Quack Bait

Quacks play on human emotion. They sell hope. They appeal to vanity, misfortune, and fear. They also rely on the still-widespread belief in magic and miracles. Otherwise-rational people become victims of quack schemes because they *want to believe*.

With quacks so skilled in manipulating emotions, it's easy to be conned. How can you protect yourself? When you see an advertisement for a sensa-

quacks
. . . .
people who pretend to have medical skills and who often sell fake cures for illnesses

INTERACTING WITH TECHNOLOGY

A MEDICAL REVOLUTION

Technology is helping medical research to expand rapidly and to expand in many directions. Scientific applications are changing the ways medical personnel understand, diagnose, and treat medical problems.

X-ray films have long been used for diagnosis. These films are now being digitized (changed to number codes) so that they can be analyzed by computers. Preliminary results indicate that the use of computer images may make it possible to detect subtle visual changes in the body at much earlier stages than is possible with X-ray film. This could mean that diseases such as cancer could be detected and treated earlier, thus improving the patient's chance of recovery.

Technology also is helping to create more effective drugs for treatment. Computers are being used to simulate the three-dimensional structure of the particular diseased molecules that are targeted for treatment. Once these structures are simulated, drugs are designed that attach themselves with a perfect fit to these molecules so that their activity can be altered. Such a specific fit offers many potential benefits to the patient. Because the drugs will be designed to target specific molecules, they will most likely be effective in low doses. This is a significant change from the drugs of today that affect a broad spectrum of molecules. The use of computers to help design drugs offers the additional benefit of being able to develop drugs more rapidly. The methods of the past often took years. Such research may now be accomplished in two to three years with the assistance of computer imaging.

Another area of research that offers exciting possibilities for medical treatment is that of electronic implants that help bypass damaged nerve cells. Electronic devices are being studied that may provide sight to persons who are blind. These devices would capture light entering the defective eye and stimulate the retina so that messages are sent to the brain to create vision. Electronic devices are also being used to stimulate muscles of paralyzed individuals and send messages to the brain to help these people to learn to use their limbs again.

Genetic research is perhaps the most controversial of the current trends in medical research. Researchers foresee the day when diseased genes can be altered to cure patients. Serious questions arise about how these tests will be used. Will we eventually use gene therapy to breed disease-free humans? Will we design super-beings with selected traits? As always, new answers will provoke new questions, questions that consumers must face.

LONG-DISTANCE HEALING WITH RADIO WAVES

A woman in Illinois, Mrs. X, noticed a small lump in her breast. She visited her family doctor, who told her that it might be cancer. He said she should enter the hospital immediately for an accurate diagnosis. Frightened, Mrs. X called her husband, who was in California on a business trip. In a day or two, Mr. X called back with "good news." She might not have to go into the hospital after all. He had found "a new miracle."

A "Radio Therapeutic Instrument" had been invented by a Dr. Ruth B. Drown in Hollywood—who claimed it eliminated the need for operations. Since Dr. Drown was temporarily in Chicago, it would be convenient to get treatment.

In Chicago, Dr. Drown took a drop of Mrs. X's blood on a blotter and placed it into a black box. She turned some knobs on the top of the box, then announced that there was no cancer. The problem was a "fungus growth" that had spread throughout the digestive system and into the liver. There was also some gallbladder "trouble," and one kidney had ceased to function. Dr. Drown said Radio Therapy could cure these problems in five months. She recommended that Mrs. X see a local doctor who used her invention.

Mrs. X made the twenty-mile trip from Blue Island to Chicago to receive Radio Therapy daily. Willing to pay the high cost of treatment but becoming too tired to make the trips, Mrs. X was told not to return. "Just stay at home," the doctor told her. "We can treat you by radio wave. That's what's so wonderful about the Drown machine. It's just as effective when the patient is miles away as when he or she's here."

After eighteen months, Mrs. X's condition had not improved. In fact, it seemed worse. Mr. X called Dr. Drown in Hollywood, who replied, "We suggest that Mrs. X have the breast removed if she feels that she is not getting hold of the trouble with our treatment. She can be treated for the condition afterwards on the instrument." Shocked, Mr. and Mrs. X visited a cancer specialist in New York. Unfortunately, the cancer had advanced too far to be operable.

tional new health or vanity product, remember the quack's favorite ploys:

- "scientific breakthroughs"
- "secret cures"
- testimonials
- "cure-alls"

Is the product touted as a "new scientific breakthrough," or with words to that effect? Many quack promotionals refer to medical studies or "reports in leading medical journals"—but they don't name the journals. Such claims are sometimes promoted in sensational popular magazines and newspapers, and claims promoted in this way are generally shams.

Does the promoter call the product a "secret cure"? Some quacks claim they are being persecuted by the medical establishment for seeking to inform the public about the value of their products. This tactic brings forth sympathy (and money) from those who cheer for the underdog.

Does the advertising list testimonials (personal recommendations) from satisfied users? Scientists view such testimonials with skepticism. Sometimes they are outright lies, but sometimes they are honest statements. People making such statements often do not realize that the product they used had nothing to do with their improved condition.

Does the product claim to be effective for a wide variety of ills? "Cure-alls" are pure quackery.

HOLISTIC MEDICINE

The holistic approach to medical care is gaining acceptance in America. Holistic (or wholistic) medicine means treating the whole person. Holistic medicine attends to mental-emotional, physical, social, and spiritual needs in order to maintain health. It emphasizes good quality of life, not just treating illness. These principles are not new, but the name is new. The realm of holistic medicine is broad, ranging from the best traditional medicine to outright quackery.

The strength of holistic medicine seems to be the concept that the body and mind together can help prevent or overcome many diseases, and this part of holism appeals to many. Using this concept, the doctor tries to make it as easy as possible for the body and mind to maintain health.

The supporters of holistic medicine include many medical doctors, but many who claim to be holistic healers are quacks who reject everything related to medical tradition. Keep in mind that a responsible doctor will not use unproven methods for treating human beings.

holistic medicine
....
a medical approach that treats the whole person; mental-emotional, physical, social, and spiritual

HEALTH CARE CONTINUES TO IMPROVE

Medical knowledge, based on science, will continue to improve the diagnosis and treatment of illness. As these medical processes become more sophisticated, we can expect improved health care by medical professionals whenever we need medical attention. A proper diagnosis and good treatment cannot make up for unhealthy living habits. Fortunately, science is also providing guidance for a healthier lifestyle too.

Summary

- Advances in diagnostics, surgical techniques, medications, and education of health care personnel have all contributed to a dramatic improvement in health care in recent years.

- Preventive medicine includes all kinds of activities aimed at the prevention or early detection of disease.

- Quacks are people who make untrue claims that they can cure illnesses. They often try to convince people with "scientific breakthroughs," "secret cures," testimonials, and "cure-alls."

- Holistic medicine involves treating the whole person—mentally, emotionally, physically, socially, and spiritually.

CHAPTER REVIEW
31

ENRICHING YOUR VOCABULARY

Number your paper from 1–7. Read each sentence below. If the sentence is true, write "true" next to that number. If the sentence is false, rewrite it to make a true statement.

1. Communicable diseases can be transmitted from one person to another.
2. Diagnosis identifies a particular condition.
3. Communicable diseases affecting large numbers of people are called epidemics.
4. Holistic medicine is not practiced by licensed doctors.
5. Immunization programs provide cures for certain diseases.
6. Preventive medicine is used in treating critically ill patients.
7. Quacks make untrue claims about curing illness.

REVIEWING WHAT YOU HAVE LEARNED

1. Why was penicillin called the miracle drug?
2. There are two types of activities involved in preventive medicine. Name these and tell how they help prevent disease.
3. List four agencies or organizations that are fighting medical quackery.
4. Describe advertising techniques used by quacks.

USING YOUR CRITICAL THINKING SKILLS

1. There have been many important developments in health care through the years. What development do you think has had the greatest effect on health care today? Why?

APPLYING WHAT YOU HAVE LEARNED

1. Prepare a report about a health problem such as arthritis or diabetes. At what ages is the problem most common? Describe symptoms, diagnosis, and treatment. Are there new advances? Where can treatment be obtained? Is it costly? Does insurance usually cover it? Is a specialist needed? Include all information helpful to consumers.

CHAPTER 32

Personal Health Considerations

OBJECTIVES

After completing this chapter, you will be able to do the following:
1. Explain what happens to the blood vessels in a person who continually eats foods containing too much fat.
2. Explain and give examples of ideal exercise.
3. Explain the health risks of smoking.
4. Explain the cause of hypertension and why it is called the silent killer.
5. Name eight things you can do to help cope with stress.
6. Explain how the AIDS epidemic is affecting our society and lifestyles.

TERMS

AIDS	migraine headache	stress
alcoholism	over-the-counter	tension headaches
HIV	(OTC) drugs	vascular headache
hypertension	personal environment	wellness lifestyle
illicit drugs	prescription drugs	
junk foods	side effects	
look-alike drugs	SPF	

Good health helps people stay happy. Bad health not only makes people miserable, it also costs money. The best way to save on medical bills while keeping a happy outlook is to develop healthy living habits.

MODERN LIFESTYLES AND HEALTH

Much of the modern lifestyle is harmful to general health. For example, regular physical exercise is needed for good health—but many of us do work that is not physically active. Instead of fresh fruits and vegetables, we often eat foods that lack vitamins and nutrients and foods that are high in fat.

Cancer and heart disease are the biggest causes of death among adults, and the modern lifestyle increases the frequency of both. Research focuses on both the treatment and prevention of these diseases, and the research shows that changes in lifestyle can help prevent both cancer and heart disease.

Science is currently explaining the relationship between lifestyle and health. We can listen and adopt healthy living habits while we are still young, and by doing these things we can look forward to healthier and longer lives.

Diet

Everyone needs a balanced diet. As recently as 1992, it was thought that a balanced diet should regularly include dairy foods, meat, vegetables and fruit, and breads or cereals. The new food guide pyramid, introduced in 1992 by the Department of Agriculture, recommends eating large quantities of breads and cereals, vegetables, and fruits—

and less meat. (Guidelines to healthy eating were covered more fully in Chapter 16.)

Americans have a greater variety of foods available than exists in any other country in the world, but we seem to have developed a taste for fatty foods. Hamburgers and french fries are favorites of millions, and these foods contain far more fat than anyone should eat in one meal. Several fast-food restaurant chains have recognized this, and they have cut down considerably on the amount of fat in their products. Even so, a burger and fries is still an unbalanced meal and should not be the main course on a regular basis.

Eating too much fat raises the levels of cholesterol and triglycerides (fatty acids) in the blood. When these levels are too high, fatty deposits are formed on the lining of blood vessels. This restricts the flow of blood, and the heart must work harder to force the blood

Diet is one of the most important factors in living a healthy lifestyle. Compare your diet with the diet suggested by the Food Guide Pyramid (discussed in Chapter 16). How does your diet compare? Does it need some improvement?

Shannon had been overweight ever since she could remember. For that matter, so were the other members of her family. They were always trying one "miracle" diet or another. There were times Shannon maintained a rigid diet, and there were other times when she gave up and binged on whatever she wanted. Basically, nothing had ever worked. Sure, she might lose ten or fifteen pounds, but she always put it right back on.

She was embarrassed about her weight problem and had never discussed it with anyone but her family. Finally, she decided to consult her doctor, who told Shannon that fad diets rarely worked for people over time. She taught Shannon how to eat a balanced, low-fat diet. She also told Shannon that physical fitness is just as important as diet when you want to slim your figure. She recommended that Shannon join a health club or the YMCA and get into a regular program of exercise. The doctor further told Shannon that weight can be affected when someone is under a lot of stress. She asked if Shannon was experiencing much stress in her life, and if she was, to seek out a friend or professional to talk it over with.

Shannon followed the doctor's suggestions regarding diet and exercise, and even went to a therapist to discuss some family problems. Within a few months, Shannon had not only lost weight, but she was feeling happier and healthier than she ever had!

junk foods

foods with little nutritional value

throughout the body. This strain can result in heart disease.

Research shows that sugar, too, increases the risk of heart disease by narrowing and hardening the blood vessels. Avoiding sugar is not as simple as passing up desserts. Most people like the taste of sugar, so manufacturers have added sugar to hundreds of food items. Check the ingredients of the items in your refrigerator or pantry, and you will likely find that most of them contain sugar. Even if the word sugar does not appear, many items contain sugar in another form, such as "corn sweetener."

Sugar is a special problem for people who have diabetes. Their bodies cannot use sugar normally; and, as a result, the amount of sugar in their blood builds up. Drugs may be used to control the problem, but doctors also prescribe special diets.

Junk Foods

The dictionary defines "junk" as something worthless or trashy. **Junk foods** are things we eat that have little food value, and many of them contain sugar. Diets high in sugar have been closely associated with tooth decay.

Sugar increases weight gain, and the average American eats more than 100 pounds of sugar and corn sweeteners each year (according to the U.S. Department of Agriculture). It is possible to become overweight without eating much sugar, but most overweight people seem to like sweets.

WEIGHT MANAGEMENT

You don't have to be trim to be healthy, but being trim is generally healthier than being overweight. Nearly everyone wants to be trim, and almost every overweight person has tried many times to lose unhealthy pounds.

If you diet, protect your health. Don't take any extreme measures to lose weight without discussing them with your doctor. For example, some people take pills to suppress their appetites, but diet pills may be addictive and can be harmful to your health. They should be taken only under a doctor's direction.

In order to lose weight safely and keep it off, you must eat the right way. Eat a balanced diet that is low in fat and calories—and eat less. You can never achieve a trim figure by eating in the same way that made you overweight in the first place.

To develop a slimmer figure, you may need to change your lifestyle. Some people develop a new eating pattern by recording the time when they eat and carefully charting every bite that goes into their mouth. After several weeks, they discover that they are most likely to eat high-calorie foods at certain times of the day. Then they schedule a non-eating activity for those times. For example, a person who likes to snack on sweets in mid-afternoon may plan to play tennis at that time.

EXERCISE AND FITNESS

The benefits of exercise amount to more than just a trim figure. In the eighties, Americans of every age took up running—in the nineties, some slowed the pace and began taking long walks. Millions more began riding bicycles for exercise—and tennis, handball, and swimming are now more popular than ever. Why? We have learned that physical fitness is the key to a healthy lifestyle. Exercise gives us more energy and often improves our social lives, and being physically fit generally makes for a happier, more satisfied life.

Staying with an exercise program isn't easy, especially after we are out of school. Career and family responsibilities often leave little time for activities like running in the park, and those who do exercise regularly place high value on its benefits.

The ideal exercise is one that uses as many muscles as possible. Swimming, walking, running, and most outdoor sports are excellent. (See Chapter 40.)

It's always best to begin slowly and work up to more vigorous exercise.

Exercising at Home

Outdoor sports can be hazardous during bad weather, but missing regular exercise for even a week or two decreases the level of fitness significantly. So try to continue exercising at home.

Copies of various exercise plans may be available in your local public library, or you may be able to buy a book or booklet for a reasonably low price in a bookstore. There are many good home exercise programs. One example is the BX Fitness Plan, developed by the Royal Canadian Air Force, which requires only a few minutes each day.

Health Clubs

Many people exercise mainly at home, but others find this monotonous and boring after a few weeks. Playing a competitive sport such as tennis, handball, or racquetball is both physically and mentally stimulating.

Many people join health clubs such as the YMCA or YWCA and enjoy activities in a variety of exercise and sports facilities. If this appeals to you, try it on a pay-as-you-go or short-term basis. Then, if you like it and can attend several times a week, you may want to join the club for three months or so. Don't sign up for a long period if you may not be able to attend regularly. Be cautious about contracts that require long-term commitments.

Exercise is not just a passing fad. Millions have learned that it does indeed improve the quality of their lives.

Keeping Well

A new concept in health care promotes a **wellness lifestyle**, and wellness

wellness lifestyle
....
a focus on several controllable factors such as balanced diet, regular exercise, and stress relief

Exercise is a critical factor in living a healthy lifestyle, and one that can be controlled. There is an almost endless variety of exercises available for people at all ability levels. Do you have a regular exercise routine? If not, you should consider starting one.

centers have cropped up all across the country. They are founded on the idea that a balanced diet, regular exercise, and a lowered level of stress make for healthy, happy people. One wellness center begins its program with a risk-of-death survey, which evaluates such health risks as weight, blood pressure, cholesterol level, driving habits, and whether the person smokes. Then the person works to correct conditions and habits that may be a threat to good health.

Medical costs in the United States were nearly a trillion dollars in 1992. Because of this, the wellness lifestyle may be the only one many of us can afford!

Risk-of-Death Survey

The Wholeness Center
1567 Jersey St.
Any Town, USA 12121

Date:_____

Name:_____ Address:_____
City:_____ State:_____ Zip:_____
Occupation:_____ Home Phone:_____ Business Phone:_____
Date of Birth:_____ Age:_____ M_____ F_____ Marital Status:_____ No. of Children:_____
Social Security Number:_____ Insurance:_____

DIETARY SELECTIONS:
Please circle any dietary selection that is appropriate for you, and grade according to the following scale:

O – Do not consume this **FM** – Consume a few times per month **W** – Consume this weekly
M – Consume this monthly   (less than weekly) **FW** – Consume this a few times per week
                              FD – Consume this a few times per day **D** – Consume this daily

Alcohol _____		Fruit _____	
Coffee _____		Whole Grains _____	
Tobacco _____		Dairy (milk products) _____	
Artificial Sweeteners _____		Fried Foods _____	
Soda _____		Refined Sugar _____	
Diet Food _____		Beef _____	
Refined Sugar _____		Poultry _____	
Eggs _____		Fish _____	
Vegetables _____		Seafood _____	

GENERAL EMOTIONAL TRAUMA:
With each of the following stress situations, please check either "P" for Past or "C" for Current.

	MILD	MODERATE	EXTREME		MILD	MODERATE	EXTREME
	P C	P C	P C		P C	P C	P C
Childhood stress	☐☐	☐☐	☐☐	Work-related stress	☐☐	☐☐	☐☐
School stress	☐☐	☐☐	☐☐	Stress of commuting	☐☐	☐☐	☐☐
Play or recreational	☐☐	☐☐	☐☐	Loss of loved one	☐☐	☐☐	☐☐
Family stress	☐☐	☐☐	☐☐	Change in lifestyle	☐☐	☐☐	☐☐
Personal relationships	☐☐	☐☐	☐☐	Change in vocation	☐☐	☐☐	☐☐
Stress of being sick	☐☐	☐☐	☐☐	Abuse	☐☐	☐☐	☐☐

How do you grade your physical health? Excellent ☐ Good☐ Fair☐ Poor☐ Getting Better☐ Getting Worse☐
How do you grade your emotional/mental health? Excellent ☐ Good☐ Fair☐ Poor☐ Getting Better☐ Getting Worse☐
If you consider yourself ill, why do you feel you are ill? _____
_____
_____

If you consider yourself well, why do you feel you are well? _____
_____
_____

Figure 32.1
....

As you read this sample Risk-of-Death Survey, think about how you would answer these questions. (You might even want to answer the questions on a separate sheet of paper.) Using your knowledge of foods, substances, and activities that are health risks, how do you rate? Are you at a high or low risk of death?

EFFECTS OF PERSONAL ENVIRONMENT

Everyday habits can lead to many health problems, including cancer. Dr. John Higginson, former head of cancer research for the World Health Organization, commented on this. He said, "We now know that 80 to 90 percent of all cancers are dependent directly or indirectly on our personal environment—smoking, alcohol intake, diet, and exposure to sun." Except for sun exposure, these factors also contribute to dozens of other health problems. Many researchers believe that stress, too, is a major cause of bad health.

personal environment
....
actions and surroundings that can be controlled by the individual

Smoking

Every cigarette steals seven minutes of a smoker's life, according to the Centers for Disease Control in Atlanta. The CDC counted 418,690 U.S. deaths in 1990 that were directly attributed to cigarette smoking—not counting cigars, pipes, and smokeless tobacco. *Cigarettes were responsible for 20 percent of all deaths in the U.S. that year, more than deaths from alcohol, drugs, car crashes, and AIDS combined.*

A study at the University of California at San Francisco found that the average smoker in California loses 15.23 years of life. In 1989, the California Medical Association reported that more people died from smoking than from AIDS, cocaine, heroin, alcohol, fire, auto accidents, homicide, and suicide combined.

If you smoke, your chances of developing lung cancer are 10 to 25 times greater than for a nonsmoker—and your risk of dying from heart disease is much higher, with 30 percent to 40 percent of all deaths from coronary

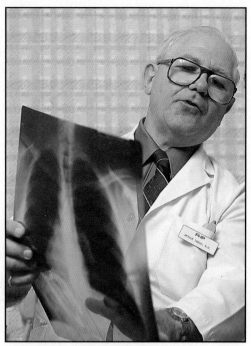

People who smoke increase the risk of respiratory problems for themselves and those around them. Because of this, many feel that people should not be allowed to smoke in any public places. What is your opinion of this?

heart disease caused by smoking. Tobacco smoking is also closely linked to stroke, cancer of the oral cavity (mouth), cancer of the esophagus, cancer of the bladder, bronchitis, and emphysema.

The good news for smokers is that the moment you quit smoking or chewing tobacco, your body will begin to repair itself and your risk of developing these diseases will begin to drop.

But you're not safe from the effects of smoking even if you don't smoke! Secondhand smoke, also called environmental smoke, comes from the burning end of a cigarette or cigar, or a pipe, and from smoke exhaled from the lungs of smokers. The Environmental Protection Agency estimates that environmental smoke each year causes up to 300,000 lower-respiratory-tract infections in infants and children under 18 months. An

EPA report in 1993 concluded that secondhand smoke kills 3,000 people each year from lung cancer alone.

According to the National Center for Health Statistics in Hyattsville, Maryland, SIDS (sudden infant death syndrome), which may be caused by secondhand smoke, kills about 7,000 babies each year in the U.S.

Statistics make it very clear that smokers do not have the right to jeopardize the health of nonsmokers, especially children. According to the EPA, "The only suitable place for smokers is outdoors, away from crowds and doorways—unless smokers can find secluded rooms with their own ventilation systems."

But people have become more aware of the dangers of smoking, and in the last decade millions of smokers have kicked the habit. One group in particular has cut back on smoking because of the health danger—doctors. In 1992, nonsmoking adults outnumbered smokers three to one. Still, smoking is considered extremely addictive and is a difficult habit to break. In 1994, it was discovered that some cigarette companies were increasing the level of nicotine in cigarettes—making them even more addictive!

Alcohol

Alcohol abuse is a common problem—and, as a group, young people are drinking more alcohol than they did in the past. Unless behavior patterns change, there will likely be more people suffering from alcohol-related diseases in the future. Alcohol may cause diseases of the stomach, liver, and heart—and the effects of drinking cause many automobile and industrial accidents. In the late 1970s, it was discovered that drinking during pregnancy sometimes affects the mental and physical development of the unborn child.

Some people become addicted to alcohol; the result is a diseased condition called **alcoholism**. People suffering from it are called alcoholics. Alcoholism creates problems in almost all areas of the alcoholic's life. Families of alcoholics especially suffer the consequences of living with an addicted person.

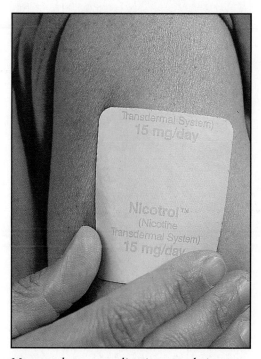

More and more medications are being dispensed through patches rather than by pill or liquid. The patches allow for a continuous supply of the drug to enter the body. Have you ever had medication dispensed through a patch?

alcoholism
....
a disease characterized by the addiction to alcohol

DRUGS

Used properly, drugs help us improve and protect our health. Used improperly, they can damage health and even threaten or destroy lives. There are three general groups of drugs:

- prescription drugs
- over-the-counter drugs
- illicit drugs

Pharmacists dispense prescription drugs following doctors' orders. However, they also are willing to answer questions about over-the-counter drugs and about such things as mixing medications.

Prescription Drugs

prescription drugs
....

drugs that can be purchased with the written order of a doctor

Prescription drugs may be obtained with an order written by a doctor. Doctors write prescriptions only after determining that the person will likely benefit from taking a certain drug. The prescription states the name, dose, and amount of the drug—and it gives directions for use of the drug. Antibiotics and tranquilizers are examples of prescription drugs.

Over-the-Counter Drugs

over-the-counter (OTC) drugs
....

drugs that can be purchased without a prescription

Drugs that may be purchased without a prescription are known as **over-the-counter (OTC) drugs**. The most common OTC drug is aspirin—and, in normal doses, it's safe, effective, and cheap.

There are many other OTC drugs that are effective for such things as cold symptoms, itching, and allergies—but some studies have revealed that only

Drug stores, supermarkets, and even discount department stores have rows and rows of over-the-counter medicines. Remember that just because a drug is sold over the counter doesn't mean it is entirely safe. Always read and follow the directions given with over-the-counter medications, and if you have any questions, ask your doctor or pharmacist.

about half of the ingredients in OTC drugs meet federal standards of safety and effectiveness. Some recent books have been written on OTC drugs by doctors and pharmacists. Ask your doctor to recommend one as a guide.

Illicit Drugs

Illicit drugs are any drugs that are obtained illegally, including prescription drugs that are obtained without a prescription. Others, such as cocaine, LSD, and heroin, are almost never prescribed legally.

The use of such harmful drugs has cost thousands of lives, especially over the past twenty years. It is also estimated that more than half of all burglaries are committed for drug-related reasons. People steal to obtain money for buying illegal, addictive drugs. Many drug addicts do not live very long.

Effects of Drugs

All drugs have a variety of effects in the body. For example, aspirin is usually taken to relieve pain or to reduce fever and inflammation. If used too often, however, it can cause stomach irritation, sometimes even ulcers. The undesirable effects of drugs are called **side effects**.

The variety of effects a drug may have in the body depends on several factors. The dose and frequency of usage are important. The age, weight,

illicit drugs
....
drugs obtained illegally

side effects
....
undesirable effects of drugs

EMERGENCY MEDICAL INFORMATION

A student passed out at school one day, and the student's family could not be reached. A doctor discovered a serious infection and was about to administer a shot of penicillin, but the doctor stopped. A different drug was given because the unconscious patient was allergic to penicillin. The patient could have suffered a bad reaction and might even have died. How did the doctor know that penicillin was the wrong drug to give this person?

In this true case history, the doctor noticed the patient's Medic Alert bracelet. On it was an engraved warning against using penicillin. When a person cannot communicate in an emergency,

the Medic Alert emblem conveys an important message.

A product that serves much the same purpose is offered by the National Safety Council. Their Medical Information Card contains microfilm that is viewed with a built-in magnifying lens. The film shows medical information about the card's owner.

Medical information displays such as these are helpful in emergencies, and they are particularly important for people who need special care. To learn how to get an emblem or card, you can write Medic Alert or the National Safety Council at the addresses shown in the Appendix.

sex, and certain genetic traits (heredity) of the person taking the drug are also important. Many people are allergic to certain drugs. If a person is taking more than one drug, the combination may cause a reaction. Some types of drugs are affected by certain types of food or drink. For example, drugs taken with soft drinks or even fruit drinks may dissolve too quickly and will not be as effective. Combining drugs with alcohol is especially dangerous and may even cause a fatal reaction. Physicians consider all these factors when writing prescriptions. Even so, undesirable side effects sometimes occur. Illicit drugs are especially dangerous because these factors, including the strength of the drugs, are not usually considered by those who use them.

Over-the-counter drugs have few bad effects when taken in recommended doses. In recent years, however, certain of these OTC drugs have been sold illegally on the street as **look-alike drugs**. Legal OTC drugs containing deconges-

tants and caffeine are being sold as amphetamines (speed). Both types of capsule have a similar appearance, and the effects are similar—but using large amounts of these drugs is extremely dangerous. The decongestants speed up the heart, and the caffeine narrows the arteries. This combination of actions can interfere with the blood supply to the brain—and when this happens, a stroke may occur. Young people have died of stroke because they've taken look-alike drugs.

AIDS

Human history is filled with plagues and epidemics that have destroyed large populations. We tend to think that modern medicine and technology will prevent such disasters from happening today. But the most recent threat, AIDS, remains unchecked. In little more than ten years, the AIDS epidemic has grown from a few cases in 1981 to a predicted thirty-four million cases worldwide by the year 2000.

look-alike drugs
....
over-the-counter drugs that are combined with other chemicals and packaged to look like illegal drugs or prescription medications

AIDS (acquired immunodeficiency syndrome)
....
a communicable disease that affects the immune system

You may have noticed that doctors, nurses, dentists, and other health care professionals almost always wear gloves when working with a patient. This is for their own protection as well as the patient's. Wearing gloves makes it less likely that germs will be spread from doctor to patient or from patient to doctor. Can you think of other reasons they might wear gloves?

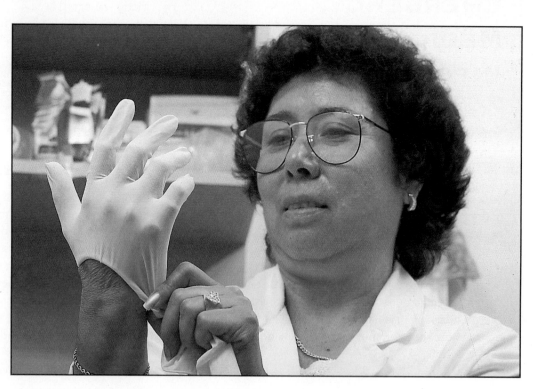

EVERYONE'S AT RISK

Alison Gertz was 16 when she became infected with HIV. She lived in Manhattan in an upper-class neighborhood. She had never had a blood transfusion and had never been an intravenous drug user. She was infected when she had sex with a man who had been a long-time friend.

Alison carried the virus unknowingly for six years. When she was 22, she was admitted to the hospital with severe flu-like symptoms. Because nothing in her background caused the doctors to suspect HIV infection, it took several weeks for them to diagnose her condition as AIDS. Alison re-mained in the hospital for several weeks before she was able to return home to her family.

Gradually, Alison realized that her dreams of leading a normal life had been changed forever. With the support of her family, she spent the next few years trying to help people understand that everyone is at risk from this disease. She spoke at schools, sharing her story and encouraging students to realize that the choices they make will determine their risk of acquiring AIDS. She helped organize fund-raising events and became the subject of a TV movie, "Something to Live for: The Alison Gertz Story."

Alison died at the age of 26. She was one of the first teens to have been identified with AIDS. She hoped that telling her story would prevent others from sharing her fate.

AIDS is caused by the human immunodeficiency virus (HIV). This virus, which was first identified in 1984, causes a breakdown of the body's defense system. Having HIV infection is not the same as having AIDS, but it leads to AIDS, usually within ten years.

You cannot get HIV infection by sharing the same space with an infected person. The virus (HIV) is fragile and can only survive in semen, blood and blood products, and vaginal and cervical secretions. HIV is most often transmitted in these three ways:

- By sexual contact involving semen, vaginal secretions, or blood.
- By the exchange of blood through needle sharing, blood transfusions, or accidents. (Two cases appear to be due to sharing a razor.)
- Mother-to-infant during pregnancy or birth.

You can protect yourself from HIV infection by making careful choices. The most effective way to prevent transmission of HIV is not to have sexual relations with anyone (abstinence). Never share a needle used by someone else for any purpose. Keep yourself informed of the latest research and information regarding this life-threatening epidemic. Remember, AIDS is transmitted by what you do, not by who you are.

SUN AND SKIN

Our skin protects us against viruses, parasites, and bacteria. If we give it reasonably good care, it serves us well. Healthy people are active and often spend some time in the sun, and the sun sends out ultraviolet rays. We cannot see them, but the damaging effects of these rays build up. Every exposure

HIV
• • • • •
human immuno-deficiency virus; the virus that causes AIDS

during your whole life has an added effect on your skin, much in the way that the tread on a tire gradually wears away. Wrinkled skin is due much more to ultraviolet radiation than age. Besides giving us an old look at an early age, ultraviolet radiation may also cause precancerous cells to develop. In recent years, the protective layer of ozone around the earth has eroded and allowed much higher levels of ultraviolet radiation to come through. In the United States, sun exposure now leads to 600,000 cases of skin cancer each year.

There is really no such thing as a healthy tan, but—just as some people choose to smoke—some pursue a fashionable tan, even when they know it's risky. One in six Americans will develop some form of skin cancer. People with blond or red hair, fair skin, blue or light-colored eyes, and who live in sunny climates are at greatest risk—along with those who have a family history of skin cancer.

Protecting Yourself from the Sun

If you must be out in the sun, wear protective clothing and apply a sunscreen lotion. The effectiveness of the lotion is expressed as the sun protection factor (SPF), which is printed on the label of the container. Most lotions list an SPF in the range of six to fifty. This means that you can remain out in the sun from six to fifty times as long as you could without the sunscreen and not get burned. Sunscreens are chemicals, not physical barriers. You need to apply the sunscreen at least 30 minutes before going out in the sun so that it can penetrate the skin for greater effectiveness.

STRESS

Stress is physical, mental, or emotional strain. Running is physical

SPF

·····

rating describing the sun protection factor of a product

stress

········

tension

Many Americans live in areas where people love to spend time in the sun. Spending time in the sun can make us feel very good, and, over time it can make us feel very bad. The occurrence of skin cancer, caused by too much exposure to the sun, is on the rise. How much time do you spend in the sun? Do you use sunscreen with a fairly high sun protection factor? Prevention now can save pain in the future.

stress, and solving difficult math problems is mental stress—both are examples of healthy stress. But emotional stress, often called distress, is harmful. It is often caused by frustration—being unable to reach our goals. Another common cause of stress is change, and life is full of changes or events that cause emotional stress.

Stress affects people in several ways. Some suffer severe headaches, and some have high blood pressure (also known as hypertension). Distress can weaken the body's immune response (defense against disease), and it sometimes appears to speed up the aging process.

Headaches

Headaches are not a new experience due to twentieth-century stress. Some ten thousand years ago, ancient "doctors" cut holes in the heads of patients with severe headaches. The purpose was to let out the demon that was causing the headache. Amazingly, some patients survived this "cure."

About 90 percent of all headaches today are tension headaches, which are caused by the tightening of muscles around the head and neck. These headaches occur most often when we are anxious or depressed because of some stressful situation, and almost everyone has tension headaches occasionally.

The other common type of headache is a vascular headache. The pain is caused by dilated (enlarged) blood vessels. The most painful headache of this type is called a migraine headache. Migraine headaches are often caused by stress, but recent research has shown that these headaches may also be triggered by certain foods.

More than five hundred million dollars are spent each year on medications to relieve headache pain, and the most common remedy is aspirin.

Hypertension

High blood pressure is called hypertension. It is known as "the silent killer." It is not painful—in fact, you can't even feel it. You may not know you have it until a doctor tells you, but hypertension is the leading cause of strokes. It is also one of the major causes of heart attacks and kidney failure.

Hypertension narrows the small arteries, causing the heart to work harder. The large arteries may lose their elasticity, become scarred, and collect fatty deposits. Sometimes clots form in arteries. In narrowed arteries, a blockage of blood flow is likely. If this occurs in an artery that supplies blood to the heart, a heart attack results. If it occurs in the brain, it causes a stroke.

Hypertension is due to a combination of factors, including heredity, being overweight, eating too much salt, and emotional stress.

Stress and Illness

Research indicates that stressful events are often related to illness. Experiments with animals show that stress suppresses the body's immune response, and research is now being done to determine if this holds true for people as well. If so, it may become possible to avoid illness by strengthening immunity during stress.

Dealing with Stress

We're all exposed to the stress (including distress) of living, but there are some things we can do to help us deal with it. Doctors who have studied the causes and effects of stress have made several suggestions:

- Exercise
- Eat balanced meals daily
- Talk about problems

hypertension
....
high blood pressure

tension headache
....
headache caused by the tightening of muscles

vascular headache
....
headache caused by enlarged blood vessels

migraine headache
....
extremely painful type of vascular headache caused by enlarged blood vessels

Figure 32.2
. . . .

There are many events that cause stress in our lives. This chart shows several of those events. The higher the number of life change units, the more stress the event causes. We have no control over many of these events, but following the stress-reducing suggestions listed on pages 355 and 356 can help keep your stress under control. How do you deal with stress?

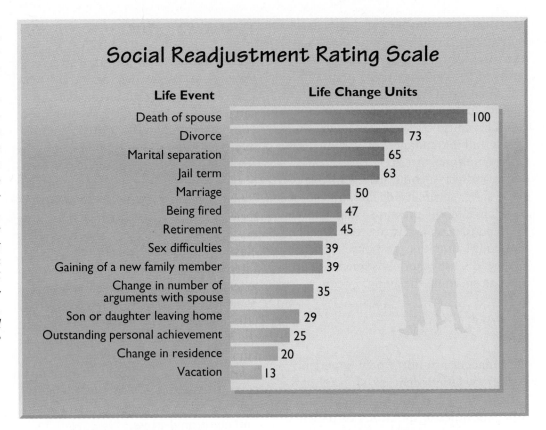

Social Readjustment Rating Scale

Life Event	Life Change Units
Death of spouse	100
Divorce	73
Marital separation	65
Jail term	63
Marriage	50
Being fired	47
Retirement	45
Sex difficulties	39
Gaining of a new family member	39
Change in number of arguments with spouse	35
Son or daughter leaving home	29
Outstanding personal achievement	25
Change in residence	20
Vacation	13

- Get enough sleep
- Have recreation
- Be willing to compromise
- Accept things you cannot change
- Help others

Work off stress through exercise. Vigorous physical exercise changes the body chemistry and reduces the effects of distress. Playing a fast game of handball or smacking a golf ball around the course really does relieve stress.

Eat balanced meals daily. Follow the food guide pyramid for supplying your body with a variety of nutrients. Foods should be low in fat and sugar.

Talk out your problems. When you are worried about problems, discuss them with a family member, counselor, teacher, minister, or a trusted friend. Another person can often help you find solutions or see problems in a new perspective.

Get enough sleep. Long days and short nights make us susceptible to stress. We become distressed by things that don't normally bother us much when we've had a good night's sleep. Almost everyone handles stress better when well rested.

Balance your school and work activities with recreation. Recreation that involves physical exercise is especially good. (See Chapter 40.) But total relaxation can also relieve stress. When coping with all of the responsibilities of life seems difficult, a little time away from responsibility may clear up the confusion.

Learn to compromise. The source of stress is often a disagreement with another person. Even when you think you're right, it's sometimes better to give in or at least compromise. Consider how important it is to have your own way, then compromise to relieve the stress whenever you can.

Learn to accept things you cannot change. We all have things we would like to change but which are beyond our control. Don't spend time worrying about them—that's self-defeating. Go on to something else. If, later on, you have a chance to make the changes you would like, you'll still remember the original problems.

Help someone with something. This will get your mind off your worries for a while and give you the sense of satisfaction that comes from helping someone.

Summary

- The best way to save on medical bills is to develop healthy living habits.
- A balanced diet includes large quantities of breads and cereals, vegetables, and fruits, with less meat.
- Junk foods have little food value, and often contain sugar.
- Physical fitness is the key to a healthy lifestyle. It gives us more energy, often improves our social lives, and makes for a happier and more satisfied life.

- Eighty to ninety percent of all cancers depend directly or indirectly on our personal environment— smoking, alcohol intake, diet, and exposure to sun.
- Cigarettes are responsible for more deaths in the U.S. than alcohol, drugs, car crashes, and AIDS combined.
- Alcohol may cause diseases of the stomach, liver, and heart—and drinking causes many automobile and industrial accidents.
- The three general groups of drugs are: prescription drugs, over-the-counter drugs, and illicit drugs.
- HIV, the virus that causes AIDS, is fragile and can only survive in semen, blood and blood products, and vaginal and cervical secretions. You can protect yourself from HIV infection by making careful choices.
- You can protect your skin from the sun by wearing protective clothing and using a sunscreen lotion.
- There are some things we can do to help deal with stress: exercise, eat balanced meals, talk about problems, get enough sleep, have recreation, be willing to compromise, accept things you cannot change, and help others.

ENRICHING YOUR VOCABULARY

Number your paper from 1–17. Beside each number, write the word or phrase that matches that definition. Choose your answers from the following list.

AIDS
alcoholism
HIV
hypertension
illicit drugs
junk foods

look-alike drugs
migraine headache
over-the-counter (OTC) drugs
personal environment
prescription drugs
side effects

SPF
stress
tension headache
vascular headache
wellness lifestyle

1. A focus on balanced diet, regular exercise, and stress relief
2. Drugs that can be purchased without a prescription
3. A communicable disease that affects the immune system
4. Drugs obtained illegally
5. Over-the-counter drugs that resemble illicit drugs
6. A disease characterized by the addiction to alcohol
7. Rating describing the sun protection factor of a product

8. Extremely painful type of vascular headache
9. Tension
10. Undesirable effects of drugs
11. Drugs that can be purchased with the written order of a doctor
12. Headache caused by the tightening of muscles
13. The virus that causes AIDS
14. High blood pressure
15. Headache caused by enlarged blood vessels
16. Foods with little nutritional value
17. Actions and surroundings that can be controlled by the individual

REVIEWING WHAT YOU HAVE LEARNED

1. What happens to the blood vessels in a person who continually eats food containing too much fat?
2. Explain what is meant by ideal exercise. Give examples of ideal exercise.
3. Discuss the health risks of smoking.

4. Why is hypertension known as "the silent killer"? What causes it?
5. Name eight things you can do to help cope with stress.
6. How is the AIDS epidemic affecting our society and lifestyles?

CHAPTER REVIEW 32

USING YOUR CRITICAL THINKING SKILLS

1. Discuss with the class ways to make the modern lifestyle healthier. Together, prepare a list of tips for healthy living.

2. Some companies offer incentives to employees to participate in weight loss programs, regular exercise programs, programs to stop smoking, etc. List the ways a company might benefit from employee participation in such programs.

3. Substance regulation is a controversial issue in our country. Discuss the following questions with your class and tally your opinions.

a. Should cigarette smoking be banned in all public places?

b. Should substances that are known health hazards be illegal? Cigarettes? Alcohol?

c. Should a seriously ill patient be allowed to use an experimental drug that has not been approved by the FDA?

d. Should the sale of vitamins be regulated to protect the consumer?

APPLYING WHAT YOU HAVE LEARNED

1. A record of your health and medical care is needed when you apply for school, a job, or health insurance. Even more importantly, it will help you get the health and medical care that you need. For your own use, prepare a chart that includes: names, addresses, and phone numbers of your doctor(s) and dentist, date of last medical checkup, date of last dental checkup, immunizations and booster shots you have had and when you had them, childhood illnesses you have had and when you had them, your blood type, any allergies, any chronic illnesses, any injuries or surgery you have had, name and type of health insurance and your policy number, and any other helpful information. Keep this record up to date.

CHAPTER 33

Obtaining and Financing Medical Care

OBJECTIVES

After completing this chapter, you will be able to do the following:
1. Explain why routine heath care is important.
2. Describe how you would go about selecting a primary care doctor.
3. Explain how medicine should be stored.
4. List three ways you can avoid medical costs.
5. Explain how you can save money on prescription drugs.
6. Name the five types of health insurance.

TERMS

coinsurance clause
coordination-of-benefits
  clause
generic drugs
health maintenance
  organization (HMO)

Medicaid
Medicare
medication
minerals
pharmacist
primary care doctor

specialists
stop-loss protection
vitamins

There are two broad divisions of medical care:

- primary care
- specialized (secondary) care

Primary care doctors are trained to provide total medical care. They must be very good at diagnosing illnesses, and they must be capable of treating most medical problems. Medical programs now require as much training for primary care doctors as for those who specialize in only one part of the body. Primary care doctors are also known as family doctors, general internists, or general practitioners.

Sometimes a primary care doctor feels that a patient with a diagnosed illness will receive better care from a specialist. Specialists have greater depth of training in one area of the body or one type of ailment.

SELECTING A PRIMARY CARE DOCTOR

In many large cities, good medical care is available in outpatient clinics of general hospitals or medical centers. However, one seldom sees the same doctor on successive visits. For general, long-term medical care, it seems wise to have your own primary care doctor. A personal doctor can serve as a counselor and friend, as concerned with keeping you well as with treating you when you become ill. You may already have a primary care doctor. If you don't, call your county medical society to learn the names of primary care doctors in your area. The society does not make recommendations, but a friend or neighbor may do that. Then consider:

- Location: You will want a doctor whose office is not too far from your home.
- Hospital affiliations: Your doctor must have hospital privileges in case you need hospitalization for surgery or for other reasons. (Hospitals are discussed later in this topic.)
- Insurance coverage: if You have health insurance, pick a doctor who is covered under your policy.
- Availability: Pick a doctor whose practice is not overloaded.
- Personality: Your emotional reaction to the doctor as a person is important.

There are other considerations, of course. The relationship between a doctor and a patient is very personal, and you must be able to trust the doctor's judgment and skills. It may be worth the price of a visit to two or three doctors just to interview them. If you do this, here are some questions to get you started. Some of these may not apply to you, and you will probably want to add questions of your own.

- Will you care for all members of my family?
- At which local hospitals do you have admitting privileges?
- What types of surgery do you perform?
- What do you do in the way of preventive medicine?
- What are your office hours? (Will the hours allow you to see the doctor without missing school or work?)
- Do you make emergency house calls?
- What are your fees?
- What doctors take your place when you are not available?

Finally, the real test of a good primary care doctor is his or her judgment of

primary care doctor

a doctor trained to provide total medical care; a general practitioner, general internist, or family doctor

specialists

doctors who have in-depth training in one area of the body or one type of ailment; this training is beyond the medical degree requirements

when patients should be referred to a specialist. You will probably have to talk to other patients about this matter.

ROUTINE MEDICAL CARE

Whether you have your own primary care doctor or visit an outpatient clinic, routine medical care is important. Basic parts of routine medical care are:

- physical examinations
- immunizations

Over 75 percent of all deaths in the United States are due to chronic (long-term) illnesses. Many of these illnesses can be prevented by regular physical checkups.

Starting in infancy, routine medical care includes a series of immunizations. See the information given in Figure

33.1 on the next page. You may be able to get these shots at your local county health office at minimum cost.

SPECIALIZED MEDICAL CARE

Specialists have intensive training in taking care of one part of the body or treating one type of ailment. You are familiar with some specialists. For example, dentists take care of teeth. Ophthalmologists take care of eyes. When we have a health problem that can *best be treated by* a specialist, the primary care doctor will make a referral.

There are many kinds of specialists. There are even sub-specialists who diagnose and treat disorders in only one very small part of the body. For example, oncologists are specialists who treat tumors. Some of them specialize even further and treat only tumors of the head and neck.

Hospitals

When thinking about medical care, consider hospitals. Some doctors care for patients at only one hospital, but you might want to have a doctor who goes to the hospital of your choice.

You might need a hospital with special services. Some hospitals have special equipment, such as kidney dialysis machines. Some hospitals specialize in certain disorders, such as cancer or drug problems. Some people want a hospital with outpatient clinics that treat people who do not stay in the hospital overnight. Some people need a hospital that can give long-term care, lasting for months. Once you know what hospital you will use, become more familiar with its services.

Almost all hospitals have emergency rooms, which are places for treating immediately anyone who is sick or hurt. Learn how to get to the emergency rooms of the hospitals nearest your home and work.

You can get information about hospitals from doctors and medical societies, or you can visit or call hospitals directly.

Medication

Medication is any substance taken to improve one's health. This includes hormones and vitamins as well as drugs.

Early medicines were compounded by a pharmacist from plants and minerals, and ingredients were not standardized. That is, if one plant or mineral wasn't available, a medicine might be made from something else. Medicines were usually in the form of powders and ointments—and they smelled and tasted awful. Pharmacists

Routine Medical Care

Disease	Suggested Immunization Schedule
Diphtheria, Tetanus (lock jaw), and Pertussis (whooping cough)	**DTP** 2, 4, 6 months 15 months, and 4-6 years (5 total DTPs before school) **Diphtheria** age 14-16 years; **Tetanus**, every 10 years for life
Polio	**OPV** 2, 4, 6 months, 4-6 years (4 total before school)
Measles Mumps Rubella	**MMR** 12-15 months (depending on geographical region) and 4-6 years (2 total before school)
Hemophilus Influenza B Meningitis	**HIB** 2, 4, 6, and 15 months (1-4 required before school)
Tuberculosis (TB) skin test	**PPD** or **TINE** at 9 months, then **PPD** 4-6 years and as needed throughout life (Does not prevent disease)

Figure 33.1

Routine medical care such as immunizations can help prevent diseases that killed many people in the past. Check with your local county health service to see if they recommend any immunizations that are not listed here. If they do, make a list to share with your class.

still make and dispense some medicines, but most medicines are now made in large quantities by pharmaceutical companies. Ingredients are standardized and measured carefully during manufacturing. Some medicines are derived from plants and minerals, and some are made from animal

medication

a substance taken to improve one's health

pharmacist

a person licensed to prepare and dispense medical drugs

glands. Living fungi are also an important source for drugs. For example, penicillin is made from bread mold.

Medicine is made in various forms. Tablets, capsules, creams, and liquids are common forms of medicine. Skin patches that allow the medicine to enter the body more slowly are being used more and more.

Before a medicine can be sold, it must be shown to be safe and effective before the Food and Drug Administration (FDA) will approve it. Medicine is tested first on animals and then on human volunteers.

Brand Names and Generic Names

Prescription drugs are usually developed by a manufacturing company, which obtains a patent from the government. The patent gives that company the sole right to make and sell the drug for seventeen years under its own brand name. During this time, the costs of developing the drug are included in the price. After the patent expires, other companies may produce and sell the drug under their own brand names, and this competition usually results in lower prices. Also, after the patent expires, companies may produce the drug under its generic (general) name. Often, generic drugs are much less expensive than the equivalent brand-name drugs.

Storing Medicine

Drugs lose strength when exposed to heat and moisture, so the medicine cabinet in a steamy bathroom is probably the worst place to store medicine. Many pharmacists suggest the top shelf of a closet. Drugs must, of course, be kept out of the reach of small children. You can ask to have prescriptions placed in special child-proof containers.

Vitamins and Minerals

Vitamins are organic compounds that the body needs in very small amounts to regulate certain biological processes. These processes allow nutrients to be released from fats, carbohydrates, and proteins. A vitamin will cure a disease or disorder only if the condition was caused by lack of that specific vitamin.

Minerals make up about 4 percent to 5 percent of the body structure. Like vitamins, they are needed in regulating many biological processes.

A truly balanced diet normally contains all the vitamins and minerals your body needs. If you do not always eat a balanced diet, you might benefit from taking supplemental vitamins and minerals. Many vitamins and minerals are lost in the water used to cook foods, and this is especially true if the food is overcooked.

If you do take vitamins or minerals, you should know that taking very large doses can be harmful. This is especially true of the fat-soluble vitamins: A, D, E, and K. These are held in the body. Other vitamins are water soluble, and excesses of water-soluble vitamins are usually excreted from the body—unless the dose is extremely high.

Vitamin and mineral tablets and capsules containing 100 percent of the recommended daily allowance are available in health food or vitamin stores. Don't pay extra for so-called natural vitamins, because they are chemically the same as synthetic (manufactured) vitamins. Your body won't know the difference. If you do take supplemental vitamins and minerals, don't think you can just eat whatever you want and stay well. There are many necessary nutrients that haven't been packaged in pills, so eating a variety of foods is the safest way to ensure good nutrition.

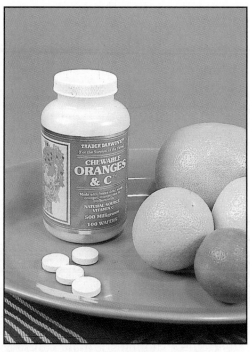

Taking vitamin and mineral supplements can help a diet that is lacking in these substances. However, the best way to get both vitamins and minerals is through a balanced diet. How is your diet? Are you getting a variety of vitamins and minerals by eating a variety of foods? How can you improve your diet?

vitamins
....
organic compounds needed by the body for growth and proper functioning

minerals
....
earth elements, some of which are necessary to maintain good health; 4%–5% of the body's structure is made up of minerals

FINANCING MEDICAL CARE

In recent years, inflation has pushed the price of food, housing, cars, and other living expenses to new highs—but the cost of health care has increased at a rate 50 percent higher than the overall cost of living. Half of all Americans have cut back on visits to their doctors and dentists because of increased costs. Even the best, most expensive health insurance plans seldom cover all medical expenses. In 1994, more than 39 million Americans had no health insurance.

AVOIDING MEDICAL COSTS

Certainly, you won't want to sacrifice your health (or your family's health) to save on medical expenses, but with health care costs expected to continue rising, how can you get the most for your medical dollars? Staying healthy, of course, is the best way. Having regular checkups and keeping off excess weight also help. Getting regular exercise, learning to handle stress, and not using tobacco and alcohol help, too. There are other steps you can take to avoid costs.

- Select a primary care doctor before you get sick. After you have been examined and your health history is up to date, you may be able to simply telephone your doctor about minor health problems. This can save money on office calls. Many doctors don't charge anything for providing information over the phone to their patients.

- Let your primary care doctor decide if and when you need to visit a specialist. Going from specialist to specialist, depending on what part of the body is showing signs of illness, is very expensive. Your primary care doctor is important because she or he knows your complete health history.

- Ask your doctor what you can safely do on your own to cut health care costs. For years, diabetics have given themselves insulin shots. Many people with hypertension regularly take their own blood pressure. You can do these and other things as well as the doctor, but don't try to diagnose your own symptoms of illness. Don't try to treat yourself without a doctor's advice.

CONTROLLING THE COST OF PRESCRIPTION MEDICINE

There are many kinds of medicines available today, and the cost of drugs has increased. There are ways of saving money on medicine:

- Shop around
- Buy generic drugs
- Buy in large quantities
- Take advantage of special discounts

Shopping Around

A newspaper reporter took the same prescription for a brand-name drug to eleven different pharmacies in the same city. You might expect that the prices for the same medicine would be similar—but they ranged from $5.85 to $27.50. The lowest price was quoted by a pharmacy in a discount department store.

In some states, pharmacies must post their prices for many common drugs. Of course, sometimes a prescription drug is needed right away for treatment. In those cases, it isn't worth risking one's health to save money by shopping around for the lowest price. For prescriptions that must be continually refilled, shopping around can save a lot of money.

Buying Generic Drugs

Generic drugs can save you money. These drugs are not sold under brand names, but are sold under names that

generic drugs
....
the chemical or general names for drugs; drugs not sold under brand names

simply describe the drugs. A generic drug is often available at a fraction of the cost of the same drug sold under a brand name. In many states, pharmacists may substitute a different, cheaper brand or a generic drug in place of the drug prescribed. If you prefer the generic or least-expensive brand of a drug, tell the pharmacist.

Buying in Large Quantities

Sometimes a medicine must be taken over a long period of time, and you can save money if the doctor writes the prescription for a large quantity. Pills and capsules are often less expensive when purchased in 100s or 500s. If you cannot purchase large quantities from your pharmacist, ask your doctor where you may fill your prescription by mail. In large quantities, savings often amount to 40 percent. However, when buying in large quantities, you will need to store medications properly to ensure adequate shelflife.

Using Special Discounts

Many pharmacies give special discounts on prescription medicines. For example, students, senior citizens, or union members may be eligible for discounts. Check with several pharmacies in your area, then take advantage of any special discounts for which you are eligible.

COUNTY HEALTH SERVICES

Check with your county health department to learn what services are available. Services offered may include low-cost immunization programs and facilities for detecting cancer. Clinics may be held for dealing with high blood pressure or vision, hearing, or speech problems. Find out if you are eligible to use the services offered.

HOSPITALI-ZATION

When your doctor says you should have an operation, ask if it's really necessary. Find out what your choices are and get a second opinion before agreeing to surgery. Do this no matter how much you trust your doctor—many unnecessary operations are performed every year. Besides costing money, every surgery requiring anesthesia places the patient at risk.

CONSUMER PROFILE

Melanie was very ill with a rare disease. Her doctor had prescribed a number of medications that she would have to take for several months. Her mother gave her injections twice a day. Purchased through the doctor's office, the vial of medication for each shot cost six dollars. There was another medicine she had to take in pill form—a bottle of 60 tables that cost over seventy dollars!

Since these medications were not covered on Melanie's insurance plan, her family tried to find some less expensive sources. By calling around town, Melanie's mother found a local pharmacy where she could get the medicine for Melanie's shots for only eighty-nine cents apiece! Then she found a local consumer buyer's club that helped people purchase medications in bulk and at a discount. Melanie's family saved 30 percent to 40 percent by purchasing her other medications through the club. It is certainly worth shopping around and buying in quantity when you can.

Ask the doctor what the fee will be—most insurance plans pay a set amount, depending on the type of surgery. If surgery is to be performed, ask if it can be done on an outpatient basis. If so, you may walk into the hospital or surgical center, have the surgery, and leave (with help) the same day. This can save thousands of dollars compared to spending even a few days in a hospital.

Many employers offer membership in an HMO (health maintenance organization) to their employees. Do you know anyone who is a member of an HMO? If so, ask them how they like the care they are provided.

If you must enter the hospital and you have a choice about the day you enter, avoid going in on Friday. If little is to be done on your case until Monday, you can save hundreds of dollars by spending the weekend at home. Ask, too, if you can save money by having some routine lab tests done before you enter the hospital.

When you are admitted to the hospital, you can save money by asking for a semiprivate room. This means that at least one other patient will occupy the same room.

HEALTH MAINTENANCE ORGANIZA- TIONS

One way to keep the cost of health care down is to join a **health maintenance organization (HMO)**. The goals of HMOs are to help you stay healthy as well as take care of you when you are sick.

There is a monthly fee, sometimes paid by employers. The monthly fee is the same no matter how many times you visit the doctor. Some HMOs require a small copayment for each visit or prescription.

Membership in an HMO covers all of your health care needs. It includes the cost of visits to doctors on the staff. It also includes the cost of medical tests, maternity care, emergency service, and hospitalization. Members of HMOs pay 10 percent to 40 percent less for health care than those with other types of health insurance.

HEALTH INSURANCE

The cost of health care increased rapidly during the 1980s, and this made health insurance a necessity for most people. The best way to plan your health insurance program is to decide which risks are the greatest threats to you and your family, then cover these risks with insurance. There are five

health maintenance organization (HMO)
....
an organization of physicians that is designed to cover all of a consumer's health care needs under a prepayment plan

types of health insurance available today:

- hospital expense insurance
- surgical expense insurance
- physicians' expense insurance
- major medical insurance
- disability insurance

Hospital Expense Insurance

The most well-known and widely held type of health insurance is hospital expense insurance. Coverage usually includes the cost of the hospital room, meals, and nursing care. There is usually a time limit for benefits. Limits are often set between 21 and 365 days, but the period of coverage may be longer. Only 3 percent of those admitted to hospitals remain longer than 31 days. Because of this, it may not be wise to pay extra for a policy that covers you for 365 days. Some policies now include some out-of-hospital costs, such as medical tests and prescription drugs.

Surgical Expense Insurance

A surgical expense insurance policy covers the cost of operations. The policy lists the amounts that will be paid for each kind of operation, so read your policy when you receive it.

Physicians' Expense Insurance

Physicians' expense insurance covers the cost of doctor visits while you are hospitalized. It is usually combined with hospital and surgical insurance as a basic policy. Some physicians' expense policies pay for visits to your doctor's office.

Major Medical Insurance

Major medical insurance is sometimes called extended benefits or catastrophe insurance. It helps pay costs not covered by basic health plans, including surgery, hospital care, doctors' fees, prescription drugs, home medical care, medical tests, psychiatric care, and physical therapy. The Health Insurance Institute recommends major medical coverage of at least $250,000 over your lifetime.

Most major medical policies include a coinsurance clause indicating expenses will be shared 80–20 or 75–25. You must pay the 20 or 25 percent, and the insurance company pays the 80 or 75 percent. Many policies also have deductible clauses. That is, you must pay a certain amount of the cost before the insurance will pay any amount. The insurance covers the rest. When comparing the cost of buying insurance, compare the amounts you would share in paying major medical expenses. Try to find a policy that limits your share to $1,000 to $2,000. This is called stop-loss protection.

Disability Insurance

Disability insurance helps replace the earnings lost because of illness or injury. Most policies limit the amount paid to about 60 percent of your usual earnings, up to a fixed amount.

Government Health Care Programs

Medicare and Medicaid are programs that provide benefits to special groups. Medicare is a federal health insurance program for people sixty-five or older and some disabled persons

coinsurance clause

an agreement whereby the insured shares costs (usually 20%–25%) with the insurance company

stop-loss protection

an insurance policy that limits a consumer's coinsurance payments

Medicare

a federal health insurance program that provides medical benefits for people aged 65 or older and some disabled people

Medicaid

a joint federal and state program that provides medical benefits for people who cannot afford to pay for health care

CHECKLIST FOR GOOD HEALTH CARE

Ultimately, you are responsible for your own health care. You can have a good health care program by using the following checklist:

___ Eat a balanced diet.
___ Use a sensible approach to losing and maintaining weight.
___ Exercise regularly and sensibly.
___ Avoid using tobacco and liquor.
___ Cope with stress.
___ Use drugs properly when needed, but don't abuse them or use illicit drugs.
___ Choose a primary care doctor or an outpatient clinic.
___ Have regular checkups.
___ Control the cost of prescription medicine and doctor bills.
___ Consider outpatient services as an alternative to hospitalization.
___ Plan for health insurance according to your needs.

join a club that offers group health insurance.

Ask about special policies or rates. For example, some companies have special policies for college students or for nonsmokers.

Don't buy policies with overlapping coverage. It's a waste of money. Most policies have a **coordination-of-benefits clause** that prevents collecting from more than one policy.

HEALTH CARE DECISIONS

Following your doctor's advice is generally wise—but if you doubt the doctor's judgment, get a second opinion. When any kind of surgery is recommended, *always* get a second or even a third opinion. Ask if the surgery is necessary or elective (optional). Ask what will happen if you do not have the surgery, and ask about the risks of that kind of surgery. When elective surgery is recommended, ask yourself how it will affect your overall quality of life.

Remember, too, that you have rights as a patient. The American Hospital Association developed "A Patient's Bill of Rights." According to this document, a patient has the right to receive considerate and respectful care. A patient also has the right to expect confidential treatment of medical records. The complete "Patient's Bill of Rights" is available from the American Hospital Association.

Above all, ask questions. This applies to all areas of health care. Ask about routine procedures, surgery, and fees. Know what your choices are. Doing this will help you make wise consumer decisions about health care.

coordination-of-benefits clause
....
a condition included in most insurance policies that states that the insured cannot collect from more than one policy

who are eligible to receive benefits from Medicare. Medicaid is a joint federal and state program. People who cannot afford to pay for health care may receive help from Medicaid.

Buying Health Insurance

Health insurance may be obtained through a group plan where you work or as an individual or family policy. Group insurance plans cost 15 percent to 40 percent less than an individual policy for the same coverage. Find out if you are eligible for a group plan where you work or through membership in a club. If not, you may want to

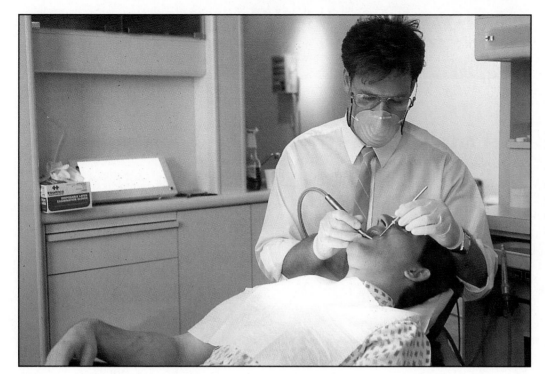

Dentists and orthodontists are health care specialists who take care of the teeth, gums, and bones of the mouths of their patients. Do you go to a dentist regularly? Do you know anyone who has been to an orthodontist? If so, did they go because they wear braces?

Summary

- There are two broad divisions of medical care: primary care (general practitioners) and specialized or secondary care (specialists).

- Routine medical care (physical examinations and immunizations) is important, whether you have your own primary care doctor or visit an outpatient clinic.

- Medication is any substance taken to improve one's health.

- If you do not always eat a balanced diet, you might benefit from taking supplemental vitamins and minerals.

- The cost of health care has increased at a much higher rate than the overall cost of living.

- There are ways you can save money on medicine: shop around, buy generic drugs, buy in large quantities, and take advantage of special discounts.

- One way to keep the cost of health care down is to join a health maintenance organization (HMO).

- There are five types of health insurance available today: hospital expense, surgical expense, physicians' expense, major medical, and disability.

- Health insurance through a group plan is less expensive than an individual policy for the same coverage.

E NRICHING YOUR VOCABULARY

Use the following words or phrases to complete the sentences below. Write the completed sentences on your paper.

coinsurance clause
coordination-of-benefits
    clause
generic drugs

health maintenance
    organization (HMO)
Medicaid and Medicare
medication

vitamins and minerals
pharmacist
primary care doctors
specialists
stop-loss protection

1. Balanced diets contain adequate supplies of

2. Insurance companies protect themselves from providing overlapping coverage with a

3. Government-supported health insurance is provided through

4. Drugs that are not protected by a trademark are called

5. Family doctors or general practitioners are names for

6. Prescription drugs are dispensed by a

7. The share of medical expense a consumer will pay is described in an insurance policy's

8. An organization designed to cover all of a consumer's health care needs is called a

9. A prescription drug or an OTC drug is a form of

10. In order to limit coinsurance payments, a consumer may purchase

11. Doctors with in-depth knowledge of a particular field of medicine are

R EVIEWING WHAT YOU HAVE LEARNED

1. Why is routine health care important?

2. Describe how you would go about selecting a primary care doctor.

3. Where should medicine be stored? Why?

4. List three ways you can avoid medical costs.

5. How can you save money on prescription drugs?

6. What are the five types of health insurance?

7. What are some services offered by county health services?

8. Describe how an HMO works.

9. What is Medicare?

10. Explain the differences between Medicare and Medicaid.

USING YOUR CRITICAL THINKING SKILLS

1. Several years ago, John received a knee injury that has continued to bother him. What should John do to find out if he should have an operation? What should he find out and do to make the best arrangements possible for having an operation?

APPLYING WHAT YOU HAVE LEARNED

1. Collect newspaper and magazine articles about recent advancements in health care. Share these with your classmates through oral reports and bulletin board displays.

UNIT

12

PROTECTING OUR ENVIRONMENT

CHAPTERS

Each of us has a personal, or near, environment. This includes our home and its surroundings—and, unless we live alone, we share this environment with others. We consider their needs and feelings when making decisions about its use.

Our larger environment is the world in which we live. Decisions about this larger environment may affect many other people, animals, and plants.

In the past, we have made some bad decisions about our natural resources (air, land, water, and energy sources) causing problems that will be difficult to solve. Now we must clean up the environment and conserve our resources. However, decisions that are good for the environment are sometimes bad for the economy. For example, concern for an endangered species has halted large construction projects and caused workers to lose their jobs. What is important to some can cause harm to others.

As responsible consumers, we must be concerned about our present quality of life, but we must also consider the impact of our decisions on the future. We must make more efficient use of our energy resources, and we must develop new sources of energy to meet the needs of our growing population. While doing this, we must prevent further pollution of our land, air, and water.

If we are well informed and alert, we can do a lot to protect our natural resources—and we can use them wisely. As citizens of the world concerned for the future, we cannot do less.

CHAPTER 34

Protecting Our Land

OBJECTIVES

After completing this chapter, you will be able to do the following:
1. List four major uses of land.
2. Name the three major sources of waste.

TERMS

erosion   recycle   visual pollution
hazardous chemicals   sanitary landfills

As you travel around in your area, do you see bottles or cans tossed along the roadside or street? Do billboards and other signs block your view of the scenery? Do you pass by fields marred with deep gullies? These are examples of pollution and abuse of our land.

USES OF LAND

During this century, more than 2.5 billion acres of land in the United States have been covered by roads, cities, airports, and industrial development. This loss of agricultural land continues. Each year we lose around 2 million more acres to nonagricultural uses.

Urban Land Use

As in most countries, the largest part of the U.S. population is concentrated on a very small part of the land. In urban areas, most land is covered by buildings, concrete, and asphalt—and it is often spoiled with litter and garbage. Sometimes land is blocked from view by billboards and advertisements. Open space is scarce. Many city planners today realize that open spaces are important to our well-being. Parks and avenues lined with trees not only make people feel better, they also help keep the air clean. These open, green spaces help keep the temperature of the city cooler in the summer, and they provide homes for animals and birds.

Most consumers have left downtown areas to live in the suburbs, where they may select homes with open areas around them. People can enjoy the green spaces and even have gardens of their own. Part of the effort to redevelop cities and encourage people to move back to the downtown areas includes reclaiming some of the land in cities for these kinds of uses.

Gardening is useful both as recreation and as a food source. More than eighty million Americans now stake out their plots each spring. They are taking part in a hobby that does more than beautify the land; it helps relieve the frustration and tension caused partly by living in a crowded, polluted world.

Recreation Lands

Every year, millions of Americans literally head for the hills. Recreation land is becoming one of our most important public resources. Most of us enjoy hiking, fishing, swimming, or simply contemplating the natural splendor of the land. Today, though, when we arrive at a vacation spot, we are likely to find it already overrun with other vacationers. For example, in 1949, only 600,000 people visited the Grand Canyon, only 12 hiked to the bottom, and less than 100 took the boat trip on the river. In a recent year, four million people visited this popular attraction. More than 850,000 of them used the recreation area for an overnight stay. Some people are working to limit the number of visitors that can make the trip down into the canyon. They feel the natural surroundings are being damaged by too many people.

The U.S. government now owns about 700 million acres of land, less than one-third of the total land area of the country. This public land is used for many purposes, including national parks—and the parks have become so popular that we are in danger of losing some of them. Some have been closed temporarily to give the environment time to revive. At others, attendance has been limited, or all motor vehicles have been banned. These practices are

Our national forests and parks have become popular vacation sites for many people. So many people like to use these facilities, that some parks and forests have had to limit the number of people allowed in. Do you think it's fair to limit the use of something owned by the government? Why or why not?

intended to keep the air clean and the grass growing.

Forest Lands

Our forests are a natural resource that serves many important functions. Trees produce oxygen and help control air pollution, and the forests serve as homes for wildlife. People use forests for recreational activities as well.

We have increased our demand for wood to burn in fireplaces and to make houses, paper, and insulation. This demand has reduced the number of trees so much that, in some areas, we have lost entire forests. Without trees to hold the soil and absorb the rain, the soil has washed away—resulting in floods and changes in climate.

Unlike many resources, however, trees can be replaced and progress is being made in doing just that. We can produce fast-growing varieties of trees on special tree farms, allowing us to replace trees almost as fast as they are cut down. Replacing trees and replac-

ing forests may be quite different. A forest lost in a cool climate, such as high on a mountain, may require a generation or more to come back.

Farmland

Of all the types of land, farmland is the type on which we depend most for our immediate survival. Drought, flood, change in climate, and improper farming damage farmland, and this damage can cause sudden food shortages, and millions of people may go hungry. Rapid growth in population makes it necessary to use our farmland wisely.

Early settlers in the United States could plant the same kind of crop every year on the same land. When the soil was worn out, they simply moved on to "new" land. Later, farmers found a different system useful. They would plant a crop one year and leave the land unplanted for three years, then they would plant the field profitably again.

Millions of acres of forests are lost to logging each year. Companies that do the logging are successfully replacing the trees that are cut down. However, it takes many years for the forest to grow back. What are your feelings about this process? Are you in favor of allowing companies to continue logging? Or should we use recycled products instead of cutting down more trees?

Today, only about one-third of the world's 7.86 billion acres of farmable land is used to grow crops. With billions of people to feed, we make heavy use of our land. By applying fertilizers and using improved farming techniques, farmers have become so efficient that they can now plant their fields each year and still reap large harvests.

But land can still be worn out or lost if it is not given proper care. In 1990, there were 51 million fewer acres of productive farmland in the United States than in 1980. Worldwide, 15 million acres of productive land are disappearing each year. One major problem is **erosion**, the wearing away of soil. Soil can be carried away by water or wind, especially if the soil is bare, but plants help hold the soil and prevent erosion, and they also absorb water. People in cities can support projects that promote planting and proper drainage. Farmland is also lost as it is converted to other uses such as the development of housing, roads, or other structures. As our population increases, more and more demands are placed on farmland—and this increases the problem of handling waste from farming.

DEALING WITH WASTES

Where does all the trash and garbage go? For most of us, remembering to place it outside in the trash can for pickup is about as much thought as we give the question. Dealing with wastes is one of our most difficult problems, and it is one that is becoming more difficult each year. Our waste is costly to dispose of, and it can create health hazards. The papers and cans along our highways remind us that pollution from our waste is ugly, but waste produces many more far-reaching problems.

erosion
....
the wearing away of soil by wind or water

When floods occur in faming areas, acres of arable farmland are lost. How do you think farmers would deal with this type of catastrophe? How do you think it would affect the economy of the area?

Sources of Waste Materials

In the United States, a total of 4 billion tons of waste are produced every year. The three major sources of waste materials are:

- agriculture
- industry
- homes

Surprisingly, the largest source of solid waste in the United States is farming. Wastes from farming are spread out over billions of acres, so they are not as noticeable as the garbage hauled from cities each day. It is estimated that over 2 billion tons of farm waste are dumped on the land or into waterways every year. This includes animal waste, vegetable stalks and hulls from crops, and greenhouse waste.

Industrial wastes, including mining, make up more than 40 percent of the solid waste. Industrial mineral waste is easy to see in big piles near mines and processing plants.

Homes and commercial establishments contribute about 180 million tons of waste per year, and a lot of this waste will be around forever. It's estimated that an aluminum can may last a billion years. Glass containers may last even longer. Archaeologists have found glass, believed to be the first ever made, that is more than 3,000 years old.

Disposing of Wastes

The question comes up again: Where does all this waste go? A few years ago, most of the solid waste from households was placed in open dumps, but these areas create **visual pollution** and cause bad odors and water contamination. They are breeding grounds for rats, flies, and cockroaches, too, so open dumps are now prohibited in most areas.

Most solid waste is put into **sanitary landfills**. Here, the waste is covered each day with soil to minimize the problems common around open dumps. Part of the waste is burned,

visual pollution
....
environmental contamination that can be seen

sanitary landfills
....
garbage disposal systems in which the waste is covered daily with a layer of soil

either at home or in municipal incinerators.

Some coastal cities continue to dump their solid waste into the ocean, and other cities have done so in the past. Sewage sludge (solids left after the water has been removed) has also been dumped into the ocean. The long-term effect of this practice is not known.

Recycling

One positive step that we consumers can take toward preserving our environment is recycling. To **recycle** means to "process again." Many concerned people today believe that the cure for our mounds of solid waste is recycling, that we should recycle as much waste as possible. Recycling saves our natural resources and keeps our environment cleaner. As the cost of new materials increases, recycling will become more profitable. We can recycle metal, glass, paper, and other products.

Many areas have curbside recycling programs in use. Typical items that are recycled are paper, glass, and plastic. Does your area have a recycling program? What items are recycled?

Metal. Aluminum cans are accepted for recycling in most areas. But steel cans, in which most of our food is packaged, are not accepted everywhere. Check the recycling centers near you to find out what materials are recycled in your area.

Glass. No-return bottles are convenient, but they are a major source of "waste glass." Each year we throw away 28 billion glass jars and bottles. In some areas, government agencies have taken steps to reduce the number of no-return bottles. Some have prohibited the sale of no-deposit containers for soft drinks and beer in a particular city or county. Others have added a tax to no-return bottles, increasing the cost and encouraging consumers to use returnable bottles. Recycling of glass has increased from about 5 percent in 1980 to more than double that now.

Paper. Americans use about 50 million tons of paper a year, which consumes about 850 million trees. We can easily recycle paper, particularly newspaper. If we recycled only 10 percent of the newspaper used in this country each year, we could save 25 million trees—yet in the United States, we burn or bury much of our paper. We are increasing our efforts to recycle paper, and estimates suggest that in 1994 Americans recycled about 29 percent of the paper they used.

Plastics. We have just begun to recycle some plastics. In 1988, only about one percent of plastics was being recycled. Most plastics are not recycled because of their complex chemistry. Plastics do not decompose (rot) when buried—nor do they burn well in most incinerators. Some even give off poisonous fumes when they burn. Certain products, such as plastic bags, can be used over and over. Other plastics can

recycle
....
to process again or
make ready for reuse

be recycled to produce new products such as insulation, carpeting, wood-like furniture, fencing, and marine fixtures.

CHEMICALS AND THE ENVIRONMENT

We use large amounts of chemicals to help grow our crops and control diseases. Chemicals are also used to con-trol flies, mosquitoes, and other pests. Over one billion pounds of pesticides were produced in the United States in the early 1990s. Consumers are concerned more and more about these **hazardous chemicals** and what they may be doing to our environment, and that concern is well-founded.

Farmers, the government, and industry buy and use the greatest amount of chemicals, but most chemicals can be bought by anyone. These are easy to get and low in cost. However, many people don't understand how to use and store chemicals properly—and they may not even bother to read the precautions on the labels. So they may use the chemicals in the wrong way or for the wrong purpose.

Disposal of the used chemicals and their containers is also a problem. Materials such as mercury, arsenic, radioactive waste, and the PCBs (poly-chlorinated biphenyls) are serious pollutants. If not disposed of properly, they can ruin our water supply. (This is discussed further in the next topic.) Chemicals can also cause serious medical problems for people exposed to them, but still we dump millions of pounds of them into our environment each year. Mercury is easily absorbed by the food chain and may cause blindness, deafness, and eventual death. The PCBs, synthetic chemicals that cannot be broken down by natural processes, were once used in electrical equipment—and PCBs may cause cancer. Safe disposal of radioactive waste also continues to be a serious problem.

CHECKLIST FOR CHEMICAL PRODUCTS

Many common products that we use every day are poisonous if eaten or swallowed. Several of these products are listed below. You can probably add to this list simply by seeing what products you have at home. Special care must be taken to store potentially harmful products safely.

- insect sprays and repellents
- bleach
- laundry detergents
- toilet bowl cleaner
- charcoal starter
- furniture polish
- air fresheners
- paint
- paint remover
- antifreeze
- floor wax
- oven cleaner
- ____ Are chemical products contained in safety packaging (example: child-resistant caps)?
- ____ Are products stored in their original containers? Are original labels on containers? Are the products locked up? Are they stored out of the reach of small children?
- ____ Are chemical products stored away from food products?

Dealing with Hazardous Chemicals

How and where to dispose of chemical wastes are big problems. Once a disposal site has been developed, transporting hazardous chemicals to that

INTERACTING WITH TECHNOLOGY

OUR ENVIRONMENT AND THE THREE Rs

Reading, writing, and arithmetic have for years formed the core of our educational programs. Environmentalists are now insisting that American consumers must learn about reduction, reuse, and recycling of materials if we are to protect our environment.

Waste disposal is rapidly becoming a serious problem in some areas of our country. Landfills near large urban areas are filling up at an alarming rate, and toxic leaks from these sites are contaminating soil and ground water. One proposal to prevent contamination is to build above-ground concrete silos to replace landfills. Incinerators provide an alternate method of waste disposal, but they create different environmental problems. Even with rigid air pollution controls, the end product at incinerator sites is ash that may often be highly toxic. What to do with this residue is a serious concern.

Reducing the quantity of garbage we generate is the first step in solving our waste-disposal problem. Manufacturers and consumers working together are finding solutions. Unnecessary packaging can be eliminated. Changing from packaging materials that are difficult to recycle to more environmentally friendly materials is another solution.

Technology and economics are joining forces to help make recycling an attractive part of the solution. Technology has been developed to recycle plastic shopping bags into paving bricks and scrap auto steel into framing materials. Computer housing materials are being recycled into roofing shingles, newspapers into floor decking and insulation, and glass into kitchen and bathroom tiles.

The tire industry is also developing successful recycling programs. Technology has developed a method of recycling tires by shredding them and removing the glass and steel belts. The recycling product can then be used to manufacture mud flaps, doormats, cushioned flooring, and railroad crossings. The most popular use of this product is the creation of rubberized asphalt for paving.

Across the country, large-scale "second hand" businesses are beginning to flourish. These industries provide a network of used goods, making the reuse of durable goods more attractive. Consumers are beginning to practice the three Rs of environmental protection—reduction, reuse, and recycling.

Many household items are hazardous to the environment and should be disposed of properly. Some cities have hazardous waste disposal sites set up around the city. Find out whether your city has disposal sites for household chemicals. Tell your family and friends about these sites and encourage them to use the sites.

site presents another problem. Each year, more than 19,000 accidents involving the shipment of hazardous materials are reported.

Many cities and some states have passed laws regarding hazardous chemicals. Some laws prohibit transportation of such chemicals into the area for the purpose of dumping. Other laws do not allow trucks to carry hazardous materials through areas with many people. Some groups have asked the federal government for better enforcement of the laws and high fines for breaking them. The average fine for dumping hazardous wastes in the wrong way is only $300, but fines as high as $10,000 have been proposed.

The disposal of hazardous waste is a problem for individual households, too. Paints, paint thinners, batteries, cleaners, and pesticides are just a few of the toxic materials found in most homes. Dumping these products down the drain or into the ground can cause serious water-pollution problems.

Check with local authorities to learn how to properly dispose of such materials, and, whenever possible, choose products that are less harmful to the environment.

YOU CAN HELP PROTECT OUR LAND

Protecting our land is a big project. It may seem that it can only be done by the government or a large organization, but there are many things you can do to protect our land. Above all, respect it and encourage others to respect it. Don't litter, and don't abuse or deface the land. Use with care the resources land offers. For example, don't cut down a tree for firewood if you can gather driftwood instead.

Sort through your trash at home, and take cans and glass products for recycling. Save and bundle newspapers, then take them to be recycled. Our resources will last longer.

Don't take chances with hazardous chemicals—read product labels carefully before you buy. Know what you are getting—then handle, use, and store it properly. Dispose of chemicals and containers in the safe manner recommended by the manufacturer.

Support, join, or lead groups working to protect our land and its resources.

For further information, contact the Sierra Club, the Department of the Interior, the Bureau of Land Management, the Department of Agriculture, or other interested agencies. (See the Appendix.)

Summary

- Decisions about our environment may affect many other people, animals, and plants.

- Decisions that are good for the environment are sometimes bad for the economy. Compromises must be made to do the most good at the least expense for all concerned.

- As concerned citizens, we must be concerned about the future and do what we can to prevent further pollution of our land, air, and water.

- Dealing with wastes is one of our most difficult problems.

- There are three major sources of waste materials: agriculture, industry, and homes.

- One positive step we consumers can take toward preserving our environment is recycling: of metal, glass, paper, and plastics.

- Check with local authorities on the proper disposal of hazardous chemicals and, whenever possible, choose products that are less harmful to the environment.

ENRICHING YOUR VOCABULARY

Number your paper from 1–5. Read each sentence below. If the sentence is true, write "true" next to that number. If the sentence is false, rewrite it to make a true statement.

1. Green spaces in an urban environment contribute to visual pollution.

2. Plants cause erosion.

3. One way we pollute our environment is to recycle.

4. Most households and industries face the problem of disposing of hazardous chemicals.

5. Sanitary landfills and open dumps create the same environmental problems.

REVIEWING WHAT YOU HAVE LEARNED

1. List four major uses of land.

2. What are the three major sources of waste?

USING YOUR CRITICAL THINKING SKILLS

1. In your area, what are the advantages and disadvantages of recycling?

2. What are the advantages and disadvantages of using chemicals around the house and on a lawn? How might some of the dangers be avoided?

3. Discuss things you can do to protect our land, in addition to the things you read about in this topic. Make a list and keep it for use in the Applying What You Have Learned activity.

APPLYING WHAT YOU HAVE LEARNED

1. Organize the class into three groups. Each group should prepare and distribute a list of suggestions for one of the following:
   • conserving and protecting our land
   • conserving and protecting our air and water
   • conserving energy

   Groups may use information from the text, lists prepared in class, and outside sources.

CHAPTER 35

Protecting Our Air and Water Supplies

OBJECTIVES

After completing this chapter, you will be able to do the following:
1. List four major sources of air pollution.
2. Explain why air pollution is greater around cities, and explain the effect this has on cities and the people in them.
3. Name some results of being exposed to excessive noise.
4. Explain why water is important to industry.
5. List the three basic sources of water pollution.

TERMS

acid rain
air pollution
asbestos fiber
carbon monoxide
Clean Air Act
decibels (db)
emission standards

Environmental Protection
   Agency (EPA)
eutrophication
Federal Water Pollution
   Control Act
hydrologic cycle

noise
particulates
phosphates
smog
water pollution
water treatment plants

Not so long ago, people used expressions such as, "as natural as breathing" or "pure as the driven snow." Today, these phrases often make no sense. In some areas, the air is so filled with impurities that breathing is considered "unhealthy." Our ground water, and even our rain and snow, may be dangerously polluted.

As mentioned before, solutions to these problems are often at odds with the economy. For example, in the 1970s, oil became more costly and hard to obtain. Some factories were faced with a difficult choice—they could close down, or they could go back to the use of coal for their energy needs. Coal produces more air pollution than oil when burned, but closing the factories puts people out of work and causes other social and economic problems.

We are making some progress in cleaning up our air and water, but it is a slow, hard process. Nevertheless, it has to be done, or our children and grandchildren will have even greater environmental pollution.

AIR POLLUTION

Waste products in the air can cause the dirty conditions we call **air pollution**. Some air pollution has been with us for a long time—even Great-grandmother had to deal with it. There were no automatic washers and dryers in her time. When she washed clothes, she hung them outside to dry, but she was always careful to take them down before the train went by. The black soot from that coal-powered train would soil her clean wash, a problem that is not a concern for most of us today.

Other sources of air pollution affect us daily, such as dust particles, poison gases, or tiny bits of solid or liquid material. These bits of material (such as soot) are called **particulates**.

Densely populated areas have the worst air pollution. If you live near a

air pollution
....
contamination of the atmosphere

particulates
....
tiny bits of solid or liquid suspended in the air

Anti-smoking laws are becoming more common across the United States. Are there anti-smoking laws in your area? If so, what are the laws? Do you agree or disagree with the laws?

city, you can sometimes feel the air pollution burn your eyes and irritate your lungs. News reports commonly include daily monitoring of the air quality levels in cities.

The earth has only a certain amount of air, about five quadrillion tons. This may sound like a lot, but we are quickly polluting it. More than three-fourths of a ton of gaseous waste per person is released into the air each day in the United States. Most of this waste is invisible and odorless, and some of it is very harmful.

Air is cleaned and circulated by changes in the weather, but this natural recycling process cannot handle all the pollution. When the pollutants are cleaned from the air by rain, they are carried to the ground. When harmful chemicals are washed from the air in this way, the rain is called **acid rain**. This "polluted" rain creates problems, too.

Sources and Effects of Air Pollution

Sometimes, air pollution can harm rural areas. For example, acid rain, the result of air pollution, has a profound effect in some rural areas. Air pollution sources, though, are largely urban. Transportation, especially the automobile, accounts for most air pollution. Industry, electric power plants (stationary source fuel combustion), and waste disposal operations are other major sources.

Air pollution affects the temperature and weather around many of our cities. The annual average temperature in large cities is about 1.4 degrees Fahrenheit (.78 degrees Celsius) higher than in the rural areas surrounding them. Scientists are not certain what the long-term effects of these temperature increases will be. They might cause droughts and coastal flooding, or the

temperature increases may have only minor effects. We do know that the probability of cloudiness and rain is 5 percent to 10 percent higher, and fog is 30 percent more likely—in the presence of air pollution. Pollutants in the air screen out the sun's rays and harm plant life.

Some pollutants, primarily chlorofluorocarbons (CFCs), are destroying the ozone layer in the atmosphere. The ozone layer is a belt of gases 10 to 30 miles high that makes life possible on earth by blocking the sun's deadly ultraviolet (UV) rays. UV exposure causes skin cancer and cataracts, damages farm crops, and kills tiny marine animals important to the global food chain. The greatest losses in the ozone layer have been over populated areas of North America, Europe, and Asia. Concern about this problem led to an international agreement to phase out the use of CFCs by the end of the 1990s—and, as early as 1993, it was found that many industries had already cut the production of these chemicals. Scientists now expect the worst of the ozone destruction to occur around the turn of the century, when the maximum load of CFCs slowly wafts up to the stratosphere. Then, as these chemicals are gradually destroyed by natural processes, the ozone layer will begin to recover. Although it will take several generations, our great-great-grandchildren will be healthier because of this generation's concern for the environment.

Costs of Air Pollution

Air pollution threatens the quality of life—even life itself. People have died because of air pollution, and it injures and destroys plant life. Over five hundred million dollars' worth of crops are lost each year in the United States due to air pollution. Billions of dollars are spent each year in attempts to reduce

acid rain
. . . .
natural washing of chemicals from the air

CONSUMER PROFILE

Emma was trying to do what she could to help protect the environment. She convinced her mother to buy "healthy" nontoxic household cleaning products, biodegradable laundry soap, and toilet paper and tissues made from recycled paper. She found a nonharmful alternative to charcoal starter, and, with a little research, found some harmless and natural methods to replace insect sprays.

Emma's friends were shocked to discover that she used hairspray in an aerosol can. The chemicals from aerosol cans are thought to contribute to the destruction of the ozone layer. Emma felt that, with all the positive things she and her family were doing, she could be allowed this one "sin." Her friends thought she was a hypocrite. What do you think?

breathing too much carbon monoxide can be fatal for anyone.

Although carbon dioxide is not a poisonous gas, large quantities of it are being added to the atmosphere each day from burning fossil fuels such as gasoline. These large quantities of carbon dioxide are causing the earth's atmosphere to heat up. The United States produces 22 percent of all the carbon dioxide that is entering the earth's atmosphere.

Hydrocarbons are pollutants made of hydrogen and carbon. These combine with nitrogen oxides (compounds of nitrogen and oxygen) to cause smog. Smog can irritate your eyes, nose, throat, and lungs; and it damages plants and speeds the breakdown of building materials.

Lead and mercury may be given off as vapors. Industrial plants, particularly those making plastics and paper, are the largest producers. These serious pollutants are also produced when

smog
......
a haze caused by the combination of hydrocarbons and nitrogen oxides

air pollution. Industry and government pay many of these costs, but costs are also passed on to the individual consumer. The smog control device for cars is just one example of these costs.

Types of Air Pollution

All types of air pollution are dangerous, depending on the degree of pollution. Some of the pollutants that threaten health the most are carbon monoxide, carbon dioxide, smog, lead, mercury, and asbestos.

carbon monoxide
......
a common gaseous waste, most of which comes from transportation exhaust

Carbon monoxide is the most common gaseous waste. Most of the carbon monoxide pollution comes from transportation exhaust. It is colorless and odorless, and it prevents our blood from carrying the oxygen that our bodies need. Even small amounts of it can cause headaches and drowsiness, and in heavy city traffic this can result in accidents. People who suffer from hardening of the arteries and emphysema (a lung disease) cannot tolerate much carbon monoxide. Of course,

Keeping your car tuned properly can not only save you money by giving you better gas mileage, it can also decrease the amount of pollution in the air. It benefits everyone to keep vehicles tuned properly.

coal, oil, or natural gas is burned. Breathing too much lead can produce tremors, and it can lead to mental health problems.

In most situations, we do not find asbestos fiber in the air. In the past, though, it was used as insulation for buildings—and this insulation remains in many buildings today. Asbestos is still in some car brake linings, too. Fibers from these sources can find their way into the air nearby, and there it becomes a health hazard. Exposure to asbestos or asbestos products over a long period of time can cause serious diseases, such as cancer and asbestosis, a lung disease.

The Fight Against Air Pollution

Times were different when Great-grandmother hurried to protect her laundry from soot. Chances are, she never thought of suggesting that the train's owner use cleaner forms of fuel. The population was small and spread out, and the number of pollution sources was small, too. So individuals and families dealt with pollution problems in their own ways.

In the 1960s, a large part of the population became more and more upset about the worsening environment and asked the government to pass and enforce laws to control air pollution. In 1970, the U.S. Congress passed the Clean Air Act. This set of regulations established strict emission standards for air pollution from cars and factories.

New technology was needed to meet these standards. Engineers developed products and equipment to limit air pollution. Today, antipollution devices are installed in new cars, and cars built after 1974 use only unleaded gasoline. Factories, too, must control the amount of pollution they emit. For example, many plants that generate electricity are now using mechanical scrubbers to remove pollutants from smoke.

asbestos fiber
·················
an air contaminant from insulation materials

Clean Air Act
·················
federal legislation that established strict emission standards for air pollution from cars and factories

emission standards
·················
the measure of contaminants being added to the air

Cars are one of the nation's greatest causes of pollution. Even though the government regulates the amounts of emissions allowed into the air by vehicles, the sheer number of vehicles continues to make pollution a problem. What ideas do you have for helping to reduce air pollution?

Emission standards have helped improve the quality of the air, but they have added to the cost of products. In this case, society decided that cleaner air was more important than lower prices. This was a compromise that needed to be made.

The **Environmental Protection Agency (EPA)** was established in 1970. Its goal was to set national air quality standards and to enforce the Clear Air Act—but in 1977, the Clean Air Act was amended. Deadlines for carrying out all of the antipollution measures were delayed. Major changes to the Clean Air Act were passed in 1990. These changes called for the phasing-out of CFCs that are destroying ozone in the atmosphere. They also set stricter standards for auto exhaust emissions and industrial emissions. Meeting these standards will be expensive but should produce cleaner air. Unfortunately, recent rules issued by the EPA make further delays in cleaning up our air a distinct possibility.

Environmental Protection Agency (EPA)

the federal agency established in 1970 to enforce the Clean Air Act

You can help clean up the environment by purchasing products that cause as little pollution as possible. Many publications are available that give pollution statistics on such items as cars. Check these statistics before you buy and you will be making a big step toward becoming a responsible consumer.

You Can Do Something About Air Pollution

Air pollution is everyone's problem. As a consumer, you can take steps to help correct and prevent it by staying well informed. Do you know of a company that is polluting the air? Then don't buy its products until the conditions are corrected. Moreover, don't buy products that pollute the air—and let the companies know why you will not buy their products.

Buy a car that gets good gas mileage. Automobile manufacturers are working on increasing the average miles per gallon delivered by future cars. Increasing it to 40 mpg from 28 mpg would prevent 440 million tons of carbon dioxide from entering the air each year. Is the car you drive burning fuel effi-ciently? If the engine is running properly, fewer pollutants will enter the air. Don't let the car sit for long with the motor running, and use lead-free gasoline or another fuel that does not create a lot of air pollution. Make sure your car has antipollution devices, and that they are working properly.

Do you use your car more than you need to? Whenever you can, use public transportation, walk, or ride a bike. If you make daily trips to work or school, consider car-pooling.

A lot of air pollution is caused by burning coal and oil to produce electricity, so cutting down on the use of electricity will help prevent air pollution. Turn off lights you don't need in your home. You will learn more about using energy wisely later in this section.

Car-pooling

A car pool is a group of people who share rides to work or to school. Members usually take turns driving, or they pay one driver a share of the driving costs. Car-pooling can save 50 percent to 80 percent of the cost of driving your own car.

The 3M Company has an effective pooling program, with many of their employees sharing rides in vans. The company estimates that each van replaces seven individual cars. With 160 vans in all, the program saved 330,000 gallons of gasoline in one year—and it reduced air pollution by ninety tons of pollutants.

Other companies offer incentives or benefits to their employees for car-pooling. If there is no such plan where you work, you can ask some of your coworkers or school friends if they're interested in forming a car pool. Or you can place a notice on a bulletin board at work or school. Some people contact others interested in car-pooling through newspaper ads. Car-pooling is economical for the individual, and it helps to improve the quality of the environment.

Other Ways to Reduce Air Pollution

Burning fuel in your home also produces air pollution. Check to see that the furnace is working properly, and use your fireplace sparingly. Don't burn leaves or trash. Some communities have laws against doing this. Do you know your community's air pollution laws? If not, learn them, obey them, and report violations by others. Write to your government representatives, and encourage them to support laws that will promote clean air.

Learn what else you can do to help ensure clean air for everyone. Many or-ganizations are concerned about air pollution, and they are good sources of information. One is the American Lung Association, another is the Environmental Protection Agency.

NOISE

We all think we know what **noise** is. To your parents, it might be any song written after 1980. (It's especially "noisy" when it flows from your room while they have guests.) To you, noise might be every syllable uttered by your little brother in the past five years. Surprise—both definitions are correct! Noise is defined as any "unwanted sound." It is also a form of air "pollution."

The intensity of noise is measured in **decibels (db)**. Figure 35.1 on the next page shows some examples. Normal conversation measures about 60 db. A rock band may soar to 120 db—long exposure to any kind of sound at this level can permanently damage your hearing. Brief exposure may cause a temporary hearing loss, which you might notice as a ringing in your ears.

Noise Outside the Home

Many sources of noise, such as trucks, motorcycles, trains, planes, and factories can harm our hearing. Continued exposure to these loud noises can also cause ulcers and high blood pressure.

Many factory workers and farmers have suffered hearing losses from exposure to the noisy equipment they operate. The Occupational Safety and Health Administration (OSHA) is charged with ensuring safety in the workplace. OSHA sometimes sets time limits for exposure to certain noise lev-

noise
....
unwanted sound, a form of pollution

decibels (db)
....
the measure of the intensity of sound

Figure 35.1

Many jobs, such as bus and truck driving, subject people to sound levels that, over time, can be harmful to a person's hearing. OSHA works with companies to ensure that all possible precautions are taken to protect employees' hearing. However, OSHA cannot protect the hearing of people who choose to listen to loud music.

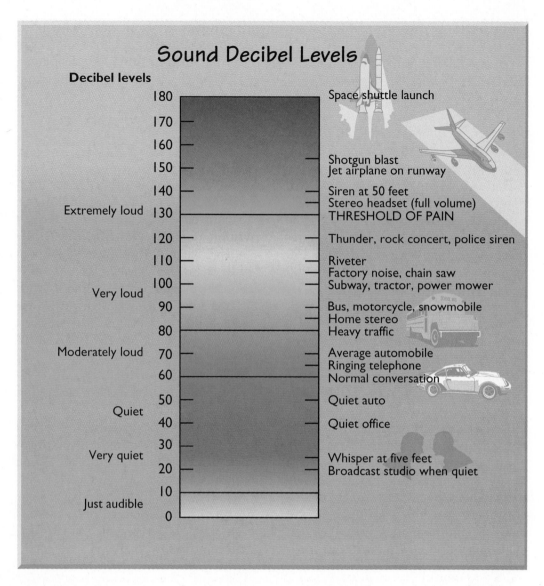

Sound Decibel Levels

Decibel levels

Decibel level	Description	Source
180		Space shuttle launch
170		
160		
150		Shotgun blast / Jet airplane on runway
140		Siren at 50 feet
130	Extremely loud	Stereo headset (full volume) / THRESHOLD OF PAIN
120		Thunder, rock concert, police siren
110		Riveter
100	Very loud	Factory noise, chain saw / Subway, tractor, power mower
90		Bus, motorcycle, snowmobile
80		Home stereo / Heavy traffic
70	Moderately loud	Average automobile / Ringing telephone
60		Normal conversation
50	Quiet	Quiet auto
40		Quiet office
30		
20	Very quiet	Whisper at five feet / Broadcast studio when quiet
10		
0	Just audible	

els, or may require companies to furnish workers with hearing protectors.

Today, many consumers, concerned about noise near their homes, are participating in local planning and development to help solve their problems. They are influencing town and state officials about where new roads and factories should be built, and some are trying to reduce noise pollution in residential neighborhoods. The EPA also works with consumers. Together, they try to help reduce noise around factories or heavy traffic areas. Some companies may not comply with government noise rules, and they can be fined or closed down until the noise is reduced.

Noise Inside the Home

Noise in the home is also becoming a major concern. People living in multifamily housing often have problems with noisy neighbors. Many of our household appliances are noisy, too. Noise in the home is usually not at a level that would cause hearing loss. It is annoying, though, and it interrupts our activities. For example, phone conversations are difficult if the noise level is

Airports are a source of noise pollution. Because of this, the government has put restrictions on the noise levels of airports, but people who live near airports still have more noise than they want. How do you think the noise levels at airports should be controlled?

above 75 db. Noise can also cause fatigue and irritability.

You Can Do Something About Noise

You can help control noise in your home in a number of ways. Above all, be considerate of others. Keep stereos, TVs, and radios at sound levels that do not disturb others. Place carpets or rugs on floors, and rubber mats under noisy appliances. Before you buy a new appliance, make sure it works quietly—then have it installed properly.

Support the efforts of groups that are concerned with noise control. For example, you may want to support the efforts of local planning groups that try to have noisy industries or transportation located away from residential areas.

Further information about controlling noise pollution is available. You may wish to contact the Federal Avia-

tion Administration, the Environmental Protection Agency, or other interested agencies.

CONSUMER PROFILE

Ben *loved* rock and roll. Fortunately for Ben, he lived near a large city where rock concerts were offered regularly. Also lucky for him, his father worked at a radio station and could get tickets for every concert that came through town. Nearly every weekend, Ben went to a rock concert. He often got seats near the front, near the speakers. As far as he was concerned, the louder the better.

Ben's parents warned him about the risk of frequent exposure to loud music. They said it could damage his hearing. Ben just said, "Yeah, yeah" and paid no attention to them. His parents asked him to wear earplugs to protect his hearing, but he never did.

Slowly, over the years, it became more difficult for Ben to hear what other people were saying. Often, he had to ask them to repeat what they said. Within ten years, Ben could no longer hear conversations on the phone. How he wished he could get his hearing back!

Much of the water in lakes, rivers, and streams is not fit for human use. It contains contaminants and, in many cases, disease-carrying organisms. Who is responsible for the condition of our water supply? What can be done to improve this situation?

WATER

Water is perhaps our most "romantic" natural resource—our oceans, lakes, and rivers have inspired countless works of art. That is fitting. After all, if there is no water, there is no life. Along with the air we breathe, water is essential for us to live.

Water is very cheap for most of us to buy. In many cities, fifteen cents will buy a ton of water for your home. Still, only 30 percent of the world's population has access to clean, piped water. Some people choose to purchase bottled water which they hope will be of better quality. Other people have to rely on wells and rivers, which may contain contaminated (impure) water—some of it may even carry organisms that cause disease.

Water Distribution

Water is a renewable resource. It circulates through the ground and enters the **hydrologic (water) cycle**, so it can be used again and again.

Although our water supplies can be used again and again, the total quantity of water available is limited. Seawater or saltwater makes up 97 percent of the supply. Only the remaining 3 percent is fresh water, and most of that is not available because it is frozen in the polar ice caps.

Further, our water supplies are not distributed evenly across the United States. For example, Southern California gets less than 1.5 percent of the state's rainfall, yet more than half of the state's population lives in that part of the state. A costly system of dams, canals, and pipelines has been built to move the water to the areas where it is needed. Because of this, people in Southern California must pay more for the water they use.

Coping with water distribution creates other problems in the preservation of our natural surroundings and wildlife. Some concerned groups of citizens object to dams and other water

hydrologic cycle
....
the sequence through which water passes from vapor in the atmosphere through precipitation and back into the atmosphere through evaporation; the water cycle

MAKING CONSUMER DECISIONS

During a recent drought, the town of Dry Gulch learned a lot about water conservation. The radio and TV aired frequent conservation announcements and tips. Citizens received educational flyers in the mail. Low-flow showerheads were available for free, and sizable rebates were offered if you installed a low-flow toilet. People were taught to not "sweep" their sidewalks with water from the garden hose. They were encouraged to not wash their cars. They were told to not leave the faucet running while they brushed their teeth. Used water from washing machines was recycled and used to water the garden. People were encouraged to stop watering their lawns. They were taught many basic facts about efficient water consumption.

The town responded very positively. Within a few months, water consumption had dropped to a third of what it had been. The town was very proud of its accomplishment. Everyone saw how wasteful their old habits had been. This low rate of water consumption continued through the following months of the drought.

When the drought was over, however, the campaign to conserve the precious resource was over, too. People drifted back into many of their old habits. They put their high-flow showerheads back on, "washed" their sidewalks again, and watered their lawns in the middle of the day when the most water is wasted. The city appeared to be happy with the increased income from people's water bills. So, all is well. Or is it? If you were in charge of this city, what would you have done at the end of the drought? Is it okay that people went back to their old habits?

projects, saying that the projects will alter the natural beauty of our waterways or threaten wildlife. These groups include the Sierra Club, Trout Unlimited, and Friends of the Earth. They were able to stop the construction of a huge dam when a threat to wildlife was discovered. Proceeding with the project would have caused a tiny variety of fish, the snaildarter, to become extinct.

Water Use in the Home

It takes about 200 gallons of water a day to support the lifestyle of the average American. About 83 gallons are used in the home. We use 24 for flushing the toilet; 32 for bathing, laundry, and dishwashing; and 25 for swimming pools and for watering the lawn. We drink about 2 gallons a day. The rest of the 200 gallons is used outside the home to produce the goods and services we use.

If you live in the city, water from your home is usually recycled through a water treatment plant. If you live in a rural area, the water is recycled by natural processes through the dumping of dirty water into the ground or a septic tank—but we must take care to avoid contaminating underground water supplies. Pesticides, paints, bleach, and other common household products that are dumped into drains or dumped on the ground contaminate our water supplies.

Water for Food Production

Producing food requires huge amounts of water. In one growing season, a single corn plant takes more than 50 gallons of water from the soil. Producing one pound of meat also requires a lot of water. It requires the water to grow ten pounds of plants, water for the animal, and water for processing the meat.

A garden requires 600 gallons of water per week for every 1,000 square feet of soil. Where rain is scarce and water rates high, you may pay a high price for your garden produce.

Water for Industry

When considering a site for building an industrial plant, investors look for a supply that is dependable and low in cost. All along our major seas and rivers, there are industrial centers that rely on water to run the plants—and they use the waterways for shipping raw materials and finished products.

Water is often used as steam heat for factories. It is used to process food, food containers, and many other consumer goods. Of course, water is used for cleaning, too.

Even goods that we don't usually think of as needing water may use large amounts. For example, it takes more than 100,000 gallons of water to produce a single automobile!

Water Pollution

In recent years, concern about the quality of our water has increased because much of our water is no longer clean and pure. Our rivers, lakes, and oceans have been polluted. The three basic sources of **water pollution** are:

- industries
- farms
- urban areas

Industrial Pollution

Over half of our water pollution can be traced to factories. Several thousand factories still dump waste water, chemicals, and other waste into our waterways. This is another area in which compromises have been made. In the past, we were especially concerned with industrial growth and not too concerned about the condition of our

Industries use large amounts of water to produce the products they sell. They also contribute to the water pollution problems in this country by dumping waste water, chemicals, and other types of waste into the water system. Should the government introduce stricter pollution standards for industries to follow?

water supply. Now that we understand the consequences of pollution, new decisions must be made.

Oil industries contribute to water pollution, too. More than 10,000 spills of oil or other hazardous substances occur each year, and oil tanker accidents pollute seawater and beaches.

Agricultural Pollution

When land is overused or used improperly, soil is washed into our streams and rivers. This becomes a problem for wildlife, and also a problem for humans who must use the water.

Farming chemicals, especially fertilizers and pesticides, present problems because these chemicals can be washed into streams, where they can poison fish and disrupt the life cycles of the stream.

Municipal Pollution

For hundreds of years, our population was small and scattered. Household sewage could be dumped directly into a river, and nature was able to handle it through its own purification process. However, the population continues to increase, and nature's ability to purify the water does not. We cannot continue our dumping practices.

We now have laws that ban the dumping of household sewage into waterways. Municipal water treatment plants are installed to process sewage and wastes, and these plants remove solid wastes and many chemicals. These plants also treat the water to ensure that it is safe for people to use. Then the water is put back into the river or lake it came from.

The amount of water a treatment plant can handle is limited. Growing cities often produce more sewage than

water treatment plants
· · · · · · ·
facilities that process sewage and wastes and remove solid wastes and many chemicals from water

Water treatment plants often cannot adequately process all of the sewage and wastes in the water being treated. This leaves some impurities in the water. Talk to someone at the water treatment plant in your area. Ask them whether there is a need for more treatment plants in your area.

their plants can treat properly, and new plants are costly to build. If a city does not have enough treatment plants, water pollution is the inevitable result.

Phosphate is another pollutant that often comes from our homes. Phosphates are natural minerals often added to household detergents to boost cleaning power. Phosphates may also come from farm drainage, animal wastes, or industrial waste.

When phosphates enter the water supply, they contribute to the growth of algae. Decomposing algae can remove oxygen from the water, causing fish to die—a process called eutrophication. It is a major problem in slow-moving waters, especially lakes. In 1958, scientists found that Lake Erie was dying from too much phosphate and sewage—so steps were taken to stop the dumping into the lake and help bring it back to life.

Population growth in coastal areas leads to increased pollution of the oceans. Worldwide, over six million tons of litter ends up in the oceans each year.

What Can We Do?

Billions of dollars have been spent on municipal water treatment plants in an attempt to improve water quality near our major cities. Laws have been passed by Congress to help improve our water. Some laws have provided money to cities for new water treatment plants, and other laws state what materials can be dumped into our waterways and in what quantities.

The enforcement of these laws is left to the states, and some states are more concerned than others. Citizens living in one state paying taxes to clean up their water rightfully complain when a neighboring state "sends its dirty water down the river" into their state.

Amendments to the Federal Water Pollution Control Act were passed in 1972, with a goal to clean up the waters of the United States by 1983. These amendments are known as the Clean Water Act. The waters were to be made clean enough for swimming and fishing. The Clean Water Act and the Water Quality Act of 1987 provided states with federal funds to:

- help communities build sewage plants
- develop additional programs to clean up water supplies
- establish stricter laws governing the use of toxic chemicals
- develop programs to control pollution in the Great Lakes and Chesapeake Bay

Many of our waters are responding to the care being taken. Their quality is better than it was ten years ago, but there is still a lot to be done.

SAVE WATER AND PREVENT POLLUTION

As a consumer, you can do a lot to protect our water. What you do can help ensure adequate and safe water supplies, now and in the future. Here are some things to do:

- Take brief showers and install low-flow showerheads.
- Don't completely fill the tub when taking a bath.
- Use a dishwasher only with a full load of dishes.
- Wash only full loads of clothes.
- Use low- or phosphate-free laundry detergents.

There are many items available to consumers that will allow you to conserve water right in your own home. Some of those items are pictured here. In some areas water companies will give rebates to customers who install water-saving devices. Do you have any of these devices in your home?

- When washing a car, use a bucket of water instead of a running hose.
- Have leaky faucets repaired.
- Install new toilets that require fewer gallons of water to flush.
- Don't throw trash into bodies of water.
- Support laws and rules that control water pollution. Urge government representatives to do the same.

You can get further information about improving and protecting our water supplies. You may contact the Environmental Protection Agency, the Department of Agriculture, or other interested organizations. (See Appendix.)

Summary

- Major sources of air pollution are: transportation (especially the automobile), industry, electric power plants, and waste disposal operations.
- Some examples of air pollutants that threaten health are: carbon monoxide, carbon dioxide, smog, lead, mercury, and asbestos.
- Some steps you can take to help correct and prevent air pollution are: stay well informed, don't buy products made by a company that pollutes, don't buy products that pollute the air, let companies know why you are not using their products, buy a car that gets good gas mileage, use public transportation or walk or ride a bike when possible, use car-pooling, cut down on the use of electricity.
- Noise pollution can harm your hearing and cause other health problems.
- The three basic sources of water pollution are: industries, farms, and urban areas.

E NRICHING YOUR VOCABULARY

Number your paper from 1–17. Beside each number, write the word or phrase that matches that definition. Choose your answers from the following list.

acid rain
air pollution
asbestos fiber
carbon monoxide
Clean Air Act
decibels (db)
emission standards

Environmental Protection
    Agency (EPA)
eutrophication
Federal Water Pollution
    Control Act
hydrologic cycle

noise
particulates
phosphates
smog
water pollution
water treatment plants

1. The combination of hydrocarbons and nitrogen oxides

2. Federal legislation to establish emission standards for air pollution

3. Unwanted sound, a form of pollution

4. Bits of solids suspended in the air

5. Facilities for the processing of sewage and wastes

6. Water cycle

7. Measure of the intensity of sound

8. Gaseous waste

9. Natural washing of chemicals from the air

10. Federal agency for enforcing the Clean Air Act

11. Impurity in the water system

12. Measure of contaminants being added to the air

13. Federal legislation setting standards of water purity

14. The removal of oxygen from the water

15. Contamination of the atmosphere

16. An air contaminant from insulation materials

17. Natural minerals that boost cleaning power of detergents

R EVIEWING WHAT YOU HAVE LEARNED

1. List four major sources of air pollution.

2. Why is air pollution greater around cities? What effect does this have on the cities and the people in them?

3. What are some results of being exposed to excessive noise?

4. Why is water important to industry?

5. List the three basic sources of water pollution.

CHAPTER REVIEW
35

USING YOUR CRITICAL THINKING SKILLS

1. Ted's car had a smoky exhaust, and Carolyn knew that installing a certain antipollution device would do much to correct the problem. Ted didn't want to buy the device. He said, "The air is already smoky—a little more smoke is not going to make any difference. I'll save my money." Carolyn told Ted that, while he might save money, everyone, including him, would end up paying. Do you agree or disagree with Ted's decision? Why? What do you think Carolyn meant?

2. You and your family are spending the summer working on remodeling your house. You are accumulating a large quantity of material that you must dispose of. Some of the materials are toxic chemicals such as paint thinner, paint stripper, etc. The simplest method of disposal would be to flush these chemicals down the drain or to throw them into your trash barrels. Are these acceptable methods of disposal? Why or why not? How else might you go about disposing of these materials?

APPLYING WHAT YOU HAVE LEARNED

1. Investigate how your area (or another area) has been affected by acid rain. Pretend you are a newspaper reporter and write an article about what you learn. Be sure the facts you present are accurate. You may wish to submit the best article to your local newspaper. The article might be considered for possible publication.

2. Gather information regarding your monthly water usage. Try to obtain this information for one year. Your family may have these records or you may be able to get them from your local water district. Create a line graph showing this information. Then do a survey of your home and your family's habits. Suggest ways in which you could conserve water.

CHAPTER 36

Consumer Use of Energy

OBJECTIVES

After completing this chapter, you will be able to do the following:
1. Explain the difference between renewable and nonrenewable energy sources, and give two examples of each.
2. Name three major groups that control energy usage.

TERMS

deregulate
hydropower
nonrenewable energy
  sources

Organization of
  Petroleum Exporting
  Countries (OPEC)
radioactive waste

regulate
renewable energy sources
solar power
thermal pollution

The people of the United States make up only about 5 percent of the world's population, yet we use more than 25 percent of the world's energy supply. The use of energy for labor-saving devices has shortened our work week and given us more time for leisure activities and the opportunity to travel. Energy keeps us warm or cool, depending on the weather and climate.

In the past fifty years, we have consumed more coal and oil than all of the people who ever lived. The energy demand in the United States is fifteen times higher than it was in 1870, but our population has only tripled.

Our energy supplies have not kept up with our energy demands, and in recent times we have imported up to 50 percent of our gas and oil. In the 1970s, countries that supplied oil either stopped or reduced their shipments and raised their prices. As a result, American consumers took a closer look at how we use or misuse energy.

ENERGY RESOURCES

All energy resources can be divided into two groups: renewable and nonrenewable. Today, we rely on nonrenewable sources for most of our energy.

Nonrenewable Energy Sources

Nonrenewable energy sources can be used up. These include coal, oil, natural gas, and uranium.

Coal. We have large deposits of coal in the United States, but there are disadvantages to its use. When coal is burned, ash and sulfur dioxide are re-leased into the air. Coal is also expensive to transport.

Underground mining of coal is hazardous—and strip-mining, which accounts for 50 percent of our coal production, causes erosion and can leave ugly scars on the land unless we spend money to restore it.

On the other hand, coal is one of the most versatile fuels. It can be burned as a solid, or it can be changed to a liquid or gas. Until 1940, coal was our major source of energy. Even today, it is used to generate more than 40 percent of our electricity.

Oil. Our oil supply is in danger. If we continue to use it at the present rate, unless we find new sources, we will run out of oil in the United States in less than 100 years. About half of the oil we use in the United States is imported, and that supply can be cut off at any time by suppliers.

We use 60 percent of our oil supply for transportation, mainly by converting oil to gasoline. We burn 20 percent of our oil for home heating and 10 percent for generating electricity.

There are several ways to take more oil from the earth, but some of these ways are costly. Oil can be produced from shale, for example, through a very expensive process. Oil supplies under the ocean floor may be tapped, but these supplies are difficult to reach, so obtaining this oil would be expensive. We as consumers could expect much of the cost to be passed on to us. Accidental spills can pollute our oceans and beaches, and spills are costly in two ways. First, we lose the oil; then, we must pay for the cleanup. Plant and animal life may also be affected.

Natural Gas. One of the fuels that have been low in cost is natural gas, because government controls have kept the price low. Gas is in great demand for home use because it is clean, and it

nonrenewable energy sources
....
energy resources, such as coal, oil, and natural gas, that can be used up

is easy to transport to homes through pipelines.

Today, oil and gas are used where coal and wood once were used, and using oil and gas has reduced the smoke and ash in the air. When oil and gas are burned, however, they give off chemical fumes and other pollutants. Here we see another trade-off.

Nuclear Reaction. Uranium 235, a metallic element that is mined, is used to generate nuclear energy, which is used mainly in running electric generators. One ounce of U-235 has more energy potential than 375 barrels of oil.

A fuel that can produce so much energy from such a small supply may seem ideal, but it has some big disadvantages. Accidents could leak radiation into the environment, and we have not found a sure way to dispose of **radioactive waste** safely.

We can bury the waste, but sometimes this affects underground water supplies. Dumping it in the sea creates hazards to sea life and to people on ships, and it may affect seafood that we eat. Storing the waste creates problems, too, because radioactive materials can remain dangerous for thousands of years. Can we keep people away from them for that long? People in nuclear energy production are working now to solve disposal problems.

Nuclear energy also creates a danger of **thermal pollution**. The huge nuclear reactors become extremely hot and they must be cooled down with water. The water itself becomes hot during this process. If it is dumped into our lakes and rivers, it can raise the temperature enough to kill some fish and perhaps upset the balance of life in the water. When cooling towers are used in nuclear plants, hot water is not

thermal pollution
....
the release of heated liquid into a body of water at a temperature that is damaging to the environment

radioactive waste
....
the unwanted and highly dangerous byproduct that occurs after a nuclear reaction

Environmentalists test the levels of impurities in the air and water. They devise ways to control the spread of undesirable materials in the environment. How concerned are you about pollution? What things have you done to help control the pollution in your area?

dumped, and the possibility of thermal water pollution is lessened.

Renewable Energy Sources

Some sources of energy are never used up. These are renewable energy sources such as the sun (solar energy) and moving water (hydropower).

Today we use solar power for limited home and water heating, but sun power might be harnessed more effectively. If it were, it would go far to meet our future energy needs.

Solar energy is attractive because the supply is not only unlimited but also pollution free. Installing solar power equipment is costly, but it reduces electric and gas bills. As a result, consumers usually find solar power worthwhile. The major problem with solar energy is that it is difficult to store for later use.

Hydropower is created by the movement of water. Dams in many parts of the United States create artificial waterfalls to generate power, and about 15 percent of our electricity is generated in this manner. Hydropower is safe for the environment, but we can do little to expand this source of energy.

Alternative fuel sources may help meet our future needs, but we need to develop better, more economical ways of producing or using them. For instance, solid wastes (trash) could be burned, and this could provide part of a city's electricity. It would get rid of waste and generate power at the same time, but it could pollute the air. Brooklyn, New York, is one large city now using incineration (burning) of waste to heat water. The ash that is left can be used as fertilizer.

Alternative fuel can be made from carbohydrates. For example, plant stalks, corn, or sea algae can be converted to alcohol in order to fuel auto-

hydropower
• • • • • • • • • • •
power caused by the movement of water

renewable energy sources
• • • • • • • • •
energy resources, such as the sun and moving water, that are never used up

solar power
• • • • • • • • • • •
energy derived from the sun

Experiments have been conducted with wind farms in California and other places. Wind farms are built on land that is considered useless and in areas that have continuous wind. Are there any wind farms in your area?

mobiles. Synthetic fuel can be produced from coal and from oil shale—but, at least for now, these fuels are expensive to produce.

Methane gas can be produced by breaking down organic matter, so human and animal wastes could be used as a fuel source. Many people are studying the possible harnessing of wind for its power, and windmills that can provide enough electricity to light thirty houses have already been built. Geothermal energy from naturally hot water under the earth's surface might also be used.

We may be able to make these alternative energy sources practical. If we could do so while continuing to practice conservation, our future energy supplies might be assured.

For more information about renewable energy sources, contact the Department of Energy or other related sources. Addresses are given in the Appendix.

Using Energy Sources

In 1994, more than 132,000,000,000 gallons of gasoline were used by motor vehicles in the United States, and gasoline use is increasing every year. Gasoline consumption is the single largest use of our energy resources, and heating and cooling our houses is the second largest use of energy.

Much of our energy is used to produce electricity, and any of the fuels we've talked about could be used in this process. It involves heating water to make steam, which turns turbines to generate electricity—which is a clean source of energy, but its production does result in some loss of energy. Whenever we convert energy from one form to another, some of it is wasted. For example, coal may be burned to produce electricity, but the electricity will not supply as much energy as the coal used to generate it.

Who Controls Energy Use? Consumers, government, and industry all influence the amount and type of energy used. As consumers, we can conserve energy by building energy-efficient houses, or we can move closer to our work to cut down on energy used for transportation. About two-fifths of all the energy used per person in the United States is under our direct control. We can control how often we drive our cars. We can choose how many lights we turn on or what kind of light bulbs we use. We can also decide how we heat and cool our homes.

We do not have full control of the remaining three-fifths of the energy we use, but we do have some influence. Our own expectations, in large part, determine how well lit our streets will be. Our expectations (or demand) determine how much food and goods should be transported to us from faraway places.

The products that we choose to produce have an enormous effect on the amount of energy that is used. For example, in just one year, U.S. farmers use over ten million tons of ammonia fertilizer. To produce just one ton, enough natural gas is burned to heat an average home for two-and-a-half months.

Government and industry can also save energy. Industry can recycle materials and water used in factories. Governments can provide efficient mass transit and encourage consumers to save energy. For example, the federal government has given tax benefits for home improvements that save energy. Installation of solar-powered heating units is an example of the kind of change the government has encouraged with tax benefits. Some governments in other countries place a very high tax on gasoline to encourage people to conserve.

All groups in our country can influence our energy future—but as a consumer, you have the final decision as to how much energy you will use.

Who Controls Energy Costs? About sixty years ago, major countries of the world met their energy needs from their own supplies, but today that is not the case. For example, the world has become heavily dependent on oil—but oil reserves are not distributed evenly around the world. A few countries have most of them. The ten major oil-producing countries banded together to form the **Organization of Petroleum Exporting Countries (OPEC).** OPEC countries have tried to agree on the price of oil, and their fixed price directly affects our economy.

Our own government also influences the cost of natural gas and oil as it **regulates** (controls) or **deregulates** prices (removes the controls). Deregulating prices allows the demand for the product to determine the supply and cost. When supplies are low, prices can go up—then companies will have more money to find additional sources. When supplies increase, prices can go down. In recent years, the prices of natural gas and oil were deregulated to increase the supplies by encouraging exploration for new sources. It also had the effect of driving up the price paid by the consumer.

Some states have utility commissions that control the price of all public utilities, including gas and electricity. The utility companies must provide information to the commission about their expenses and profits. Then the utility commission either approves or denies requests for rate increases. Generally, consumers have a chance to present their views about rates to the commission.

Homes are being built that contain many energy saving devices such as more efficient heating and cooling systems. Look at the checklist on the following pages. Which of the suggestions listed could you do to improve the energy efficiency of your home?

Commissions may also have the power to set other policies for the utility companies. For example, some states have special policies to protect consumers in the winter. Some consumers might not be able to pay their bills. For consumers whose yearly income is below a certain level (which changes yearly), *Lifeline* rates have been established so that utility companies may not be allowed to shut off gas or electricity during cold weather.

ENERGY CONSERVATION

New sources of energy are becoming harder to find, so it is important for us to conserve as much of our present energy as we can. We are already taking measures that affect our lifestyles. Just a few years ago, most of the cars on our highways were big "gas guzzlers" that traveled only eight or ten miles on a gallon of gas. Today, we expect cars

Organization of Petroleum Exporting Countries (OPEC)
....
the ten major oil-producing countries that have banded together and agreed on the price of oil

regulate
....
to establish restrictions or controls

deregulate
....
to remove restrictions or controls

CHECKLIST FOR ENERGY-SAVING HOUSING UNITS

Housing can be designed and built with many energy-saving features. You might be able to incorporate these features in a brand-new housing unit, or you may want to check for them before buying an existing unit. Most of these features can also be added to a unit that is already owned. Consider the following energy-saving features:

___ insulation in attic, at least six inches thick

___ insulation in outside walls, at least three and a half inches thick

___ insulation in floors

___ insulation in basement walls

___ caulking and weather stripping around windows and doors

___ storm doors

___ automatic setback on thermostats (for sleeping hours)

___ energy-efficient furnace and air conditioning

___ solar heating and cooling

___ energy-efficient water heater

___ small windows

___ adequate attic ventilation

___ trees for shade or windbreak

___ proper orientation of housing unit

You Can Help Conserve Energy

Heating
- Keep all parts of the home-heating system clean.
- Turn the thermostat to its lowest setting when you are gone for more than a day.
- Lower the thermostat to no more than sixty-eight degrees Fahrenheit (twenty degrees Celsius) for the day. Keep it at sixty degrees Fahrenheit (sixteen degrees Celsius) or lower for the night (10:00 P.M. to 6:00 A.M.).
- Use an electric blanket at night so you can reduce room heating.
- Use drapes or insulated shades.
- Heat only those rooms you use frequently.
- Use a fireplace sparingly.
- Make sure windows and doors close tightly.
- Change furnace filters often.
- Insulate your home and consider solar heating.
- Use storm windows.

Air-conditioning
- Adjust room air-conditioner vents upward where the air is warmer.
- Close heating system registers when using a room air conditioner.
- Avoid unnecessary lighting.
- Use shades and drapes to keep out the sun and retain the cooled air.
- Keep windows closed and use doors sparingly.

- Turn off air-conditioning when you are gone for several days.
- Set air-conditioning thermostats no lower than seventy-eight degrees Fahrenheit (twenty-six degrees Celsius).

Lighting
- Make the best use of natural lighting.
- Avoid excessive lighting.
- Install three-way bulbs.
- Dust light fixtures regularly.
- Turn off incandescent lights when you leave a room, even if only for a few minutes.
- Use fluorescent tubes in home lighting fixtures where possible.

Refrigerators and Freezers
- Plan to take out or put in as many items at one time as you can.
- Defrost non-frost-free models often enough to avoid excessive ice buildup. The ice can act as an insulator.
- Keep freezers and freezer compartments filled.
- Cover foods.

Dishwashers
- Wash only full loads.
- Allow dishes to air-dry when possible.

Ovens and Ranges
- Use as little water as possible to cook food.
- Use a pan that fits the size of the burner.
- Boil water in a covered pot.
- Bake as many items at one time as you can.
- Consider using a microwave oven.
- Do not preheat the broiler or the oven unless absolutely necessary.
- Do not use your range or oven to heat the kitchen.
- If you have a pressure cooker, use it whenever possible.
- Use smaller cooking appliances, such as toaster-oven, crockpot, electric frying pan, instead of the range.
- Keep the oven door closed while baking.

Clothes Washers and Dryers
- Use the least amount of water for the washing job to be done.
- Do not overload your washer.
- Use warm or cold water instead of hot water whenever possible.
- Clean the lint filter after each load.
- Try to run the dryer only when you have full loads.
- Do not overdry the clothes.

Hot Water
- Set the water heater temperature no hotter than needed.
- Use insulation around the water heater.
- Use hot water sparingly.

Manufacturers have responded to the energy problem by improving the efficiency of their products. Large appliances such as refrigerators have an energy guide that tells how energy efficient the products are. Visit an appliance store near you and read the energy guides on some products. What type of information is listed?

to be smaller and more fuel efficient. In our cities, huge houses often were homes to single families. Now, many of these homes are being turned into apartments for several families.

Energy Conservation in the Home

The average American home uses the equivalent of thirty-five barrels of crude oil each year. In the past, energy was cheap, which allowed us to design and construct buildings with little regard for energy usage. Today, energy is costly, but we can take many steps to reduce energy costs. The checklist on pages 410–411 offers some suggestions, most of which can be applied easily regardless of your type of housing.

Water heating, air-conditioning, lighting, and appliances account for part of the energy use in our homes—but the major portion is for heating. So we must try hardest to conserve in that area. When the cost of oil was low, we might have set our thermostats at seventy-five degrees on chilly winter days. Now we try to keep the temperature in the sixties and put on a sweater. We can expect to make more changes like this, gradually, well into the future.

Summary

- All energy resources are either renewable and nonrenewable. Today, we rely on nonrenewable sources (such as coal, oil, natural gas, and uranium) for most of our energy.
- The sun (solar energy) and moving water (hydropower) are two examples of renewable energy sources.
- Gasoline consumption is the largest use of our energy resources. Heating and cooling our houses is the second largest.
- There are many things each of us can do to help conserve energy and protect the environment.

E NRICHING YOUR VOCABULARY

Use the following words or phrases to complete the sentences below. Write the completed sentences on your paper.

hydropower
nonrenewable energy sources
OPEC

radioactive waste
regulate and deregulate
renewable energy sources

solar power
thermal pollution

1. Moving water and the sun are examples of
2. Coal, oil, and natural gas are examples of
3. One disadvantage of nuclear power is the safe disposal of
4. The price of oil throughout the world is controlled by
5. One nonpolluting source of power is
6. Governments control energy prices as they
7. Dams are built to create
8. Industries that use large quantities of water for cooling create

R EVIEWING WHAT YOU HAVE LEARNED

1. What is the difference between renewable and nonrenewable energy sources? Give at least two examples of each.
2. What three major groups control energy usage?

U SING YOUR CRITICAL THINKING SKILLS

1. How does the use of energy affect your way of life? Compare with your classmates the types of energy sources used for heating and cooling your homes, for cooking, and for various other activities. Discuss the advantages and disadvantages of using the various types.
2. Together with your classmates, make a list of ways to conserve energy.

A PPLYING WHAT YOU HAVE LEARNED

1. How has pollution affected your community? Investigate the extent of land, air, or water pollution (choose one) in your community and what the effects have been. Prepare a report on what you learn, including costs (such as for cleanup) wherever possible.

UNIT

13

PERSONAL AND CAREER DEVELOPMENT

CHAPTERS

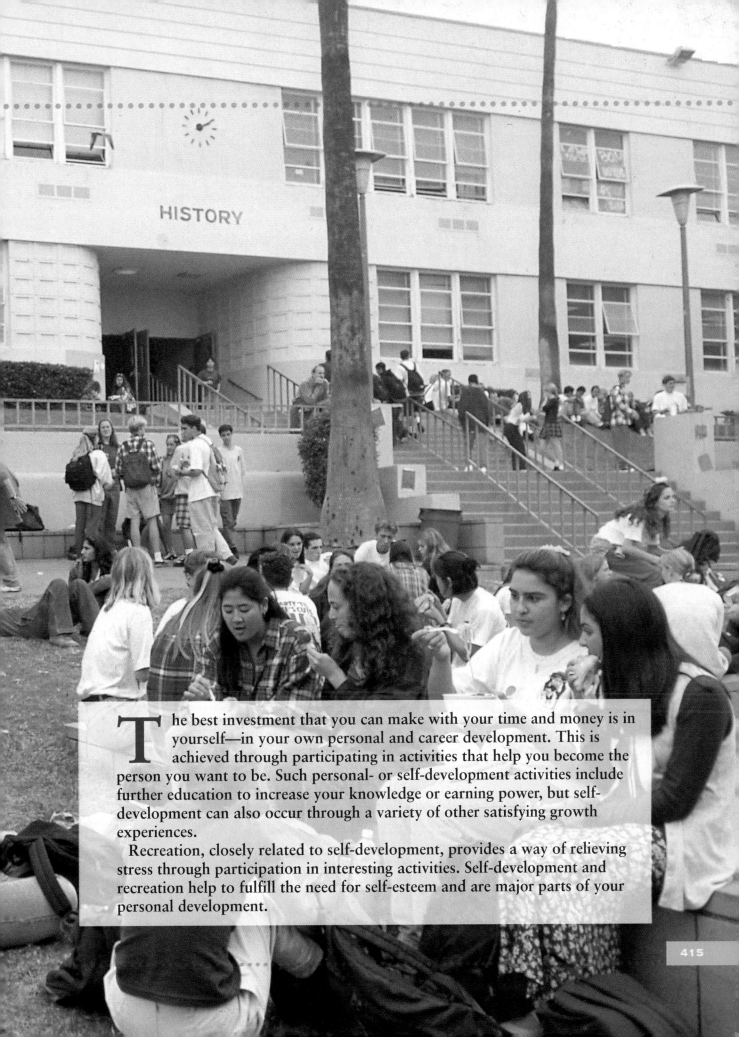

HISTORY

The best investment that you can make with your time and money is in yourself—in your own personal and career development. This is achieved through participating in activities that help you become the person you want to be. Such personal- or self-development activities include further education to increase your knowledge or earning power, but self-development can also occur through a variety of other satisfying growth experiences.

Recreation, closely related to self-development, provides a way of relieving stress through participation in interesting activities. Self-development and recreation help to fulfill the need for self-esteem and are major parts of your personal development.

415

CHAPTER 37

Lifestyle and Careers

OBJECTIVES

After completing this chapter, you will be able to do the following:
1. Name the five elements that make up lifestyle.
2. Explain how people can identify careers related to their interests.
3. Explain how a person can discover his or her aptitudes.
4. Define the process of setting a realistic goal.
5. List four ways of obtaining information on careers.
6. List eight things one should consider when gathering information about careers.

TERMS

aptitude
fringe benefits
interest inventory

Occupational Outlook Handbook
work environment

Life is full of activities and relationships, and the way we spend our time and money in these activities and relationships is what we call lifestyle. We hear a lot about lifestyle on TV or read about it in popular magazines, about how our lifestyles are changing—but as we consider lifestyle, there are really only two kinds of people. There are those who actively make their own lifestyles, and those who just let happenstance determine their lifestyle.

DEVELOPING A LIFESTYLE

People who make their own lifestyles look ahead, do some *dreaming about* the future, then *plan* for their futures. They set realistic goals and accept the responsibility for developing their own lifestyles. They *take control* of their lives. Others do some dreaming about parts of their lifestyles, but they don't understand the relationship between responsibility and lifestyle, and they don't set realistic goals. Instead of *making their own* lifestyle, they just let things happen. Lifestyles do change,

faster for some than for others, but those of us who are assertive enough to take control of our lives early in life are much more likely to satisfy the higher levels of human need.

The Elements of Lifestyle

For most people, our lifestyle consists of five types of relationships, or lifestyle elements, as follows:

- family
- friends
- leisure activities
- spiritual well-being
- work (career)

Our lifestyle elements are interconnected and each element affects the others. The last element, work, is where many of us don't really take control of our lives. Surveys indicate that more than half of working adults have not planned the development of their careers, but have simply accepted whatever jobs were available that paid enough to cover living costs and seemed like bearable work activity.

All of the activities we do, whether or not we like them, make up our lifestyle. Hobbies such as cooking, computer keyboarding classes, and even walking the dog in the evening all make up lifestyle. Have you given any thought to your lifestyle? Are you satisfied with your lifestyle? If not, what changes do you plan to make?

Whether by our own design or by chance, the time and money we invest in each lifestyle element varies greatly. Some of us become so career oriented that we neglect our families and have no time for recreation. Some are so content with family relationships that they don't reach out to make other friends. Lifestyle "patterns" have been used to illustrate various preferences for different lifestyle elements. (See Figure 37.1.)

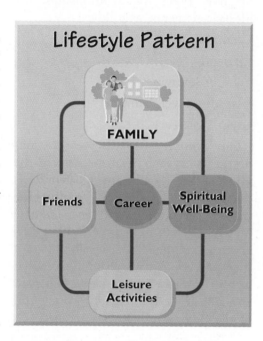

The money we earn pays for the necessities of life: food and water, housing, safety, clothing, health care, and education. Many of us make friends among those we meet in our work activities, and this helps fulfill our need for companionship. In addition to meeting these basic needs, the work we do helps provide our identity as a person. A teacher is called a *teacher*, not someone who *works at teaching*. In a social setting, when we introduce people, we might say, "This is Sarah Peterson. Sarah's an engineer." We wouldn't say that Sarah works at engineering. In fact, the work we do has such an impact on our lives that some well-known psychologists have said work *determines* a person's way of life.

You probably accept the fact that the kinds of work we do have an important impact on lifestyle, but have you thought about how long this influence continues? Once we change our identities from students to workers, work will continue to influence, even control, our lifestyles for the rest of our lives.

During our working years, the time devoted to work and related activities accounts for half of our waking hours. Students in high school today can expect to work outside the home for twenty-five to forty-five years. Many women (and some men) will interrupt careers while their children are young and then, after several years, return to jobs outside the home. Only a small percentage will never enter the job market at all.

WORK—ITS EFFECT ON LIFESTYLE

Did you notice that work (career) is at the center of the lifestyle pattern? That's because our work tends to be the central activity around which we plan our daily lives. In fact, the work we do to earn a living helps fulfill all of the five basic human needs discussed in Chapter 2.

Career Planning

In early America, people had little choice of careers. Sons learned the kind of work done by their fathers and continued in those occupations all their lives. Few women worked outside the home. Now, many more career choices are available, and career planning has become an essential part of each person's decision of what he or she wants.

Yet, many adults working today did very little career planning. Some spent more time planning a summer vacation or even a one-night party than they spent planning a working career. Because work is such an important part of life, for so long, shouldn't we do all we can to make our working lives as pleasant and rewarding as possible? This takes planning.

MAKING CAREER DECISIONS

There are many decisions that you will have to make as you prepare for the world of work. But before you can make these decisions, you will have to do some investigation. To begin, you need to learn some things about yourself, investigate some career fields, and set some goals. Along the way, you will want to pick up some job-hunting skills. For example, do you know how to locate and apply for a job? You may decide to find a part-time or summer job to get some experience.

Getting to Know Yourself

Although you will have to make many decisions as you near the time when you begin full-time employment, the most important one is probably your choice of a career goal. Your career goal will determine where and for how long you will go to college or pursue other post-high school education. So, before you get too involved in researching the demands and rewards of a variety of careers, spend some time taking inventory of yourself. Consider your lifestyle preferences for the future,

It's difficult to think about a career if you aren't sure of your own likes and abilities. If you are concerned about the environment and like being outdoors, maybe a career as an environmentalist would suit you. Take time to think about what the ideal job situation would be for you.

along with your values, interests, aptitudes, and personality.

Daydream Your Future Lifestyle. Picture yourself five years from now. What lifestyle activities and relationships would be most satisfying? Extend your "dreaming" some ten, then twenty years, and imagine the lifestyle you would find most satisfying. If it's a frugal lifestyle, then perhaps earning a lot of money is not important to you. If your lifestyle goal looks expensive, then you will want to consider careers that provide good incomes. This look into the future may also reflect some of your present interests.

Consider Your Values. Until we are about fifteen or sixteen, our values are generally adopted from what's important to other family members. Then, through observation and thought, we begin setting our own values.

The work you do to earn a living should not conflict with your basic values. Such a conflict can cause a lot of frustration, and the stress may eventually be harmful to your health. For example, if spending time at home with your family is especially important to you, you might be unhappy in a job that required long periods away from home. If attending Sunday church services is especially important to you, you probably wouldn't choose a career that required you to work on Sundays.

The following are among the basic values often considered important (also see Chapter 2). How would you rank them, in order of what is important to you?

- fame
- wealth
- power

- religion

- family (happy home life)
- health
- aesthetics (appreciation of fine arts)
- creativity (inventiveness)

- friendships
- humanitarianism (helpfulness to others)

Think about the kind of work done by adult family members and adult friends. Is there someone you know who does work that would make you happy? What kind of work would make you unhappy because of your values?

Consider Your Interests. Your present interests can provide clues to the kind of work activities you would find interesting. Of course, interests tend to change a little over the years, especially because they depend on what you've been exposed to. You may never have been exposed to certain kinds of work or leisure activities—so you really don't know whether you would find those activities interesting. The most useful kind of exposure, of course, is to actually experience work activities that you think might be interesting. Many

Working with children can be a very fulfilling and rewarding career. However, it's not for everyone. Is working with children something you like to do? If so, there are probably many volunteer opportunities that will allow you to work with children.

young people do this through volunteer work or a school-sponsored work-experience program. Instead of working at a minimum-wage job in a fast-food restaurant, they accept non-paid assignments that give them a chance to rub elbows with workers and try out work activities in careers they are considering for their own life's work. After they've tried out the work activities of several careers, they are better prepared to make realistic career choices.

Many interests develop as a result of classes taken in high school, college, or adult education programs. Sometimes recreational activities point the way to a satisfying career. You may have doubts about how your interests relate to choosing a career goal. If so, you might benefit from an **interest inventory**, which is much like a test, except that there are no right or wrong answers. Ask your teacher or counselor if you may take an interest or activity preference inventory.

Discover Your Aptitudes. An **aptitude** is a capacity for learning, a talent. If you have an aptitude for math, it probably didn't take you long to learn the basics of mathematics. Mental aptitudes, as for reading, math, and science, may be indicated by the grades you earn in school. Some physical aptitudes are indicated by speed, coordination, and strength on the athletic field.

Many specialized aptitudes necessary to learn certain job skills are not easily recognized. For example, do you know whether you have good spatial and form perception—aptitudes that would make it easier for you to learn drafting and architecture? You may have aptitudes for a variety of skills, and learning about them is helpful when you consider career goals. An aptitude test can help you identify your aptitudes.

Many schools provide aptitude tests when students request them. If your school doesn't, you may take the General Aptitude Test Battery at your local office of the Department of Employment. This test battery measures several different kinds of aptitudes; and after the test has been scored, the results will be explained to you. You will also learn how your aptitudes relate to success in a variety of careers.

Appraise Your Personality. An honest appraisal of your own personality is also important in considering which career goals would be realistic. Some careers, such as sales, require an outgoing personality because you would have contact with a lot of people. There are other careers, such as scientific research or computer programming, that involve less contact with people. So examine your preference for working with other people, data, or things.

Of course, many other elements of personality affect the ability to succeed in a career. Among these are willingness to do a full day's work for a day's pay, and a genuine desire to succeed. Others are common sense, courtesy, a sense of humor, honesty, effective use of voice, and care for personal appearance.

Researching Careers

Setting a realistic career goal is a matching process. You match your unique set of needs and traits with the demands and rewards of a career. After you have taken inventory of yourself, you will be ready to consider some career fields.

Where to Look. Before studying any careers in depth, look at the broad range of careers. You've picked up bits of information about many careers from personal observation in daily life and through movies, TV, books, and magazine articles. If you have taken an interest inventory or an aptitude test,

interest inventory
....
a type of nongraded test that helps pinpoint and rank a person's favorite activities or interests

aptitude
....
a natural ability for learning; talent

Talking with people you come in contact with often, such as store owners and professional people, can give you some good ideas about careers. Ask people what about their job they like most and what they like least. You might start with members of your family or friends. Does anyone you know have a job that you find interesting?

you have probably learned about some careers you hadn't thought about before. Reading books about careers can help. In some books, all occupations are organized into clusters (groups), such as business, medical, and communications careers.

There are many ways of looking at careers, but the most efficient way is to begin with a look at the big picture—clusters of related careers. Then, narrow your focus to several specific careers for careful study.

There are also several ways to research specific careers. You can read about them in the *Occupational Outlook Handbook*. Your counselor or librarian probably has a copy. If your school has a career information center, many kinds of career information are available: books, pamphlets, perhaps even filmstrips or movies.

People to See. You can get firsthand information on a career that seems interesting by interviewing someone who works in that career. For example, engineering and journalism

There are many publications that will give you an idea about what careers are available, the requirements for the job, outlook, and many other details about the job. Check with your school or city library for these publications and spend some time reading. You may find a job that interests you that you didn't even know existed!

Occupational Outlook Handbook

....

a government publication that is updated every two years, which describes about 250 occupations in detail

may be fields that you would like to learn more about. If so, call up an engineer and a journalist. If you are hesitant to do this, ask your counselor or work-experience coordinator to help. When you call a person about his or her career, mention your interest in the career and ask for an appointment to discuss his or her career and the work he or she does. Most people are happy to share their feelings as well as facts about their careers.

Questions to Ask. Before your appointment, outline the questions that you will want to ask. (See Figure 37.2.) The following items are usually important in matching your needs and traits to any career goal:

- *Duties and responsibilities*–What work activities and responsibilities are required of those in this career?
- *Aptitudes and abilities*–What skills are required for beginning workers?

Career Decisions and Goals

Comparison of Needs/Traits with Career Demands and Rewards

Career Under Consideration _____

Career Activities

My Preferences _____   Career Duties and Responsibilities _____
_____   _____
_____   _____
_____   _____

Data-People-Things

My Preferences _____   On-the-Job Relationships _____
_____   _____
_____   _____
_____   _____

Aptitudes and Skills

My Strengths _____   Needed in this Career _____
_____   _____
_____   _____
_____   _____

Personal Qualities

My Strengths _____   Needed in this Career _____
_____   _____
_____   _____
_____   _____

Education and Training

Before Entering Career, I Will Have   Required for Entry in this Career
Completed _____   _____
_____   _____
_____   _____

Lifestyle Goals

My Lifestyle Goals _____   Beginning Salary _____
_____   Salary After 5 years _____
_____   Salary After 10-15 years _____
_____   Hours of Work _____
_____   Conditions of Work _____
_____   Outlook (need for workers in this career
_____   during the next 5, 10, 20 years) _____
_____

Figure 37.2
....
You may want to copy the information in this figure onto another sheet of paper and use it when you are researching careers. The Occupational Outlook Handbook *will give you information about many of the things listed here for many different careers. Other information you may get from taking an interest inventory or aptitude test.*

In which jobs are certain aptitudes considered helpful?

- *Education and training*–What kind and how much education and training are required of beginning workers? Is more training required for advancement? Where can the needed education and training be obtained, and at what cost?
- *Data-people-things*–Do those in this field work mainly with data (facts), people, or things, or combinations of two or all three of these?
- *Personal qualities*–What personal qualities are important for someone to become successful in this career?
- *Work environment* –Where is the work done? What are the working conditions?

- *Salaries and fringe benefits*–What is the average beginning salary? About how much is the salary after working for five, ten, or fifteen years? What are the **fringe benefits**? These may include vacations, company-paid insurance, and other benefits besides salary.
- *Career outlook*–What is the expected need for new people in this field? Where will the jobs be? Will the demand for workers continue?

Analyzing Information. After you have researched the careers that interest you, begin to match your needs and traits with the demands and rewards of each career. Review your notes from your inventory of needs and traits, and compare them with notes on career de-

fringe benefits
....

something, such as vacations or company-paid insurance, that is provided by an employer, which is above and beyond the salary

work environment
....

the place a job is done, which includes the people, conditions, and equipment involved in the job

Making Consumer Decisions

Rudy was a law student with a wife and a young daughter with whom he loved spending time. On weekends, when he wasn't doing something with his family, Rudy really enjoyed mountain climbing with his buddies. When he graduated from law school, Rudy was hired by a very successful law firm at a rather high salary. He was excited about his new job and ready to work hard to be successful.

In the first week of his new job, Rudy's boss asked him to work on the weekend to "complete a critically important" project for a meeting on Monday. Rudy didn't like the idea that he would miss the weekend with his family, and he had planned a climb for Sunday; but he wanted to please his boss, so he said yes. He thought that his willingness would make a good impression and that it might earn him some "points" on his three-month evaluation.

On that weekend, Rudy found that most of the other lawyers in the firm were there, too. He started to notice, during the week, that few of the others took lunch breaks. One evening, he stayed late to finish something and when he left the office, he noticed that many of the other lawyers were still there. Finally, he pulled one of the newer lawyers aside to discuss this. This lawyer said, "What you have seen is how it is. The *only* way to get ahead in this firm is to work your tail off. That means evenings and weekends. Most of the lawyers here have no time for hobbies or leisure and spend little time with their wives. You'll be well rewarded for your work—steady increases in salary, lots of fringe benefits, fame, and fortune. You'll get used to it."

Of course, Rudy wants to be successful in his career and to do well at his first job, but his family and leisure time are also important. What should Rudy do? Describe a plan of action you would advise for Rudy.

mands and rewards. Analyzing all this information to see what would be the best match is sometimes easier if you make a comparison chart. Even so, you may not be comfortable with what appears to be the best match on paper. Often, it's best to narrow the choice of careers down to two or three, then continue to gather information for months or even years before reaching your decision.

The Value of Work Experience. Even after thorough research, you may not be sure about a career choice, and an excellent way of getting more information on specific careers is through part-time or volunteer work. If your school has a work-experience program, ask the coordinator for assistance in locating a paying or nonpaying job in a career field that you want to learn more about. Many schools can set up nonpaid *exploratory* work-experience assignments in local businesses that allow you to try out many of the work activities of a career. Because the company is not paying you a salary, you are allowed to explore a variety of work activities. Even after you have made your career choice, working in the career of your choice can provide valuable experience.

Gaining work experience now can be a great advantage later. Volunteer or paid work experience can help you know what types of careers you like and dislike. It can also be a source of background experience for future careers. Are you participating in a work experience program now? If not, talk with your school counselor or work experience coordinator about getting involved in a program.

Summary

- Lifestyle is made up of all your activities and relationships.

- Those people who are assertive, who take charge of their lives and plan for their futures, are much more likely to feel satisfied with their lives.

- There are five elements to lifestyle: family, friends, leisure activities, spiritual well-being, and work.

- Work tends to be the central activity of our daily lives and helps provide our identity as a person.

- Career planning is essential to making our working lives pleasant and rewarding.

- Choosing a career goal is one of the most important decisions you will make about yourself.

- It is important to match your values, interests, and aptitudes to your choice of work.

- When researching careers, some valuable resources are books, pamphlets, and people already working in the field.

- An excellent way of getting more information about a specific career is to do part-time or volunteer work in that field.

CHAPTER REVIEW
37

ENRICHING **Y**OUR **V**OCABULARY

Number your paper from 1–5. Beside each number write the word from the following list, along with a brief definition.

aptitude
fringe benefits
interest inventory

Occupational Outlook Handbook
work environment

REVIEWING **W**HAT **Y**OU **H**AVE **L**EARNED

1. Name the five elements that make up lifestyle.

2. By what means can people identify careers related to their interests?

3. How can a person discover his or her aptitudes?

4. Define the process of setting a career goal.

5. List four ways of obtaining information on careers.

6. What eight things should be considered when gathering information about careers?

USING **Y**OUR **C**RITICAL **T**HINKING **S**KILLS

1. Why is work considered the central activity of lifestyle for most people?

2. With other members of your class, develop a list of things to do during the summer to give you experience that would be helpful in researching careers. Your list can include paying jobs, volunteer work, recreation, and education. The activities could be aimed at specific job-related skills or general personal development.

APPLYING **W**HAT **Y**OU **H**AVE **L**EARNED

1. Interview two people who work in different careers. Include these questions in your interviews:

   a. What are the usual work activities in this career?

   b. What are the usual working conditions?

   c. What is the beginning salary?

   d. What are the opportunities for advancement?

   e. What education and training are required?

   f. What special aptitudes or skills are required or helpful?

   g. What are the main benefits of working in this career?

   h. What are the main disadvantages?

   i. Will there likely be a demand for workers in this career during the next five, ten, or fifteen years?

CHAPTER 38

Finding and Applying for a Job

OBJECTIVES

After completing this chapter, you will be able to do the following:
1. Name five sources of leads for job openings.
2. List what types of information should be noted when you hear about a job opening.
3. Name three things you should bring along when job hunting.

TERMS

application form
employment agency
interview

job lead
job lead card

personal data sheet
work permit

Many young people, when they decide they want a job, begin by going from door to door, but this is not an efficient way to find a job. Whether you are looking for your first full-time job after you are out of school or a part-time job while you are in high school, a little planning will save you a lot of time.

In this chapter, you will learn some proven methods that will make your job hunt both more efficient and effective. You will learn where to look for job leads, how to follow them up with an application, and how to prepare for and conduct yourself in a job interview.

FINDING JOB OPENINGS

Begin by finding some job leads—information about where there are jobs available. Then you can spend your time applying for jobs that you already

know exist. The first step is to talk with everyone you know who might produce a job lead. Follow up all leads, even if someone gives you incomplete information. Usually, it just requires a couple of phone calls to fill in the missing information. Finding the right job requires finding as many job leads as possible and then following up promptly on each one.

Good sources of information about job openings are your own family and friends. They may hear about job openings where they work. They may have other adult friends who know of a company that is looking for someone with your qualifications. Have you ever wondered whether it is appropriate to contact influential family friends when looking for a job? It is of course, if you are qualified to do the work. Most businesses don't advertise many of their best jobs. They fill them with friends of company employees.

Your school is another good source of job leads. Businesses interested in interviewing students for temporary or

job lead
....
information about a job
that is available

It is important to be organized and accurate when looking for a job. Job lead information is only helpful if it is correct. So, make sure you copy information correctly. Writing down an incorrect address, telephone number, date, or time for an interview could cost you a terrific job!

part-time work often call the local schools. Does your school have a work-experience office? If so, most employers will call this office when they have job vacancies to fill. Also, check with your business teacher and your counselor.

Job openings for many local businesses can be found by looking in your local newspaper. Acquire a recent edition of your local paper. Look in the classified ads under "Help Wanted." Are any jobs listed there that would be of interest to you? How would you go about responding to the ad?

The help-wanted ads of your local newspaper are good sources, too. Many employers list job openings in the classified ad section. You can learn a lot about the local job market by reading these ads regularly. Make it a habit to read the help-wanted ads. When you see an ad that looks like a job you might like, apply as soon as possible. If you wait even a day or two, someone else may already have the job. Employment agencies match workers with jobs. Most cities have a public employment agency whose services are free because they are tax supported. Private employment agencies also pro-vide assistance in finding jobs, but there is usually a fee for their services. If you use a private employment agency, be sure you understand what fees you will be charged. You may be required to pay a percentage of your first few months' salary to the agency.

USING JOB LEAD CARDS

A **job lead card** is an index card on which you record important information about an available job. When you hear about a job opening, write down the name of the person to whom you should apply, and the company's name, address, and telephone number on the card. Write the source of the lead in the lower left corner. Use the back side of the card to record whatever you do to follow up on the lead. Record the date when you call to request an interview and the time and date of the interview. Also, write down the name of the person you are to see, and, if necessary, directions to the company's office. Later, write down your impression of the interview and whether you are offered the job.

Use a second card to write down information about the company, such as the product it makes, the service it provides, or other important information. Staple this second card to your job lead card. Just before your interview, review your notes about the company.

APPLYING FOR JOBS

Follow up each lead you get as quick-ly as possible. If you don't, someone else will already be working on the job

job lead card
....
an index card that contains important information about an available job

employment agency
....
a company that matches workers with available jobs

application form

· · · · · · · · · · · · · · · · · · ·

a document people are required to fill out when applying for a job; it typically contains questions about the person and his or her qualifications for the job

personal data sheet

· · · · · · · · · · · · · · · · · · ·

an outline of the personal information needed to fill out an application form; it may include dates of schooling, names, addresses, and references

by the time you get around to calling for an interview. Between the times when you are following up on job leads, continue to look for new job leads as well. You increase your chances of getting just the right job every time you get a new lead.

Whether you are looking for your first job or your twentieth, the application process is much the same. Usually, you will have to fill out an application form. An **application form** consists of one or two pages of questions about you and your job qualifications. An employer uses the information you write on the form to decide whether to extend an interview invitation.

Most application forms ask the same or similar questions. One good way to prepare for the job application process is to prepare a **personal data sheet**, which answers the common job application questions. A personal data sheet is simply an outline of the information

you may need when you fill out job application forms. It includes exact dates you attended a former school, names and addresses of previous employers, and names and addresses of references. Take your personal data sheet with you when you go to apply for a job.

Remember that when you apply for a job, what you write and how you write it will be an employer's first impression of you. Fill out the form as completely and as neatly as possible. Don't skip any questions. Usually, you can take the application form home, where you can complete it on a typewriter. Since you might need to fill out the form at the employer's office, remember to take a pen with you.

Except for occasional work, such as gardening or babysitting, you will have to have a Social Security card. It is illegal for an employer to pay you until you have given your employer your Social Security number.

Your application form will tell the employer whether you are right for the job. Be sure your application is neat and accurate. If the employer can't read something or if the employer checks on any of the information listed and finds that it is incorrect, you probably won't get a chance to explain or correct the error, because you won't hear from the employer again.

Congress passed a law in 1988 that required every person five years of age or older who is claimed as a dependent on federal tax form 1040 to have a Social Security number. So, chances are, you already have a card.

If you don't have a Social Security card, get an application form at your local Social Security office or from your school work experience office. Fill out the application and mail it right away. If you don't have a Social Security number, you may miss out on a job that you would have really liked. Take your Social Security card (or just the number) along with you when you are applying for a job.

Federal and state laws regulate the work conditions and the working hours of students under sixteen or eighteen. If you are under sixteen, you will need a **work permit**—a form necessary before you can legally begin work. Some states require work permits for all employees under eighteen.

In some states, work permits must specify the exact job duties and hours of work. Ask your counselor where you can get a work permit. Find out about this now, and you will avoid a delay when you do find a job.

MAKING THE MOST OF INTERVIEWS

Your sole purpose in filling out application forms is to convince an employer to interview you. An **interview** is a formal meeting in which you and the employer discuss the job and your qualifications. It is nearly always during the interview that an employer decides whether to hire you. Yet, the first minute is the most critical. Make a good impression in the first minute,

interview
....
a formal meeting in which the person applying for a job and the employer discuss the job and the applicant's qualifications for the job

work permit
....
a form needed by underage employees, which allows them to work legally

In many cases, you will be interviewed by more than one person, maybe an entire panel of people. This may make it more difficult to remain calm during the interview. Do you have enough confidence to "sell" yourself to a panel of potential employers?

Common Questions Asked During an Interview

1. What type of work are you looking for?
2. Have you done this type of work before?
3. Why are you leaving your present job?
4. How often were you absent from your last (or present) job?
5. What did you dislike about your last (or present) job?
6. How did you get along with your boss and co-workers?
7. What are your greatest strengths? your greatest weaknesses?
8. What do you hope to be doing in five years?
9. How do you feel about this position?
10. Can we check your references?
11. How does your experience qualify you for this job?
12. How well do you take direction?
13. Can you take criticism without feeling hurt or upset?
14. Can you work under pressure?
15. Do you like detail work?
16. Do you prefer working alone or with others?
17. Have you ever been fired or asked to resign?
18. What type of people do you find difficult to work with?
19. How well do you work with difficult people?
20. What salary do you expect?

Figure 38.1
. . . .

Making sure you can answer these questions and others like them will give you an advantage when you have a job interview. Take a sheet of paper and write answers to these questions. Then add to your list any additional questions you think would be appropriate.

and that will cause the interviewer to feel positive about you throughout the interview.

Prepare

Preparing for the interview will boost your confidence and help you make that important first impression a favorable one. Learn what to say and how to say it ahead of time, and you will communicate it more effectively. Maybe your teacher will let you and your classmates practice interviewing one another, or get a friend to play the role of interviewer and ask you questions. Use the list of interview questions in Figure 38.1, and add your own based on the type of job you are seeking. Keep in mind that many interviewers ask such questions as, "Why do you want to work for this company?" or "What interests you about working here?"

Learn something about the company, and you will be able to phrase your questions and answers in ways that are more pleasing to the interviewer. Give special attention to information that fits with your education, interest, or experiences. Then, remember to use this information during the interview.

Dress Appropriately

How you dress for a job interview is very important. If you're interviewing for a sales or an office job, dress the way the best-dressed workers already on the job dress. This will help you make a good first impression. If you're applying for a job at a horse stable, then clean jeans would be appropriate. Appropriate clothing shows respect for the employer and gives you a big advantage during that critical first minute of the interview. Appropriate clothing is important, but personal cleanliness and neatness are even more important to most employers. Before your interview, shower, wash your hair, clean and trim your nails, and brush your teeth. Avoid strong-smelling lotions or perfume. Makeup for women should be used sparingly.

Arrive Early

Arrive for your interview appointment about ten minutes early. Start getting ready early and allow some extra time if you have to travel across town—traffic might delay you. On your way to the interview, mentally review what you've prepared.

Go Alone

Always go to an interview alone. Some young people have taken along a friend for support, but this always makes a bad impression on employers.

Smile!

When you meet the person who will interview you, *smile*. It helps more than anything to create a favorable first impression. The second thing you can do to create a good impression is to shake hands properly. Wait for the interviewer to offer his or her hand, then grasp the person's hand firmly—but not too hard. A weak handshake is disappointing, but don't make it a test of strength either.

If you are interviewed in an office, wait until you are asked to sit down. If you have books, a purse, or other articles with you, place them beside your chair. Sit alertly, make eye contact with the interviewer often, and answer questions honestly and completely.

The interviewer will set the tone, pace, and style of the interview. Some people are very serious and conduct interviews that are strictly business. Others are more cheerful, perhaps even humorous, and conduct interviews with a lighter touch. Adapt your responses to the interviewer's style, but don't try to be funny. An interview *is* serious business.

Make Eye Contact

As the interview progresses, look the interviewer in the eye most of the time. Shift your eyes sometimes so you don't appear to be staring. Many employers think applicants who can't maintain good eye contact are insecure or perhaps concealing something.

Answer Questions Thoughtfully

Most interviewers will ask questions about your education, experience, job preferences, and goals. When you are asked a question, give yourself time to compose an answer that is thoughtful. When you answer questions, and later, when you ask your own questions, speak clearly and loudly enough to be heard. Give complete answers, but don't ramble. Refer to your notes or your personal data sheet if needed.

Ask Good Questions

Usually, after the interviewer has asked most of his or her questions, you will be invited to ask some questions. If not, and there is a pause in the conversation, ask if you may ask a question (you won't have to limit it to one). Use your first question or two to show your sincere interest in the company, in the job, and in the employer's needs. You will want to know as much as possible about the job so that you can decide whether to accept it if it's offered to you. The subject of money may or may not be discussed by the interviewer. If not, it is all right to ask how much the job pays—but wait until near the end of the interview.

The interviewer may offer you the job or say that you will be called in a few days. If nothing is said about how you can learn whether the job will be offered to you, ask if you may call back in a few days to learn of the decision.

When It's Over, Go!

Try to sense when the interview is almost over. Most interviewers will say something like, "Well, I believe I have all the information I need." It's all right to ask one or two brief questions at this point, but don't delay your exit more than a minute or two. Be sure to thank the interviewer for his or her time before you leave.

After you are home, write a letter thanking the interviewer for taking time to discuss the job with you. (See Figure 38.2.) In the letter, emphasize your interest in the job. Since most people don't write thank-you letters, you will have an advantage.

If you take time to evaluate the experience, you can profit from every interview. Ask yourself questions like, "Did I mention everything about my qualifications that might help me get the job?" or "How would a little more planning and preparation have helped?"

CHECKLIST FOR ACQUIRING A JOB

The following is a summary checklist of important steps in acquiring a job:
1. ___ Decide on a kind of work that you can do well.
2. ___ Check all available sources of job leads.
3. ___ Make notes on all job leads and follow up on each lead immediately.
4. ___ Before each interview, learn some things about the company. Then you will be able to show intelligent interest in the company during the interview.
5. ___ Dress appropriately for interviews.
6. ___ Take a pen and pencil, your Social Security card, and a work permit (if required) to all interviews.
7. ___ When asked to fill out an application, complete the form in ink (or, if possible, take it home and use a typewriter).
8. ___ Arrive for the interview ten minutes early, and go alone.
9. ___ Introduce yourself, and state which job you wish to apply for. Do not offer to shake hands unless the interviewer extends her or his hand first.
10. ___ During the interview, remain standing until you are asked to be seated—then sit alertly. Answer all questions completely and truthfully.
11. ___ If you are not offered the job, ask if you may call in a few days.
12. ___ Write a follow-up letter to the interviewer.

Summary

- Some sources of information about job openings are family and friends, your school work-experience office, local state employment office, help-wanted ads in the newspaper, and private employment agencies.

- Job lead cards help organize your job hunt, as they provide a record of needed information about all the leads you have acquired, and they can be easily re-sorted.

- Preparing a personal data sheet will help you to organize your thoughts

Follow-up letter

1715 Bliss Street
Winfield, KS 67156
April 26, 19–

Ms. Julie Atkins
Kennedy Accounting Services
1700 South Main Street
Arkansas City, KS 67005

Dear Ms. Atkins:

Thank you for the interview yesterday afternoon regarding the position as bookkeeper.
I enjoyed talking with you and learning more about your bookkeeping needs.

Having discussed this position in greater detail, I am more interested in the job than
ever. I also feel even more certain that I can fulfill your needs.

If I may provide any further information for your consideration, please call me at home
any afternoon after three. My number is 221-4565.

Sincerely,

Mizuko Matsusko

Mizuko Matsusko

Figure 38.2
. . . .
*A follow-up letter
may cause an
employer to decide in
your favor if there are
other applicants being
considered for a job.
Before you leave the
interview, be sure you
know who you will
send the letter to and
that you can spell the
person's name
correctly. Attention to
details such as these
will impress the
potential employer.*

and prepare you for filling out job
application forms and also help in
answering questions in job
interviews.

- When you have an appointment for
a job interview, prepare ahead, dress
appropriately, arrive early and go
alone, smile and make eye contact
with the interviewer.

- As the interview progresses, answer
questions thoughtfully, ask good
questions about the company and
the job, and leave when you sense
the interview is over.

CHAPTER REVIEW
38

E NRICHING YOUR VOCABULARY

Number your paper from 1–7. Read each sentence below. If the sentence is true, write "true" next to that number. If the sentence is false, rewrite it to make a true statement.

1. An application form is a record of your work history.
2. An employment agency is one source of job leads.
3. An interview is an informal meeting with a fellow worker.
4. There are many sources of job leads.
5. A job lead card is a listing in the classified ads.
6. A personal data sheet contains information about prospective employers.
7. Workers under the age of sixteen are required by law to have work permits.

R EVIEWING WHAT YOU HAVE LEARNED

1. Name five sources of leads for job openings.
2. When you hear of a job opening, what information should be noted about it?
3. What three things should you take along when job hunting?
4. Suppose that, at the end of a job interview, the person interviewing you says nothing about how you will learn whether you will be offered the job. What should you do?

U SING YOUR CRITICAL THINKING SKILLS

1. What are the advantages and disadvantages of going door to door when looking for a job?
2. Locate a job opening in your community that might interest you. Then prepare a job lead card for this job. Use the back of the card to tell how you could follow up this lead.

A PPLYING WHAT YOU HAVE LEARNED

1. Role-play a job interview. Prepare two lists of questions. What questions would you ask if you were the interviewer? What questions would you ask if you were the person being interviewed?
2. One method of finding out more about the job market and the skills that employers are seeking is to do information interviews. Go to your local library, bookstore, or career center and read about information interviewing. Then select an employer with whom you would like to arrange an interview. Write a letter requesting an information interview.

CHAPTER 39

Evaluating Alternatives in Education

OBJECTIVES

After completing this chapter, you will be able to do the following:
1. List the six steps to follow when choosing a college or university.
2. List several post-high school educational alternatives to college.

TERMS

apprenticeship
college

community college
trade school

tuition
university

Many older people who are very successful in life had little or no formal education beyond high school. In the early 1900s, only 5 percent of the college-age men and women attended college. College then was generally considered important only for rich men's sons as they "prepared for life." Now college is considered vital to success in many careers, and more than 50 percent of recent high school graduates enrolled in universities, colleges, or community colleges.

Still, there are worthwhile alternatives to enrolling as a full-time college student. You may decide that working part time while going to school part time is the best plan for you. Your decision will depend on your lifestyle and career goals—and your finances. You might choose one of the trades as your career goal, and you may want to prepare for your career by attending

a trade school or by beginning an apprenticeship.

COLLEGES AND UNIVERSITIES

Some years ago, a college was a post-secondary school for students who wanted to study one particular field. There might be a college of education and a completely separate college of agriculture. A university was a group of these "colleges" at one place.

The difference between colleges and universities has become blurred in recent years. Most colleges now offer study in a variety of fields, but universities still tend to be larger than most colleges. In some states, the tax-supported universities have different

College is not for everyone, but if your goal is to attend college, plan ahead. Do some research to find the colleges that offer a degree in the field of your interest. Find out as much as you can about cost and reputation for each college. Do you know anyone who attends these colleges? Talk with them and ask questions about the colleges.

(usually higher) entrance requirements than the state colleges.

Selecting a College or University

There are hundreds of colleges and universities in the United States. Whatever your lifestyle and career goals, there are probably a dozen or so schools that could give you a good start toward success. How do you go about selecting the schools to which you will apply?

Consider Reputation. Choose schools that have good reputations for preparing students in the career you have chosen. If you don't yet have a career goal, then choose schools that are strong in several fields that interest you. For example, if you are considering secondary teaching

and journalism, then you might choose a college with strong departments in both of these fields.

Consider Financial Resources. Your financial resources should be considered from the beginning, but keep in mind that there are many scholarships, grants, and loans available to qualified students. (See Chapter 12 and Figure 39.1.)

Generally, state-supported colleges and universities are less expensive to attend than private schools. In the middle 1990s, tuition (the price for instruction), fees, and books for a year at college ranged from about $2,000 to more than $12,000. The lower costs were at state-supported schools, and the higher costs were at private universities. Those who lived at school spent another $3,400 to $5,000 for room and board. All other expenses averaged

tuition
....

the cost of attending a school; this does not include the price of books, housing, or expenses not relating to instruction

How Much You Must Save Each Month for College

| Child's Age | Real Annual Return | | | |
	0%	2%	4%	6%
0	$405	$339	$281	$229
2	449	384	325	273
4	503	439	381	328
6	571	510	453	399
8	662	604	548	495
10	787	733	680	630
12	971	923	875	829
14	1266	1228	1190	1152
16	1818	1800	1782	1763

Assumptions: Your child will enter a four-year private college at the age of 17; today's cost for this college is $100,000. (If he or she will be living at home and going to a state college, you may need to save as little as one-forth of the above amounts.) Real annual returns are returns in excess of the rate of inflation for college tuition. Your payments must increase each year at this rate of inflation; e.g., if your monthly payment is $1,000 this year, you'll have to save $1,050 per month next year if college costs rise by 5%.

Figure 39.1
....

Costs for college can be overwhelming, especially if no advance planning was done. This chart shows how much must be saved each month to have $100,000 for college. It might be too late for you to benefit from this information, but it could help your parents plan ahead for a younger brother or sister, or it might even help you plan ahead for your own child. Have you given thought to how you will finance your college costs?

Talking over the plans you have for after high school can help you better understand yourself and what you want in life. Talk with someone who will give you honest advice and who can help you find information you need. Who can you talk with about your plans for the future?

from $500 to $2,400 for the year. Projected yearly costs for the year 2000, including tuition, room and board, books, fees and transportation, range from about $18,000 to as high as over $50,000.

Read College Catalogs.
The approximate cost of attending most colleges and universities can be found by reading several college guides in your public library. Each of these describes many colleges, their offerings, admission requirements, and other information. Look for more specific information in individual college catalogs. Your school counselor probably has a selection of catalogs that you may use, and you can write directly to the registrars of colleges and universities for others.

Discuss Your Goals and Plans.
Talk about your goals and college plans with your counselors, parents, and teachers. Discuss them with someone who has already achieved success in the career for which you will prepare. Talk with friends who are now in

college and ask them about the schools they attend.

Visit Campuses.
Visit the campuses of the schools that seem most promising and try to spend a few days on each campus. The fall of your senior year is the best time. Try to arrange with the admissions office or with friends to stay with some undergraduates. Visit some classes, but also take in some social activities, eat in the cafeteria, listen, and observe. This is your chance to evaluate the school.

Apply to Several Schools.
When you decide you would like to attend a particular college, you will need to complete an application package. Many colleges and universities have four or five times as many applicants as they can accept. So it is wise to apply to several schools. Most students narrow their choices to about five or six schools for actual application. If they are accepted by more than one, they have the final choice of where they will enroll.

Average Earnings of Persons, by Education Attainment and Gender

	Male	Female
Less than 9th grade	$19,632	$12,570
High school graduate	$28,230	$19,336
Some college, no degree	$33,758	$22,833
Associate degree	$35,500	$25,554
Bachelor's degree or more	$50,747	$33,144

Figure 39.2
. . . .

When it comes to earnings, going to college may not make as big a difference as you might think. This chart shows average earnings by males and females according to their education. Is there a discrepancy between amounts earned by males and females? Why do you think this is so? (Source: U.S. Bureau of the Census, 1992.)

EDUCATIONAL ALTERNATIVES

Your career goal may call for less than a four-year college program, or maybe your high school grades aren't quite good enough to get you into the college of your choice. Some people may even be frightened of going to a four-year college or university. Also, a college degree does not necessarily ensure higher earnings. (See Figure 39.2.) For all of these cases, there are educational alternatives.

Community Colleges

Community colleges are sometimes called "junior colleges" or "city col-leges." Attending a two-year college is less expensive than attending a four-year college or university. You probably have a community college nearby, perhaps in your home town. If so, you can live at home and save the cost of room and board while attending college.

When you enroll in a community college, you can even begin a four year college program leading to a bachelor's degree. However, you must take courses that a four-year college or university will accept when you transfer after your first two years. Contact a counselor to help you plan your program if you wish to transfer.

Trade Schools

If you attend a **trade school**, you will take courses only in your chosen field. Many schools allow you to choose morning, afternoon, or evening classes. Class time is often spent in job-like settings solving real work problems.

Private trade schools charge tuition ranging from a few hundred dollars to several thousand dollars for a complete program. The length of the term depends on the skills you wish to learn. For example, truck-driving courses last from one to eight weeks, and medical technician courses last from forty-eight to seventy-two weeks. Most trade-school courses can be completed in less than two years, and you can usually begin full-time work sooner than if you attend a two-year college.

If you are interested in learning more about trade schools, talk with your high school counselor.

Apprenticeship Programs

An **apprenticeship** program is a system of on-the-job training combined

trade school
. . . .
an education institution that offers courses in a specific field, such as computer repair or medical technician

community college
. . . .
a two-year, post-secondary school that offers courses that lead to an associate degree; often called junior or city colleges

apprenticeship
. . . .
a system of on-the-job training combined with formal classroom instruction conducted by experienced trade instructors

Apprenticeship programs are opportunities to earn while you learn. If you don't have an interest in going to college, this may be an alternative for you. Find someone who is currently working as an apprentice or someone who has worked as an apprentice in the past. Ask questions to learn all you can about this type of program.

CONSUMER PROFILE

Dylan spent a year or so in college, then dropped out. After that, he drifted from job to job without a plan. This was not very satisfying, so he made himself sit down and do some serious thinking about his future. He was interested in computers. When he researched this field, he read books and pamphlets at the library and talked to some people working in the computer profession. He learned that, in the computer field, many opportunities were available.

However, Dylan didn't have the money for a four-year college program and didn't want to spend that much time in school. Instead, he chose to attend a local private business school that offered a one-year program in computer technology. Dylan did very well at the school and graduated with excellent grades and strong letters of recommendation from his teachers.

A small local software company was impressed with Dylan's letter of application and his success at the business school. They hired him at a salary and position at the bottom of the ladder, but he was in the door and quickly proved himself and his talents. Within two years, Dylan had climbed up the ladder and was a manager in the company. Planning, determination, hard work, and a year at the business school sure paid off!

with formal classroom instruction by experienced trade instructors. Training normally runs from two to five years, depending on the trade. Graduation from high school is usually required for acceptance into an apprenticeship program. Apprentices (learners) are full-time employees, but they are paid only a percentage of the rate for skilled workers. As the apprentice increases his or her skills, the rate of pay is also increased.

An apprenticeship is a cooperative effort by employers, schools, employee organizations, and an apprenticeship agency. Apprenticeships can be established for training new workers in many careers. The most popular programs include training in machine shop, painting, plumbing, carpentry, and sheet metal.

Nontraditional Educational Programs

Successful people continue their education throughout their lives, either to learn new employment skills or for personal growth. They do so through a great many alternatives to the traditional educational programs. Most of these alternatives can be combined with full-time employment. Among them are adult evening classes and learning "networks" (connected to a computer through your TV).

Other educational alternatives are correspondence courses and courses on cassette tapes. Some colleges even allow you to complete most of your studies for a bachelor's degree at home. Your public library can put you in touch with dozens of educational opportunities. Your local YMCA and YWCA probably sponsor a variety of classes for your recreational education.

Many jobs require ongoing training and education. For example, new advances are constantly being made in the medical field, so employees in that field must keep up with those changes. When researching a career, find out if ongoing training and education are required.

Summary

- These days, a college education is considered vital to success in many careers.

- Some things to do that will help you select a college or university are: consider the school's reputation, consider financial resources, read college catalogs, discuss your goals and plans with people who could help, visit campuses and apply to several schools.

- Some alternatives to a four-year college are community colleges, trade schools, apprenticeship programs, and nontraditional educational programs such as correspondence courses and adult evening classes.

CHAPTER REVIEW 39

ENRICHING YOUR VOCABULARY

Read the following pairs of sentences. Write the sentence that correctly uses the underlined word or phrase.

1A. An apprenticeship is a volunteer job that allows the worker to learn about a possible trade.

1B. An apprenticeship combines training, classroom instruction, and employment.

2A. Colleges and universities are post-secondary schools.

2B. Colleges and universities are state-supported schools.

3A. Work in a community college can lead to a bachelor's degree.

3B. A community college offers a bachelor's degree.

4A. A trade school offers a bachelor's degree.

4B. A trade school provides training in a particular field.

5A. Tuition is the term used to describe all college expenses.

5B. Tuition pays for the cost of instruction.

REVIEWING WHAT YOU HAVE LEARNED

1. List the six steps to follow when choosing a college or university.

2. What are some post-high school educational alternatives to college?

USING YOUR CRITICAL THINKING SKILLS

1. Considering the area in which you live, what are the advantages and disadvantages of attending a community college?

2. Bob will be graduating from high school next year. His parents are willing to help pay for a college education, but Bob does not know what he wants to study. What would you recommend that Bob do to help him make a decision about post-secondary education?

APPLYING WHAT YOU HAVE LEARNED

1. Interview two people who are now attending two different colleges. Ask the main advantages and disadvantages of attending each college. Also, ask the approximate total yearly cost.

CHAPTER 40

Applying Consumer Principles to Recreation

OBJECTIVES

After completing this chapter, you will be able to do the following:
1. Name two benefits of recreation.
2. Explain how people can discover interesting recreational activities.
3. Name five ways a person can acquire outdoor recreational skills.
4. Name three advantages of at-home recreation.
5. List several questions you should ask yourself when you are interested in an activity that requires special equipment or clothing.
6. Name three things you can learn by writing to the chamber of commerce in an area you wish to visit.

TERMS

active participant
creative recreation
flextime

hostels
overbook

spectator sports
vicarious participation

TIME FOR RECREATION

Recreation is mainly for fun, but some people today think they don't have time for fun. Many are so involved in their careers that they seldom take time for recreation, and some must work two jobs to meet their financial responsibilities.

Work fulfills human needs through productive activity, but recreation refreshes the mind and body so that when we return to our work or studies we are more productive. Recreation also increases our self-esteem. Thus, recreation gives us a more positive outlook on life and improves our personal relationships. A satisfying lifestyle usually includes some time for recreation.

flextime
....
a schedule provided by some companies that allows employees to have a choice of the hours they work

Most of us have about as much time available for recreation as we spend at school or work. The average workweek is less than forty hours, and weekends, paid vacation, and holidays provide blocks of time to use as we like. Many people especially enjoy the occasional three-day holiday weekends—and because of this, some companies have gone to a four-day workweek. Each week, people work more hours per day for four days in order to get a three-day weekend. This plan also saves 20 percent on transportation to work for the employees and additional cost savings for the employer. Other companies are trying **flextime**, a plan that provides flexible scheduling so that workers have a choice of the hours they work. For example, in some companies, employees may choose to begin work at seven and leave work at four, or they may come to work at ten and work until seven in the evening. This avoids driving to and from work during rush-hour traffic, and saves time—especially in larger cities.

None of us can spend all of our nonwork time in recreation, because some time is taken up by traveling to and from work, eating, personal care, shopping, and certain household chores. Counting holidays and vacations, that still leaves about a third of our lifetime to do with as we like, and those who know how to use this time for recreation enrich their lives immensely. Those who don't may become bored with life and even complain that there's "nothing to do" when they have free time.

If you have ever felt bored for lack of something to do, perhaps you can learn how to benefit from recreation. Some

Recreation comes in many forms and offers many different benefits. If you have not developed any recreational interests, try some of the things mentioned in this chapter. You may find an activity you'll participate in the rest of your life.

forms of recreation are free or inexpensive, others are quite expensive. Americans spend large amounts of time and billions of dollars on recreation every year.

SETTING RECREATION GOALS

As with any endeavor, to get the most satisfaction from the time and money you invest in recreation, it is best to set goals. You know some of the things you like doing in your leisure time, but there may be dozens of other activities that you will enjoy once you try them.

How do you discover interesting new ways of relaxing or being creative? You can talk with friends about the things they enjoy doing, and you will get even more ideas by checking out books on recreation at your local library. Newsstands, too, have many magazines that are loaded with recreational ideas.

Influences on Recreation Goals

Your recreational activities will be influenced by your age and sex, your

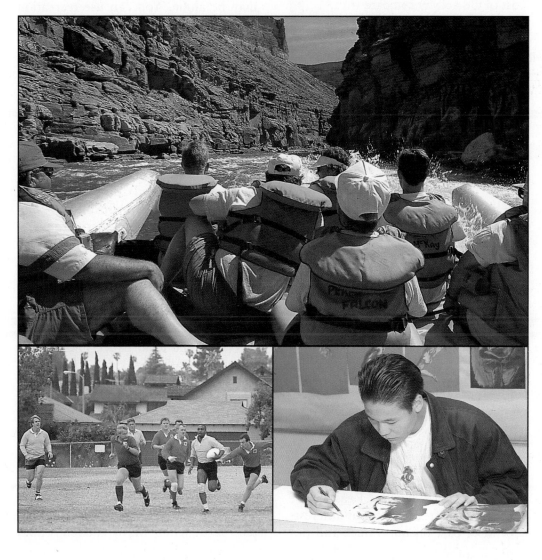

Recreational activities range from very physically active to inactive and from activities that are done alone to those that require many participants. Whatever your preferences are, there is an activity that will suit you. What types of activities do you find most appealing?

CHECKLIST FOR PLANNING RECREATION EXPENSES

The amount of money you can spend for recreation usually depends on how much is left after other expenses have been paid. (See Chapter 8.) Few of us can spend as much as we would like on recreation—so, just as with other consumer products, we gain greater satisfaction when we plan our spending to reach our recreation goals. As you plan, use the following checklist:

___ Does the activity cost a lot?

___ Do I have time to participate in this activity?

___ Is the activity one I can do or enjoy often?

___ Will the time or money spent interfere with other recreation that might be more satisfying?

___ Does the activity require continued spending? Am I likely to get money back from my investment?

___ How does the cost of this activity compare with other forms of recreation that might be nearly as satisfying?

___ Can the activity be enjoyed with a group or alone, or both ways?

___ Does the activity require a lot of equipment?

___ Am I likely to consider the activity well worth the time and money spent?

---

active participant
....

one who takes part in a sport or other recreation

spectator sports
....

activities, such as professional baseball and basketball, that involve watching others perform

vicarious participation
....

taking part in activities by watching others perform

---

family status, where you live, and your income. They will also be affected by your interests and experiences, and you may be influenced to try out the favorite recreational activities of friends. The important thing is to spend most of your leisure time doing things you enjoy.

Where you live determines the facilities available for recreation. Rural areas may lack tennis and handball courts, but they may have weekend activities such as rodeos in which you can participate. Larger cities have museums and live theater as well as all kinds of sports facilities.

What makes us interested in particular recreational activities? Reasons are hard to identify because our interests depend in part on our values and our

---

personalities. For activities such as playing a musical instrument, our aptitudes are important. To develop an interest, we need exposure, and our recreational activities often depend on our financial resources.

RECREATION ALTERNATIVES

Recreation today has many forms. Some require great physical activity, while others are enjoyed quietly. You can be an **active participant**, or you can be a spectator. You may be involved with many other people, or you may be alone. You can use recreation to improve your body and your mind; and whatever forms of recreation you choose can make your life more interesting.

Recreation as a Spectator

Spectator sports, such as professional baseball and football, are perhaps the most obvious forms of **vicarious participation**, but there are many other kinds of recreation that involve watching others perform. These include live theater, movies, concerts, and TV shows. Listening to a stereo is essentially nonparticipating.

The sports page, the theater or movie section of the local paper, and the TV listings usually provide comprehensive information on recreation for spectators.

Recreation as a Participant

There are hundreds of different kinds of recreational activities in which people participate. Many people, both

If you live near the ocean, scuba diving might be an activity you will enjoy. Before you start diving, though, you will need to take lessons from a certified instructor. Then it is important to take all necessary safety precautions. Just because an activity is recreational doesn't mean it isn't dangerous.

Bicycling is an activity that provides good, outdoor exercise. It can be done alone or in groups. Are there any bicycle clubs in your area? Would you be interested in riding with them?

young and old, prefer pastimes that involve strenuous physical activity. They may enjoy sports such as tennis or handball. Others, though not inclined to exercise vigorously, enjoy a variety of outdoor activities, such as fishing or croquet. An important element of recreation for many is the feeling of being creative, so they may paint pictures or act in drama groups.

Many recreational activities, both social and solitary, take place at home. And vacations away from home may include participation in all kinds of recreational activities.

Recreation for Physical Fitness

The value of regular exercise to the body was discussed in Chapter 32.

When it is considered recreation, exercise benefits the mind, too. Select one or two of the activities listed below that you haven't tried but that you think would be fun.

- basketball
- rugby
- soccer
- hockey
- football
- volleyball
- softball
- golf
- walking
- running
- swimming
- bowling
- handball
- racquetball
- badminton
- tennis
- table tennis
- weightlifting
- bicycling
- skating
- skiing

Outdoor Recreation

Perhaps the most restful form of recreation is simply enjoying the great outdoors. You've probably tried several of the outdoor activities shown here. Nearly everyone goes on picnics, for example. Pick out one or two of these activities that you haven't tried that seem interesting, then, first chance you get, expand your recreation in a new direction!

- picnics
- fishing
- gardening
- hiking

- astronomy
- boating
- nature study
- bird watching
- horseback riding
- camping
- backpacking
- mountain climbing

Such things as camping, backpacking, and exploring nature may be new to you, but there are several ways of acquiring sound outdoor skills. One way is to join a group or club. Some, such as the Sierra Club, promote a variety of outdoor activities. Other clubs are more specific. Examples are hiking clubs, mountain-climbing clubs, and cross-country skiing clubs. Check on the outdoor organizations in your community.

Another way to acquire outdoor skills is to enroll in a class. In many communities, a variety of outdoor recreation classes are sponsored by local junior colleges or adult-education programs. The classes that are most worthwhile include field trips. You can apply your newly learned skills in the appropriate setting.

creative recreation
· · · · · · · · · · · · · · · · · ·
a hobby or pastime, such as painting or cooking, that yields a product of some sort

Gardening can be a very rewarding pastime. There are many different types of gardening to choose from, too. Vegetable gardening can supply fresh produce for your family. Flower gardening can provide gifts for friends and perhaps awards at flower shows. Do you have a "green thumb"?

You can learn outdoor skills in other ways, too. Talk with people who are outdoor guides or visit with friends and acquaintances who have outdoor experience. Read about outdoor recreation in books and magazines. Sometimes, stores that sell outdoor equipment hold "clinics" on specific activities such as backpacking and skiing.

Creative Recreation

Most of us have felt the satisfaction of creating something ourselves. Often, things we make, such as jewelry, leather goods, or pottery, mean more to us than if we had bought them or received them as gifts. **Creative recreation** provides double benefits. The activities are stimulating in themselves, and often result in products of which we can be proud.

Consider the following list. Which creative activities haven't you tried?

CONSUMER PROFILE

When Reina had her second child, she quit her job as a graphic designer. The budget was tight with only her husband's income, but it was important to them that she be at home with their two children. Being a creative and artistically talented person, she naturally started doing some craft projects in her free time.

She discovered a craft that uses a special kind of clay and started making jewelry, refrigerator magnets, picture frames, and other items. The pieces were colorful, clever, decorative, and people loved them. Before long, she had quite a collection of these handmade items. She took samples to a local gift shop, which bought them immediately. She now has items in a number of gift or art stores and has a growing second income for her family. What a perfect match of job to person. Her new art business fits her lifestyle, values, aptitudes, and interests to a T!

INTERACTING WITH TECHNOLOGY

THE CHANGING ROLE OF THE SPECTATOR

Technology is bringing changes to the entertainment media, and many of these changes are putting more control into the hands of consumers. This control ranges from being able to access entertainment more directly to actually playing a part in the outcome of productions.

In the near future, home-shopping services will allow consumers to listen to excerpts of CDs from interactive music catalogs. These CDs could then be ordered electronically and shipped from storage warehouses. The technology currently exists to actually transmit the music electronically so that consumers could record their own CDs. In less than five minutes, consumers could record an album's worth of music.

At the present time, some retailers are gearing up to provide copies of albums, CD movies, and books on demand. The customer will make a selection from an extensive catalog, and in a matter of minutes the choice will be transmitted and recorded or printed.

A more dramatic change in the entertainment media will come from the technology that allows the consumer to interact with the material and shape its outcome. Computers that are connected to CD players will allow the listener to customize the music. Changes in the tempo and mood of the music will be possible. Listeners will be able to repeat favorite sections over and over. They will be able to create a video to accompany the music, drawing from a catalog of stored images. It will be possible to create videos that allow the consumer to "play" the musical instruments of the performers. The computer will supply an environment, the consumer will choose the path.

Perhaps one of the most thrilling applications of interactive media is that of high-tech films that immerse the viewer in the action. Special movable seats used in ride films allow the viewer to dodge, dive, and enter the story. Entertainment modules are being designed for installation in shopping malls that immerse the individual in a highly participatory film experience. The "viewers" will become participants in life-size video games. Strapped into race cars, spaceships, or underwater vessels, and surrounded by controls, they will engage in the action in the films. They will race opponents, attack enemies, and explore unknown territory. The experiences are vivid and exciting, and developers are betting that consumers will be willing to pay for them.

Which of these seem most interesting to you?

- painting
- photography
- leather work
- sewing
- needlework
- flower arranging
- playing music
- jewelry making
- creative writing
- creative cooking
- weaving
- dancing
- acting
- singing
- pottery

Classes are offered in many kinds of creative recreation. Most communities offer a variety of these classes through local colleges or adult education. You may have already taken classes in art, photography, sewing, or furniture making while in school.

Recreation at Home

For many people, most recreation time is spent at home, often including many hours of TV watching, but there are lots of things to do at home that provide active participation.

There are several advantages to at-home recreation. It is usually less ex-pensive than going somewhere else for recreation. Shorter periods of time can be used for at-home recreation since no time is used in travel, and most people are relaxed in their own homes. From the list below, pick one or two activities that you have never done but would like to try.

- reading for pleasure
- social gatherings, such as teas or card clubs
- sewing, knitting, crocheting
- indoor gardening
- raising fish in an aquarium
- collecting things, such as antiques, stamps, ceramic figures, art, or anything else that appeals to you
- table games, such as cards, chess, and many others

Special Equipment and Clothing

Many recreational activities need little or no investment of money, but oth-

Cooking is creative recreation that can produce good things to eat. Many people have turned their love for cooking into a business such as catering. Have you ever taken a cooking class? Did you enjoy it? Why or why not?

ers require special equipment or clothing that can be very expensive. Learn all you can about equipment and clothing needs. Your sources of information on specific recreation activities—classes, books and magazines, or visits with enthusiasts—should be able to supply information. What's the minimum investment required to take part? What are the important features of each needed item? Are there different brands and models? Which is the best value? Where is the best place to buy or rent equipment and clothing?

When you first try out a new activity, get by with as little investment in equipment and clothing as possible. Then, if you decide it's not a satisfying form of recreation, you won't wind up with a lot of expensive items that you will never use. For example, boating, fishing, skiing, hunting, golfing, and camping require special equipment—and some of it is quite expensive. Unless you already know that you like a particular type of recreation, rent any special equipment or clothing you will need. Wait until you have tried out a new activity and know you will be doing it on a regular basis before you spend much on equipment. Then you will have firsthand experience on which to base decisions about the equipment and clothing to buy.

Boats can usually be rented at lakeside. Fishing equipment can be rented in equipment stores near lakes, rivers, and the ocean. Skiing equipment and clothing can almost always be rented from shops at ski resorts, but you may get a better price by renting them from a local sporting goods store and taking them with you. Hunting and camping equipment can often be rented from local sporting goods stores as well. Golf clubs can usually be rented at the pro shop on any golf course.

When you decide you want to buy special recreation equipment or clothing, follow the "Checklist for Decision Making" in Chapter 3. If your funds are limited, consider buying used equipment—or trading something you no longer need for the equipment that you do need.

Planning a Vacation

Whether you spend a long weekend, two weeks, or a whole summer, a vacation is a chance to get away from the usual routine and spend some time in a different environment. Vacations can be relaxing, or they can be filled with excitement. Usually, a vacation is adventurous. Sometimes it's a combination of all three.

To get the most out of whatever you want from a vacation, you will need to do some planning and make some decisions. The first decisions are *what* you want to do, *where* you want to go, and *when* you want to go. These decisions, of course, will depend on how much time and money you have (or are willing) to spend. Then, plan for living accommodations while you're away, special attractions you want to see, and transportation you will use. Do you want a travel agent to handle things for you, or would you prefer to make your own arrangements?

Using the Services of a Travel Agency

If you are not an experienced traveler, you may decide to let a professional travel agent help with your vacation plans. An agent can answer questions on accommodations, tours, and car rentals; and most agents are familiar with schedules and fares for air, train, and bus transportation. They will let you know when special low rates are in effect. Travel agents are paid commissions by the airlines, railroad, hotels,

There are many ways to plan vacations. You can do all of the planning yourself, or you can let a travel agent do the planning for you. Have you ever helped plan a vacation? Did you work with a travel agent, or did you do it yourself?

and others—so you will not usually be charged for their services.

If you decide to use the services of a travel agent, tell him or her your vacation wishes. Say what you want to do, where and when you want to go, and about how much money you want to spend.

You may wish to take a planned sightseeing trip with a group. Group trips are economical. For one flat fee, everything can be arranged for you—transportation, living accommodations, and tours. Usually, some meals are included in the fee, and a guide travels with you. You have less independence with a group than when traveling on your own, but you also have fewer travel details to be concerned with.

Planning Your Own Vacation

You may want to spend your vacation at the home of friends or relatives, and this requires only minimal plan-

ning. You will probably write a letter or call to indicate your time of arrival (and departure). If you will be driving, pick up an up-to-date road map. If you plan to travel by plane, train, or bus, you must make reservations and pick up your tickets—or you can have your travel agent do that for you.

Check Out the Area. If you will be traveling to an area that is unfamiliar to you, write to the state tourist office or to the chamber of commerce in any city you will be visiting. They will send information on sights to see and things to do. You will also get suggestions on suitable clothing to bring along (according to the local climate)—and you will probably receive a map of the immediate area, too.

Arrange for Accommodations. If you plan to stay in a hotel or motel, call ahead for reservations. From anywhere in the United States, you may call 1-800-555-1212 and learn whether any hotel or motel has a toll-free number. Give the operator the name of the hotel and the city in which it is located.

When planning for accommodations, don't overlook the budget motels. Some don't have phones in the rooms, and you may have to pay a dollar or so for a color TV, but you can often cut your motel costs by half or more. When you make reservations at a hotel or motel, ask whether there are any special rates for which you qualify—such as family rates or special weekend rates. Also, ask whether there are any special meal plans for guests. To secure a reservation, you may have to mail a check or use a credit card to cover at least one night's lodging.

Alternatives to hotels and motels are available, such as hostels (supervised lodging for youth) and camping. Students who like to travel but have limited funds have been staying at hostels in many countries for years. This alternative is even less costly than budget motels. Before you can stay in a hostel, you must join the American Youth Hostels Association. (The address is 1108 K Street NW, Washington, DC 20005.) Your membership is good in all fifty-nine countries that have hostels affiliated with the International Youth Hostel Federation.

Another alternative is the bed and breakfast inn. These are usually large, private homes in which the owner has set aside one or even several bedrooms for nightly rental by travelers. The price per night is usually less than for a hotel and it includes breakfast. These accommodations are advertised in travel magazines and bed and breakfast guides.

If you really want to save money on accommodations, consider camping. When camping for the first time, many people rent most of the equipment they will need. Then, if all goes well, they may buy their own things for future trips. The costs of a tent, sleeping bags, cooking utensils, lanterns, and other gear can add up to a substantial amount—but camping equipment lasts for years. If you figure the cost over ten years or so, it amounts to a small fraction of the cost of staying in a hotel or motel.

hostels
....
supervised lodging, usually for young people

Camping can be an economical vacation and a good way to "get away from it all." If you enjoy outdoor sports such as fishing, boating, or water skiing, camping might be a good activity for you. Does your family camp? Do they use tents, campers, or motorhomes?

You will pay a small charge for staying overnight in national and state parks. Many campgrounds are free. If you plan to camp while traveling across country, buy a good camp guide—then make reservations well in advance of your departure.

Planning Your Transportation

Your choice of transportation for a vacation depends on several factors, including:

- the amount of time you have to spend
- how you want to spend the time—traveling around or staying at your destination
- the amount of money you have to spend

Most people choose to drive cars (or similar vehicles) or to travel by bus, train, or plane. Ships are rarely used except for cruise vacations.

Traveling by Car. If your vacation spot isn't too far from home or if you have the time, going by car is often preferable. (If you go camping, you may need a larger vehicle, such as a van, to carry all your gear.) The big advantage of driving is the freedom it gives you. You can travel as fast or as slowly as you want, and you can make side trips whenever you like. Traveling by car is comparatively economical, too, especially if several people are traveling together.

Before starting out on vacation, always have your car checked carefully by your regular mechanic. Having your car break down is no fun anywhere, but it's especially frustrating when you're in a strange city or, worse yet, on the open road.

Your regular car insurance should provide coverage throughout the United States and Canada, but if you drive into Mexico, you will have to buy Mexican insurance. This is available at insurance company offices in the U.S. border towns where you enter Mexico.

If you or someone in your family belongs to an automobile or motor club, such as the American Automobile Association (AAA), the club can be very helpful in providing maps, outlining vacation routes, and other special services. AAA provides members with comprehensive tour books (updated yearly), which list places to go and things to see in the area you will be visiting. These tour books also list hotels, motels, and restaurants, along with information about each listing.

Traveling by Bus. If you are traveling alone, going by bus may be preferable. Since someone else will take care of the driving, you will be free to look at all the scenery along the way, and traveling by bus is economical. However, you can't take any side trips, and you have little independence until you reach your destination. Unless you are going on a chartered or deluxe bus, reservations aren't usually required, but arrive early at the ticket counter to be sure you get a seat. You may take as many as three bags weighing a total of 150 pounds. Buses used for travel between cities are air-conditioned, have rest- rooms, and usually stop for meals or just to allow passengers to "stretch their legs" about every three hours. Even so, some people find long bus trips tiring.

Traveling by Train. The cost of traveling by train is greater than going by bus, but it is usually less expensive than flying. Train service has improved over the last few years. Amtrak (discussed in Chapter 22) owns and operates most trains in the United States. Requests for information or reservations are easily handled by its nationwide computer system. If you decide to go by train, remember that the cost of meals is not included in the cost of your ticket.

Traveling by Plane. Your time may be short, or the distance you're traveling may be long. You may not care to see the country along the way. In any of these cases, you will want to travel by plane. Airfares are constantly changing. Travel agents can often advise you as to the best fare available, and there is no fee for this service.

First-class fares are high. The first-class section of a plane is at the front, where seating facilities are more spacious than in coach class, but coach-class passengers get nearly the same service for a much lower price. If you want to save money, ask if any economy-class fares are available. If you are willing to fly at night, ask about special night fares.

Always make reservations well in advance. Ask your travel agent to make flight arrangements for you. Or call the airline yourself. Some people make reservations but then don't show up to take their flights. Because of this, the airlines often overbook—they accept more reservations for a flight than there are seats on the plane. Then, if everyone shows up for a flight, there are too many passengers—and some passengers must be "bumped." Usually, those bumped are the last to arrive at the gate. If you are at the gate fifteen minutes before the plane is scheduled to leave and you are bumped, airline rules require that your ticket price be refunded. Then you must be placed on the next available flight *at no cost*.

You may want to check on the amount of luggage you are allowed. This varies with the type of flight, but on most flights within the United States, you may take three bags. You may keep one of the bags with you if it will fit under your seat. If you take

Air travel offers a quick way to get places. If your time is more limited than your money, you might want to travel to your vacation spot by air. Do you enjoy flying? Where have you flown?

more than the basic allowance, you will be charged a fee.

Summary

- Recreation is a valuable part of our lives. It refreshes the mind and body, increases self-esteem, gives us a more positive outlook, and improves our personal relationships.

- To get the most satisfaction from the time and money you invest in recreation, it is best to set goals.

- Recreation comes in many forms, such as spectator, participant, outdoor, indoor, physical activity, creative, and at home.

- It is best to wait until you have tried a new recreational activity and know you will be doing it regularly before you invest much money in equipment.

- When planning a vacation, be sure to get information about the area you will be traveling to and make necessary reservations well ahead of time.

- For vacation transportation, people choose either car, bus, train, plane, or sometimes ship. Based mostly on time and money, each method has its pros and cons.

overbook
· · · · · · · · · ·
a practice of airlines in which they accept more reservations for a flight than there are seats on the plane

ENRICHING YOUR VOCABULARY

Use the following words or phrases to complete the sentences below. Write the completed sentences on your paper.

active participant
creative recreation
flextime

hostels
overbook

spectator sports
vicarious participation

1. When people use recreation to achieve physical fitness, they must be an
2. Reasonable accommodations for traveling youth can be found at
3. Photography is a form of
4. Some employees can choose their work and recreation hours with a type of scheduling called

5. Television, ball games, and concerts are forms of recreation that allow for
6. Free air travel may be awarded due to an airline's policy to
7. Professional baseball and hockey are considered to be

REVIEWING WHAT YOU HAVE LEARNED

1. Name two benefits of recreation.
2. How can people discover interesting recreational activities?
3. Name five ways a person can acquire outdoor recreational skills.

4. Name three advantages of at-home recreation.
5. Name three things you can learn by writing to the chamber of commerce in an area you wish to visit.

USING YOUR CRITICAL THINKING SKILLS

1. Consider the recreational activities available in your area. Which activities are economical?

Which activities are expensive? Choose one activity. What are the costs involved?

APPLYING WHAT YOU HAVE LEARNED

1. Choose a place where you'd like to go in the United States that is more than 500 miles from your home. Figure the round-trip costs for at least three forms of transportation. Also,

determine about how long your travel time would be. Prepare a chart showing this information.

Consumer Information Sources

Advertising

Direct Marketing Association
11 W. 42nd Street
New York, NY 10036-8096
1-212-768-7277

Federal Trade Commission
Advertising Practices
601 Pennsylvania Avenue, NW
Room 4001
Washington, DC 20580
1-202-326-2222

National Advertising Division
of the Council of Better
Business Bureaus
845 Third Avenue
New York, NY 10022
1-212-754-1320

United States Postal Service
Chief Postal Inspector
475 L'enfant Plaza West, SW
Washington, DC 20260
1-202-268-2000

Appliances

Consumer Product Safety
Commission
4330 East West Highway
Bethesda, MD 20814
1-301-504-0580

Banking

American Bankers Association
1120 Connecticut Avenue, NW
Washington, DC 20036
1-202-663-5000

Board of Governors of the Federal
Reserve System
Division of Consumer and
Community Affairs
Twentieth and C Streets, NW
Washington, DC 20551
1-202-452-3000

Federal Deposit Insurance
Corporation
Office of Consumer Compliance
Programs
550 Seventeenth Street, NW
Washington, DC 20429
1-202-393-8400

Clothing

American Apparel Manufacturers
Association
2500 Wilson Boulevard
Suite #301
Arlington, VA 22201
1-703-524-1864

American Textile Manufacturers
Institute, Inc.
1801 K Street, NW
Suite #900
Washington, DC 20006
1-202-862-0500

Federal Trade Commission
Correspondence Office
6th Street and Pennsylvania Ave.,
NW
Room #692
Washington, DC 20580
1-202-326-2000

Communications

Federal Communications
Commission
Consumer Assistance Office
Washington, DC 20552
1-202-418-0200

Consumer Information —
General

American Council on Consumer
Interests
240 Stanley Hall
University of Missouri
Columbia, MO 65201
1-314-882-7786

Consumer Federation of America
1424 Sixteenth Street, NW
Washington, DC 20036
1-202-387-6121

Consumer Information Catalog
Consumer Information Center
Pueblo, CO 81009
1-719-948-3334

National Consumer League
815 15th Street, NW
Suite 928
Washington, DC 20005
1-202-639-8140

Credit

Federal Trade Commission
Credit Practices
601 Pennsylvania Avenue, NW
Washington, DC 20850
1-202-326-2222

National Foundation for
Consumer Credit
8611 2nd Avenue
Suite #100
Silver Springs, MD 20910
1-301-589-5600

Drugs

Food and Drug Administration
Department of Health and Human
Services
5600 Fishers Lane
Rockville, MD 20857
1-301-443-3170

Education

Department of Education
Office of Public Participation &
Special Concerns
600 Independence, SW
Washington, DC 20202
1-202-708-5366

National Education Association of
the United States
1201 Sixteenth Street, NW
Washington, DC 20036
1-202-833-4000

Energy

American Gas Association
1515 Wilson Boulevard
Arlington, VA 22209
1-703-841-8400

Department of Energy
1000 Independence, SW
Washington, DC 20585
1-202-586-5000

Department of Energy Technical
Information Center
Post Office Box 62
Oak Ridge, TN 37831
1-615-576-2268

Environment

Bureau of Land Management
Office of Public Affairs
Department of Interior
1849 C Street, NW
Room 5600
Washington, DC 20240
1-202-208-5717

Department of Agriculture
Office of the Consumer Advisor
Administration Building
14th & Independence Avenue, SW
Washington, DC 20250
1-202-720-2791

Department of the Interior
1849 C Street, NW
Washington, DC 20240
1-202-208-3100

Environmental Protection Agency
Public Inquiries Center
401 M Street, SW
Washington, DC 20460
1-202-260-2090

Federal Aviation Administration
Community & Consumer Liaison
Division
Department of Transportation
400 7th Street, SW
Washington, DC 20590
1-202-366-4000

Sierra Club
730 Polk Street
San Francisco, CA 94109
1-415-776-2211

Food

Department of Agriculture
Office of the Consumer Advisor
Administration Building
14th & Independence, SW
Washington, DC 20250
1-202-720-8732

Food and Drug Administration
Department of Health and Human
Services
5600 Fishers Lane
Rockville, MD 20857
1-301-443-3170

Food Marketing Institute
Consumer Affairs
800 Connecticut Avenue, NW
Suite #400
Washington, DC 20006
1-202-452-8444

National Food Processors
Association
Consumer Affairs
1401 New York Avenue, NW
Suite 400
Washington, DC 20005
1-202-639-5900

Health Care

American Hospital Association
840 North Lake Shore Drive
Chicago, IL 60611
1-312-280-6000

American Medical Association
515 N. State Street
Chicago, IL 60610
1-312-464-5000

Medic Alert Foundation
International
2323 Colorado
Turlock, CA 95380
1-209-668-3333

National Association of Anorexia
Nervosa and Associated Disorders
Box 7
Highland Park, IL 60035
1-708-831-3438

National Health Information
Clearinghouse
P.O. Box 1133
Washington, DC 20013-1133
1-800-336-4797

National Safety Council
1121 Spring Lake Drive
Itasca, IL 60143-3201
1-708-285-1121

Veterans Administration
Consumer Affairs Staff
810 Vermont Avenue, NW
Washington, DC 20420
1-202-273-5400

World Health Organization
1501 New Hampshire, NW
Washington, D.C. 20006
1-202-861-3200

Housing

Department of Housing and Urban
Development
HUD Information Center
451 7th Street SW
Washington, DC 20410
1-202-708-1422

Farmers Home Administration
Department of Agriculture
14th & Independence Avenue, SW
Washington, DC 20250
1-202-720-4323

Insurance

Insurance Information Institute
110 William Street, 24th Floor
New York, NY 10038
1-212-669-9200

National Association of
Professional Insurance Agents
Consumer Relations
400 North Washington Street
Alexandria, VA 22314
1-703-836-9340

Local Organizations

Better Business Bureau
(Check the phone book for the
nearest office.)

Federal Information Centers
(Check the phone book for the
Center nearest you. Federal
Information Centers answer
questions about federal and
sometimes local agencies and
programs.)

Safety

Consumer Product Safety
Commission
Public Inquiries
Washington, DC 20207
1-301-504-0580

National Highway Traffic Safety
Administration
Department of Transportation
400 7th Street, SW
Room #5319
Washington, DC 20590
1-202-366-0123

Occupational Safety and Health
Administration
Office of Information
Department of Labor
200 Constitution, NW
Room #N3647
Washington, DC 20210
1-202-219-8148

Underwriters Laboratories
333 Pfingsten Road
North Brook, IL 60062
1-312-273-4255

Transportation and Travel

AMTRAK
Customer Relations
60 Massachusetts Avenue, NE
Washington, DC 20002
1-202-906-3000

Automotive Consumer Action
Program
15873 Crabbs Branch Way
Rockville, MD 20855
1-301-670-1110

Department of Transportation
Consumer Affairs Officer
400 7th Street, SW
Washington, DC 20590
1-202-366-4000

Federal Aviation Administration
Community & Consumer Liaison
Division
Department of Transportation
800 Independence Avenue, SW
Washington, DC 20591
1-202-267-3277

Interstate Commerce Commission
Office of Consumer Protection
12th & Constitution, NW
Washington, DC 20423
1-202-927-7119

Glossary

A

accessories items such as throw rugs, pillows, or plants that are not essential but add beauty

accidental death an unexpected death that happens without intent or possibly through carelessness

acid rain natural washing of chemicals from the air

active participant one who takes part in a sport or other recreation

AIDS (acquired immunodeficiency syndrome) a communicable disease that affects the immune system

air pollution contamination of the atmosphere

alcoholism a disease characterized by the addiction to alcohol

alternatives different choices

American Gas Association a private nonprofit organization that sets standards for gas appliances governing use, durability, and safety

amortization schedule payment plan for repayment of principal and interest

Amtrak passenger train service in the United States, which is operated by the federally subsidized National Railroad Passenger Corporation

analogous color scheme a color scheme that uses two or more related colors to create a naturalistic and comfortable environment

Annual Percentage Yield (APY) the actual return on $100 invested for one year at a given rate

annual percentage rate (APR) the amount credit costs expressed as a yearly percentage

anorexia nervosa an eating disorder caused by physical and emotional problems, which causes a person to eat very little or not at all in order to lose weight

application form a document people are required to fill out when applying for a job; it typically contains questions about the person and his or her qualifications for the job

apprenticeship a system of on-the-job training combined with formal classroom instruction conducted by experienced trade instructors

aptitude a natural ability for learning; talent

arbitration a process in which a complaint is referred to an impartial person whose decision the consumer and seller must agree to accept and comply with

asbestos fiber an air contaminant from insulation materials

assets the value of all things owned

automatic teller machine (ATM) a computerized machine that allows deposits and withdrawals to be made when the bank is closed or from another city or state

automatic transfer a method of savings in which money is taken from the paycheck by the bank and deposited in a savings account

B

balanced diet eating habits that include foods that provide the right amounts of protein, carbohydrates, and fat

bank statement a monthly accounting of checking account activity and balance provided by the bank

bankrupt having debts that are greater than the ability to repay over a period of time

Bankruptcy Reform Act of 1978 a law that allows for two types of bankruptcy; one in which the debtor may file a plan to repay debts from future earnings, and another in which the debtors' assets are sold and the money is used to repay as much of the debt as possible

bankruptcy a situation in which a person or company is unable to repay debts

banks institutions for the safekeeping of money and the transferring of money and credit

bargains good buys

basic coverage homeowners' insurance that protects the home against 11 perils stated in the policy

Better Business Bureaus organizations supported by local businesses for the purpose of assisting consumers with information and complaints

biased information information that comes from a personal and sometimes prejudiced outlook

blank endorsement a signature on the back of a check with no instructions

bonds interest-earning "IOUs" sold by governments or corporations to raise money

boycott organized refusal to buy certain products as a means of sending a message to the producer

broad coverage homeowners' insurance that protects the home against 17 perils stated in the policy

bulimia a dietary problem in which people crave food constantly. They overeat—then, before the food can be absorbed by the body, they cause themselves to vomit—and the body never gets adequate nutrition. Bulimia can lead to serious health problems.

business cycle periods of prosperity and recession

buying on contract an arrangement in which the seller holds the title to the property while the buyer makes the monthly payments to the seller

C

calories units that measure the amount of energy provided in foods

canceled checks checks that have been identified as paid

capital money invested in business

carbon monoxide a common gaseous waste, most of which comes from transportation exhaust

care labels laundering or cleaning instructions that must be permanently attached to textile products

case goods wood, plastic, metal, or woven furniture items that have no upholstered parts

cash-and-carry a store policy that allows the customers to pay for a product and take it with them

caveat emptor let the buyer beware

certificate of deposit a savings account in which money is deposited for a given period of time

certification seals stamps of approval indicating that products have met certain established standards

chain store one of several stores under common ownership

check a document for transferring money

check register a record of checks and deposits for a checking account

class-action suit a case in which many consumers have similar complaints against the company or person

Clean Air Act federal legislation that established strict emission standards for air pollution from cars and factories

coinsurance clause an agreement whereby the insured shares costs (usually 20%–25%) with the insurance company

collateral security for a loan

college an institution of higher learning that offers a course of study that leads to a bachelor's degree

collision insurance insurance that covers the cost of repairing a vehicle if it is damaged in an accident with another vehicle or if it runs into another object

commercial banks full service banks offering a wide range of financial services

communicable diseases illnesses that can be transferred from person to person

community college a two-year, post-secondary school that offers courses that lead to an associate degree; often called junior or city college

commuter service public transportation between cities and their suburbs or nearby cities

comparison shopping checking several sources for prices and quality of an item to determine the best buy

compatibility having the ability to work with other components; how well an item will go with other items

competition producing the best product or service at the best price

complementary color scheme a color scheme that brings together contrasting colors such as purple and yellow or blue and orange for a visually stimulating environment

comprehensive insurance insurance that covers the cost to repair a vehicle that is damaged by fire, flood, earthquake, hurricane, hail, a collision with an animal; it also covers the loss of a stolen vehicle

condominium a multiple housing structure in which owners purchase individual units and shares of the common areas

constraints restrictions

consumable items that will be used up or thrown away after use

Consumer Action Panel (CAP) a group of persons not employed in a particular industry that is responsible for handling consumer complaints in that industry

Consumer Price Index (CPI) monthly government list of how much average prices have gone up or down

Consumer Product Safety Act legislation that established the Consumer Product Safety Commission, which enforces the Flammable Fabrics Act

Consumer Product Safety Commission federal agency responsible for establishing product safety standards

Consumer Reports and *Consumer's Research* magazines that publish annual buying guides with name-brand ratings for a variety of consumer products

consumer complaint an expression by a consumer of dissatisfaction with a product

consumer demand the quantity of goods or services that buyers will purchase at a given price

Consumers Union independent nonprofit organization that tests consumer products for quality and price

consumers users of goods and services

Consumers' Bill of Rights a list that states that consumers have the right to safety, to be informed, to choose, and to be heard

contract an agreement between two or more people that is enforceable by law

convenience foods foods, such as those that are frozen or microwaveable, that have a large amount of processing and so are more easily prepared, but which are also more costly

cooperative a multiple housing structure in which owners purchase shares of the entire building

coordination-of-benefits clause a condition included in most insurance policies that states that the insured cannot collect from more than one policy

cosigner person guaranteeing payment of a loan

coupons certificates good for money off regular prices

creative recreation a hobby or pastime, such as painting or cooking, that yields a product of some sort

credit allowing goods and services to be used now with a promise of payment in the future

credit cards cards used to charge purchases to an account

credit contract a legally binding agreement that includes all information pertaining to a loan

credit rating records that are kept by credit report companies, of how well you pay your bills

credit unions nonprofit institutions offering financial services for members only

creditors the people or companies to whom money is owed

D

debit cards cards used to deduct payment from checking accounts

debtors people who owe debts

debts money owed

decibels (db) the measure of the intensity of sound

decision-making process a series of steps that will lead the decision maker to a final choice

decision matrix a form used to evaluate and compare products

deductible clause a part of an insurance policy that tells how much the owner must pay toward damage or replacement of a vehicle (the deductible) before the insurance company will pay

defaults fails to pay in full

deferred-payment plan an arrangement that allows consumers to buy now and pay later, use a layaway plan, or use a "90 days same as cash" plan

deficit spending spending more money than is taken in

dehydrated dried

demand quantity of goods buyers will purchase

dependents those who rely on your earnings for all or part of their support

deposit slip a form to accompany a deposit so that it is credited

deposit to place money into an account

depreciation the declining value of a car, boat, or other vehicle, due to age

depression period of low business activity and high unemployment

deregulate to remove restrictions or controls

diagnosis identification of the presence of a particular illness as well as the cause of that illness

disability insurance insurance that will help cover expenses when a person can't work due to a physical or mental condition

discount supermarket warehouse supermarket that sells food at reduced prices and often in large quantities

discretionary spending using your money according to your own good judgment

down payment initial payment on a credit purchase

durability the anticipated length of service without repair

E

eclectic decorating a trend in decorating that combines a variety of styles in the same room

economy a system of producing and distributing goods and services

emission standards the measure of contaminants being added to the air

employment agency a company that matches workers with available jobs

empty calories a term that describes those foods that are high in calories but low in nutritional value

Energy Guide a label required on all new appliances that tells the relative energy efficiency of a particular model and gives the estimated annual operating costs

energy efficiency the ratio of energy consumption to use

energy efficient uses minimum amounts of energy for heating, cooling, etc.

Environmental Protection Agency (EPA) the federal agency established in 1970 to enforce the Clean Air Act

epidemic an illness that spreads quickly through a population and affects a large number of people

Equal Credit Opportunity Act a law that states that a lender cannot deny credit because of race, sex, color, religion, national origin, age, or marital status

erosion the wearing away of soil by wind or water

eutrophication the removal of oxygen from the water by decomposing algae

expiration date last date a food product is acceptable for intended use

extended warranty an agreement that allows the buyer of a product to pay a fee to have the product's warranty extended for a longer period of time; a service contract

F

Fair Credit Reporting Act a law passed in 1970 that gives people the right to see their credit record and to correct any errors that may be on it

Fair Debt Collection Practices Act a law that controls debt-collecting practices

Fair Packaging and Labeling Act a law specifying what must be on a food label

family life cycle the various stages families go through; those stages may include beginning families, childbearing families, families with preschool children, families with school-children, families with adolescents, families as launching centers, families in the middle years, and aging families

family two or more persons who are related by blood or marriage and who often live together

farmer's market a direct point of sale between customers and the farmer

fast foods foods that can be prepared and served quickly, often with little regard for nutritional value

Federal Reserve Bank System (FRBS) federal organization that controls the amount of money available for loans

Federal Water Pollution Control Act federal legislation that sets standards for water purity

federal budget the plan for spending federal tax money

federal debt amount of money owed by the federal government

FICA (Federal Insurance Contribution Act) established payroll deductions for the Social Security system

finance charges the amount that credit costs, which must be paid back over the length of a loan

financial services the functions performed by banks

fixed expenses payments such as rent and insurance that are the same amount each time you pay them

fixed-rate mortgage a loan in which the rate of interest and payment remain the same over the lifetime of the loan

flame-retardant resistant to burning or likely to burn at a reduced rate

Flammable Fabrics Act legislation that regulates the use of textiles that are likely to burn

flexible essential expenses payments for necessary items, such as food and clothing, that vary from month to month

flextime a schedule provided by some companies that allows employees to have a choice of the hours they work

floor sample an item that has been on display in a retail store

Food Guide Pyramid a guide to daily food choices developed by the U.S. Department of Agriculture

food additives substances added to foods to enhance appearance, nutritional value, or shelf life

food cooperatives groups established for buying foods in large quantities

food habits a person's ideas, beliefs, attitudes, and practices that relate to foods

foreclose to take legal action to take possession of a home for failure to meet mortgage payments

foreclosure the event in which the buyer is unable to make monthly housing payments, which may allow the lender to take possession of the property

fraud the cheating or tricking of consumers

free enterprise the practice of allowing a capitalistic economy to function with minimum government regulation

fringe benefits something, such as vacations or company-paid insurance, that is provided by an employer, which is above and beyond the salary

full endorsement a signature on the back of a check with "pay to order" instructions

full warranty an agreement that covers all repair or replacement costs (parts, labor, shipping) during the warranty period

full-service banks commercial banks

function the intended use of an item

Fur Products Labeling Act legislation that sets standards for the labeling of items of clothing made from animal fur

G

generic brands products with no brand names

generic drugs the chemical or general names for drugs; drugs not sold under brand names

goals aims or purposes that a person intends to accomplish or achieve

going-out-of-business sale a sale that may or may not be legitimate, but which indicates that a business will not be open for returns (or anything else) after the sale is over

goods products for sale, merchandise

grace period time during which interest is not charged

grades quality ratings given to meat, eggs, and dairy products by the U.S. Department of Agriculture (USDA)

GRAS (Generally Recognized As Safe) a list of food substances tested and proved to be safe by the Food and Drug Administration

guarantee a written contract (warranty) spelling out consumer rights

guaranteed insurability allows the option to purchase additional life insurance coverage without a physical exam at some specified point in the future

guaranteed renewability ensures that term insurance can be renewed when the current term expires, regardless of the person's physical condition

H

hazardous chemicals harmful chemicals found in products

health food stores stores that sell natural foods—foods grown without the use of artificial fertilizers or other chemicals

health maintenance organization (HMO) an organization of physicians that is designed to cover all of a consumer's health care needs under a prepayment plan

HIV human immunodeficiency virus; the virus that causes AIDS

holistic medicine a medical approach that treats the whole person; mental-emotional, physical, social, and spiritual

Home Owners Warranty (HOW) guarantee on a new home

hostels supervised lodging, usually for young people

house brands private-label items found only in one chain of supermarkets

household any person or group of persons living together in a housing unit

housing shelter or lodging provided for people

housing unit part of a structure or an entire structure in which one or more people live

hydrologic cycle the sequence through which water passes from vapor in the atmosphere through precipitation and back into the atmosphere through evaporation; the water cycle

hydropower power caused by the movement of water

hypertension high blood pressure

I

illicit drugs drugs obtained illegally

immunization program a system of administering vaccinations, which are doses of medicine that stimulate the immune system to help fight off infectious diseases

implied warranty the unwritten guarantee that a product can be used for its intended purpose and will give reasonable service

imports products sold in the United States that come from other countries

impulse buying purchasing items that we would like but had not planned to buy

in-home consultation decorating advice given by a decorator who comes to the home

independent store a store owned and operated by an individual or a group of individuals

Industrial Revolution a time in the late 1600s when economic changes were brought about by the production of large quantities of goods for sale for profit

inflation the rising cost of goods and services

infomercial an advertising presentation that lasts from 30 minutes to an hour and is designed to look like an informative television program

inspected checked to ensure proper labeling and wholesomeness

installment credit contract to purchase a product by paying in equal periodic payments

intercity public transportation public transportation in the form of buses, planes, and trains, which provides service between cities within the United States

interest inventory a type of nongraded test that helps pinpoint and rank a person's favorite activities or interests

interest money that is earned on deposits

interest rate price paid to borrow money

interview a formal meeting in which the person applying for a job and the employer discuss the job and the applicant's qualifications for the job

invest to use money to make more money

investments a way of using current income to produce more income at some point in the future

J

job lead card an index card that contains important information about an available job

job lead information about a job that is available

junk foods foods with little nutritional value

L

law of supply and demand relationship between quantity and price

lease legal document stating the responsibilities of property owners and tenants

legal action hiring a lawyer to settle one's claim

lemon law a law that varies from state to state, but which usually defines a lemon as a new car, truck, or van that has been in the garage at least four times for the same repair or is out of service for a total of 30 days during the first year

liabilities amounts owed

liability insurance insurance that covers costs resulting from bodily injury and property damage to others

life expectancy (of household equipment) the length of time you can expect an item to last

lifestyle the typical way a person or group of people lives

limited warranty a written guarantee that covers only the costs specified in the contract

line of credit agreement to loan a specified amount of money on demand

liquidity a measure of how accessible money is

location neighborhood or community in which a housing unit is situated

long-range goals financial goals involving large sums of money and requiring more than five years to complete

long-term consumer credit loans for large or costly purchases

look-alike drugs over-the-counter drugs that are combined with other chemicals and packaged to look like illegal drugs or prescription medications

M

Magnuson-Moss Warranty Act federal law passed in 1975 requiring that warranties be written in ordinary language

maintenance fee money charged by condominium associations for the upkeep of common areas

manufacturer overruns excess production from the maker or producer

marketplace the world of trade and business

mass transit local public transportation in large urban areas

master plan a plan that can be completed in stages

Medicaid a joint federal and state program that provides medical benefits for people who cannot afford to pay for health care

medical payments insurance insurance that covers injuries suffered while riding in your own car or someone else's; it also covers guests riding in your car

Medicare a federal health insurance program that provides medical benefits for people aged 65 or older and some disabled people

medication a substance taken to improve one's health

Metroliners high speed Amtrak trains that travel between New York City and Washington, DC

mid-range goals financial goals that can be reached in one to five years

migraine headache extremely painful type of vascular headache caused by enlarged blood vessels

miles per gallon (mpg) the number of miles driven divided by the amount of fuel used

minerals earth elements, some of which are necessary to maintain good health; 4%-5% of the body's structure is made up of minerals

minimum balance the lowest balance in an account during a given accounting period

mobile home factory-built housing that can be moved

modern style having clean, simple lines

modular house housing unit constructed of rooms that have been built in a factory and shipped to a location for final assembly

money market savings account a savings account with a variable interest rate, restricted withdrawals, and a required minimum balance

monochromatic color scheme a color scheme that uses several shades of one color to provide a unified and sophisticated interior

monopoly a condition in which a business gains control of a product or service and there is no competition

month-to-month rental agreement a contract that allows the renter or rental company to change or cancel the contract on thirty days' notice

mortgage a loan secured by a home

multifamily housing unit a structure, such as an apartment, a condominium, or a cooperative, that provides housing for a large number of people in a relatively small area

multipurpose furnishings items, such as a sleeper sofa, that can serve more than one purpose

mutual funds an investment tool that pools the money of many small investors into one large fund

N

national brands brands of food that are available nationwide

natural fibers plant fibers such as cotton, and animal fibers such as wool and silk

natural foods foods that do not contain additives or have excessive processing

net worth the difference between the value of all things owned and the value of all owed

no load mutual fund a mutual fund that can be purchased directly from a company and which has no commission costs

no-fault insurance insurance in which the driver's own insurance company pays for his or her accident costs no matter who caused the accident

noise unwanted sound; a form of pollution

nonrenewable energy sources energy resources, such as coal, oil, and natural gas, that can be used up

nutrients the items in foods, such as vitamins and minerals, that the body needs to function properly

nutrition labeling a listing of the kinds and quantities of nutrients in a product

nutritionists people who study foods and their effects on the body and help develop diets that are necessary for good health

O

obesity excessive fatness; the condition of being more than 20% over a recommended weight

Occupational Outlook Handbook a government publication that is updated every two years, which describes about 250 occupations in detail

oligopoly a situation in which a few producers control the market for a product

on-site repair service repair services located in the store where a purchase is made

open dating date placed on a product that indicates peak performance

Organization of Petroleum Exporting Countries (OPEC) the ten major oil producing countries that have banded together and agreed on the price of oil

origination fee a fee charged for starting the paperwork on a loan

outstanding checks checks that have been written but have not been paid

over-the-counter (OTC) drugs drugs that can be purchased without a prescription

overbook a practice of airlines in which they accept more reservations for a flight than there are seats on the plane

P

pack date the date a food was processed and packaged

particulates tiny bits of solid or liquid suspended in the air

passbook accounts savings accounts

pawnshops businesses that provide loans in exchange for collateral

paying yourself first putting money in savings for later use before paying for essential and nonessential items

payroll deduction plan an employer plan that allows employees to have money deducted from their earnings and put into a savings account before they receive their pay check

personal data sheet an outline of the personal information needed to fill out an application form; it may include dates of schooling, names, addresses, and references

personal environment actions and surroundings that can be controlled by the individual

personal preferences the things that an individual likes and/or dislikes

personal style your own preferences in color, furniture types, and decorating schemes

pharmacist a person licensed to prepare and dispense medical drugs

phosphates natural organic compounds often added to household detergents to boost cleaning power

pluralistic society a community or nation that has people of different ethnic, social, and religious groups

prescription drugs drugs that can be purchased with the written order of a doctor

preshopping getting objective information about an item and making preliminary decisions before shopping for that item

preventive maintenance service done to keep a car or other vehicle running well

preventive medicine care taken to stop or reduce the risk of disease; this can include a change in diet, exercise, and screening tests

primary care doctor a doctor trained to provide total medical care; a general practitioner, general internist, or family doctor

principal money borrowed

prioritize listing needs in order of importance

processor in the food industry, the people or companies that prepare and package food products

producers suppliers of services and makers of goods

product recall a notice to consumers to return, repair, or discard an unsafe item

product standards stated requirements for types of products

productivity amount of output per unit of input

profit money remaining after expenses are paid

progressive tax tax that increases in relation to increased earnings

propaganda techniques that are designed to control thoughts and actions by deceiving the audience or by distorting the truth

prospectus a written description of the philosophy, objectives, earnings, and current financial status of an investment such as a mutual fund

prosperity economic condition in which people have money to spend

pull date the last date a food can be offered for sale but not the last day it can be eaten

Q

quacks people who pretend to have medical skills and who often sell fake cures for illnesses

R

radioactive waste the unwanted and highly dangerous by-product that occurs after a nuclear reaction

rating territories areas that states are divided into, by which insurance rates are determined

real estate land and any structures built upon it

recession period of reduced business activity

Recommended Daily Allowance (RDA) a guide developed by the National Academy of Sciences-National Research Council, which details the amounts of such things as vitamins and minerals that should be eaten daily to maintain good health

reconcile to match the balance in the check register to the bank statement

recovery increase in sales and production following a recession or depression

recycle to process again or make ready for reuse

regular savings account a savings account with a fixed interest rate and unrestricted deposits and withdrawals

regulate to control the production, distribution, sales, and advertisement of products; to establish restrictions or controls

reinvested put back into the business

reliability resistance to wear

renewable energy sources energy resources, such as the sun and moving water, that are never used up

rent-to-own option an agreement by which all rental payments go toward the purchase price of a piece of furniture

repossess to take back the goods purchased because of failure to repay the loan

restrictive endorsement a signature on the back of a check with instructions limiting what can be done with the check

retailer in the food industry, the people or companies that sell food to consumers

revolving account charge account that allows an individual to make partial payments and add to the balance due up to a specified amount

riders special features, which are optional, that are added to a basic insurance policy

risk the chance of losing all or part of the money invested

S

sales credit purchase of a product with agreement to pay later

sanitary landfills garbage disposal systems in which the waste is covered daily with a layer of soil

savings and loan associations financial institutions that offer similar services to a bank but that operate under different regulations

savings banks state-chartered banks offering fewer financial services than commercial banks

savings money put aside in savings accounts or investments for future use

seconds damaged or flawed clothing

security deposit money a renter pays in advance to cover possible damages to a rental housing unit

service charge fee paid to the bank for checking services

service contract an agreement by which the consumer prepays for repairs of an item purchased; repair insurance

service credit use of a service with agreement to pay later

services activities or accommodations required by buyers

shelf life the length of time a product can be safely stored

short-range goals financial goals that can be accomplished in less than one year

short-term consumer credit installment credit, credit card credit, revolving accounts

sick leave employers' payment to employees who are unable to work because of illness; it is usually limited to 5 to 10 days per year

side effects undesirable effects of drugs

signature card a card kept on file at the bank to verify the signature on checks

signature loans loans given with no collateral required

single-family housing unit a house

small-claims court a special court in which consumers and sellers with small claims (usually less than $1,500) present their case to a judge who makes the final decision

smog a haze caused by the combination of hydrocarbons and nitrogen oxides

solar power energy derived from the sun

special coverage homeowners' insurance that protects the home against all perils with the exception of those that are specifically named in the policy

specialists doctors who have in-depth training in one area of the body or one type of ailment; this training is beyond the medical degree requirements

specialty shops stores that offer only certain products

spectator sports activities, such as professional baseball and basketball, that involve watching others perform

SPF rating describing the *s*un *p*rotection *f*actor of a product

standard of identity ingredients common to a particular food product such as catsup

standard of living level of necessities and comforts that a group of people expect to be able to buy

start-up costs costs that must be paid by those who move into a house or apartment; costs may include deposits that must be made to utility companies

status symbols expensive items that show off a person's financial position

stocks shares in a business

stop-loss protection an insurance policy that limits a consumer's coinsurance payments to $1,000-$2,000

stress tension

subsidy money furnished by the government to help pay some cost

suggested retail prices product prices that are recommended by the manufacturer, which usually differ from the actual selling prices

supermarket a type of large volume food store that accounts for 80 percent of food sales

synthetic fibers fibers made using chemicals

T

tariff a price charged to keep prices of imported goods competitive with U.S. products, so foreign companies must raise the prices of their products to cover the cost of the tariff

technology a scientific method that makes practical use of human knowledge and is applied to such things as consumer products

tenant renter

tension headaches headache caused by the tightening of muscles

term life insurance life insurance that provides benefit payments if the insured dies within a specified period of time, usually one or more years ("the term"); the insured has the option of renewing the policy at the end of the term

term the length of time for which money is borrowed

test drive driving a vehicle to evaluate its performance

Textile Fiber Products Identification Act legislation that regulates the labeling of fiber content of textile products

the "Blue Book" the *Kelly Auto Market Report*, which lists average prices for used cars

thermal pollution the release of heated liquid into a body of water at a temperature that is damaging to the environment

title a document that shows legal ownership

traction friction or holding power

trade school an education institution that offers courses in a specific field, such as computer repair or medical technician

trade-in an item, often a vehicle, that is applied toward the purchase of another item of the same type

trade-off an exchange of one thing for another

traditional style furnishings with classic lines that often include wood carving

transporter in the food industry, the people or companies that move food between the other steps of the industry

tread the part of a tire that makes contact with the ground

Truth-in-Lending Act a law passed in 1968 that requires lenders to state the interest rate and dollar cost of loans

Truth-in-Savings Law requires that financial institutions must state the annual percentage yield of all investments

tuition the cost of attending a school; this does not include the price of books, housing, or expenses not relating to instruction

U

U.S. Savings Bonds an investment vehicle that can be purchased at a discount and held until maturity

Underwriters Laboratories (UL) a private nonprofit organization that tests products for safety

unemployment the state of being without a job involuntarily

uninsured motorist insurance insurance coverage against injury by a hit-and-run driver or a driver who has no insurance

unit pricing the cost of food per unit of measurement

universal product code (UPC) electronic label that identifies the processor, package contents, and price of a product

university a higher-learning institution similar to a college, but which usually has programs leading to bachelor's, master's, and, in many cases, doctorate degrees

upholstered furniture furniture covered with padding and fabric

V

vacuum gauge a device on some vehicles that indicates when fuel use is high or low

values the things a person feels are important or believes are right or wrong

variable-rate mortgage a loan in which the interest rate and/or terms may be changed periodically

vascular headache headache caused by enlarged blood vessels

veneer a thin panel of hardwood laminated to a core of plywood or pressed board

vertical integration a situation in which one group controls all the steps in the food marketing system

vicarious participation taking part in activities by watching others perform

visual pollution environmental contamination that can be seen

vitamins organic compounds needed by the body for growth and proper functioning

W

warranty a written guarantee that is legally binding

water pollution impurity in the water system

water treatment plants facilities that process sewage and wastes and remove solid wastes and many chemicals from water

wellness lifestyle a focus on several controllable factors such as balanced diet, regular exercise, and stress relief

whole life insurance life insurance that pays benefits whenever the insured dies, and which does not have to be renewed

wholesaler in the food industry, the people or companies that sell food to consumers

withdraw to remove money from an account

wood products plywood or pressed wood

Wool Products Labeling Act legislation that requires a sweater to be labeled cashmere, mohair, etc.

work environment the place a job is done, which includes the people, conditions, and equipment involved in the job

work permit a form needed by underage employees, which allows them to work legally

worker's compensation income protection provided by some employers that covers both the medical expenses and lost salary due to a job-related illness or accident

Index

Photo Credits/Acknowledgements

All Interior photography provided by Dana C. White and Elisa Haber of Dana White Productions, Inc. except:

p. 125—David Hanover Photography
p. 174—David Hanover Photography
p. 190—David Hanover Photography
p. 338—Superstock
p. 339—Superstock
p. 351—David Hanover Photography

p. 371—David Hanover Photography
p. 379—Superstock
p. 380—Superstock
p. 383—Superstock
p. 406—Superstock

We would also like to thank the following for their help and cooperation in completing this photo program:

Aaron Bros. Furniture
Airport Pharmacy of Santa Monica
Armstrong's Home & Garden
Art's Pawn Shop of Santa Monica
Adray's
Bank of America
Bo-Jay's Pizza
Bright & Associates Advertising
Broadway Department Stores
Stephanie Brizendine
Carlson's Appliance Center of
    Santa Monica
Chico's Clothing Stores
M. Cole Clothing Stores
Gloria Davis
Daniel Freeman Memorial Hospital
Fritto Misto Restaurant
Dr. William Hohl
Harmony Huhn
Eddie Jacobs
The Melissa & John Levoff Family

Los Angeles International
    Airport
Love Tennis
The McLaughlin Family
Martin Minkardo
George Meyer TV Repair
Mission Produce
The Charlotte & Manuel Myers
    Family
Orchard Hardware
Pacific Stock Exchange
James Paik
Pavilions Markets
J.C. Penney's
Peterson Automotive Museum
Pepperdine University School of
    Business and Management
Valmore Riera
Thomas Richards Company
Santa Monica College
Santa Monica High School

Santa Monica Orthopedic and
    Sports Medicine
Santa Monica Place
ScubaHaus of Santa Monica
SD Color Labs
Sheridan Toyota of Santa Monica
Sizzler Restaurants
Sports Connection
Stokes Tire of Santa Monica
Supergo/Bikecology
Carolyn Thacker
Felicia Torrence
Venice Family Clinic
Video and Audio Center of
    Santa Monica
Ted Washington
Wells Fargo Bank
Wherehouse
Windward School
Natalie, Michael and
    Andrew White